Ordering Medieval Society

THE MIDDLE AGES SERIES

Ruth Mazo Karras, Series Editor
Edward Peters, Founding Editor

A complete list of books in the series
is available from the publisher.

Published in cooperation with the
Max Planck Institute for History, Göttingen.

Ordering Medieval Society

Perspectives on Intellectual and Practical Modes of Shaping Social Relations

Edited by

BERNHARD JUSSEN

Translated by

PAMELA SELWYN

PENN

University of Pennsylvania Press

Philadelphia

10 9 8 7 6 5 4 3 2 1

Published by
University of Pennsylvania Press
Philadelphia, Pennsylvania 19104-4011

Library of Congress Cataloging-in-Publication Data
Ordering medieval society : perspectives on intellectual and practical modes of shaping
social relations / edited by Bernhard Jussen ; translated by Pamela Selwyn.
    p. cm. — (The Middle Ages series)
    Includes bibliographical references and index.
    Contents: Counting piety in the early and high Middle Ages / Arnold Angenendt ... [et
al.] — Counting piety in the late Middle Ages / Thomas Lentes — Perceiving social
reality in the early and high Middle Ages / Otto Gerhard Oexle — Liturgy and
legitimation, or How the Gallo-Romans ended the Roman Empire / Bernhard Jussen —
Inventing a social category / Joseph Morsel — (Royal) favor : a central concept in early
medieval hierarchical relations / Gerd Althoff — Satisfaction : peculiarities of the
amicable settlement of conflicts in the Middle Ages / Gerd Althoff — Peace through
conspiracy / Otto Gerhard Oexle.
    ISBN 0-8122-3561-4 (alk. paper)
    1. Social History—Medieval, 500–1500.   2. Civilization, Medieval.   3. Europe—Social
conditions—To 1492.   I. Jussen, Bernhard.   II. Series.
HN11 .O73 2000
306'.09'02—dc21   00-039284

Contents

Illustrations

Introduction

Bernhard Jussen

The title of this book, *Ordering Medieval Society*, immediately poses the question: Who is doing the ordering? On the one hand, the subjects are medieval people themselves who—within the framework of their cognitive possibilities—organized their world mentally and practically. On the other hand, the subjects are, of course, those present-day historians who—again within the framework of their cognitive possibilities—mentally and practically organize the remains of what once was (and which is forever past), constructing "history" on this foundation. Both the historical and the contemporary subjects proceed from their own specific perspectives. Thus, if we wish to understand their models, we need to familiarize ourselves with their cognitive categories. This book is directly concerned with the categories (and practices) of medieval people. More indirectly, it also treats the categories of historians, presenting to an English-speaking audience the products of a scholarly culture that, while sharing many of the parameters of international medieval studies, also refers to a tradition of discussion that developed in Germany and has no international counterpart.

However much we may invoke the international nature of scholarship nowadays, and the growing similarity of methodological principles and basic epistemological stances, historical knowledge continues to be organized primarily on a national level. Academic job markets and professional associations are national and react to national requirements. Systems of higher education, the shape of disciplines, and the composition of the student body differ greatly from country to country. The expectations placed on historians vary from the United States to Germany, and from Germany to France or Poland. Scholarly production inevitably reflects these varying demands and organizational forms in the questions scholars ask, their styles of writing and argumentation, and the answers they propose. Conferences, journals, and discussions may be international, and members of the scientific community may jet tirelessly around the world, but national scholarly cultures perpetuate themselves all the same.

This has a simple consequence for our practical work, which may be easy to accept in theory, but is rarely remarked upon in practice. Historical knowledge cannot be transported directly over national borders or across the Atlantic. We must always take into account that historians work within different national scholarly cultures and that the histories they produce, and the way they present their arguments, can be explained to a large extent by the scholarly culture in which they live. This is neither good nor bad, but simply an inevitable condition of historical knowledge, and one that we should constantly keep in mind. Thus, scholars who look beyond their own academic world must always ask whether the scholarly cultures on the other side of the fence have developed questions, approaches, and conclusions that could expand their own scholarly horizons. Centers of national history abroad, such as the German Historical Institute in Washington or the Mission Historique Française en Allemagne in Göttingen, but also binational conferences of medievalists[1] and, not least, translations, serve this end. The task of internationalizing medieval studies (and cultural studies more generally) is less one of creating a uniformity of discourses than of increasing our sensitivity to different national contexts of argumentation.

This book will introduce one of these discussions—an amalgam of international questions and specific scholarly traditions. Certainly, one could view the contributions in this volume as expressions of the international trend, now well established, which—after the end of the primacy of structural approaches to history—once again places individuals and their perceptions at the center of interest. This reading would not be incorrect. At the same time, however, the work of these medievalists was conceived in opposition to a position that does not exist within Anglo-American or French medieval scholarship: what is known in German as constitutional history (*Verfassungsgeschichte*). It was this typically German conflict that inspired these authors to develop their distinctions, questions, and arguments. Today, we can see that these efforts have illuminated certain institutional phenomena of medieval society that have received little or no attention in international research.

Examining Medieval Social Groups

Current research on "Social Groups in Medieval Society"[2] or "The Political Significance of Group Ties in the Early Middle Ages"[3] refers—at least in Germany—to the tradition founded by the medievalist Karl Schmid. In the 1960s, Schmid provided the decisive impetus for attempts to understand medieval society by examining concrete groups and interpreting their practices and symbolic expressions. In diametric opposition to the dominant view at that time (in Germany at any rate), he proceeded from the assumption that classes, strata, and estates are not historical actors. The reality of estates, strata, and classes is the reality of the patterns of interpretation that people used to understand their respective societies and to enforce norms. In this sense, one of the central challenges for historians is to grasp the complex and ever changing "potential relationships between interpretive schemes and reality" (Chapter 3).

In the 1960s, Schmid put this apparently simple insight into scholarly practice, arguing that "monasticism and the nobility" were not active subjects, but rather "appeared in the form of monastic and noble communities," that is, as persons or groups of persons.[4] At first, historians applied this impulse to those forms of group formation that have always dominated the scholarly view of the Middle Ages: kinship and monastic groups. The most significant product of this research was the detailed history of a monastic group and its lay surroundings over a period of some three hundred years: the five-volume account of the monastic community of Fulda.[5]

If the present volume does not document the work on kinship and monastic groups, it is in part because English-speaking scholars are already familiar with this research. There is a more important reason, however: research on the Middle Ages as a culture of groups does more than merely place the study of kinship on a new footing. Rather, its particular strength is that it takes us beyond a fixation on medieval kinship. As soon as we look seriously at group cultures, it becomes clear that the popular notion of medieval society as "archaic," and thus largely organized along kinship lines, is an erroneous one.

The first step toward this insight comes automatically, since looking at social groups forces us to redefine the research fields of "the nobility" and "kinship." Schmid's famous 1957 essay "Zur Problematik von Familie, Sippe und Geschlecht, Haus und Dynastie beim mittelalterlichen Adel" (On the Problem of Family, Clan and Lineage, House and Dynasty Among the Medieval Nobility) was extraordinarily influential in this area.[6] From this perspective, kinship studies is concerned with the following questions: Under what conditions and in what composition did groups conceive of or represent themselves as "kin" at a particular moment, and how did this conception or representation change over time? Thus, the topic of kinship is removed from biology and transferred to the level of imagination or discourses. Research on kinship deals with, or at least aspires to deal with, the concepts of historical groups.[7] Research on the nobility must, analogously, proceed from the question of when and how particular individuals and groups were perceived as "noble" or as part of the nobility and how they translated this perception into symbolic forms (Chapter 5).

Such a subsumption of the research fields of kinship and the nobility under the broader field of "social groups" has far-reaching consequences: if we understand "kinship" solely as a historically determined concept for structuring groups, it becomes apparent that even in the early Middle Ages, this was by no means the only possible way of thinking about group structures. The sources present us with many situations in which groups did not organize themselves using the concept of kinship. Instead we find forms of organization that were so fundamentally different from kinship—but also feudal—ties that they severely disrupt the usual image of a static, hierarchical, and feudal Middle Ages.

Social Ties Beyond Kinship

Thanks in particular to the mediation of Georges Duby,[8] aspects of Schmid's ideas became known outside of Germany and were integrated into anthropological research on kinship. What the international reception of Schmid's work did not take into account, however, was that the issues he raised challenged a central orientation of German medieval studies, "constitutional history," which has no counterpart outside of Germany. In the style of legal history as defined by nineteenth-century scholars Georg Waitz and Heinrich Brunner, this branch of history studies the political and social institutions of the Holy Roman Empire, with a primary interest in the central authority.[9]

When German historians began to conceive of early medieval society as a conglomerate of interacting groups they were bound to come into conflict with the dominant mode of German medieval scholarship, and to measure their own argumentation against this tradition. Thus it is impossible to overlook that in Schmid's reconceptualizations and those of the succeeding generation the German tradition of constitutional history was an omnipresent opponent. The contributions by Gerd Althoff and Otto Gerhard Oexle in this volume, in particular, represent two different responses to the inspiration offered by Schmid, and two different departures from the constitutional history tradition.

Gerd Althoff expressly sees his work "in a long tradition of constitutional history research such as has been and is characteristic of German medieval scholarship." He views his studies of institutional history as the fruit of a critical grappling, and ultimately a break, with this tradition. In order to further develop the approaches suggested by Schmid, he has adopted impulses from current Anglo-American and French anthropology, particularly from research on ritual.[10] In recent years he has uncovered the social weight of institutional phenomena ignored by constitutional history—particularly of a specifically early medieval type of ritual friendship (*amicitiae*) that established formally egalitarian group ties. Using numerous early medieval sources, he was able to demonstrate how nobles utilized the egalitarian social form of *amicitia* among themselves to form alliances. In the early tenth century, the East Frankish king Henry I (d. 936) systematically adopted this custom in order, with the help of *amicitiae*, to give the vertical relationship between the king and the nobility the symbolic form of horizontal social ties. Whenever conflicts arose, Henry I offered his opponent *amicitia*, that is, a cooperative rather than hierarchical representation of their relationship.[11]

In Chapters 6 and 7 of the present volume, Althoff sketches two further central institutions that are generally overlooked by medievalists: "(royal) favor" and "satisfaction." These institutions of hierarchical order and conflict resolution regulated the relationship between the king and those around him—particularly the powerful nobles—and bound the superior and inferior parties alike to a strict set of rules of proper conduct.

In order to be successful within this system, one needed not only the favor of one's lord, but also the support of as many others as possible who were active at court. And there were reliable means and rules for acquiring such support. It would surely not be incorrect to imagine the atmosphere at such courts, along with their medieval critics, as a . . . struggle of all, by whatever means, for the favor of the ruler. Interestingly enough, the result of this situation was not the absolutist position of the lord or king who could have granted or withdrawn his favor at will. Instead, the lord had to orient his bestowals of favor to the rank and position of his followers if he did not wish to provoke the collective solidarity of all against his one-sided display of preferences.[12]

Althoff's aim, which is quite compatible with the tradition of constitutional history, is to discover what was "specific about medieval rule," but he places the emphasis on "the pre-state specificity of medieval rule." Proceeding from the assertion that "what was lacking in medieval conditions in contrast to those of the modern age" was "the monopoly on the use of force, the separation of powers and the state," Althoff asks, "what existed in their stead and how order was preserved even without these institutions that seem so fundamental to coexistence nowadays."[13]

Chapters 6 and 7 may be viewed as elements in a framework of potentially promising answers, as must the previously sketchy institution of the "mediator." Until now, medievalists have overlooked that the institution of the mediator, the arbitrator in the amicable settlement of disputes, was not merely a phenomenon of neighborly relations, but also fundamental to conflicts within the ruling strata in particular.[14] Phenomena of this type are especially well suited to helping us rethink the traditional concepts of constitutional history. After all, these institutions are far removed from the perceived objects of constitutional history, and yet they belong at the center of what this research was looking for in the first place.

Otto Gerhard Oexle has chosen another path in order to further the study of social groups methodologically and theoretically. He has returned our attention to the period around 1900 and the beginnings of German cultural studies. In the work of early German cultural theorists and historians, particularly Max Weber and Georg Simmel, but also Otto Hintze, Ernst Troeltsch, and Otto von Gierke, he found some important points of reference for a medieval scholarship oriented toward patterns of conduct and interpretation. His return to this tradition led him to ask questions and propose systematic categories that not infrequently diverge from the medieval history that draws its influences from current French or Anglo-American anthropology.[15]

In the *coniurationes*, Oexle studies a central type of early medieval group formation that plays scarcely any role in current international research (Chapter 8, "Peace Through Conspiracy").[16] Since Roman late antiquity and particularly since the sixth century, we find local "guilds" (*conjurationes, geldoniae*) organized on the principle of equal representation that constituted themselves by means of reciprocal promissory oaths. Very diverse groups used this legal form to organize extensive mutual aid outside of family networks: local groups (villagers, men and women, laity, and clergy) as well as sectoral groups (clerics, serfs). These early guilds already maintained funds for mutual aid in emergency situations (sickness and disability, fire damage, the commemoration of the dead), sociability, and poor relief.

It is characteristic of Oexle's research perspective that he studies these groups as "sworn associations" just like merchant or artisan guilds, brotherhoods, journeymen's associations, early universities, or medieval urban communes: his systematic interest began with the groups' legal form, their organization on the principle of equal representation, and the oaths used to constitute them.[17] It was precisely the legal form of the reciprocal oath, he argues, that created a specific political and social culture—particularly in the shape of peacekeeping and group-specific law. In the tradition of Max Weber, Oexle brings out this egalitarian political and social culture as a specific phenomenon of occidental history. As a group culture present since the early Middle Ages, it engaged in perpetual conflict with hierarchical patterns of thought and action and belonged to the great dynamizing motors of Western history.

In short, research on groups serves as a corrective to our image of a hierarchical, "feudal" Middle Ages, confronting it with the powerful presence of organizational forms such as the ritual friendship, the conspiracy, and the guild. These social forms were precisely not hierarchical, and individuals were not "born into" them. Instead, they rested on the idea of free contract and were—at least formally—structured along egalitarian lines.

It is easy to see the use of such correctives to the image of a hierarchical, feudal Middle Ages. With the tradition of free and voluntary forms of political and social organization in mind, it is easier to understand the thought patterns and models which contemporaries could use to cope with new problems. Thus, for example, in the case of the founding of cities (Chapter 8) or the early universities, we can see how individuals utilized this very model of the freely organized association that had already appeared in the *amicitiae* and the early medieval guilds. Models of social organization based on voluntary contract could be adapted much more easily to new circumstances. In situations of conflict and disorganization they could be mobilized far more quickly than the models of kinship or of monarchical structuring from above (Part III).

Conceiving—Transforming—Stabilizing

The diversity of the egalitarian and hierarchical legal forms which medieval individuals used to forge groups could only be discovered by scholars who set out to examine phenomena such as kinship or the nobility not as historical "facts," but rather as historical mental constructs—a form of social knowledge specific to a time and place. This approach shifted objects of study that had previously been the province of intellectual history to the center of social history.

By moving back and forth between models and the conduct of groups, we can hope to gain information about how permanent social ties arose, when they worked and when they did not, how identities were formed, which concepts the values and basic attitudes of the different groups were condensed into, how individuals assumed their roles in various groups, how these groups provided themselves with a profile both internally and externally, and how conflicts were handled and law and peace secured.

How did society function as a conglomeration of heterogeneous groups? How did something like cultural stability emerge between collective thinking in models and the daily struggle over political and social organization? In addressing these questions, the present volume seeks to introduce research trends that have developed specifically in Germany, and which have received little or no attention within English-language scholarship until now.

The research approaches presented here already imply that medieval modes of conceiving, transforming, and stabilizing society cannot be studied separately from each other, since it is precisely their interdependence that is the object of scholarly interest. Nevertheless, each of the three aspects entails its own methodological problems, and the emphasis shifts depending upon the questions asked. Thus studies of guilds and friendships and of techniques for preserving peace and law (Chapters 6–8) are primarily concerned with the enormous cultural efforts involved in stabilizing medieval society (Part III). Chapter 8 on the forms of peace through conspiracy in particular shows the difficulty of assigning categories. A good portion of this chapter from Part III could also be linked to Part I (Conceiving), which is concerned with medieval schemes for interpreting society.

In Part I, Otto Gerhard Oexle maps out the theoretical and methodological framework and discusses the central research problems in his "contribution to a history of social knowledge" (Chapter 3). Here he takes up the (mainly French) studies from the 1970s and 1980s that address the functional tripartition of society from around the year 1000 into those who pray, those who fight, and those who work with their hands. Oexle criticizes the tendency to declare these patterns of interpretation, which scholars have studied in the form of *mentalités* or the imaginary, to have been mere ideological inventions of the ruling class and to deny them any relationship to reality. Using the history of this famous example, he outlines how relationships between interpretive schemes and reality must be understood as central objects of a history of social knowledge.

There are many possible relationships between reality and knowledge, which Oexle seeks to distinguish according to typology. Thus the constant defamation of egalitarian groups by representatives of the authorities appear as an expression of a central opposition within medieval forms of knowledge about society: it was inevitable that the egalitarian groups, given their view of themselves, would come into conflict with those who argued in terms of hierarchical patterns of interpretation. Such an example, in which differing ways of conceiving reality meet, can help us to elucidate the connections between objective reality and knowledge about it in a differentiated manner, asking how reality conditions knowledge, and how knowledge helps to constitute reality.

The authors of the first two chapters belong to a wholly different scholarly tradition from Oexle and Althoff. Arnold Angenendt, Thomas Braucks, Rolf Busch, and Hubertus Lutterbach (Chapter 1) and Thomas Lentes (Chapter 2) received their primary academic socialization in Catholic theological seminaries, which in Germany are part of the general state universities, to be sure, but which retain a strong denominational stamp. Here the authors received a thorough training in Catholic exegesis, the foundations of theology, dogmatics, and liturgy, with which they now work in the field of social history. Thanks to these dual roots in theological and historical debates, they are able to find meanings in medieval patterns of thought and behavior that usually remain hidden to historians.

The inspiration behind Arnold Angenendt's research may also be described to a certain extent as typically German, since from the beginning his work has been directed against the notion—stubbornly handed down within German Catholic scholarship—that the early Middle Ages "was, from the standpoint of church history, in an important sense a Germanic period" (according to the influential church historian Joseph Lortz). A central aim of Angenendt's work, which culminated in the recently published voluminous *Geschichte der Religiosität im Mittelalter* (History of Religiosity in the Middle Ages), has been to make up for the failure to renew Catholic church history after 1945, and more particularly to free our historical images of "Germanicisms."[18] The second problem of reception that concerns Angenendt relates to the history of theology, which is still being written as if the seven hundred years between Augustine and the twelfth century had never existed. Apparently, scholars interested in theology and ideas completely lack the foundations necessary to understand the forms of thought and action of the fifth to eleventh centuries. The "objective of an account of the Middle Ages from the perspective of the history of religion," which Angenendt has been pursuing for over twenty years, is largely directed against this tradition.[19]

The enormous utility of his research for social history becomes clear in the first two chapters of the present volume: In a diachronic overview of the history of Christian religiosity from the New Testament to the late Middle Ages, the authors examine the dominant medieval form of piety: counted piety. To be sure, it is a commonplace of medieval studies that piety was quantifiable in the Middle Ages. Jacques Chiffoleau's study of bookkeeping on the hereafter (*La comptabilité de l'au-delà*) is twenty years old, and very well known.[20] Chapters 1 and 2, however, place the meaning of these pious practices within the broader context of the history of religion. They investigate the formation, functioning (Chapter 1), and decomposition (Chapter 2) of that religious imaginary which led to a literally quantifiable religiosity: the triad of quantification of the sins, exchange rates for different modes of penance, and penance by proxy; the redefinition of the Eucharist in the early Middle Ages; the importance of the priest's "clean hands"; and the enormous success of the private Mass (*missa specialis*) in the early Middle Ages, to name only the most important phenomena. Chapter 2, in particular, repeatedly underlines the constant shift of religious argumentation between ethical and quantitative considerations, between the orientation toward nonquantifiable intentions and that toward countable acts.

Thus, on the whole, Parts I and III emphasize the procedures of institutions—lasting behavioral patterns, systems of rules for decision making, bestowals of meaning, and symbolic representations. Part II (Transforming), in contrast, focuses on less permanent procedures, the at once mental and practical reordering of social relations. This refers to situations of cultural disorganization (Chapter 4) and to constellations in which the social positions actually assumed no longer correspond to the patterns of interpretation and are, in a sense, "readjusted" by the people involved (Chapter 5).

A prime example of cultural disorganization is Gaul between antiquity and the Middle Ages. Unlike Roman Africa, for example, in Gaul the cultural system was not changed "from above" as the result of conquest. From about 400 onward, the Gallic elites found themselves confronted with the fact that the emperors, around whom the entire system of political legitimation revolved, were no longer present. The Roman interpretive schemes lost their power to legitimate and establish norms, and since the Merovingians did not become recognizable as the new central authority until the sixth century, the inhabitants of Gaul were left to their own devices for a good century. This gives us the opportunity to observe how a provincial society, confronted with the fading of the imperial ideological framework, negotiated new criteria for authority and legitimate power in the period between "antique" and "medieval" Gaul. The most successful product of these negotiations was episcopal rule, a new institution of local power. The creation and establishment of this form of authority by the increasingly delegitimated imperial aristocracy provides a good case study of institutionalization as primarily a struggle over symbols. Episcopal rule took shape during a long struggle over orders of procession and articles of clothing, chairs, hairstyles, shoes, languages, and redefinitions of the categories of time and space.

An especially subtle example of how mental classifications and nomenclature were modified in reaction to a concrete political configuration is the establishment of the nomenclature surrounding "the nobility" in late medieval Franconia (Chapter 5). In order to counteract the measures of the territorially oriented princes, which appeared to endanger traditional social relations, the aristocracy homogenized the terminology they used to refer to themselves. Previously called *fürsten*, *grafen*, *herren*, or *ritter*, in the mid-fifteenth century they "invented" the homogeneous term "the nobility," and very soon the social imaginary organized itself around this new term. Joseph Morsel argues that these lexical and semantic innovations were a decisive move in the resistance to incorporation within the territorial state. The new nomenclature contributed decisively to the sociogenesis of the nobility, which constituted a fundamental force in the society and political system of the modern age.

It should be mentioned in closing that Joseph Morsel has worked as a medievalist in Germany for many years, is a specialist on the history of the German nobility and of kinship, and is extremely well versed in the perspectives sketched in this introduction. His contribution, however, combines these perspectives with the legacy of his French scholarly background, which owes much to the sociology of Pierre Bourdieu. His essay (like the others, of course) reveals the peculiarities of scholarly nomenclature, and in each terminology—despite translation into English—the reader will easily recognize the various authors' preferred scholarly "fathers." Readers will also note repeated overlaps of themes, and a convergence of the questions and answers proposed by the authors.

Notes

1. American/German: *Imagination, Ritual, Memory, Historiography: Conceptions of the Past*, ed. Gerd Althoff, Johannes Fried, and Patrick Geary (Cambridge, in press); British/German: *Political Thought and the Realities of Power in the Middle Ages. Politisches Denken und die Wirklichkeit der Macht im Mittelalter*, ed. Joseph Canning and Otto Gerhard Oexle (Göttingen, 1998). French/German: *Mittelalterforschung in Frankreich und Deutschland heute*, ed. Otto Gerhard Oexle and Jean-Claude Schmitt (Göttingen and Paris, in press); Russian/German: *Das Individuum und die Seinen*, ed. Yuri Bessmertny and Otto Gerhard Oexle (Göttingen and Moscow, 2000).

2. This is the title of a long-term project directed by Otto Gerhard Oexle at the Max Planck Institute for History in Göttingen; cf. *Die Repräsentation der Gruppen. Texte— Bilder—Objekte*, ed. Otto Gerhard Oexle and Andrea von Hülsen-Esch (Göttingen, 1998).

3. This is the subtitle of Gerd Althoff's synthesis of the scholarship on early medieval groups, *Verwandte, Freunde und Getreue. Zum politischen Stellenwert der Gruppenbindungen im früheren Mittelalter* (Darmstadt, 1990).

4. Karl Schmid, "Über das Verhältnis von Person und Gemeinschaft im frühen Mittelalter," *Frühmittelalterliche Studien* 1 (1967): 225–49, quotation on 248; Schmid's most important essays are collected in Karl Schmid, *Gebetsgedenken und adliges Selbstverständnis im Mittelalter. Ausgewählte Beiträge* (Sigmaringen, 1983); on Schmid's work see the posthumous appreciation by Otto Gerhard Oexle, "Gruppen in der Gesellschaft. Das wissenschaftliche Oeuvre von Karl Schmid," *Frühmittelalterliche Studien* 28 (1994): 412–23.

5. *Die Klostergemeinschaft von Fulda im früheren Mittelalter*, ed. Karl Schmid, 5 vols., Münstersche Mittelalter-Schriften 8/1–3 (Munich, 1978); Michel Parisse provides a sort of French-language guide to the larger work in his "La communauté monastique de Fulda," *Francia* 7 (1979): 551–65.

6. Karl Schmid, "Zur Problematik von Familie, Sippe und Geschlecht, Haus und Dynastie beim mittelalterlichen Adel. Vorfragen zum Thema 'Adel und Herrschaft im Mittelalter,'" in *Gebetsgedenken*, 183–244.

7. How far we still are from culturalist kinship research has recently been demonstrated by Joseph Morsel and Anita Guerreau-Jalabert, in particular; cf. Bernhard Jussen, *Artificial Kinship as Social Practice: Godparenthood and Adoption in the Early Middle Ages* (Newark, Del., 2000), chap. 1.

8. Georges Duby, "Structures de parenté et noblesse dans la France du Nord au XIe et XIIe siècles" (1967), reprinted in Duby, *Hommes et structures du Moyen Age* (Paris and The Hague, 1973), 267–85.

9. For a fundamental critique of German constitutional history, see Frantisek Graus, "Verfassungsgeschichte des Mittelalters," *Historische Zeitschrift* 243 (1986): 529–89. Otto Gerhard Oexle offers a brief, critical overview of the history of German "mainstream" medieval studies in "Was There Anything to Learn? American Historians and German Medieval Scholarship: A Comment," *Annual Lecture 1995, German Historical Institute, Washington, D.C.* (Washington, D.C., 1996), 23–44; see also Patrick Geary, "Medieval Germany in America," in ibid., 9–31.

10. See esp. Gerd Althoff, *Spielregeln der Politik im Mittelalter. Kommunikation in Friede und Fehde* (Darmstadt, 1997).

11. Gerd Althoff, *Amicitiae und pacta. Bündnis, Einung, Politik und Gebetsgedenken im beginnenden 10. Jahrhundert* (Hanover, 1992).

12. Gerd Althoff, "Die Bösen schrecken, die Guten belohnen. Bedingungen, Praxis und Legitimation mittelalterlicher Herrschaft," *Menschen im Schatten der Kathedrale: Neuigkeiten aus dem Mittelalter*, ed. Gerd Althoff, Hans-Werner Goetz, and Ernst Schubert (Darmstadt, 1998), 1–99, 27.

13. Althoff, "Die Bösen schrecken," quotations 3–4.

14. Gerd Althoff offers a sketch in "Vermittler," in *Lexikon des Mittelalters* 8 (Munich, 1997), 1555–57. For a more extensive account, see Hermann Kamp, *Friedensstiftung und Vermittlung im Mittelalter* (in press).

15. See Otto Gerhard Oexle, "Kulturwissenschaftliche Reflexionen über soziale Gruppen in der mittelalterlichen Gesellschaft: Tönnies, Simmel, Durkheim und Max Weber," in *Die okzidentale Stadt nach Max Weber. Zum Problem der Zugehörigkeit in Antike und Mittelalter*, ed. Christian Meier (Munich, 1994), 115–59; and "Les groupes sociaux du Moyen Age et les débuts de la sociologie contemporaine," *Annales É.S.C.* 47 (1992): 751–65.

16. See Otto Gerhard Oexle, "Conjuratio und Gilde im frühen Mittelalter. Ein Beitrag zum Problem der sozialgeschichtlichen Kontinuität zwischen Antike und Mittelalter," in *Gilden und Zünfte. Kaufmännische und gewerbliche Genossenschaften im frühen und hohen Mittelalter*, ed. Berent Schwineköper, Vorträge und Forschungen 29 (Sigmaringen, 1985), 151–214.

17. Otto Gerhard Oexle, "Gilde und Kommune. Über die Entstehung von 'Einung' und 'Gemeinde' als Grundformen des Zusammenlebens in Europa," in *Theorien kommunaler Ordnung in Europa*, ed. Peter Blickle (Munich, 1996), 75–97.

18. Arnold Angenendt, *Geschichte der Religiosität im Mittelalter* (Darmstadt, 1997); quotation from Joseph Lortz, 2.

19. Ibid., 24.

20. Jacques Chiffoleau, *La comptabilité de l'au-delà: Les hommes, la mort et la religion dans la région d'Avignon à la fin du moyen âge (vers 1320–vers 1480)* (Rome, 1980).

PART I

CONCEIVING

ONE

Counting Piety in the Early and High Middle Ages

Arnold Angenendt, Thomas Braucks, Rolf Busch, and Hubertus Lutterbach

Images of Counting: The Ledger and the Scales

This essay will focus on the counting and accumulation of acts of piety rather than the significance of numbers in the history of medieval piety more generally (that is, number allegorism or gematria). The model of accounting and the scales is the most useful approach for understanding this practice of counting and weighing. Historians of religion have remarked that the idea of a celestial account book exists in "three types, of which the 'book of fate' and the 'books of works' are common to all religions, while the 'book of life,' in the sense of a register of the citizens of Heaven, proves to be a biblical Christian image."[1] The less these books were understood in metaphorical terms, the more realistic the "bookkeeping" became. The vita of St. Martin already includes an enumeration of deeds: his fellow monks experienced the temptations of the devil, during which the devil listed the misdeeds of each; Martin, however, contradicted the devil, firmly asserting that old sins were canceled out by a pious way of life.[2] The "Books of Works," particularly those containing lists of "lifetime deeds," suggest accounting even more clearly. Bede recounts the tale of a royal liege man visited on his deathbed by two angels, who showed him a splendid but terribly small book in which everything good he had ever done was recorded; then, however, demons stormed into the room with a book so heavy they could scarcely carry it, in which all his misdeeds were "recorded there in black letters."[3] A person's deeds were listed, checked, and weighed. The number and the consequent weight were the decisive factors. A further metaphor was that of the scales, an image that is not frequently documented for the early church, however.[4] The example of a vision of the East Anglian peasant Thurkill from the year 1206 shows how realistically medieval people imagined the weighing process:

One part of the scale hung . . . before the Apostle Paul, the other . . . before the devil. The apostle had two weights beside him, one large and one small. . . . The devil similarly possessed two weights, one large and one small. . . . One after another, the wholly blackened souls stepped with great fear and trembling up to the scales to see how their deeds, the good and the evil, would be weighed there. For these weights, which were employed by the Apostle and the Devil on either side of the hanging scales, measured the works of the individual souls according to their merits. And so it happened that the Apostle's weights sometimes inclined the scales to his side when they showed the good works of one of the souls present. Occasionally, however, the Devil's weights were heavier, when they indicated the evil works of another soul; then they pulled the entire scale with the Apostle's weights over to the Devil's side.[5]

The speaker here may have been a villager, but this phenomenon was by no means restricted to popular religion. Boniface had already reported a vision in which demons and angels participated in the weighing process, "the demons bringing charges against them and aggravating the burden of their sins, the angels lightening the burden and making excuses for them."[6] The scales have been omnipresent in iconography since the twelfth century.[7] They were used to weigh good against evil deeds. Here, at the latest, we see the important place that counting and quantification assumed within Christian piety over the course of the early Middle Ages.

The New Testament

The New Testament, in contrast, mentions numbers, but not counting, in connection with religious acts. In the Gospel according to Luke, the disciples call upon Jesus: "Lord, teach us to pray!" Jesus then taught them the Our Father, a prayer which—according to Luke—contained but four lines (Lk. 11:1–4); Matthew cites seven lines (Mt. 6:9–15). They are preceded by the admonition not to "heap up empty phrases as the Gentiles do; for they think that they will be heard for their many words" (Mt. 6:7). True prayer was a different matter altogether: "But when you pray, go into your room and shut the door and pray to your Father who is in secret" (Mt. 6:6). As in the case of prayer, almsgiving and fasting—the other two of the three acts pleasing to God—were also internalized and banished from the public gaze, because they were meant for the eyes of God alone. We need only recall the now proverbial dictum, "do not let your left hand know what your right hand is doing, so that your alms may be in secret" (Mt. 6:3–4). The Gospel presents the example of the poor widow who can only afford to throw two small coins into the offertory box; in reality, though she has "put in more than all those who are contributing to the treasury" (Mk. 12:42–43). Fasting, too, is removed from the public sphere, "that your fasting may not be seen by men but by your Father who . . . sees in secret" (Mt. 6:18). These words were all uttered with critical intent, for they referred to an omniscient and all-seeing God who judged people by their hearts alone: thus one should love him, and one's neighbor, with all one's heart (Mk. 12:30). Just as good arises from the heart alone, so, too, does evil (Mk. 7:21)—hence the maxim, "Blessed are the pure in heart" (Mt. 5:8).

The words placed by the New Testament in Jesus' mouth were doubtless sharpened for critical effect: prayers did not need many words to be effective, and alms might consist of worthless pennies. At any rate, counting was unnecessary. One received the same dinar whether one had worked all day or only one hour (Mt. 20:1–6), for even this one dinar was a gift of pure grace. Thus in the end, "when you have done all that is commanded you, say, 'We are unworthy servants'" (Lk. 17:10). The classicist Albrecht Dihle commented on these postulates with the maxim, "In granting this grace, God is not bound by a humanly comprehensible yardstick of previous meritorious compliance with the law."[8] Such a lack of commitment must appear arbitrary to all notions of justice—and the gods are generally thought of as guardians of justice.[9] It was, however, precisely because Jesus did not feel bound by an iron justice that he could exercise mercy: one did not have to make atonement to him; he could forgive the greatest debt without any previous penance, as recounted in the parables of the lost sheep (Lk. 15:3–7) and the prodigal son (Lk. 15:19–32). As in the parable of the merciless creditor, the only precondition was that he whom God had forgiven an immeasurable debt was prepared to forgive his fellow men their, in reality, very minor debts: "'should not you have had mercy on your fellow servant, as I had mercy on you?'" (Mt. 18:32). Only a lack of mercy toward one's fellow human beings aroused the wrath of God, leading to judgment and damnation.

Numbers do appear in the New Testament, but they are not supposed to be used for counting. Instead, they are meant to convey the message that demands on behavior cannot possibly be grasped in numbers, and that counting is therefore absurd. Accordingly, when asked how often one must forgive one's brother (seven times), Jesus shifts the answer to the plane of the countless: "'I do not say to you seven times, but seventy times seven'" (Mt. 18:21–22). Jesus takes quite a similar approach to retribution. The underlying principle is that of talion or reciprocity, which Niklas Luhmann calls the first legal principle.[10] As Albrecht Dihle has shown,[11] Jesus put this retributive principle out of commission in the sentence: "the measure you give will be the measure you get" (Mt. 7:2). The intention is as clear as it is simple: because one would, naturally, like to claim more than one's due according to the talion, one is tempted to make "immeasurable" demands on interpersonal repayment. This means that the talion is overcome by the talion. And so it is with numbers: they are only mentioned in order to portray all counting as inappropriate.

Gifts and Return Gifts

The circumstance that God—as the Bible says—does not respond to force and is not obliged to reward good deeds, is quite unusual within the history of religion, for it calls into question a virtually fundamental religious law: the well-known *do ut des*, which has been referred to as the "shortest formula for the contractually conceived equilibrium . . . between gods and human beings."[12] The French sociologist of religion Marcel Mauss (d. 1950) taught us to view the significance of this exchange of gifts in a new light. Exchange applies to everything; it is a "system of total services,"[13] or, to put it even more clearly, a law of precise debits and credits. This applies particularly to relations with the gods: "it is believed that purchases must be made from the gods, who can set the price of things."[14] As an example, Mauss cites an epigrammatic poem from the Scandinavian *Edda*, whose refrain is "A gift in return for a gift."[15] Applied to religion this means that it is "Better not to ask / than to overpledge / As a gift that demands a gift / Better not to send / than to slay too many."[16] The consequence, as Hans Hattenhauer put it from the perspective of the history of religion, was that "The reciprocal relations between human beings, like those between them and the higher powers, were kept in equilibrium by means of gifts. . . . The principle of 'do ut des / I give, that you may give' is the indestructible foundation underlying all archaic legal cultures."[17]

Wherever the religious law of gift and return gift holds sway, a system of absolute justice and precisely calculated retribution develops. All beings, both earthly and celestial, are obliged to do their part. Thus clear measurements of transgression and guilt, mercy and forgiveness arise. The merit due to a good deed is as readily measurable as the penance due after a sin has been committed. In this manner of thinking, it is the very nature of religion to pay close attention to maintaining this equilibrium. The symbols of this view of religion are, once again, the ledger and the scales.[18] The scales must be in equilibrium if the existence of the world and of one's own life is not to be endangered. Well-being can only be expected if good outweighs evil. Roman religion, in particular, maintained a strict balance, since after all the "view of history as the work of the gods, who reveal themselves by demanding, rewarding and punishing [is] . . . the only form of theology that Rome has to offer."[19]

In contrast, the generosity demanded in the New Testament is founded in God's rich gifts to humankind, for which he expects nothing personal in return, but only the "offering of thanks." Yet God does not merely dispense with return gifts. Rather, he expects the recipients of benefits to pass them on to their neighbors: " 'You received without pay, give without pay' " (Mt. 10:8b). This act of transmission should, however, be free from any expectation of a return gift: " 'And if you do good to those who do good to you, what credit is that to you? . . .

And if you lend to those from whom you hope to receive, what credit is that to you?' " (Lk. 6:33f). This stance represents a clean break with the balance of gift and return gift, thus permitting the development of social behavior.

To be sure, the religious expectation of rewards was soon to attain a new significance within Christianity as well. The entire process of salvation could, of course, already be regarded as a "sacred exchange" (*sacrum commercium*),[20] if a "wondrous" one; since almighty God took all that was negative upon himself and left all that was positive to puny man. Thus Pope Leo the Great (d. 461) preached, "For He [Jesus Christ] came into this world as the rich and merciful merchant of Heaven, and, in a wondrous trade, entered into a commerce of salvation [*commercium salutare*], by taking on what was ours and distributing what was His, giving honor for disgrace, salvation for pain, life for death; and He, who had at His command more than twelve thousand of the host of angels to expel his persecutors, preferred to take upon Himself our weakness than to exercise His power."[21] Augustine had already spoken of the "merchant" Jesus Christ: "O good merchant, buy us! I say it, buy us, so that we must give thanks to you for buying us."[22] It is thus God who pays, not humankind!

This exchange was rooted in the person of Jesus Christ himself, in his simultaneous status as God and man, which made possible the relations of exchange with human beings in the sacraments, especially baptism and the Eucharist. Yet, the idea of *commercium* would soon approach a *do ut des* among Christians as well. The givers were now human beings and God was supposed to give them what he had in return. This notion then shaped the various acts of piety and was ultimately used to justify counting. A mode of thinking that emphasized redress appeared early in asceticism and penitence. The shift from grace to reward is already apparent in Tertullian: God must, for the sake of justice, punish every evil and reward every good deed. Thus, Tertullian was able to express the postulate that "a good deed makes a debtor of God."[23] Heaven is the reward for earthly toil. For, according to Ambrose of Milan, "no one who has not fought for it legitimately may receive the prize. And thus there is no glorious victory without laborious struggle."[24] For those who were particularly zealous— monastics—this idea was transformed into the firm expectation that ascetic merits could guarantee sure rewards: *ubi maior lucta maior est corona* (the greater the struggle, the larger the crown).[25]

Alms in particular produced a steadfast attitude of expectation: soon people could no longer imagine giving them without receiving some reward.[26] Preachers enticed the faithful with prospects of heavenly exchanges: "Make a trade with Christ! Why not give a portion of your goods to Him who prepared you an eternal reward? Why should He who has given you everything not receive the tithe? God offers heaven for your earthly wealth. . . . Then the Father, Lord and friend with whom you have made a heavenly exchange will answer: 'Earthly things have I received, eternal ones will I return; I have received what is mine, and give myself in exchange.' "[27]

Pope Gregory the Great already extolled the opportunity to place God in one's debt by giving alms.[28] It was a *sacrum commercium*, a trade that brought salvation, and the expectations of reward, Peter Damian believed, were sure to be fulfilled: "What one gives to God on Earth is accepted in Heaven; one may expect one's reward from that place whereto the offered gift preceded one. . . . A lucky exchange, by which man becomes the lender and God the debtor."[29] This is the source of the much lamented medieval "egotism of salvation": alms were given not out of love for the poor but out of a desire to assure oneself a place in heaven.[30]

From the perspective of *commercium*, the Eucharist was particularly amenable to combination with the idea of exchange: "Lord, with joy we bring earthly gifts to your altars, in order that we may receive heavenly ones; we give temporal [gifts] in order that we may receive eternal ones."[31] The universal religious expectation of exchange indeed began to change the nature of the Mass, since people assumed that the Mass was the sacrifice during which the Church presented the body and blood of Christ to God as an offering, and that God could not refuse his son's renewed sacrifice and was compelled to answer. As a consequence, people began to compute the value of the Mass. Thus, we might say the following of the medieval concept of the Mass: the fact that "the medieval theology and piety of the Mass were intensely concerned with the value of the Mass . . . and with the question of the fruits of the Mass . . . and their bestowability is connected with the understanding of the Mass as a sacrifice by the Church."[32]

The idea of compensation and the question of the measurability of the works of grace were the factors that allowed counting to penetrate the various areas of medieval piety. Medieval piety counted and weighed in a wide variety of ways, but not without opposition. After all, the sentence God ponders not how much, but from how much (*Non pensat Deus quantum, sed ex quanto*) retained its validity.[33] This conflict, like the hopes that the pious placed in counting at various times in the Middle Ages, will be the subject of the following section.

Penance and Counting

New Testament Foundations: Boundless Repentance and Endless Forgiveness

The writings of the New Testament use numbers to clarify the proper treatment of sin and guilt. These numbers do not, however, serve the quantification of (penitential) acts. Instead, they are intended to express the sinner's boundless desire to change his ways and the endless forgiveness owed to him. From the beginning, a reluctance to accept the salvation bestowed upon one by baptism and refusing it without subsequent repentance were regarded as deeply sinful and dangerous to the community, and ultimately as causes for excommunication.[34] Thus, according to Luke's Gospel, there is more rejoicing in heaven over a single sinner who repents than over ninety-nine righteous persons who have no need of repentance (Lk. 15:7). Luke's parable of the woman who loses one of her ten silver coins and then finds it again contains a similar lesson: " 'In the same way, I tell you, there is joy before the angels of God over one sinner who repents' " (Lk. 15:10). The forgiveness owed to the sinner is likewise computed symbolically; it is the unconditional duty of a Christian to search for those who have gone astray rather than to hold them to account with precisely measured sanctions (Mt. 18:12–14). This principle also influenced the procedure described in Matthew 18:15–17, which provided the basis for later congregational penances (showing the sinner his fault in private, then before three witnesses, and finally before the congregation) by shifting the "emphasis [of the procedure] from the realm of legal thinking to [that of] the pastoral and ecclesiological."[35] On a deeper level, what is at stake here is the endless forgiveness of the sinner. Matthew emphasizes this again in terms of the number seven: "Then Peter came up and said to him, 'Lord, how often shall my brother sin against me, and I forgive him? As many as seven times?' Jesus said to him: 'I do not say to you seven times, but seventy times seven' " (Mt. 18:21–22). The readiness to forgive is clearly expressed in Peter's question, "but it seeks the limit in a quantitative sense." Jesus' answer, as a "game with numbers, rejects limits and demands an endless readiness to forgive."[36] Luke's Gospel states accordingly that "if your brother . . . sins against you seven times in the day, and turns to you seven times, and says, 'I repent,' you must forgive him" (Lk. 17:4). Thus Luke, too, stresses the unconditional willingness to forgive the sinner: "The measure of readiness to forgive should know no bounds."[37]

In keeping with the New Testament demand that sinners repent as well as the injunction to forgive them, total repentance and boundless forgiveness were also the leitmotifs of the early church's treatment of guilt and sin. Given the concern for the individual, quantified penances were not to be expected: thus, the *Didache*, a church order of around 100 A.D., accordingly admonished sinners to confess and those around them to seek reconciliation: "Confess your transgressions to the congregation, and do not come to your prayers with a guilty conscience. That is the path of life."[38] Furthermore, "let no one who has a dispute with his neighbor come together with you until they have become reconciled again, so that your offering may not become unclean."[39] Above all, "cause no division, but rather make peace among the conflicting parties. Judge justly, and be no respecter of persons when you find someone guilty of an offense."[40] The ancient church sought to advance its communal penitential procedures not in order to punish sinners, but to improve them, and in the name of the love between them and the congregation: "Institutionalized canonical penance was developed in the second half of the second century to promote reconciliation."[41]

THE ANCIENT CHURCH: INDIVIDUAL EVIDENCE FOR A PREDETERMINED SCHEDULE OF PENANCES

The church soon found itself confronted with particularly grave ethical offenses, the *crimina capitalia*, above all fornication and idolatry, which went well beyond the minor misdemeanors of everyday communal life. Because people who had fallen into such sins had departed in an especially serious manner from the duty to love God and their neighbors (which they had accepted at baptism) and distanced themselves from the Christian community, the councils of the ancient church imposed precise and generally long penances in such cases. The "penitential letters" of Basil the Great reflect this very practice.[42] While the fourth- and fifth-century decrees of the Gallican councils describe the prescribed penances generally as *a communione separari* or *abstineri a communione*, from the sixth century onward they increasingly list clearly defined penances, which usually refer to capital offenses involving the unworthy conduct of office by clerics (bishops, presbyters, deacons, and so forth). Only rarely did the Gallican council fathers respond to the *crimina capitalia* of the Christian laity with predetermined penances. The number of years of penance imposed on clerics guilty of serious sins indicates that they were excluded either from office or from communion. To be sure, the years of penance varied from offense to offense; generally, however, if an exact time period was mentioned, offenders were excluded from office for between three months and two years,[43] but in most cases for no more than one year.[44] The same may have applied to exclusion from communion: the duration of penitence fluctuated between two months and one year, but was generally set at one year.[45] Only in rare cases did conciliar legislation stipulate fasting,[46] the payment of six ounces of silver or solidi[47] or one hundred blows[48] in place of temporary exclusion. Despite this prescribed measure of penance, the ancient church principle according to which the bishop alone decided what penance was appropriate for an individual sinner remained valid in the cases cited here as well. As Cyrille Vogel notes, "although some conciliar canons in antiquity prescribe a precise duration of penitence for certain sins, the bishop reserved the right to modify the prescribed duration of the penance for the good of sinners."[49]

Adalbert de Vogüé has pointed out that the monastic penance exercised by the cenobites of late antiquity "imitated completely the penitential discipline of the [ancient] church," but was at the same time distinct from it by virtue of its greater strictness: "This refinement of the collective conscience, which apparently regarded slight misdemeanors as grave faults, also meant that the time allowed for a change of heart was imposed with the greatest severity."[50] Although both the superiors of monasteries and the bishops were permitted to set penances as they saw fit in individual cases, the few exactly prescribed penances in the monastic rules show that these were imposed for even minor offenses and rarely lasted longer than a few days. Pachomius, for example, imposed a three-day public penance for house superiors who allowed a brother to go missing. A brother who spoke disparagingly of another was to be excluded from the community for seven days and permitted only bread and water.[51] The scale of penances of the *Regula Quatuor Patrum* from the abbey of Lérins ranged from a three-day exclusion for superfluous talking to a two-week punishment for laughing and frivolous speaking.[52] According to the monastic rule of Aurelian of Arles, the penalty imposed on a sinner must never exceed thirty-nine blows of the cane.[53] The penances in the Italic *Regula Magistri* from the first quarter of the sixth century range from one to two days, and only in one case ten days.[54] Only the monastic rule of the southern Gallican bishop Ferriolus of Uzès (d. 581) contains more extensive penances: while the penance for laughing in church was three days of fasting, a brother guilty of intemperance and overindulgence in wine had to pay with thirty days of penance. Disrespectful talk about a fellow monk carried the penalty of six months' exclusion from communion and the Pax.[55] Other penances were to be tailored to the gravity of the misdeed; the number of days of fasting imposed for arriving late to vigil were to correspond to the number of hours of prayer missed.[56] If a brother left the monastery without permission, his penitential fast was set at twice the number of days of his absence.[57]

In short, despite the occasional exact prescription of penances in the conciliar texts and monastic rules, the ancient church left the imposition of penances to the responsible bishops or superiors. They alone were believed to be in a position to set penances tailored to the individual sinner, taking all of the circumstances of the case into account.

The Early Middle Ages: The Tariffed Penance

In the early Middle Ages, the penitential practice of the early church diminished in influence. The penitentials, a literary genre that came to the Continent from Ireland in the seventh century, played a central role here. By making the tariffing of almost every sin a guiding principle, the penitentials moved away from the earlier practice of evaluating individual cases by bishops or the superiors of monasteries. At the same time, tariffing meant that numbers attained an importance unprecedented in the history of Christian penitence. Cyrille Vogel, a historian of the liturgy, defines the penitentials as "texts of varying size . . . which contain lists of sins, each of which is accompanied by a tax or tariff of expiation. In most cases, this consists of a precise number of days, months or years of fasting. . . . These lists . . . are always formulated with an astonishing casuistic care. The peculiarity of the penitential rests in this taxation or tariffication."[58] These characteristics cannot be explained simply in terms of the penitentials' highly particular point of view. Rather, the penitentials signal a deep break between the piety of the ancient church and that of the early Middle Ages. In regard to penitence, we can demonstrate this epochal change using the example of several offenses already discussed in the *Traditio Apostolica* of Hippolytus of Rome, a church order of the early third century, which were later also treated in the penitentials: "When you eat and drink, do so with dignity and not to the point of drunkenness,"[59] admonishes the *Traditio Apostolica*. The *Paenitentiale Cummeani*, an early Irish penitential, and numerous later penitentials, also discuss this area of offenses, but in a casuistically detailed form, with a precise penitential tariff for each separate offense: "He who suffers from overfilling his belly and the pain of overeating does penance for one day. If he suffers to the point of vomiting, without being ill, he does penance for seven days. If he also vomits up the host, he does penance for forty days."[60] The *Paenitentiale Cummeani* further stipulates that "those who have taken an oath of holiness and become drunk on wine or beer . . . atone for their offense by drinking only water for forty days, laypersons however for only seven days."[61] The *Traditio Apostolica* also admonishes the faithful always to take communion on an empty stomach: "Each believer should make an effort to receive the Eucharist before he has eaten anything else."[62] Referring to the commandment to have an empty stomach, virtually every penitential since at least the eighth-century *Iudicia Theodori* states that "whoever receives the *sacrificium* after eating does penance for seven days."[63] Finally, the *Traditio Apostolica* recalls that "you have received the chalice . . . as an image of the blood of Christ. Therefore do not spill any of it, so that no alien spirit, in contempt for you, might lap it up."[64] The penitentials, in contrast, stipulate that whoever spills a drop of the *sacrificium* onto the altar out of carelessness must do three days' penance.[65] Whoever offers up the chalice and spills it onto the earth must do ten days' penance.[66] The *Paenitentiale Laurentianum* distinguishes between the chalice from which something is spilled onto the altar during the offertory (*quando offertur*)—which entailed seven days' penance—and the chalice spilled during the actual celebration of the Mass (*dum solemniter missa celebratur*)—which demanded forty days' penance;[67] other penitentials limit themselves to the spilling of the chalice during the Mass, for which they impose thirty days' penance.[68] Anyone who dropped something from the chalice at the end of the Mass was to do thirty days' penance in some cases and forty in others.[69] We find a corresponding treatment of instructions from the ancient church among monastics. Thus, the rule for nuns written by Donatus (d. before 660), a disciple of Columbanus, refers back (among other texts) to the rule for nuns of Caesarius of Arles (d. 542) and the Rule of Benedict of Nursia (d. 546), both of which promote the ancient church's flexible imposition of penances. Donatus borrows numerous descriptions of offenses verbatim from these Rules, but in many cases replaces the imposed penances, which the late antique monastic instructions mention at most in very general terms, with precise penitential tariffs. An example of a text that Donatus borrows from the Rule of Caesarius may help to illuminate this shift. The Rule of Caesarius stipulates that no one may perform a task of her own without being instructed to do so, and that all work must instead be performed collectively; Columbanus' disciple Donatus adopts this description of the offense, but adds that, in case of violation, the offender must undergo a penance of one hundred blows.[70]

To recapitulate, tariffing, as a general characteristic of early medieval penitence, not only runs through the penitentials, but also left its traces in the monastic Rules in a manner that departed from the traditions of the ancient church.

A study of the frequency and significance of the numbers used for the tariffing of penances, which would be a worthwhile addition to the history of medieval piety, remains a desideratum; in light of the general lack of critical editions, especially of the most significant penitentials, we do not yet possess a reliable textual basis for such an undertaking. Thus in regard to the penitential tariffs, Reinhold Haggenmüller, who has studied the manuscript transmission of the penitentials attributed to Bede and Egbert, and unearthed a total of seventy-four copies "containing more or less extensive parts of these penitentials,"[71] notes that "the Bede-Egbert penitentials do not, to be sure, bear the stigma of anonymity, but rather the names of highly regarded authors. At the same time, the individual stages of the transmission, and even the individual manuscript groups, like the separate representatives of the manuscript groups, suggest differing, indeed even alternative, penances."[72]

Despite this lacuna, even an initial examination of the scale of penances permits some individual observations, which are of particular interest for the history of theology. Thus, the penitentials largely continue to rely on the number seven, which is used in the New Testament to describe unlimited forgiveness,[73] but transform it into a precisely stipulated penitential tariff. In the penitentials, the New Testament number symbolizing God's boundless love becomes an arithmetical exercise in recompense and atonement for damages: "A small boy who eats stolen food does penance for seven days."[74] Similarly, someone who became drunk on wine or beer also did seven days' penance. A seven-day penance likewise awaited those who had eaten so much that they had to vomit.[75] The development from a symbol of abundance to a tariffed measurement is evident for the number forty, which was originally associated not with a period of penance or fasting but with a period of reconciliation with God and one's fellow human beings: "[In the ancient church] one may note that the number forty was not understood as a precise mathematical figure, but rather as a [biblical] symbolic one. . . . Thus it was unimportant whether this period lasted exactly forty, forty-one or even only thirty-nine days. . . . As soon as one began to emphasize one particular element of this forty-day preparatory period—more precisely, the act of fasting [as a compensatory act, which was performed in the name of inward preparation]—one also began to calculate the exact number of fast days."[76] Correspondingly, we encounter the forty-day tariff penance, or the twenty-day version derived from it, everywhere in the penitentials: "Whoever steals food, does forty days' penance; whoever does so frequently, three times forty days,"[77] or "A ten-year-old boy who steals does seven days' penance; if he is twenty years old and commits a petty theft, he does twenty or forty days."[78] The penitentials also contain other scales of penance behind which we may suspect the number symbolism of the New Testament at work. An example is the number three, which is considered the symbol of "the triune Creator" or a "characteristic of the Redeemer."[79] Whether such a theologically motivated recourse to New Testament symbolism is also probable in light of the otherwise highly concrete information in the penitentials remains a matter for speculation. The way in which the individual penitentials treat Old Testament precepts in particular should make us skeptical. From the vantage point of proverbial repentance piety,[80] the Book of Proverbs transmits a maxim that seeks to elucidate the ever present possibility of repentance for the faithful: "for a righteous man falls seven times and rises again; but the wicked are overthrown by calamity" (24:16). The *Paenitentiale Finniani* takes up this vivid precept in order to set a seven-year penance for a fornicating cleric who fathers a child. "Holy Writ already states: just as the righteous man falls seven times and rises again, so too may the cleric who has fallen be called 'righteous' once again after having done penance for seven years."[81] Also remarkable are the extensive explanations of the number seven as a penitential tariff measure in the *Paenitentiale Bigotianum*, according to which the number seven was a symbol of the present life and, with reference to the Creation story, the day when the world was completed.[82]

In contrast to the heartfelt piety of the prophets, some pre-exilic works of the Old Testament reflect a mental horizon that distinguished between ritual cleanness and uncleanness. The periods of exclusion from the community that are mentioned at least occasionally in this context and expressed in numbers refer to the reestablishment of purity, for example after menstruation and childbirth; the number seven dominates, and refers to the number of days which a person had to stay away from camp or the marriage bed while he or she was unclean (for example, Lev. 14:8, 9, 38–39: exclusion of lepers; Lev. 15:13: discharge from the body; Lev. 15:24: sexual relations with an unclean woman; Num. 19:11–12, 16: touching a dead body). The early medieval penitentials reflect these periods in the penitential tariffs and the accompanying offenses.[83] In rarer cases, we can also trace the adoption of arithmetical prescriptions of penances from the Old Testament based on other figures. Thus, according to Leviticus, "If a woman conceives, and bears a male child, then she shall be unclean seven days. . . . Then she shall continue for thirty-three days in the blood of her purifying. . . . But if she bears a female child, then she shall be unclean two weeks, as in her menstruation" (12:2–5). Similarly, in the *Paenitentiale Cummeani* we read that "after childbirth the man withholds himself (from his wife because of her uncleanness) for thirty-three days, after the birth of a daughter for sixty-six days."[84] The *Paenitentiale Bigotianum* provides a variant stipulation: "It is already written in the book of Leviticus that a woman is unclean when she has given birth to a child. Yes, she is not merely unclean, but doubly unclean; for it says in the Bible that she remains unclean for two times seven days. . . . When she bears a boy, the child should be circumcised on the eighth day and then she is considered clean."[85]

The examples cited here demonstrate, particularly using the number seven, that in adopting numbers the penitentials oriented themselves toward the Old and New Testaments, but in so doing altered the original meanings. Many additional questions remain, however. How can we explain the widely varying yardsticks used to set penances for which the Bible provides no evidence from penitential practice? Is it conceivable—and the adoption of the number seven as recourse to the Creation story might suggest it—that, in taking numbers from Holy Writ, the penitentials sometimes oriented themselves more toward the symbolic value of the numbers than to the context of meaning of penitential practice? A further question concerns the biblical contexts from which numbers were borrowed, and what conclusions we may draw for the early medieval concept of penitence, on the one hand, and of Scripture, on the other. To what extent can we assume that the numbers to which the penitentials refer when imposing penances were taken from the Bible, even if it is nowhere explicitly stated? Yet another question relates to the extent to which the penitentials transmit numerical evidence reflecting "cosmic piety." Particularly striking is the number 365,[86] which we encounter frequently in eighth-century commutations, and which, as a number that was considered to be cosmic, was often used for converting and quantifying prayers, particularly in the late Middle Ages.[87] To be sure, the theological roots of this number reach back to the early Middle Ages. Thus, an Irish table of commutation sets up a relationship between the total number of joints in the human body, 365, and the number of "penitential works" that had to be sent after a dead person in order to free him or her from eternal perdition: "A commutation for rescuing a soul out of hell: 365 Paters and 365 kneelings and 365 blows of the scourge every day for a year, and a fast every month—this rescues a soul out of hell. For it is in proportion to the number of joints and sinews in the human body."[88] By taking it upon themselves to say the Lord's Prayer and endure genuflection and scourging on each of the 365 days of the year, the faithful liberated the dead person joint by joint until, at the end of the year, he or she was freed with all 365 joints from the eternal inferno. Another commutation refers, in the manner described, to the conversion of a one-year penance in the face of mortal danger: "If there be danger of death, the following is a commutation of a year of penance when accompanied by intense contrition: to chant 365 Paters, standing with both arms extended toward heaven and without the elbows ever touching the sides, together with fervent concentration on God. And the words [of the prayers] are not spoken aloud. And to recite the Beati in a stooping position with thy two arms laid flat by the sides. Or the whole body is stretched out along the ground face downwards and both arms laid flat by the sides."[89] The underlying principle that the penance imposed after the commission of a sin must be applied to all 365 joints of the body can apparently be found in many of the penances that ran for one year, that is, 365 days. For example, "if a wife leaves her husband and later returns to him, he should take her back and she should atone for one year on [a diet of bread and water]," or "a boy who puts his intention of fornication into practice with a girl will do penance for one year."[90] In the face of a grave sin entailing a penance of several years (for example, seven years, generally for perjury or fornication by a cleric), the penance must be imposed multiply upon each of the 365 joints of the body, in this case seven times. Underlying this logic is the principle that the penitentials apply to the apportionment of penance: "Whoever sins with the body, makes amends with the body."[91] This concept constituted the root of corporal penitential practices in the penitentials, particularly the tariffed fasts, vigils, and scourgings—a subject largely neglected up until now by historians of religion and theology.

It was part of the logic of the penitential tariffs described here that penitents could also convert their tariffed penances into penitential units of their own choosing through commutation and redemption. Cyrille Vogel has even referred to these alternative possibilities as "a necessary corrective to the tariffs foreseen by the Libri Paenitentiales." [92] Only with these aids were the sometimes impossible penances involving fasting—which were imposed for even the most minor offenses—practically, and above all quickly, manageable. An eighth-century Irish table of commutation provides an extensive justification for the existence of such lists: "The sages enumerate four reasons why the commutations are practiced: 1. for a speedy separation from sin with which one has been united; 2. for fear of adding to the [unatoned] sin in the future; 3. for fear that one's life may be cut short before the end of the penance decided by a soul-friend [as a proxy]; 4. in order to be free to approach the Body and Blood of Christ by restricting the period of penance." [93] The penitentials particularly passed down tables of commutation that converted fasting penances into stricter and thus temporally restricted forms of penance. One of the earliest pieces of evidence for the interchangeability of penances, which served not the ethical improvement of the sinner but only necessary compensation, has come down to us under the title "De arreis" within the *Canones Hibernensis*. [94] The notes on commutation all proceed from a duration of one year. The equivalent penances are organized in ascending order, whereby the harshness of the "penitential work" diminishes with the temporal extension of the replacement penance. To be more precise, one year of penance with a fast of bread and water could be replaced by:

Three days and nights without sitting and with little sleep during which one
    recited 150 psalms with the ten Cantica and hourly prayers; in addition
    twelve genuflections and raised hands during horary prayers
To lie three days in a grave with a dead saint, without food, drink, or sleep,
    chanting the Psalms and the Hours after confessing one's sins to a priest and
    taking a (not more precisely defined) vow
Three days in a church without sleeping or sitting as well as additional chanting
    without pause of the Psalms and Cantica, furthermore twelve genuflections
    with each horary prayer after confessing to a priest and making a promise
Twelve days and nights of fasting eating twelve rusks of the amount of three
    loaves of bread
Twelve times three days (fasting)
One month (that is, thirty days) in great pain (*in magno dolore*), from which
    however no one would die
Forty days and nights on bread and water as well as two particular fast days every
    week; forty psalms and forty genuflections with each of the horary prayers
Fifty days on bread and water as well as sixty psalms and sixty blows at each of the
    horary prayers
One hundred days on bread and water as well as regular horary prayers

Similar equivalencies were a self-evident component of most penitentials.[95] The mathematical precision, however, which the *Paenitentiale Remense* reveals in calculating psalms and genuflections, is unusual indeed:

1 day of fasting = 50 psalms with genuflection, or 70 without.
1 week of fasting = 300 psalms with genuflection, or 420 without.
1 month of fasting = 1,200 psalms with genuflection, or 1,680 without.[96]

The preceding examples—which we use here only to indicate that tariff penances of whatever quantity or "penitential unit" (purchasing the freedom of slaves, almsgiving, masses, and so forth) were also taken into account in the commutation stipulations—point to the need for a systematic study of the commutation of penances. Generally, we need to ask what conclusions the tables of commutation allow us to draw about medieval penitential piety in regard to numbers and counting. More precisely, to what extent can we demonstrate an unchanged reception of commutation stipulations, such as we have already shown for the above-mentioned equivalencies in the *Paenitentiale Remense*? Conversely, what changes in the equivalencies do we find over the course of the transmission process, and what traditions do they point to? These questions open up for discussion both the issue of how binding these stipulations were in the process of transmission and the possibility that the value placed upon different means of penance may have varied regionally.

Within the system of tariff penances, with its characteristic bookkeeping mentality, there was an ultimate logic to sinners' ability to satisfy the imposed penance by selecting proxies to atone on their behalf: "Whoever does not know the Psalms and cannot fast may choose a righteous man to perform this for him and take upon himself the penance and labors, and for one day of [penance by proxy] let him give one dinar to the poor."[97] The possibility of transferring necessary spiritual acts to another person (who received a monetary reward for it) facilitated the incorporation of the Mass, in particular, into the system of penance by proxy; the laity paid the priest to say the Mass in compensation for their penance.[98] These examples underline the potential value of a study of all redemptive acts for a history of the counting of penances. At present, however, such a project faces insuperable barriers: "A complete overview of the transmission of the various redemption texts cannot be gained using the existing editions, since the composition of the texts in copies of the Excarpsus Cummeani and Paen. Remense that have come down to us vary sharply . . ., and since the editions of the Paenitentialia Ps.-Bedae and Ps.-Egberti as well as of the Paen. mixtum by Schmitz and Wasserschleben account for only a randomly chosen segment of the transmission in each case."[99] When it comes to the counting of penitential piety in particular, it may safely be said that "the redemptions and commutations are highly variable in their forms and equivalencies."[100]

THE STANDARDIZATION AND BROADER INFLUENCE OF THE PENITENTIALS

The influence of the penitentials, which were originally circulated as private texts, that is, outside of canon legislation,[101] is reflected in the fact that these catalogues of penances were expressly taken into account on several occasions by ninth-century Council assemblies. On the one hand, the Councils—for example that held in 813 in Châlon-sur-Saône—demanded that the penitentials be repressed, indeed destroyed, because they contained obvious errors from uncertain sources and signified death for souls.[102] In 829, the Council fathers of Paris demanded that each bishop should have his diocese searched for penitentials; these little texts (*codicelli*) should, to the extent that they ran contrary to canonical authority, be abolished altogether and committed to the flames.[103] On the other hand, the Council texts recommend that the divergent penance tariffs contained in the circulating penitentials should at least be unified in a standardized "norm penitential." Bishop Halitgar of Cambrai put this suggestion into practice. The final part of his five-volume work on penitence, in particular, emulated traditional penitentials in pairing every offense with a tariffed fasting penance.[104] Given that Halitgar sought to unify the scale of penances for individual offenses, and that the study of the manuscripts of Bede's and Egbert's penitentials still reveals largely divergent penitential tariffs for the ninth to twelfth centuries, we should maintain a certain skepticism about the reception of the commutations unified by Halitgar.

The epochal quality of Halitgar's penitential, then, lies in the fact that he received an official ecclesiastical commission to unify the penitential tariffs of Irish origin. The counting of penitential piety was apparently already so entrenched in the life of the Church that people only dared to discuss the level of penitential tariffs or the conversion rate. The penitential system, with its emphasis on settling accounts, had long since become irreversibly established in many areas of early medieval piety. This development was not without consequences for early medieval literacy. Thus, the *interrogationes examinationis* of a capitulary from the year 803 expected that priests "should know and understand how to use the penitential."[105] Another capitulary of the same period stipulates that the priest should be "instructed in the Canones and know his penitential well."[106] According to the *Capitula Ecclesiastica* of 810, the priest should even be able to give detailed information on the precise usage of the penitential.[107] Other church assemblies listed the instruments and books, including penitentials, which priests were supposed to bring with them when they reported on their pastoral activities before the regular meetings of the synods. Examples include the capitulary of Ghaerbald of Liège,[108] the capitulary of Haito of Basel,[109] the *Capitula episcopi cuiusdam Frisingensia*[110] and the so-called *Admonitio synodalis*.[111] Beyond the numerous manuscripts in which many penitentials have come down to us, at least a few medieval inventories demonstrate that penitentials belonged to the basic fixtures of parishes.[112] The idea that the spread of quantified penitential piety helped to stimulate the spread of literacy may be illustrated by examining the records of prayer fraternities. Prayer fraternities were established in order to fulfill the atonement due to God after one's death. These associations of living and dead monks, clerics, and laymen were founded with the purpose of offering mutual support through the precise fulfillment— mainly by prayer and the celebration of masses—of duties specified in writing. The union of donation, penance by proxy, and entry into the commemorative book was also the foundation of probably the most famous mortuary association, that of Attigny (776/777). The participants promised to offer each other spiritual aid in case of death. In the case of bishops and abbots, this meant one hundred masses or psalters, and in the case of clerics, thirty of either. The bookkeeping mentality propagated by the penitentials also influenced the spread of votive masses,[113] as well as the system of donations and alms,[114] and, finally and particularly, the emergence of indulgences. The system of indulgences returns to the practice, seldom criticized but frequently permitted in the penitentials, of tariffed penances being performed by paid proxies, a practice referred to in the above-mentioned *Excarpsus Cummeani* as a possibility for redemption. What is more, within the logic of the penitentials, the indulgence goes even one step further by offering penitents security even for those sins to which they had forgotten to confess, and for which they had thus not atoned according to the penitential tariff. Even if the roots of indulgence in the early medieval system of penitential tariffs have not yet been studied in great detail, it is apparent that within the tradition of commutations, indulgences ensured the performance of those penances that penitents could no longer manage in their own lifetimes.[115] Above all, though, the massive spread of indulgences in the high and late Middle Ages brought forth new written media, which precisely recorded the relationship between services and reciprocal services, and were to exercise a powerful influence on high and late medieval piety. As a high point in the counting of penitential piety, the indulgence was a thorn in the side of the Reformers. Because of its incompatibility with both the boundless repentance demanded of sinners in the New Testament and the unlimited forgiveness owed to them, the indulgence helped provoke the outbreak of the Reformation.

Counting Alms

Alms as Penance and Commutation in the Penitentials

In early Christianity, almsgiving was already regarded as a meritorious pious exercise; alms were considered particularly important for gaining forgiveness for postbaptismal sins.[116] The forgiveness of sin at baptism would have remained worthless, Cyprian of Carthage (d. 258) emphasized, had God not "opened a path to salvation through the works of mercy, so that we might wash away the stains of sin through alms."[117] However much the additional possibility of atonement through alms may have been propagated in the penitential parenesis of the ancient church, though, the penitent's religious and moral attitude remained decisive. The efficacy of penance was dependent on true repentance and a change in one's mode of living. Characteristically, Augustine taught that it was not enough to give alms for one's misdeeds while at the same time continuing in one's habits of sin.[118] Almsgiving was regarded primarily as a visible expression of a penitential state of mind, but not accorded any value as a means of atonement in its own right.

The ancient church doctrine of the expiatory effect of alms remained central in the early Middle Ages, but an obvious shift of emphasis occurred, which affected the practice of almsgiving as penance. This change becomes tangible in the stipulations of the penitentials and their system of tariffs. We should note first of all that alms were seldom applied in the casuistical provisions of the penitentials. Where they are mentioned, however, there is often a correspondence between the misdemeanor and the penance imposed. Thus, for example, Columbanus' seventh-century penitential stipulates that a penitent who committed perjury out of greed should "sell all of his goods and give to the poor, turn to God, put aside all worldly things and serve God in a monastery until his death."[119] The *Paenitentiale Remense*, which was composed in the first half of the eighth century in northeastern France, directs those who, out of ignorance, hoarded superfluous goods for the future to give them to the poor; those who did so out of evil intentions, in contrast, should be healed by almsgiving and fasting, following the judgment of a priest.[120] According to the late eighth-century *Paenitentiale Merseburgense*, "whoever grasps the property of others evilly, through strength or some other quality, and steals it, should do penance for three years, one of them on bread and water, and give many alms."[121] The stipulations cited here are typical examples; alms generally represented the penance for sins rooted in penury and greed or related to the theft and destruction of property. It was no accident that almsgiving was regarded as the proper expiation, since the idea was based on the principle, already formulated by John Cassian and propagated in the penitentials, of *contraria contrariis curare*,[122] according to which a sin should be atoned for by the opposite good work. Yet, this mode of applying salutary penances to sins by no means became decisive for the imposition of penances, so that we cannot speak of a "medicinal" notion of penitence.[123] For example, many penitentials, including the *Burgundense, Bobbiense, Parisiense simplex, Sletstatense, Oxoniense I, Floriacense, Hubertense*, and *Sangallense simplex*, also impose almsgiving as a penance for drunkenness or sexual offenses.[124] We should note furthermore that fasting was the most important penance in the penitentials.[125] A specified exercise in fasting was the penance imposed for the great majority of misdemeanors, without any recognizable salutary correspondence between the sin and the expiatory act, or any intention of morally improving the sinner. This is even truer of the commutations, which treat fasting, prayer, and alms as interchangeable penances.

In contrast to the casuistical differentiation of misdeeds and assigned penances, alms were of the greatest significance for the commutation lists. A fundamental shift of emphasis had occurred, particularly in the commutations, when compared to their value within the ancient church. Almsgiving now served not only penitence but also the "cancellation" of fixed terms of repentance. Money payments and other material services—understood as alms—could now replace extended periods of fasting imposed upon sinners. The *Paenitentiale Remense*, for example, states, "Let whoever cannot do penance in the manner described above give 26 solidi in alms during the first year, 20 during the second, and 18 in the third, that is 64 solidi."[126] The figures quoted here represent the penance of one year in relation to a corresponding sum of money in alms: assuming the solidus or sou to be worth twelve denari,[127] a value that the commutation expressly sets as alms in exchange for one day of penance,[128] this appears to yield a well-organized catalogue of conversion, according to which the sum of twenty-six solidi for the first year represents the equivalent of 312 days of penance. Adding Sundays, which were penance free, this would amount to about the number of days in a year. The same is true of the sum of twenty solidi for the second year: converted into denari, this yields a sum of 240, to which we must add the Sundays and the periods from Christmas to Epiphany and Easter to Whitsun, which the commutation designates as penance free for the second year.[129] In order for the eighteen solidi (216 denari) demanded in the third year to fill the penitential year on the basis of the mode of calculation used here, a number of holy days deemed penance free elsewhere in the commutation had to be added to those named for the first two years.[130] Arithmetical precision down to the last detail was impossible, to be sure, but in each case the figures in the commutation come quite close to replacing the days of penance in a year by the payment of alms. This exchange of the means of penance reveals a telling break with the notions of the ancient church: almsgiving neither served the purpose of counteracting a sin by means of the opposite good deed, as can be found in some provisions in the penitentials, nor did it express a penitential attitude or efforts at moral improvement. Rather, it was considered a compensatory act that was objectively capable of making up for the misdeeds committed.

Deeds of Donation: Almsgiving and Heavenly Rewards

Apart from information on commutations, the penitentials also contain recommendations for almsgiving: the oblation *super Dei altare*, the distribution of alms to the needy, purchasing the freedom of, and freeing, slaves, and donating land to the Church.[131] The practice of atoning for one's sins and securing the salvation of one's soul by donating land, in particular, became a central element of early medieval piety, as scholars have argued. People sought access to the liturgical memorialization of monks and canons, in *Liber vitae* and necrologies, by means of donations to monastic or spiritual communities.[132] Deeds recording the donation of land repeatedly mention their purpose as *pro remedio animae*; *arengas* and explanatory formulas interpret it as retributive compensation. The guiding concepts may be illustrated using records from the monastery at St. Gallen, which include some eight hundred documents on parchment from the period up until the beginning of the tenth century, containing around six hundred donations *pro remedio animae*.[133] An *arenga* that recurs frequently in St. Gallen, and is widespread in this and variant forms, states in ideal-typical terms, "If we give something of our property to the places of the saints or as alms to the poor, we may be sure that this will be rewarded in eternal blessedness."[134] In another arenga, Christ appears as a *remunerator*, whose agreement to a gift surely entails compensation.[135] The conviction that good will be rewarded is summarized succinctly in the formula *pro aeterna retributione*, of which we find some one hundred examples before the year 900 alone.[136]

This motif is rooted in the eschatological expectation of compensation by Christ the judge, and was of secondary significance in early Christianity, as a look at the visual arts reveals. The few early Christian depictions of judgment are dominated by the idea of the coming Kingdom of God: "The idea of salvation is so much in the foreground that it plays the central role in the Last Judgement."[137] To be sure, the concept of a last judgment was firmly anchored in patristic literature. It mainly served as a warning there, however; the discussion of reward and punishment was seen as a mighty incentive to ethically responsible behavior.[138] The emphasis shifted in the early Middle Ages. Now, judgment was passed wholly in the spirit of retribution for good and evil behavior. Before pronouncing judgment on salvation or damnation, the divine judge undertook a strict weighing of deeds, and good deeds had to stand up to evil ones.[139] To be sure, this expectation of judgment is only rarely made explicit in the deeds of donation, and scarcely developed in a clear manner. These documents nevertheless contain certain key words that provide some idea of the Last Judgment to come and of its forensic nature. They speak briefly of *cogitavimus de diem iudicii*.[140] One mid-ninth-century deed adds the phrase *cogitans futuram peccatorum discussionem et retributionem justorum* in justification of the donation,[141] while other documents mention future procedures for examining conduct and rewarding individuals for the merits they have amassed.[142] Finally, donations and alms were interpreted as effective means of preparing for the Last Judgment: "Whatever we have given in the places of the saints or to the poor as alms, will, we do not doubt, be compensated eternally by the just and most high judge, who says: What you have done to one of the least of my brothers you have done to me."[143]

Against the background of examining one's conduct over a lifetime, donation was regarded above all as an expiatory offering for sins committed. The expiatory purpose of land donations is generally marked by simple phrases, such as *in remissione peccatorum* or *pro peccatis meis* in the section of the deed leading up to the *dispositio*.[144] At the same time, the widespread and much used formulas featuring the term *venia*[145] as well as expressions such as *delictorum meorum non inmemor*[146] or *recordatus multitudinem peccatorum meorum*[147] point to sins as the occasions for the donation. Furthermore, the texts take up the motif of the forgiveness of sins, speaking variously of redemption from sins or the redemption of the soul. These expressions already possessed an extraordinary significance in the ancient church: the expressions *redemptio peccatorum* and *redemptio animae* were set terms for the penitential exercise of cleansing oneself of sin by giving alms to the poor or making donations to the Church.[148] Authors particularly invoked the words of the Old Testament, such as Daniel 4:24 (*peccata tua elemosynis redime*) and Proverbs 13:8 (*redemptio animae hominis divitiae suae*), to support this practice. Thus, the arenga from a deed of 852, which is remarkable for its individual form, states: "After mankind was afflicted by the mark of sin and banished from the joys of Paradise because they were guilty of disobedience, God recommended to the world this remedy among many, that men could redeem their souls from Hell by their wealth, as he said through Solomon: a man's riches may ransom his soul."[149]

We frequently encounter the author's expectation of attaining rewards from the divine judge. Expressions containing the word *merces* or *praemium*, in particular, refer to Heaven as a reward for alms.[150] Arengas occasionally use the motif more explicitly, noting that one may attain eternal reward through one's wealth.[151] The texts also impress upon the reader that those who well know how to handle worldly goods properly could turn their transitory goods into everlasting reward.[152] Here the idea of *commercium*, for which the patristic literature prepared the ground, and which entered the liturgy,[153] becomes significant for deeds of donation as well. The arengas present the donation of land as an earthly-heavenly exchange by means of which one could purchase everlasting property with one's worldly goods. An individually worded arenga, which refers to Luke 6:38 and Matthew 19:29, reads, "I . . . Wolfhart am exhorted through divine inspiration to buy everlasting with earthly property and to acquire lasting goods for transitory ones. Mindful of the salutary instructions: Give and you shall receive, and: No one who leaves his house and his land for my sake will not receive a hundredfold reward, I convey. . . ."[154] From this perspective, it is understandable when one arenga admonishes each person to keep documentation of his property as long as he lives, "for the fleeting light of life is worth nothing unless one can use present goods to buy everlasting ones."[155]

Contemporaries believed that all of this was substantiated by the Bible, and a number of deeds contain phrases borrowed from the Old and New Testaments that (usually woven into an arenga) are recalled as divine postulates. Those most frequently encountered are Sirach 3:33 (*ignem ardentem extinguit aqua et elemosyna resistit peccatis*), Luke 6:38 (*date et dabitur vobis*) and 11:41 (*date elemosynam et ecce omnia munda sunt vobis*), as well as Proverbs 13:8 (*redemptio animae viri divitiae suae*).[156] Just as these words had belonged to the inventory of treatises and sermons on almsgiving since the early patristic period, they now became relevant for the composition of deeds of donation. From a programmatic standpoint these sentences, by supporting the expectation of retribution, expiation, and heavenly reward, expressed the prospects associated with donation. Thus, the view that God deemed alms and the renunciation of property in favor of the Church to be meritorious offerings must have appeared to donors to be well anchored in Scripture.

The few examples from St. Gallen that we have cited here make it clear that the motivations for donations were strongly shaped by sin and the need for atonement as well as by the expectation of God's retribution for and reward of human deeds. We find articulated here not so much individual penitential attitudes as the bookkeeping mentality as a motive force behind human action. Just as misdeeds unrelentingly demanded compensation, the authors of the documents discussed here counted on their donations being accepted as retributive exchange. This finding can be generalized; the elements sketched here appear throughout the documents, although they have not yet received the attention they deserve. To be sure, the arengas and justificatory formulas, which were largely dismissed in the older literature as trivial commonplaces,[157] have gained in reputation since the path-breaking work of Heinrich Fichtenau,[158] since their "value for our knowledge of medieval thought and behavior is no longer disputed."[159] The new questions raised have scarcely been pursued in relation to early medieval documents, however. The conceptual horizon dominated by notions of "counting piety" that we find expressed in arengas and formulas has failed to arouse the interest of scholars. Although the context within which donations emerged and exerted influence has other dimensions as well,[160] the vast number of donations *pro remedio animae* owe much to the effects of the bookkeeping mentality.

Counting Masses

THE MASS AS AN EXPIATORY AND SAVING SACRIFICE

The changes in the understanding and practice of Christian worship that began during late antiquity and reached their conclusion in the early Middle Ages are well known. The "Eucharistia" of the ancient church became the "Mass," and the "thanks for" became a "sacrifice for."[161] The petitions of the faithful for salvation and forgiveness of their sins as a blessing from God moved to the foreground. To be sure, Ambrose and Augustine had already attributed to the celebration of the Eucharist a certain utility for the living and the dead,[162] but early medieval theology went several steps further. The offerings of the faithful as well as the effect of the sacrifice of the Mass in bringing about salvation and the forgiveness of sins—whether for those making the offering themselves and their desires, or for the dead—became the pillars of the practice of the Mass. One made the offering and attached one's desires and petitions to it in the hope that God could not leave them unfulfilled in the face of this sacrifice.[163] Angelus Häußling has expressed this concisely as "The sacrifice of the Mass, however, becomes a 'Means to.' "[164] Thus not only were many pleas associated with the sacrifice of the Mass—as was the case in the various intercessions in the canon of the Roman liturgy—but the sacrifice was also deployed for many purposes. This practice found expression in the numerous and diverse formulas of the votive Masses.

VOTIVE MASSES AND SERIES OF MASSES

The early Middle Ages witnessed a rapidly growing number of Masses, a multiplication of altars in the churches and an ever greater proportion of priests among the monks in the monasteries. This development and its causes have been discussed from various perspectives.[165] What does seem certain is that the votive Masses played a significant role here. Their formulas occupy a central place in the sacramentaries—both in terms of their numbers and their assignment to the services held during the week—as an examination of these books reveals.

The *Bobbio-Missal* contains a total of sixty formulas for the Mass, including fourteen for votive and requiem Masses;[166] in its "Liber tertius," the *Altgelasianum* offers fifty-seven formulas for votive and requiem Masses alongside the Sunday Masses and a few further prayers;[167] and the *Sacramentarium Rhenaugiense* contains thirty-two such formulas.[168] The widely distributed *Supplementum Anianense* assembles thirty-six formulas for votive and requiem Masses in all.[169] Many of the ninth-century Gregorian sacramentaries increased the number of these Masses still further; one sacramentary from Cologne provides a total of eighty-nine,[170] and a sacramentary from Saint-Amand one hundred.[171] The most extensive collection, however, can be found in the Fulda sacramentary: it contains 161 different formulas for votive and requiem Masses.[172]

The votive Masses were celebrated at all stages of life and for various individuals and groups; the *Supplementum Anianense*, for example, contains formulas for Masses said for kings or for one specific king, for the king at the time of a synod, for the priest himself, for the *uotum* of an individual, for the salvation of the living, for one's close friends, for the abbot and the congregation, for travelers, for mariners, for the sins, in wartime, for peace, for emergencies, in cases of cattle epidemics, disputes, against unjust judges and contradictors, for rain or fine weather, against storms, for a sick person, for a dead person, for a dead person recently baptized, for the dead who yearned for but had not attained repentance, on the anniversary of a death, for many dead people in the cemeteries, for the salvation of the living, and for the dead.[173] Votive Masses were by no means celebrated only once; rather, the sacramentaries reveal the emergence of additive series of Masses, which required the celebration of a certain number of Masses. Thus, for example, we find series of seven Masses in honor of Mary and all the saints or for the priest himself, which were sometimes expressly assigned to individual days of the week.[174] The Fulda sacramentary also contains a series of seven Masses for the days of the week to be said in times of tribulation, and a series of four Masses for the sins, which were to be celebrated on Monday, Tuesday, Wednesday, and Friday.[175] Apparently, the observance of the precisely measured number was intended to ensure the workings of grace. Thus, we should also ask whether a series of three thematically similar votive Masses held one after the other was intended only as an equivalent alternative, or as an additive series of Masses.

COUNTING MASSES

While the series of Masses already hint at the significance of counting for the early medieval piety surrounding the Mass, it becomes even more evident in the case of the commemoration of the dead. The Mass became an instrument by means of which one hoped to atone for the sins of the dead and to shorten their time in purgatory.[176] Pope Gregory the Great offered the justification for this practice. As evidence, he recounted the story of a deceased bathhouse attendant whose sins were expiated by a priest saying seven masses for him on seven consecutive days. In a second tale, the monk Justus was freed from purgatory by a sequence of thirty masses on thirty days.[177] While the series of seven or thirty of the Gregorian Masses had originally been limited to the care of the dead, they were later extended to all sorts of occasions. Addressing the fundamental logic that underlay the success of the Gregorian Masses, one scholar has remarked that "what these Masses . . . have in common is the promise of absolutely certain success, whether they were said for the dead or the living."[178]

The counted masses played a pioneering role in the prayer fraternities.[179] We repeatedly find agreements indicating that one hundred or thirty masses, but also seven or three, should be celebrated in case of death.[180] The interests of the living were also included in such arrangements regarding masses, however. The "Statuta Rispacensia, Frisingensia, Salisburgensia," for example, stipulates that the entire clergy should fast, recite a litany, and celebrate masses on the fourth and sixth days of the week for "the soundness and prosperity and firmness of God's entire Church, and also for the eternal salvation of the Christian people and the everlasting life of their souls, as well as for the life, salvation, and stability of the empire, the lord, the king and his children."[181] The 840 Synod of Le Mans also decided that fifty psalms could be chanted as the equivalent of the Litany and the Mass.[182] We encounter other frequencies for such Masses, such as daily,[183] or every Wednesday, as well.[184]

In the last-mentioned cases, the frequency of masses followed a pattern: the salvation they procured, or their expiatory effect, was constantly being reassigned to the living in a periodically recurrent rhythm, whereby differences in duration could be attributed to the efficacy of an individual mass. In the practice of penance, however, the efficacy of the Mass was itself quantified and introduced as a commutation service for other penitential works. Around the end of the eighth century, at the latest, we find masses being incorporated into these lists as a means of expiation.[185] In the *Sacramentarium Rhenaugiense*, which was written shortly before 800, we find a telling phrase in a formula entitled *Missa uotiua*, which belonged to a Mass for the living and the dead: the priest now also celebrated the Mass for those "who had confessed to him their own crimes and misdeeds before God's majesty."[186] The background was that the person confessing had given alms to the priest celebrating the Mass, for which the latter in return said the Mass as a penance on the other's behalf. This sacramentary itself contains a table of commutation for money, psalms, and masses: "For one solidus 100 psalms or three masses; for one ounce 150 psalms or three masses; for six ounces six psalters and three masses; for one pound twelve psalters and twelve masses."[187] The list does not appear to be exact—it may well contain scribal errors, but we might also attribute this to a social gradation of tariffs. Lists containing quite precise calculations have also come down to us, though: "The celebration of a mass may redeem twelve days, ten masses four months, twenty masses eight months, thirty masses twelve months."[188]

Masses were also counted in times of trouble. In a letter written to Bishop Ghaerbald of Liège during the famine year 807, for example, Charlemagne ordered three three-day fasts because of the infertility of the soil, the threat of famine, the unfortunate climate, epidemics, and wars. Apart from the precise dates, Charlemagne also sent Ghaerbald extensive instructions for the penitential works to be performed on those days. Aside from fasting and alms, each priest should say Mass on each of the days named, that is, three times three masses, and every cleric, monk or nun should chant fifty psalms on each day.[189] Finally, the masses for the king or for him and his family were counted. When the Council of Arles decided in 813 that masses should be celebrated for Charlemagne and his children in all episcopal sees and in all bishoprics every day so long as he lived, they expressly stated that these masses were in recompense for his benevolent deeds.[190] Apart from such masses that accompanied the life of the monarch, we also have evidence of counted masses characterized by astonishingly high numbers. Thus, for example, the monks of Fulda promised Emperor Louis one thousand masses in the year 828.[191] Hrabanus Maurus informed Louis the German in a letter that the 847 Council of Mainz had decided that masses should be celebrated and psalms chanted for him, his wife, and his children, the sum of which he mentioned as thirty-five hundred masses and seventeen hundred psalters.[192]

The Written Word and the Counting of Masses

The significance of the written word for the early medieval liturgy cannot be overestimated. Not only was great emphasis placed on correct liturgical books,[193] but a very great number of such books arose, since each participant in the liturgy was given his own book: the sacramentary, which contained the prayers for the chief celebrant; the lectionary, which contained the texts for the lessons; and the antiphonary, which contained the versicles to be sung by the choir.[194] Thus, for example, the inventory of one church mentions three sacramentaries, three lectionaries, one old gospel book and two antiphonaries, alongside the books of the Bible in several volumes and commentaries.[195]

In the sacramentaries, the various formulas of the "missae generales pro vivis et defunctis"[196] take us to the heart of the practice of counting masses and the writing associated with it. In the *Bobbio-Missal* we already encounter such a formula, entitled *Missa pro uiuos* (!) *et defunctis*,[197] whose opening oration is characteristic. For the sake of clarity, it may be useful here to cite the first oration in its entirety: "Thy majesty, most benevolent Father, we ask for our brothers and sisters, also for all of our benefactors and for those who have entrusted their prayers to us, both for the living and for those released from the pay of death, whose alms we have received for distribution and whose names we have written down in commemoration and whose names are recorded on the holy altar. Grant mercifully that this sacred offering may serve the forgiveness of the dead and the salvation of the living and that thy faithful, for whom we make this sacrifice, may be aided by the remission of thy mercy."[198]

We encounter the formulas of the Mass for the living and the dead (benefactors, confessants, and so forth) in many later sacramentaries; while they may be found in most eighth-century Gelasian sacramentaries, they are present in practically all of the Gregorian sacramentaries written in the ninth century. The latter often contain several—occasionally as many as five—different formulas for the living and the dead. In addition, these may also be found in memorial books or agreements on prayer fraternities, a clear sign of their "rootedness in life." It also becomes evident that they themselves were counted. The *Liber memorialis* of Remiremont begins with a pact agreeing to a daily mass for the benefactors.[199] The 840 Synod of Le Mans stipulates that a *Missa generalis pro vivis et defunctis* was to be held twice a week for the bishop and those in his care.[200] The practice of listing the beneficiaries of these masses had also become a matter of course, and such lists appear elsewhere in the sacramentaries, for instance as insertions into the *Memento* of the living within the canon of the Mass, which was used in every celebration of the Mass.[201] Thus, the logic of counting masses was also fixed in writing: the mention—if only in cumulative form—of a name in many masses guaranteed a greater participation in the salvation they effected.

The very expressions used in these formulas ("whose names are recorded here in the Book of Life," or "whose names are recorded on the holy altar")[202] point to a further group of liturgical books, which were of fundamental import for the early medieval practice of piety: the *Libri vitae*.[203] It is well known that they emerged from the diptychs of the ancient church,[204] and in the early Middle Ages entire codices were compiled with long series of names. The best known of these is the record book of the Reichenau prayer fraternity, which lists some 40,000 names.[205] In the ancient church, entering a name into the diptychs was primarily an "expression of the ecclesiastical community," a "symbol of inscription in the books of Heaven."[206] Although this view lived on in the notion that, parallel to the recording of a name in the *Liber vitae*, God also inscribed it in the heavenly Book of Life,[207] in the early Middle Ages reading the diptychs (aloud) acquired a different emphasis: the recipient of the salvation effected by the Mass was designated by the recitation of his name. This reflected the notion that those who were named would benefit particularly from the efficacy of the Mass. The mention of a name, the unmistakable mark of the individual, guaranteed the presence of the named persons, even if they were not physically present, and permitted them to benefit from the forgiveness of sins effected by the Mass.[208]

In order to ensure the presence of names in the Mass, efforts were made to inscribe them as close as possible to the site of the holy events. On the occasion of his coronation as emperor, Charlemagne presented Saint Peter's in Rome with a golden paten inscribed with his name.[209] People inscribed names on the altar table itself, but also on the church walls or on the columns surrounding the altar.[210] Furthermore, the texts of the various orations in the sacramentaries reveal that there were several types of lists of names. For example, various orations distinguish between lists of names for the living and those for the dead. Priests also kept personal lists of names in addition to the official records of a particular church, and we thus find mentions of those persons recorded *in libello memorialis mei*.[211] We also see names recorded in the margins of the sacramentaries themselves. In the *Bobbio-Missal*, for instance, the name *munubertus* was written on the lower edge of the page of a Mass for the living and the dead.[212] They sometimes also include entire lists of names, such as lists of bishops,[213] or lists of kings, bishops, and others, as in the "Nota historica" of the Prague Sacramentary.[214] One episcopal capitulary required that every priest keep the names of all members of the cathedral clergy as well as the country clerics, both living and dead, in diptychs on the altar.[215]

Looking at early medieval piety and the forms of writing associated with it, from the sacramentaries with their votive masses to the various ways of recording names in a holy place or for liturgical use, we can only agree with Hagen Keller that "Christianity placed written culture unconditionally in the service of 'life' — but of 'true' life in the Christian sense of the word, i.e., eternal life or the striving to attain it."[216]

CRITIQUES OF COUNTING MASSES

The sacrificial theology of the Epistle to the Hebrews (9:23–28), according to which there is but one sacrifice, Christ's death on the Cross, highlights the problematic nature of such a quantification of masses. Even the early medieval texts of the Mass were familiar with the idea that this sacrifice redeemed the entire world.[217] And yet only a specific, quantifiable efficacy was attributed to the Mass in which Jesus' sacrifice was "present." This is evident particularly in the incorporation of the Mass into the system of penitential tariffs. This dilemma runs through the entire Middle Ages and into the present day, repeatedly occasioning criticism and confronting theologians with a practically insoluble task.[218]

The early Middle Ages already witnessed critiques of this piety of the Mass, particularly at problematic points in practice. In his liturgical history, Walafrid Strabo criticizes the widespread belief "that the only way to perform a full memorial for the offerers is for them to make a separate offering for each individual."[219] A provision made by the Roman Council of 826 went in a similar direction: priests should not be persuaded by the words of individual offerers to refuse the oblations to others. They were, after all, the intermediaries between God and humankind and had to perform their prayers generously, otherwise the Redeemer, however full of mercy, could not accept the *vota* of the many peoples and loosen the bonds of sin.[220] Another point of criticism related to the celebration of masses in exchange for alms, or, to be more precise, for money. Thus the 813 Council of Châlon-sur-Saône opposed the greed of priests and demanded that they seek the salvation of souls rather than earthly rewards. The faithful must not be forced to make donations; instead, the oblations should be made voluntarily.[221]

Critical voices were also raised in the high Middle Ages. Pope Alexander II (1061–73) spoke out against the proliferation of masses celebrated on a single day: "Let it suffice for a priest to say one mass each day, since Christ suffered but once and yet saved the entire world."[222] Some religious orders also initially rejected this practice. The Cistercians invoked the Benedictine Rule, which did not mention the saying of many masses for the salvation of souls.[223] Saint Francis ordered the brothers to celebrate the Mass only once daily, even when several priests were present.[224] Yet, neither order maintained this practice for long. Similarly, theologians could not agree on the efficacy of many masses for the individual. Some expressed the opinion that a special mass said for an individual was no more efficacious than a mass devoted to several persons. The majority, however, attributed a particular efficacy to individual masses—thus giving precedence to the dominant practice of piety. We may cite Thomas Aquinas as an example. Replying to the question of whether the Eucharist possessed unlimited efficacy, he said that "although the power of Christ, which is contained in the sacrament of the Eucharist, is unlimited, its efficacy is limited. . . . Therefore it is unnecessary that the full penitence of the persons dwelling in the place of purification be accomplished by a single sacrifice, just as no one is released from the entire satisfaction that he owes for his sins by a single sacrifice. Therefore the obligation to say several masses may occasionally be imposed for the satisfaction of a single sin."[225]

Notes

This chapter, with Chapter 2, is slightly abridged from Arnold Angenendt, Thomas Braucks, Rolf Busch, Hubertus Lutterbach, and Thomas Lentes, "Gezählte Frömmigkeit," *Frühmittelalterliche Studien* 29 (1995): 1–71.

1. Leo Koep, "Buch IV (himmlisch)," in *Reallexikon für Antike und Christentum*, 2 (1954), 725–32, 725.

2. Sulpicius Severus, *Vita sancti Martini* 22, ed. Jacques Fontaine, Sources chrétiennes 133 (Paris, 1967), 301–2.

3. Bede, *A History of the English Church and People*, trans. Leo Sherley-Price, rev. R. E. Latham (Harmondsworth, 1968), 295–98, quotation 296.

4. Josef Schmid, "Waage," in *Lexikon für Theologie und Kirche* 10, 2nd ed. (1965), 903–4, 904.

5. *Visio Thurkilli*, ed. and trans. into German by Paul Gerhard Schmidt (Weinheim, 1987), 36–39.

6. Boniface, *The Letters of Saint Boniface*, trans. Ephraim Emerton, no. 10, 26.

7. Schmid, "Waage," 903–4.

8. Albrecht Dihle, "Gerechtigkeit," in *Reallexikon für Antike und Christentum*, 10 (1978), 233–360, 307.

9. Albrecht Dihle, *Die Goldene Regel. Eine Einführung in die Geschichte der antiken und frühchristlichen Vulgärethik*, Studienhefte zur Altertumswissenschaft, 7 (Göttingen, 1962), 22–25.

10. Niklas Luhmann, *Rechtssoziologie*, vol. 1 (Reinbek bei Hamburg, 1972), 154–57.

11. Dihle, *Goldene Regel*, 72–79.

12. Karl Hoheisel, "Do ut des," in *Handbuch religionswissenschaftlicher Grundbegriffe*, vol. 2 (1990), 228–30, 229.

13. Marcel Mauss, *The Gift: The Form and Reason for Exchange in Archaic Societies*, trans. W. D. Halls, foreword by Mary Douglas (London, 1990), 5–6.

14. Mauss, *The Gift*, 16.

15. Edda, Hávamál 46, 6, ed. Ivar Lindquist, in *Die Urgestalt der Hávamál. Ein Versuch zur Bestimmung auf synthetischem Wege*, Lundastudier i Nordisk Språkvetenskap 11 (Lund, 1956), 15; *The Elder Edda: A Selection*, trans. Paul B. Taylor and W. H. Auden (New York, 1970), 43.

16. Edda, Hávamál, 145, 1–5, 26; *The Elder Edda*, 57.

17. Hans Hattenhauer, *Europäische Rechtsgeschichte* (Heidelberg 1992), 13.

18. Schmid, "Waage," 903–4.

19. Antonie Wlosok, "Römischer Religions- und Gottesbegriff in heidnischer und christlicher Zeit," *Antike und Abendland* 16 (1970): 39–53, 44.

20. Martin Herz, *Sacrum commercium. Eine begriffsgeschichtliche Studie zur Theologie der römischen Liturgiesprache*, Münchner Theologische Studien, II/15 (Munich, 1958).

21. Leo the Great, *Sermones* 54, 4, ed. J. P. Migne, PL 54 (Paris, 1881), 321A.

22. Augustine, *Sermones* 130, 2, ed. J. P. Migne, PL 38 (Paris, 1841), 726.

23. Tertullian, *Liber de paenitentia* II, 11, ed. J. G. Ph. Borleffs, Corpus Christianorum, Series Latina 1 (Turnhout, 1954), 323[44]: "Bonum factum deum habet debitorem."

24. Ambrose of Milan, *De officiis ministrorum* I, 15, 58, ed. J. P. Migne, PL 16 (Paris, 1880), 44D.

25. Artur Michael Landgraf, *Dogmengeschichte der Frühscholastik*, vol. I/2 (Regensburg, 1953), 98–104.

26. Thomas Sternberg, "Orientalium more secutus. Räume und Institutionen der Caritas des 5. bis 7. Jahrhunderts in Gallien," in *Jahrbuch für Antike und Christentum*, Ergänzungsband 16 (Münster, 1991): 31–32.

27. Caesarius of Arles, *Sermones* 31, 5, ed. Germanus Morin, Corpus Christianorum, Series Latina 103 (Turnhout, 1953), 138.

28. Gregory the Great, *Registrum epistolarum* I, 13, ed. Dag Norberg, Corpus Christianorum Series Latina 140 (Turnhout, 1982), 14[13]: "Ita ergo facite, ut et Deum uobis faciatis pro rebus talibus debitorem"; see also ibid., I, 60, 71[11].

29. Petrus Damianus, *De elemosyma* 6, ed. J. P. Migne PL 145(Paris, 1853), 219BC.

30. Michel Mollat, *The Poor in the Middle Ages: An Essay in Social History*, trans. Arthur Goldhammer (New Haven and London, 1986), 259ff.

31. *Sacramentarium Veronense* 91, ed. Leo Cunibert Mohlberg, Rerum ecclesiasticarum documenta, Series maior, Fontes 1, 3rd ed. (Rome, 1978), 12.

32. Hans Bernhard Meyer, "Abendmahlsfeier II (Mittelalter)," in *Theologische Realenzyklopädie*, vol. 1 (1977), 278–87, 285.

33. Collection of *quaestiones*, British Museum Harley lat. 658, fol. 74v, quoted in Landgraf, *Dogmengeschichte der Frühscholastik*, 96.

34. In regard to St. Luke's Gospel, see Gerhard Schneider, *Das Evangelium nach Lukas*, vol. 2, Ökumenischer Taschenbuch-Kommentar 3, 2 (Gütersloh, 1977), 324–25j.

35. Joachim Gnilka, *Das Matthäusevangelium*, Part 2, Herders theologischer Kommentar zum Neuen Testament, 1 (Freiburg i. Br., Basel, and Vienna, 1988), 139.

36. Gnilka, *Matthäusevangelium*, 145.

37. Schneider, *Evangelium nach Lukas*, 346.

38. *Didache* 4, 14, ed. Georg Schöllgen, Fontes Christiani, 1 (Freiburg i. Br., 1991), 114–15.

39. *Didache* 14, 2, 132–33.

40. *Didache* 4, 3, 110f.

41. Reinhard Meßner, *Feiern der Umkehr und Versöhnung*, Gottesdienst der Kirche. Sakramentliche Feiern 1/2 (Regensburg, 1992), 65.

42. Basil of Caesarea, "penitential letters," epp. 188, 199, 217, ed. J. P. Migne, PG 32 (Paris, 1886), 663–84, 715–32, 793–810.

43. For example, Concilia Epaonense (a. 517) 4, in *Concilia Galliae a. 511–a. 695*, ed. Carolus de Clercq, Corpus Christianorum, Series Latina 148A (Turnhout, 1963), 25 (two or three months' separation from office and communion for bishops and presbyters who hunted); Conc. Narbonense (a. 589) 8, in ibid., 255 (two years' removal from office for clerics and other officeholders who stole church property).

44. Concilia Aurelianense (a. 538) 1 in *Concilia Galliae a. 511–a. 695*, 114 (delayed convocation of a synod by a metropolitan bishop); Conc. Aurelianense (a. 538) 19, in ibid., 121 (the treatment of an excommunicated person by a cleric); Conc. Aurelianense (a. 541) 10, in ibid., 134 (ordination of a person who has violated canon law).

45. Conc. Epaonense (a. 517) 4 in *Concilia Galliae. a. 511–a. 695*, 25 (two or three months' exclusion for bishops or presbyters who hunted). Further examples of a one-year exclusion from communion may be found in Conc. Aurelianense (a. 549) 17, in ibid., 154 (a bishop who did not punish injustices); Conc. Arelatense (a. 554) 4, in ibid., 171 (dismissal of a deacon or subdeacon by a presbyter without the bishop's knowledge).

46. Conc. Epaonense (a. 517) 29 in *Concilia Galliae. a. 511–a. 695*, 31.

47. Conc. Narbonense (a. 589) 4.9 and 14, in *Concilia Galliae. a. 511–a. 695*, 254–57.

48. Ibid., 15, in *Concilia Galliae. a. 511–a. 695*, 257.

49. Cyrille Vogel, "Composition légale et commutations dans le système de la pénitence tarifée," *Revue de droit canonique* 8 (1958): 89–318 and 9 (1959): 1–38 and 341–59, here 8 (1958): 291.

50. Adalbert de Vogüé, *Die Regula Benedicti. Theologisch-spiritueller Kommentar*, Regulae Benedicti Studia, Suppl. 16 (Hildesheim, 1983), 220.

51. Pachomius, Iudicia 1, ed. A. Boon, *Règles et épitres de S. Pachôme*, Bibliothèque de la Revue d'histoire ecclésiastique 7 (Louvain, 1932), 63–64.

52. *Regula Quatuor Patrum* 5, 2–6, ed. Adalbert de Vogüé, in *Les règles des saints pères*, vol. 1, Sources chrétiennes 297 (Paris, 1982), 202.

53. Aurelian of Arles, "Regula ad monachos," 41, ed. A. Schmidt, *Zur Komposition der Moenchsregel des heiligen Aurelian von Arles* 1, Studia Monastica 17 (1975), 252.

54. *Regula Magistri* 19, 13–17, ed. Adalbert de Vogüé, Sources chrétiennes 106 (Paris, 1965), 94: arriving late to serve at table (forfeit of one-fourth of the bread during the meal for seven or ten meals equals ten days at one meal per day).

55. *Regula Ferrioli* 24, 13–15, ed. D. Vincent, "La Regula Ferrioli: Texte critique," *Revue Mabillon* 60 (1982): 137; 22, 5, 136; 25, 5, 137–38.

56. Ibid., 13, 132.

57. Ibid., 20, 6–8, 135.

58. Cyrille Vogel, *Les "Libri Paenitentiales*," Typologie des sources du moyen âge occidental, 27 (Turnhout, 1978), 28.

59. *Traditio Apostolica* 28, ed. Wilhelm Geerlings, Fontes Christiani 1 (Freiburg i. Br., 1991), 281.

60. *Paenitentiale Cummeani* 1, 6–8, ed. Ludwig Bieler, in *The Irish Penitentials*, Scriptores Latini Hiberniae 5 (Dublin, 1963), 111: "Qui autem superfluam uentris disten-tionem doloremque saturitatis sentit, I diem. Si autem ad uomitum infirmitate sine, VII diebus. Si uero sacrificium euomerit, XL diebus."

61. *Paenitentiale Cummeani* 1, 1, in *The Irish Penitentials*, 109–11: "Inebriati igitur uino siue ceruisa contra interdictum Saluatoris . . . si uotum sanctitatis habuerint, XL diebus cum pane et aqua culpam deluant, laici uero VII diebus."

62. *Traditio Apostolica* 36, in *The Irish Penitentials*, 293.

63. *Iudicia Theodori* D77, ed. Friedrich Wilhelm Hermann Wasserschleben, in *Die Bussordnungen der abendländischen Kirche* (Halle a. d. Saale, 1851; reprint Graz, 1958), 245: "Qui acciperit sacrificium post cibum VII diebus peniteat."

64. *Traditio Apostolica* 38, ed. Wilhelm Geerlings, 297.

65. *Paenitentiale Ambrosianum* 9, 12, ed. Ludger Koerntgen in *Studien zu den Quellen der frühmittelalterlichen Bußbücher*, Quellen und Forschungen zum Recht im Mittelalter, 7 (Sigmaringen, 1993), 270; *Paenitentiale Halitgarii* V (*De dissensibus sacrificium*), in S II, 298: "Perfundens aliquis calicem super altare, quando auferuntur linteamina, VII diebus poeniteat."

66. *Paenitentiale Bobbiense* 50, ed. Raymund Kottje, in *Paenitentialia Minora Fran-ciae et Italiae saeculi VIII–IX*, Corpus Christianorum, Series Latina 156 (Turnhout, 1994), 71: "Si quando infert calicem, et effuderit in terram, X diebus peneteat in pane et aqua."

67. *Paenitentiale Laurentianum* 53, in S I, 790: "Perfundens aliquid super altare de calice quando offertur, VII dies peniteat aut si abundantius VII dies peniteat. Qui autem perfundit calicem dum solemniter missa celebratur, XL dies peniteat."

68. *Paenitentiale Pseudo-Egberti* 3, 53, in *Die Bussordnungen der abendländischen Kirche*, 339: "Qui effuderit calicem suum inter missam suam, XXX dies jejunet"; *Paeniten-tiale Vallicellanum* I (Cod. E15) 122, in S I, 334; the length of penance was set at seven days.

69. For example, *Paenitentiale Cummeani* 11, 6, in *The Irish Penitentials*, 131: "Qui effudit calicem in fine sollemnitatis missae, XL diebus peniteat."

70. Caesarius of Arles, *Regula ad virgines* 29, 1–2, ed. Adalbert de Vogüé and Jean

Courreau, Sources chrétiennes, 345 (Paris, 1988), 208; *Regula Donati* 9, 2–4, ed. Adalbert de Vogüé, in "La Règle de Donat pour l'abbesse Gauthstrude. Texte critique et synopse des sources," *Benedictina* 25 (1978): 254.

71. Reinhold Haggenmüller, *Die Überlieferung der Beda und Egbert zugeschriebenen Bußbücher*, Europäische Hochschulschriften, III 461 (Frankfurt am Main, Berne, New York and Paris, 1991), 128.

72. Haggenmüller, *Die Überlieferung*, 299.

73. Seven as a "sacred number" or more precisely as the "number of forgiveness" has an Old Testament background: the Day of Atonement will be celebrated on the tenth day of the seventh month after seven times seven years (Lev. 25:8).

74. *Paenitentiale Cummeani* 10, 10, in *The Irish Penitentials*, 128.

75. Ibid., 1, 1.6, 110–12.

76. Hans Jörg auf der Mauer, "Die Vierzig Tage vor Ostern. Geschichte und Neu-gestalt," *Liturgischer Dienst* 47 (1993): 6–23, 13.

77. *Paenitentiale Cummeani* 1, 12, in *The Irish Penitentials*, 112.

78. Ibid., 1, 13, 112.

79. Heinz Meyer and Rudolf Suntrup, *Lexikon der mittelalterlichen Zahlenbedeut-ungen*, Münstersche Mittelalter-Schriften, 56 (Munich, 1987), 214.

80. On the significance of inner conversion, see Peter Welten, "Buße III," in *The-ologische Realenzyklopädie*, vol. 7 (1981), 434–39.

81. *Paenitentiale Finniani* 21, in *The Irish Penitentials*, 80: "Ita clericus qui cecidit eodem modo in septimo anno post laborem penitentie debet accipere clericatus officium sicut ait scriptura: Septies cadit iustus et resurgit, id est post septem annos penitentie potest iustus uocari qui cecidit."

82. *Paenitentiale Bigotianum* 20, in *The Irish Penitentials*, 200.

83. For numerous examples relating to the seven-day abstinence from receiving communion, see Hubertus Lutterbach, "The Mass and Holy Communion in the Medieval Penitentials (600–1200): Liturgical and Religo-Historical Perspectives," in Charles Caspers (ed.), *Bread of Heaven: Customs and Practices Surrounding Holy Communion* (The Hague, 1995), 61–82.

84. *Paenitentiale Cummeani* 31, in *The Irish Penitentials*, 116: "Post partum abstineat, si filius, XXXIII, si filia, LXVI."

85. *Paenitentiale Bigotianum* 17–19, in *The Irish Penitentials*, 200.

86. K. Meyer believed that the number 365 could be traced back to an Irish origin. See "An Old-Irish Treatise *De arreis*," *Revue Celtique* 15 (1894): 485–98.

87. See the contribution by Thomas Lentes in this volume, at n. 23 in the text.

88. "The Old-Irish Table of Commutations," ed. D. A. Binchy, in *The Irish Peniten-tials*, 278.

89. Ibid., 31, 281.

90. *Paenitentiale Finniani* 42–45 and Prol. 4, in *The Irish Penitentials*, 90 and 74.

91. For example *Excarpsus Cummeani*, in S II, 604: "Qui per corpus peccat, per corpus emendet."

92. Vogel, *Les "Libri Paenitentiales*," 53.

93. "The Old-Irish Table of Commutations" 6, in *The Irish Penitentials*, 278.

94. *De arreis* 1–12, in *The Irish Penitentials*, 162–66.

95. Vogel, *Les "Libri Paenitentiales*," particularly 50–51.

96. *Paenitentiale Remense*, ed. Franz Bernd Asbach, in *Das Poenitentiale Remense*

und der sogen. Excarpsus Cummeani. Überlieferung, Quellen und Entwicklung zweier kontinentaler Bußbücher aus der 1. Hälfte des 8. Jahrhunderts (Regensburg, 1975), 11.

97. *Excarpsus Cummeani* 1, in S II, 603: "Et qui psalmos non novit et jejunare non potest, elegat justum, qui pro illo hoc impleat et de suo precio aut labore hoc redimat, id per unumquemque diem de precio valente denario in pauperibus eroget."

98. For example, *Paenitentiale mixtum Bedae-Egberti* 46 in S II, 699; on the Mass in the system of penances and the commemoration of the dead see below, "Counting Masses."

99. Ludger Körntgen, *Studien zu den Quellen der frühmittelalterlichen Bußbücher*, Quellen und Forschungen zum Recht im Mittelalter, 7 (Sigmaringen, 1993), 157–58.

100. Vogel, *Les "Libri Paenitentiales,"* 53.

101. Raymund Kottje, "Bußbücher," in *Lexikon des Mittelalters*, vol. 2 (1983), 1118–21, 1119.

102. *Conc. Cabillonnense (a. 813)* 38, ed. Albert Werminghoff, MGH Concilia 2, 1 (Hanover and Leipzig, 1904), 281: "Modus autem paenitentiae peccata sua confitentibus aut per antiquorum canonum institutionem aut per sanctarum scripturarum auctoritatem aut per ecclesiasticam consuetudinem, sicut superius dictum est, imponi debet, repudiatis ac penitus eliminatis libellis, quos paenitentiales vocant, quorum sunt certi errores, incerti auctores, de quibus rite dici potest: Mortificabant animas, quae non moriebantur, et vivificabant animas, quae non vivebant."

103. *Conc. Parisiense (a. 829)* 32, ed. Albert Werminghoff, MGH Concilia 2, 2 (Hanover and Leipzig, 1908), 633.

104. *Paenitentiale Halitgarii* V, in S II, 286f.

105. "Interrogationes Examinationis" 3, ed. Alfred Boretius, in MGH Capitularia Regum Francorum 1 (Hanover, 1883), 234–35, 234.

106. "Capitula in dioecesana quadam synodo tractata" 4, in ibid., 236–37, 237.

107. "Capitula Ecclesiastica" 20, in ibid., 178–79, 179.

108. "Capitula Ghaerbaldi" 9, in ibid., 242–43, 243.

109. "Capitula Haitonis" 6, in ibid., 362–66, 363.

110. "Capitula Frisingensia" 32, ed. Emil Seckel, "Studien zu Benedictus Levita II," in *Neues Archiv für ältere deutsche Geschichtskunde* 29 (1904): 287–94, 292–93.

111. "Admonitio synodalis" 97, ed. Robert Amiet, in "Une 'Admonitio synodalis' de l'époque carolingienne. Etude critique et édition," *Medieval Studies* 26 (1964): 41–99, 68.

112. Inventory of the Treasure of Thannkirchen (county of Wofratshausen), no. 89, from the era of Bishop Anno of Freising (d. 875), ed. Bernhard Bischoff, in *Mittelalterliche Schatzverzeichnisse*, vol. I, Veröffentlichungen des Zentralinstituts für Kunstgeschichte in München 4 (Munich, 1967), 94.

113. See "Counting Masses."

114. See "Counting Alms."

115. See the first section of the essay by Thomas Lentes in this volume.

116. W. Schwer, "Almosen B. Christlich," in *Reallexikon für Antike und Christentum*, vol. 1 (1950), 302–7.

117. Cyprian, *De opere et eleemosynis*, ed. Wilhelm Hartel, Corpus Scriptorum Ecclesiasticorum Latinorum, 3/1 (1868), 371–94, 373–74.

118. Augustine, *De civitate Dei* 21, 27, ed. Bernhard Dombart and Alphons Kalb, Corpus Christianorum Series Latina 48, 801.

119. *Paenitentiale Columbani* 20, in *The Irish Penitentials*, 104: "Si quis laicus pe-
riurauerit, si per cupiditatem hoc fecerit, totas res suas vendat et donet pauperibus et
convertatur ex integro ad Dominum et tundatur omni dimisso saeculo et usque ad
mortem serviat Deo in monasterio." This stipulation is repeated almost verbatim in the
Continental penitential tradition. See, for example, *Paenitentiale Remense* 7, 11, 47.

120. *Paenitentiale Remense* 10, 5, 59: "Thesaurizans superflua in crastinum tempus
per ignorantiam tribuat illa pauperibus, si autem per contemptum arguentium elymosina
et ieiunio sanetur iudicio sacerdotis."

121. *Paenitentiale Merseburgense* (Me 1) 21, in *Paenitentialia Minora Franciae et Italiae*, 131–32: "Si quis per postestatem ut quolibet ingenio res aliena malo ordine inuaserit
vel tollerit, III annos peneteat, I ex his in pane et aqua, et multas elemosinas faciat."

122. John Cassian, *Conlatio* 19, 14, ed. Michael Petschenig, Corpus Scriptorum Ecclesiasticorum Latinorum 13, 2 (Vienna, 1886), S. 547–550. Cf. the prologue to the *Paenitentiale Cummeani*, in *The Irish Penitentials*, 110.

123. See, for example, Meßner, *Feiern der Umkehr und Versöhnung*, 165–66.

124. See the examples in Kottje (ed.), *Paenitentialia Minora Franciae et Italiae*, 15, 40
or 113.

125. Bernhard Poschmann, *Die abendländische Kirchenbuße im frühen Mittelalter*,
Breslauer Studien zur historischen Theologie 16 (Breslau, 1930), 12.

126. *Paenitentiale Remense*, 12: "Et qui non potest sic agere penitentiam, sicut superius diximus, in primo anno eroget in elymosinam solidos XXVI et in secondo XX et in
tertio XVIII, hoc sunt solidi LXIII."

127. Philip Grierson, *Coins of Medieval Europe* (London, 1991), 219.

128. *Paenitentiale Remense*, 12.

129. Ibid., 12.

130. The list of over twenty penance-free days is contained in ibid., 14.

131. *Paenitentiale Pseudo-Egberti* 4, 60, in *Die Bussordnungen der abendländischen
Kirche*, 341 Paenitentiale Remense, 13.

132. Otto Gerhard Oexle, "Memoria und Memorialüberlieferung im früheren Mittelalter," *Frühmittelalterliche Studien* 10 (1976): 70–95.

133. *Urkundenbuch der Abtei St. Gallen*, ed. Hermann Wartmann, 4 vols. (Zurich and
St. Gallen, 1863–1899); on this see Michael Borgolte, "Gedenkstiftungen in St. Galler
Urkunden," in Karl Schmid and Joachim Wollasch (eds.), *Memoria. Der geschichtliche
Zeugniswert des liturgischen Gedenkens im Mittelalter*, Münstersche Mittelalter-Schriften
48 (Munich, 1984), 578–602, 581.

134. *Urkundenbuch der Abtei St. Gallen*, vol. 1, no. 119, 112: "Si aliquid de rebus nostris
ad locis sanctorum vel in ælemosinas pauperum conferimus, hoc nobis procul dubio in
aeterna beatitudine retribuere confidimus."

135. *Urkundenbuch der Abtei St. Gallen*, vol. 1, no. 307, 284.

136. See, for example, ibid., nos. 70–78, pp. 68–75.

137. Beat Brenk, *Tradition und Neuerung in der christlichen Kunst des 1. Jahrtausends.
Studien zur Geschichte des Weltgerichtsbildes*, Wiener Byzantinistische Studien 3 (Vienna,
1966), 75.

138. Helmut Merkel, "Gericht Gottes IV (Alte Kirche bis Reformationszeit)," in
Theologische Realenzyklopädie, vol. 12 (1984), 483–92.

139. Arnold Angenendt, "Theologie und Liturgie der mittelalterlichen Totenmemoria," in Schmid and Wollasch, *Memoria*, 79–199, 123–31.

140. *Urkundenbuch der Abtei St. Gallen*, vol. 1, no. 301, 278.

141. *Urkundenbuch der Abtei St. Gallen*, vol. 2, no. 450, 68.

142. *Urkundenbuch der Abtei St. Gallen*, vol. 1, no. 219, 209: "cogitans ultimam discussionem reproborum et remunerationem electorum."

143. *Urkundenbuch der Abtei St. Gallen*, vol. 2, no. 442, 60: "Quicquid vero locis sanctorum vel in pauperibus in elemosinam conferimus, hoc sine dubio credimus nobis aeterna retributione a justissimo judice repensari, ipso dicente: Quod uni ex minimis meis fecistis, mihi fecistis."

144. See, for example, *Urkundenbuch der Abtei St. Gallen*, vol. 1, no. 153, p. 145 and no. 193, p. 183.

145. Ibid., no. 21, p. 25: "Igitur ego in nomine Podalus in amore domini nostri Jesu Christi et remissione peccatorum meorum, ut veniam delictis meis consequi merear in futuro." See also ibid., no. 179, p. 169.

146. *Urkundenbuch der Abtei St. Gallen*, vol. 1, no. 348, p. 323.

147. Ibid., no. 39, p. 41.

148. Alfred Stuiber, "Die Diptychon-Formel für die nomina offerentium im römischen Meßkanon," *Ephemerides Liturgicae* 68 (1954): 127–46.

149. *Urkundenbuch der Abtei St. Gallen*, vol. 2, no. 418, 38: "Humano genere peccatorum maculis sauciato atque ob culpam inobedientiae a paradisi gaudiis dejecto inter cetera curationum medicamenta etiam et hoc Deus mundo remedium contulit, ut propriis divitiis homines suas animas ab inferni tartaris redimere potuissent, sicut Salomonem dicitur: Redemptio animæ viri propriæ divitiae ejus." See also the Arenga in ibid., no. 407, 28.

150. *Urkundenbuch der Abtei St. Gallen*, vol. 1, no. 197, p. 187; vol. 2, no. 470, p. 86.

151. *Urkundenbuch der Abtei St. Gallen*, vol. 1, no. 33, p. 36.

152. Ibid., no. 195, p. 185: "Ille bene possidit res in sæculo, qui sibi de caduca ista conparat premia sempiterna."

153. See above following n. 30.

154. *Urkundenbuch der Abtei St. Gallen*, vol. 2, no. 491, 107: "Ego . . . Wolfhart divino admonitus, ut terrenis facultatibus mercarer aeternas et bonis transitoriis mansura conquirerem. Memor itaque illius salutaris praecepti: Date et dabitur vobis, et: Non est, qui relinquat domum aut agros propter me, qui recipiat centies tantum, trado. . . ."

155. *Urkundenbuch der Abtei St. Gallen*, vol. 1, no. 90, p. 85.

156. Ibid., no. 155, p. 146; vol. 2, no. 505, p. 119 and no. 408, p. 29.

157. Cf. the view of Hermann Henrici (*Über Schenkungen an die Kirche*, Weimar, 1916, 25) for whom "the pious formula in the Arenga" is a "mere vacuous phrase"; see also Philippe Jobert, *La notion de donation. Convergences: 630–650*, Publication de l'université de Dijon 49 (Paris, 1977), 205–6.

158. Heinrich Fichtenau, *Arenga. Spätantike und Mittelalter im Spiegel von Urkundenformeln*, Mitteilungen des Instituts für Österreichische Geschichtsforschung, Ergänzungsband 18 (Graz and Cologne, 1957).

159. Heinrich Fichtenau, "Forschungen über Urkundenformeln," *Mitteilungen des Instituts für Österreichische Geschichtsforschung* 94 (1986), 285–339, 307.

160. See Michael Borgolte, "Die Stiftungen des Mittelalters in rechts- und sozialhistorischer Sicht," *Zeitschrift der Savigny-Stiftung für Rechtsgeschichte. Kanonistische Abteilung* 74 (1988), 71–94.

161. Josef Andreas Jungmann, "Von der 'Eucharistia' zur 'Messe'," *Zeitschrift für*

katholische Theologie 89 (1967), 29–40; Rupert Berger, *Die Wendung "offerre pro" in der römischen Liturgie*, Liturgiewissenschaftliche Quellen und Forschungen 41 (Münster, 1965).

162. Ambrose, *De sacramentis* 4, 28, [German] trans. and with an introduction by Josef Schmitz, Fontes Christiani 3 (Freiburg i. Br., 1990), 152; Augustine, *Enchiridion* 110, ed. E. Evans, Corpus Christianorum, Series Latina 46 (Turnhout, 1969), 108–9.

163. Arnold Angenendt, "Missa specialis. Zugleich ein Beitrag zur Entstehung der Privatmesse," *Frühmittelalterliche Studien* 17 (1983), 153–221.

164. Angelus Albert Häußling, *Mönchskonvent und Eucharistiefeier. Eine Studie über die Messe in der abendländischen Klosterliturgie des frühen Mittelalters und zur Geschichte der Meßhäufigkeit*, Liturgiewissenschaftliche Quellen und Forschungen 58 (Münster, 1973), 252.

165. Angenendt, "Missa specialis," 153–63 and 208–12; Otto Nussbaum, *Kloster, Priestermönch und Privatmesse*, Theophaneia 14 (Bonn, 1961); Häußling, *Mönchskonvent und Eucharistiefeier*, 174–348; Cyrille Vogel, "Une mutation culturelle inexpliquée. Le passage de l'Eucharistie communautaire à la messe privée," *Revue des Sciences Religieuses* 54 (1980): 231–50.

166. *The Bobbio-Missal: A Gallican Mass-book* (Ms. Paris. Lat. 13246), ed. Elias Avery Lowe, Henry Bradshaw Society 58 (London, 1920; reprint, 1991).

167. *Liber sacramentorum Romanae aeclesiae ordinis anni circuli (Sacramentarium Gelasianum)*, ed. Leo Cunibert Mohlberg, Leo Eizenhöfer, and Petrus Siffrin, Rerum Ecclesiasticarum Documenta, Series maior, Fontes IV (Rome, 1960).

168. *Sacramentarium Rhenaugiense. Handschrift Rh 30 der Zentralbibliothek Zürich*, ed. Anton Hänggi and Alfons Schönherr, Spicilegium Friburgense 15 (Fribourg, 1970).

169. Jean Deshusses (ed.), *Le sacramentaire grégorien: Ses principales formes d'après les plus anciens manuscrits*, 3 vols, Spicilegium Friburgense 16, 24, and 28 (Fribourg, 1971–1982), vol. 1, 424–72.

170. Cologne, Bibliothek des Metropolitankapitels, ms. 88, f. 105r–171v. For a summary of the contents, see Deshusses, *Le sacramentaire grégorien*, vol. 3, 46–47. Later additions have not been taken into consideration in counting the formulae.

171. Paris, Bibliothèque Nationale, ms. lat. 2291, f. 133v–172v und 193r–196v. Summary of the contents in Deshusses, *Le sacramentaire grégorien*, vol. 3, 39–41.

172. *Sacramentarium Fuldense saeculi X*, ed. Gregor Richter and Albert Schönfelder, Quellen und Abhandlungen zur Geschichte der Abtei und Diözese Fulda IX (Fulda, 1912).

173. See, for example, the titles of the votive Masses and Masses for the dead in the *Supplementum Anianense* (Deshusses, *Le sacramentaire grégorien*, vol. 1, 424–72).

174. One sacramentary from Saint-Amand contains a series of seven Masses *in honore dei genetricis et omnium sanctorum* (Deshusses, *Le sacramentaire grégorien*, vol. 2, 56–63).

175. *Sacramentarium Fuldense*, nos. 365–71 and nos. 372–75, pp. 234–39.

176. Angenendt, "Theologie und Liturgie der mittelalterlichen Totenmemoria," 156–64.

177. Gregory the Great, *Dialoge* IV, 57, 3–16, ed. Adalbert de Vogüé, Sources chrétiennes 265 (Paris, 1980), 184–94.

178. On the "Gregorian masses," see Adolph Franz, *Die Messe im deutschen Mittelalter. Beiträge zur Geschichte der Liturgie und des religiösen Volkslebens* (Freiburg, 1902), 218–25, 244–91, here 248.

179. Angenendt, "Missa specialis," 203–8.

180. *Concilium Attiniacense a. 762 vel 760–762*, in MGH Conc. 2, 1, 72[30]; *Concilium Dingolfingense a. 770*; B. *Notitia de pacto fraternitatis episcoporum et abbatum Bawaricorum*, in ibid., 96[32]; *Concilium Baiuwaricum a. 805*, in ibid., 233[15].

181. *Concilia Rispacense, Frisingense, Salisburgense a. 800*; A. *Statuta Rispacensia, Frisingensia, Salisburgensia* c. 5, in MGH Conc. 2, 1, 208[9].

182. *Concilium Cenomanicum*, 12 May 840, in MGH Conc. 2, 2, 784[21].

183. Synod of Pavia, a. 850, c. 2, in MGH Conc. 3, 220[18].

184. Synod of Savonnières, 14 June 859, c. 14, in MGH Conc. 3, 462[4].

185. For a compilation of such lists, see Vogel, "Composition légale et commutations dans le système de la pénitence tarifée," 30–31.

186. *Sacramentarium Rhenaugiense*, no. 1316, 267.

187. *Sacramentarium Rhenaugiense*, no. 1370b, 281.

188. Regino of Prüm, *De synodalibus causis et disciplinis ecclesiasticis* II, 454, ed. F. G. A. Wasserschleben (Leipzig, 1840, reprint Graz, 1964), 392.

189. Karoli ad Ghaerbaldum episcopum epistola, Nov. 807, in MGH Capitularia Regum Francorum 1, 245–46.

190. *Concilium Arelatense* a. 813 (Praefatio), in MGH Conc. 2, 1, 249[12].

191. *Fuldaer Brieffragmente*, 4, ed. Ernst Dümmler, MGH Epp. 5 (n.p., 1974), 518[9].

192. Synod of Mainz, Oct. 847; Epistola Rabani Magonciacensis Archiepiscopi cum coepiscopis suis ad Hludowicum regem, in MGH Conc. 3, 160[8].

193. Arnold Angenendt, "Libelli bene correcti. Der 'richtige Kult' als ein Motiv der karolingischen Reform," in Peter Ganz (ed.), *Das Buch als magisches und als Repräsentationsobjekt*, Wolfenbütteler Mittelalter-Studien 5 (Wiesbaden, 1992), 117–35.

194. Cyrille Vogel, *Medieval Liturgy: An Introduction to the Sources*, trans. and rev. by William Storey and Niels Rasmussen (Washington, D.C., 1986).

195. *Brevium exempla ad describendas res ecclesiasticas et fiscales*, 5, 251, 23.

196. In our assignment of the votive Masses to this group as well as in the means of referring to them here, we follow Deshusses, *Le sacramentaire grégorien*, vol. 2, 233–50.

197. *Bobbio-Missale*, nos. 438–40, 130–31.

198. *Bobbio-Missale*, no. 438, 130.

199. *Liber memorialis von Remiremont*, ed. Eduard Hlawitschka, Karl Schmid, and Gerd Tellenbach, MGH Libri memoriales 1 (Dublin and Zurich, 1970), 1–4.

200. *Concilium Cenomannicum*, in MGH Conc. 2, 2, 785[16].

201. For examples of such an interpolation into the *memento vivorum*, see Deshusses, *Le sacramentaire grégorien*, vol. 1, no. 6, 87; no. 6*, 687; vol. 2, no. 3100, 241; Fernand Cabrol, "Diptyques (Liturgie)," in *Dictionnaire d'archéologie chrétienne et de liturgie*, vol. 4.1 (Paris, 1920), 1045–94, 1061–63.

202. Deshusses, *Le sacramentaire grégorien*, vol. 1, no. 6*, 687: "quorum nomina hic in libro uitae scripta esse uidentur"; ibid., vol. 2, no. 3079, 235: "quorum nomina ante sanctum altare tuum scripta esse uidentur."

203. Leo Koep, *Das himmlische Buch in Antike und Christentum. Eine religionsgeschichtliche Untersuchung zur altchristlichen Bilsdersprache*, Theophaneia 8 (Bonn, 1952); Arnold Angenendt, "Theologie und Liturgie der mittelalterlichen Totenmemoria," 188–96.

204. Cabrol, "Diptyques," 1045–1058.

205. *Das Verbrüderungsbuch der Abtei Reichenau*, ed. Johanne Autenrieth, Dieter Geuenich, and Karl Schmid, MGH Libri memoriales et necrologia N.S. 1 (Hanover, 1979).

206. Otto Stegmüller, "Diptychon," in *Reallexikon für Antike und Christentum* vol. 3 (1957), 1138–49, 1146, and 1148.

207. As the petition in an oration put it, "ut nomina famulorum famularumque tuarum quae hic piae dilectionis officio pariter conscriptimus, in libro vitae miserationis tuae gratia iubeas conscribi." Deshusses, *Le sacramentaire grégorien*, vol. 2, no. 3051, 229.

208. Berger, *Die Wendung "offerre pro" in der römischen Liturgie*, 228; Otto Gerhard Oexle, "Die Gegenwart der Toten," in *Death in the Middle Ages*, ed. H. Braet and W. Verbeke, Medievalia Lovaniensia, Series 1, Studia 9 (Louvain, 1983), 19–77.

209. Liber pontificalis 377, ed. L. Duchesne, in *Bibliotheque des Écoles Françaises d'Athènes et de Rome*, vol. 2 (Rome 1981), 7–8.

210. *Die Altarplatte von Reichenau-Niederzell*, ed. Dieter Geuenich, Renate Neumüller-Klauser, and Karl Schmid, MGH Libri memoriales et necrologia N.S. 1 Suppl. (Hanover, 1983); for further examples, see Oexle, "Die Gegenwart der Toten," 46–47.

211. Cabrol, "Diptyques," 1062.

212. *Bobbio-Missale*, 120, n. 5; further examples in ibid., 120, n. 2.

213. Several examples of lists of bishops in the sacramentaries may be found in the summaries of contents provided in Deshusses, *Le sacramentaire grégorien*, vol. 3, 19–59.

214. *Das Prager Sakramentar*, ed. Alban Dold and Leo Eizenhöfer, Texte und Arbeiten 38–42 (Beuron, 1949), 124*–125*; cf. the commentary, 17–28.

215. Paul Willem Finsterwalder, "Zwei Bischofkapitularien der Karolingerzeit. Ein Beitrag zur Kenntnis der bischöflichen Gesetzgebung des neunten Jahrhunderts," *Zeitschrift für Rechtsgeschichte. Kanonistische Abteilung* 14 (1925): 336–83, 379–80.

216. Hagen Keller, "Vom 'heiligen Buch' zur 'Buchführung'. Lebensfunktionen der Schrift im Mittelalter," *Frühmittelalterliche Studien* 26 (1992): 1–31, 12.

217. Deshusses, *Le sacramentaire grégorien*, vol. 2, no. 1836, 44: "Haec oblatio domine ab omnibus nos purget offensis, quae in ara crucis etiam totius mundi tulit offensa."

218. Erwin Iserloh, "Der Wert der Messe in der Diskussion der Theologen vom Mittelalter bis zum 16. Jahrhundert," in his *Kirche—Ereignis und Institution. Aufsätze und Vorträge*, vol. 2: *Geschichte und Theologie der Reformation* (Münster, 1985), 373–413.

219. Walafrid Strabo, *Libellus de exordiis et incrementis quarundam in observationibus ecclesiaticis rerum* 23, ed. Alfred Boretius and Victor Krause, MGH Capitularia 2 (Hanover, 1897), 500[26]: "Sed et in hoc error non modicus videtur, quod quidam putant se non posse aliter plenam commemorationem eorum facere, pro quibus offerunt, nisi singulas oblationes pro singulis offerant."

220. *Concilium Romanum a. 826*; B. *Canones concilii Romani, Forma uberior et forma minor* 17, in MGH Conc. 2, 2, 575[1].

221. *Concilium Cabillonense a. 813*, c. 6, in MGH Conc. 2, 1, 275[15].

222. *Decretum Gratiani* III, dist. 1, c. 53, ed. Emil Friedberg, in *Corpus Iuris Canonici* I (Leipzig, 1879), 1308.

223. "Exordium parvum" 15, ed. Jean de la Croix Bouton and Jean Baptiste van Damme, *Les plus anciens textes de Citeaux. Sources, textes et notes historiques*, Citeaux—Commentarii Cistercienses—Studia et Documenta 2 (Achel, 1974), 77–80, 77; Joachim Wollasch, "Neue Quellen zur Geschichte der Cistercienser," *Zeitschrift für Kirchengeschichte* 84 (1973): 188–232, 230–32.

224. "Schreiben an das Kapitel der Minderbrüder" 3, ed. Kajetan Eßer and Lothar Hardick, in *Die Schriften des heiligen Franziskus*, Franziskanische Quellenschriften 1 (Werl, 1951), 103.

225. Thomas Aquinas, *Summa theologica*, Suppl. q. 71 a. 14 ad 2; *Die deutsche Thomasausgabe*, vol. 35, ed. Albertus-Magnus-Akademie (Heidelberg, 1958), 131.

TWO

Counting Piety in the Late Middle Ages

Thomas Lentes

The counting of piety reached a high point in the late Middle Ages, in quite diverse ways. The seeds planted in the early Middle Ages were now cultivated and perfected: a veritable arithmetic of salvation[1] incorporated ever broader groups of the faithful[2] and became more firmly entrenched as the written word gained in significance. At the same time, however, there was increased criticism of counting, and an attempt to replace outer works with heartfelt piety and self-cultivation. This attitude affected the very way in which numbers were treated, and numbers and counting were now also used to develop the inner human being.

The Arithmetic of Salvation—Heightening and Perfecting the System

Counting was virtually omnipresent in late medieval piety. Religious life was not merely marked by quantification and multiplication; rather, counting appeared as an essential component of the practice of piety. An outstanding example of this is the rosary, which could be said using a string with beads or knots to count the number of prayers required. Such forms of counted repeated or serial prayers were extremely popular in the fifteenth century and accordingly existed in a wide variety of forms. We have evidence of prayer forms and corresponding prayer strings with 50, 63, 100, and even 150 prayers.[3] These repeated prayers were by no means directed exclusively to Mary, nor did they limit themselves to the metaphor of the wreath of roses.[4] Thus rosaries were said to the Eucharist, the various saints, Jesus Christ and the individual stations of his Passion, as well as to the Holy Trinity and the various feasts of the church calendar.[5] Apart from the wreath of roses, other serial prayers were intended to produce crowns, entire garments, necklaces, mantle fasteners, paradise gardens, and many other things in honor of the saints.[6] Prayers said on earth, the faithful hoped, would become ornaments for the saints in the hereafter.[7]

The vita of the Dominican nun Beli von Lütisbach of Töss shows just how realistic such notions were and how tightly they were bound up with precisely measured acts of prayer. One night she had a vision of the Mother of God clad in a snow-white gown. Mary sat down beside Beli on the bed and said to her: "I am your mother from the kingdom of heaven, whom you have so honored, and this is the dress you made for me with the English salutation (the Hail Mary) which you so often speak in veneration." Beli examined the gown and was bewildered to find that it had no sleeves. When she asked about this Mary explained: "You say 150 Aves every day; if you say 50 more, then I will have a complete gown of your making."[8] The garments of the saints had their price and the instructions for prayer were well apprised of them. Thus, for example, a text about a mantle for Mary from the Unterlinden convent at Colmar recorded the "costs in prayer" of the individual parts of the mantle, and in some cases computed the sums: the damask for the mantle "should cost 30,000 Hail Marys . . . the golden stars thereon . . . cost 12 times all their sequences, which come to 3180 verses. Similarly, the silk with which the mantle is sewn costs 1000 Magnificats."[9]

Prayer became, in effect, a currency with which the various parts of the furnishings of heaven were paid for by the faithful. There was a fairly good balance between the efforts people put in and the merits they earned. By praying to the saints, those who prayed hoped to gain their saving protection for themselves or to free poor souls from purgatory. Services performed were directly related to the hope of merit. A Cologne prayer book, for example, promises those who venerated the 1,200,000 drops of blood shed by Christ "as many ineffable joys in heaven as there were drops of blood."[10] This connection between the frequency and the efficacy of prayer is a guiding principle of the instructions in late medieval prayer books. The mention of the frequency of prayer was intended to ensure that the prayer would be heard; thus one of many instructions for prayer promised: "Whoever speaks this prescribed prayer for thirty days . . . will have his wish . . . granted by the mother of all mercies; and this has often been proven."[11]

Indulgences took arithmetic to new extremes. The authors of prayer books, for example, calculated how many indulgences could be expected for how many acts of piety. A promise of indulgence made in a prayer book from the Dominican convent of St. Nicholas in undis at Strasbourg is representative of the rich body of evidence that has come down to us: "Whoever reads the psalter of Our Lady with zeal daily, [gains] 34 years, 30 weeks and 3 days indulgence; and that is 174 years and 80 days for each week; and whoever reads it daily for an entire year has 8,949 years of indulgence."[12] Such projections, like the multiplication of the most diverse indulgence figures, already provoked the opposition of many contemporaries,[13] and in the modern period they have also been interpreted as "exaggerations"[14] and a "fantastical pursuit of numbers."[15] They are, nonetheless, completely understandable within the logic of penitential piety as it was established in the early Middle Ages.[16] If sins not atoned for had to be expiated after death, then people had to take precautionary measures while still on earth. No one doubted, to be sure, that guilt and atonement were weighed against each other very precisely. The debit account, however, displayed a trio of unknowns, which indicated that there was no final guarantee that one would actually have expiated all one's sins by the end of one's lifetime. On the one hand—according to an anonymous "Didactic Dialogue on the Souls in Purgatory"—those people ended up in purgatory who died before atoning for their trespasses, along with those "whose confessors had imposed too light a penance" and, finally, those who had forgotten their sins.[17] In the light of this unknown factor, it is understandable that the pious tried to accumulate "countless" indulgences. It was, thus, not a "fantastical pursuit of numbers" that motivated the faithful to collect indulgences, but simply concern for their well-being in the hereafter. The fear of unknown residual punishments, which they would have to make up for in the beyond, encouraged them to accumulate inordinate numbers of indulgences to compensate for even the most obscure penalty.

Such a calculated access to salvation also meant that the faithful sought to test the efficacy of their prayers. Quite in keeping with the scheme of service and counterservice, we find numerous late medieval accounts of visions in which the persons praying were told how many souls had been released from purgatory by their prayers. Such figures are constantly repeated in the "Revelations of Adelheid Langmann." Adelheid asked Christ, for example, whether poor souls had been saved by her piety. She received the answer straight away that "some 30,000 souls had been released from bondage and as many sinners repented and the same number of pious folk became firmer in their faith."[18] Such figures on the fruits of grace resulting from acts of piety may be found in the works of many female German-speaking mystics in the Middle Ages.[19] The most extensive figures are probably those given for Christine Ebner, whose efforts were calculated to have effected the redemption of 23,710,200 souls.[20] In a vision of Gertrude of Helfta, it was Jesus himself who explained the connection between prayer and the gifts of grace. Christ distributes the prayers of men and women "as means of grace for souls," and he accordingly asks Gertrude, "Won't you give me your surplus of merit, so that I may increase my gifts?"[21] Piety had become an arithmetical art here, one tied to excessive promises of grace.

The consequence of such an arithmetic of salvation was that all of the numbers of salvation were counted and calculated, listed and weighed against the corresponding acts of piety with the greatest possible precision. The prayer books offered veritable lists containing the individual numbers of salvation. Thus a manuscript from a Cologne convent devotes ten pages to the following figures and provides corresponding instructions for prayer: the number of months, weeks, days, and hours that Jesus spent in the womb; the number of years, months, weeks, days, and hours that he spent on earth; the numbers of the Passion—how many steps Jesus had to take, the hours between his prayer on the Mount of Olives and his death; the servants who accompanied him on the various stations; how many times he was spat upon and slapped; the number of thorns in the crown of thorns, and of Jews who cried "Crucify him!"; the number of scourgings and hammer blows when he was nailed to the cross; the months, weeks, days, and hours he spent on earth between the Crucifixion and the Ascension; the drops of blood he shed; the number of tears wept by Mary, and so forth. The various projections and sum totals demonstrate how very seriously the compilers of such lists took the precise recording of the figures. Thus at the end of the Cologne list we find a calculation of the total of Jesus' wounds (thirty thousand) as well as the number of blows (seventy thousand) that he received.[22]

If we compare the number of prayer verses that were to be spoken on the various parts of the Passion, we find mathematically precise correspondences. The calculation of Jesus' time in the womb, for example, begins with the information that he spent nine months there. It goes on to calculate that "there were 39 weeks and 3 days."[23] The required prayers consisted of two Te Deums, which contained 54 verses. Then the number of days was calculated: "the days were 276," in honor of which one should recite the Te Deum nine times and the 148th Psalm (which has 15 verses) once. If we multiply the 29 verses of the Te Deum by 9, we obtain the number 261; adding the 15 verses of the psalm produces the number 276. Thus one verse was recited for every day that Jesus spent in the womb. Such computations, with the corresponding prayers, were then produced for any number of periods and events in the life of Jesus. The key, namely, that the corresponding number of verses should be recited for each event mentioned, was then also revealed in the list itself: "The days of a year are 365; the human body has the same number of parts and our Lord suffered particular torment in each part." If one said thirteen Te Deums, one spoke "one verse for each suffering."[24] The meaning of such instructions is obvious: because one hoped to enjoy Christ's saving grace by saying prayers on all the stations of his earthly life, one sought to account for even the smallest detail of that earthly life.

The most widespread numerical prayers were those on Christ's wounds. The key figures here were the numbers of wounds, either 5,460 or 5,490, which had been revealed in visions.[25] The story of how these prayers were handed down remains to be written, but the tradition most likely goes back to Mechthild of Hackeborn and Gertrude of Helfta, and the prayers were popularized by Ludolph of Saxony.[26] In the proem to the section of his *Vita Christi* dealing with the Passion, Ludolph recounts how a female recluse was told "the amount and number of all of Christ's wounds." A celestial voice had revealed the number to her with a corresponding devotional exercise: "there were 5,490 wounds on my body; if you wish to venerate them, then repeat the Lord's Prayer fifteen times daily with the English salutation in memory of my suffering; after a year has past, you will have saluted each wound reverently."[27] The calculation was correct for leap years ($366\times15=5490$); in the other years—as Ludolph noted—only 5,475 prayers had to be spoken.[28] He ends with a mnemonic verse to help the faithful remember the number of Christ's wounds: Once upon a time, it is written, a gentle heavenly voice was sent to refresh an old woman's despondent heart, speaking as follows: "Multiply 500 times 11, subtract 10, and when you awake again, you will know all of Christ's wounds."[29]

It was the devil who suffered most from the numerical prayers on the wounds of Christ. He and the evil spirits were accordingly loud in their lamentations. After the "fifteen Paternosters on all the wounds of Jesus" had been revealed to a nun, for example, legend has it that a hermit living in the woods heard evil spirits utter a terrible cry. When questioned by him they replied: "An old chatterbox of a woman sits in these woods, and she has invented a prayer that so well pleases the highest God that we have been greatly harmed by this prayer. Through it we have lost everything that was once in our power."[30] Ultimately, the evil spirits believed that God had unlawfully disturbed their bookkeeping: "Not since God destroyed Limbo have so many souls been stolen from us as by this prayer. We had a great sinner for thirty years. When he died we came, eager to take his soul. But this prayer saved him."[31] Counting prayers thus foiled the devil's plans.

While these devotional exercises weighed acts of piety against the hoped-for gifts of grace, the act of grace itself became quantified in the celebration of the Mass. The Mass as a work for the dissemination of grace was considered quantifiable. Authors could, accordingly, state precisely how many and which gifts of grace could be distributed through the celebration of a mass. This notion found literary expression in the various treatises on the fruits of the Mass, which were widespread in vernacular versions.[32] The simplest version of such quantification is reflected in the promise "that each mass will cause a poor soul to be freed from purgatory and a sinner to repent."[33] The quantification of salvation was to have a lasting effect on the Mass stipends: one of the most frequently posed questions about the Mass centered on the problem of whether a mass that was celebrated for many people could be just as efficacious as one offered for a single person. The answer was clear for those who thought in quantitative terms: the more beneficiaries of a mass, the less efficacious it was; and accordingly the practice arose of providing stipends with the express admonition to pray only for the donor during the mass in question. Because theologians and pious laypersons alike understood the celebration of the Mass as an act whose effects on human beings were objectively quantifiable, they tried to prevent too many people from enjoying the fruits of the Mass.[34] Repeated criticisms of this practice from the early Middle Ages on had little effect.[35] The privatization of the fruits of the Mass went so far that, in the course of the fourteenth and fifteenth centuries, the opinion that the efficacy of a mass for an individual was greater the fewer people participated in it came to dominate among theologians.[36] Even a single conse- crated host could be incorporated into this quantification. Thus Gertrude of Helfta, for example, reports that when receiving the Eucharist she tried "to bite the host into as many small pieces as possible." Her objective, she wrote, was "for the Lord to release as many souls from Purgatory as there were pieces of the host in her mouth." Christ agreed to this dissection of the wafer, and indeed even went further than she. "You shall receive far more for the price of this life-giving sacrament than you dare to ask."[37] The sacrament was the price that had to be paid for the deliverance of the souls.

The counted prayer did not remain limited to the individual practice of piety. It played an equally important role in communitary memorial prayers, for example in Dominican convents. The number of prayers to be recited by individ- ual nuns as well as the entire convent was listed in prayer books and *ordines defunctorum*.[38] Strict attention was paid to the observance of the exact figure. The *ordines defunctorum* set out in detail the number and times of the various memorial prayers according to the different groups of persons for whom prayers were to be said, the different times of the ecclesiastical year, and the prayers to be recited in the chapter or during handicraft work. Such lists also provided the sum total of prayers that a nun had to recite if she did not intend to say the memorial prayers daily, but rather cumulatively on a particular day. The following list, for example, was given for the weekly chapter prayer:

. . . the weekly prayer in the chapter
. . . for holy Christendom: for the Holy Trinity 3 Paternosters and for the worthy
    Mother of God 1 Salve Regina
For our convent: for the sweet heart of Christ, 3 Paternosters and 1 Salve Regina
For our ailing sisters, 1 Paternoster and 1 Salve Regina
For the harvest, 3 Paternosters and 1 Salve Regina
For all those who request our prayers, 1 Paternoster and 1 Salve Regina
For our father confessor, 1 Salve Regina
For the town, 1 Ave Maris stella
For the convent's angel, 1 Te deum laudamus
For St. Matthew, 1 Te deum
For St. Nicholas and St. Elizabeth, 1 Te deum laudamus
For St. Dominic, 1 Paternoster
For all whom we owe intercession, 5 Misereres.

This was followed by the instructions for the cumulative prayer:

> . . . this is the number of weekly prayers in the chapter for those who wish to say all their prayers at once:
>
> . . . 634 Paternosters, 312 Salve Reginas, 52 Ave Maris Stellas, 206 Te deum laudamus, 260 Misereres.[39]

It would be hard to overestimate how widespread the practice of counting prayers was among the most diverse social groups. Nuns and monks, clerics and laypeople, learned and unlearned all counted as they prayed. Theologians of stature such as Gabriel Biel[40] as well as protagonists of the *devotio moderna*, such as Thomas à Kempis,[41] acknowledged the salvational efficacy of counting prayers. In his *Sermones de vita et passione Domini*, Thomas à Kempis, for example, exhorted the faithful to count and contemplate all of Christ's wounds; through this contemplation, he promised, they would participate in the *thesaurus ecclesiae* and be released from all punishments.[42] Finally, well knowing that he could not cite biblical accounts, Thomas put the exact number of Christ's wounds into mnemonic verse in a prayer: "Septuaginta quinque quatercentum milia quinque: Tot fertur Christus pro nobis vulnera passus" (5,475: this is how many wounds Christ suffered for our sake).[43] Gabriel Biel preached the same figure (5,475) and added the corresponding devotional exercise.[44] The same holds true for prayer books written by laymen, whether they were of noble origins[45] or belonged to Humanist circles:[46] all of them display numerous traits of counting. Laypersons, too, recorded how many prayers they had recited. For Wilhelm Werner, one of the counts of Zimmen, the Zimmen family chronicle listed the prayers he said every day:

> His daily prayers were a Confiteor, In te domine speravi, Miserere, Paternoster, Ave Maria together with four collects de sancta Trinitate, In quinque vulnera, one Salve with the offertorio. In the evening, when the Ave Maria rang out, he said the usual three Ave Marias, then one Paternoster and Ave Maria, so that the Almighty would heed his blessed Mother, one that he would have a happy and blessed end, one for his two wives, the landgravine of Leuchtenberg and the countess of Lupfen, one for his father and mother, one for his brothers, sisters, friends, and benefactors, one for the souls of the people who had died in the current year, one for the many miserable souls in the four bishoprics of Mainz, Speyer, Konstanz, and Worms, one for the soul that had been longest in purgatory, one for the next soul to enter purgatory, one for the next soul to leave purgatory, one for the soul suffering the greatest pain in purgatory, and finally one for all the souls of Christian believers. His mother taught him to pray thus for the poor souls, promising him that if he performed these prayers daily with devotion he would grow so old that a mosquito could knock him over. And this later proved true. He said such prayers from his youth until the end and doubtless thereby attained lasting health until the end of his days.[47]

A recent historian has attributed "an almost utilitarian benefit analysis"[48] to this "quantitative religiosity"; and even people on the low end of the social scale were no less vigilant than the count cited above. In the minutes of an interrogation from the 1680s, for example, a simple horse herder, Conrad Stoeckhlin, provided the following information on his devotional practices.[49] His friend Jacob Walch had appeared to him several times after his death and warned him of the consequences of paying for sins not atoned for in life with a sojourn in purgatory. "Give heed and confess and do penance for your sins here on earth, so you do not end up where I am, for I must walk around here on earth for three years, and afterward suffer four years pain and torment in purgatory."[50] As preparation for the hereafter Walch admonished his friend to say the rosary nine times a day;[51] an angel also imposed an additional penance on him: he should instruct his wife and children to recite 30,000 Aves, that is "Our Lady's Mantle," quarterly.[52] The practice, common in Dominican convents, of collectively praying a mantle for Mary, is visible here as the practice of a family of low social position.[53] In both cases the number of prayers was distributed over the individual members,[54] doubtless in order to ensure the salvation of the entire group, whether monastic community or family.

One cannot, however, understand quantified piety only in terms of the crossing of social borders; it led in turn to the foundation of spiritual communities which exploded all boundaries of estate. An outstanding example are the confraternities, such as the confraternity of St. Ursula in Strasbourg.[55] Here, men, women and children, nuns and monks, simple clerics, and holders of ecclesiastical and secular office came together and contributed their prayers to the confraternity. Each contributed in a manner appropriate to his or her estate.[56] Clerics, monks, and nuns mainly chose masses and Latin prayers, and all sorts of other pious acts, such as scourging, giving alms and pilgrimages. The confraternity recorded the following services that were performed on behalf of the Dominican monastery at Berne, "other priests and also the venerable prioress on the island in Berne with her Sisters": "58 masses, 21 psalters, 260 times the 10 psalms spoken on the Cross *Deus deus meus*, 30 courses of Our Lady, 1000 times the seven psalms, 13,513 *Te deum laudamus*, 1000 *Gloria in excelsis deo*, 5150 *Laudate dominum omnes gentes*, 222,000 *Pater* (with) *Ave Maria* and 71,600 *Ave Maria*, 86,000 *Gloria Patri*, 1716 *Salve Regina*, 100 rosaries, 11,000 *Laus tibi domine*, 10,000 *Credo in deum*, 100 flagellations, 52 poor people fed, 300 alms given, 5 pilgrimages, 163 Masses dedicated, and otherwise many thousand antiphonies and Psalms recited and good works performed."[57] In comparison to the clerics, laypeople, as a collective account for 290 Zurich citizens shows, restricted their activities to prayers such as the Paternoster, the Ave Maria, the Credo, and other prayers that the laity knew by heart: "290 secular persons at Zurich provided our little ship well with spiritual interest and annuities; namely, they gave 436,700 Paternosters and Ave Marias and 200,800 Ave Marias, 1574 rosaries, 14,357 Salve, 676 Miserere, 200,982 Credo in deum, 12 Magnificat, 12,100 Gloria Patri, 12 Nunc Dimittis, 1000 Veni sancte, 30 vigils, 86 masses, and another 13,000 Paternoster and Ave Maria, and many pilgrimages with other blessed works and prayers."[58]

The very phrase "spiritual interest and annuities" hints at the contemporary understanding of pious acts: through prayer and other pious works one sought to pay the ferryman who was to guarantee that the ship of St. Ursula and her companions would have a safe journey to the hereafter. The minimum requirement was the recitation of 11,000 Paternosters and the same number of Aves in honor of St. Ursula and her 11,000 companions, which had to be performed once in a lifetime as "a wage and shipping fee."[59] The confraternities' main theological idea was the new notion of the *thesaurus ecclesiae* which had been developed for indulgences. While theologians had been preaching since the mid-thirteenth century that the Church possessed a storehouse of grace that was available to all, living or dead,[60] the confraternities transferred this to the collection of stored-up grace in the confraternity.[61] That, at least, was the intention of the Strasbourg confraternity of St. Ursula: "This skipper . . . said that the spiritual gifts and treasures (of the confraternity) should grow greatly from day to day and increase through the grace of God in that each [member] should renew the little ship yearly with numerous small gifts, so that all who follow may participate all the more in the gifts and treasures of this little ship until the end of the present world."[62] The tradition of monastic prayer alliances, which the confraternities carried into the world of the laity,[63] thus received new impulses from contemporary theology. The confraternities were a treasure-house (*thesaurus*) to be managed by all members within the treasure-house of the Church as a whole.

Controlling Counting Through Prayer Strings and Literacy

What we see behind all of these examples is a logic of piety that sought to ensure individual and collective salvation through counting, bookkeeping, and quantification. Such an arithmetical ascertainment of salvation also created its own media for ensuring that one's performance could also be verified. In the late Middle Ages the rosary was widespread; it could be used to check one's own individual devotional performance. As Gislind Ritz demonstrates in her study of the Christian prayer counting string, it had many more functions than that of a mere instrument for meditative repeated prayers. Rather like an abacus, it was also used as an (ac)counting tool with which the faithful sought to "oversee the prescribed or intended number of prayers to be said." Ultimately it served not merely to help count prayers; it was also an instrument of "registration, incorporating the element of a permanent notification of merit."[64]

The written word played a similar role. As important as the confraternity's spiritual treasures were for their salvation, both members and leaders were extremely anxious to fix these treasures in writing. In order to do so they used all available forms of writing: enrollment in the Strasbourg confraternity involved a registration letter announcing the new member's entry and duties to the prioress of St. Nicholas. One of these documents, the 1594 registration letter of the subprior of the Benedictine monastery of Gengenbach, has survived in the Strasbourg Municipal Archive.[65] In it the subprior promises to read 100 masses yearly beyond the number stipulated by his order, as well as to say 11,000 Paternosters and Aves once every two years and to translate the confraternity's record book into Latin and correct the German version.[66] Upon entry, the confraternity members also agreed to provide an account of their pious acts. In a letter, new members informed the prioress of what treasures they had brought with them into the confraternity. The prioress then ordered a summary register of the individual treasures.[67] This process resulted in the confraternity record book, which was many pages long and listed all of the spiritual gifts brought in by members. As a list of treasures, the confraternity record book was intended to ensure the confraternity's success in effecting mercy. The book's importance is also underscored by the fact that—as in the case of the subprior of Gengenbach—copying, correcting, and translating were themselves considered meritorious acts, which could in turn be recorded in the enumeration of treasures.[68]

The desire to record, thus perfected, demonstrates how seriously people took the need to keep proper books on their pious performance. To be sure, this desire to record was not limited to the confraternities. Monasteries and convents, too, found written forms to safeguard and supervise their spiritual achievements. A list has survived from the convent of St. Nicholas in Strasbourg which precisely records which nun prayed to St. Anne for how long on which day for a New Year's greeting. The prayer book of Elizabeth of Ursa from the Unterlinden convent has also been preserved.[69] It contains not so much prayers for Elizabeth's private use as a record of prayers spoken collectively. Elizabeth recorded how many prayers the convent said in which emergencies (war, the imperial election, famine, the threat of fire) and how these were credited to the individual nuns. Elizabeth's prayer book was thus a bookkeeping journal of communal prayers and was intended at most to safeguard the knowledge of certain "prayer recipes" for future generations.

A brief glance at the modern period shows the lasting effects of the use of the written word in both safeguarding and handing down such arithmetical prayer recipes and recording individual prayer. The *Gertrudenbüchlein*, based on the devotional exercises of Gertrude of Helfta and Mechthild of Hackeborn, has appeared in a large number of editions since the early modern period.[70] Apart from many references to indulgences, the book also contains a prayer on all of the 5,460 wounds of Jesus, for example.[71] Typically enough, the book states that one must not necessarily observe the stipulated time period of one year for one's devotional exercise. Rather, one could say the prayer cumulatively; the number, however, was more important than the time: "For this prayer has no particular time limit, instead it is only necessary to fulfill the number."[72] The same was true of a small prayer book, the so-called "Spiritual Shield" of which several copies survive in the collection of devotional works (Prälat-Schreiberschen-Andachtsbuch-Sammlung) of the University and State Library at Münster.[73] They all come from the nineteenth century, but bear a seventeenth-century ecclesiastical imprimature.[74] The title already reveals the status accorded to the written word: *A Spiritual Shield Against Spiritual and Physical Dangers to Be Carried at All Times; Containing Very Strong Blessings and Prayers . . . for the Comfort of All Christian Believers Especially Those Traveling by Land or Water, so That They May Be Preserved from Many Dangers Through the Power of This Shield Carried with Them*.[75] The prayer book as such was thus already considered a protective charm which exerted its powers even if one did not actually use it to pray. The book's content also portrays the written word as having quasi-magical properties: thus, for example, it informs the reader of which letters protect against disease, promising that "if one writes these letters over a door, all those who live in the house will be preserved from the Plague."[76] Finally, the *Gertruden-büchlein* also operates with numbers: one finds details of indulgences as well as lists with the number of torments suffered by Christ and the corresponding promises that God and his saints would hear one's prayers. Numbered prayers and the use of writing for protective purposes come together here: "To all those who say seven Paternosters and seven Aves and one Credo every day until they have completed the [number of the] above-mentioned drops I will grant the five following Indulgences and Mercies in honor of my bitter suffering and death."[77] But the promises were effective even without the prayers being spoken: The above revelation was found in the Holy Sepulchre at Jerusalem, and whoever carries it with him cannot be harmed by the evil foe; he is protected from sudden death and will not perish terribly. Similarly, a pregnant woman who carries it will have an easy birth. This salutation has 800 years of indulgence."[78] The number prayers—particularly when they were found in such prominent places as the Holy Sepulchre—appear to have been associated with such dignity that their mere possession in writing was thought to have a saving effect. The written word retained the status of heavenly power even in the modern period.

One cannot overestimate the significance of the written word, which had long since taken hold in large areas of the organization of everyday life, for the increasing unity and systematic nature of arithmetical piety in the late Middle Ages. The indulgence, in particular, with its compelling quality and broad dissemination, would be inexplicable without the increasing significance of writing, which was further heightened by the new medium of printing. The success of the indulgence began with the expansion of the papal chancery into a "well-organized dispatch department,"[79] which developed a highly differentiated and functional system of registers and certificates. Using the example of the Portiuncula indulgence, Karlheinz Frankl has demonstrated how quickly the high degree of organization led to the dissemination of indulgences.[80] Beginning in 1392,

Portiuncula privileges left the papal chancery for all purposes and all churches without distinction. First distributed in Italy, we can then trace the indulgence from the fifth year of the pontificate of Boniface IX (1393) in all countries obedient to Rome. . . . The distribution of this indulgence reached its height at the turn of the century, in the years 1400 and 1401. The register records some two thousand Portiuncula indulgences until their revocation in 1402. Evidence from recipients has increased this number by a further fifty. One must also assume a goodly number of certificates that still await discovery in the archives. The indulgence could be gained from Oslo, Stockholm, and Uppsala to the Apulian boot, from Drogheda in Ireland to the eastern frontiers of Roman Christianity.[81]

If the papal chancery maintained a system of registers and certificates in order to safeguard the distributed treasures of grace, the recipients of indulgences developed their own records to safeguard the promise of indulgence: churches, convents, and monasteries began to keep their own registers and lists to document the indulgences granted to them.[82] The certificates of indulgence themselves were publicly displayed in order to increase their credibility by documentary means; it is quite likely that the faithful even touched the certificates and seals to assure themselves of their efficacy.[83] The pious were so anxious for documentary proof that prayer book scribes sought to authenticate the indulgences promised therein by noting that they themselves had, after all, seen the certificate in this or that church with their own eyes.[84] Furthermore, in the churches, inscriptions in stone or surrounding pictures informed the beholder how many years' indulgence could be gained by which religious act—generally a prayer.[85] Such figures, in turn, spawned their own forms of writing. The most famous example is the "Indulgentiae urbis Romae,"[86] a list of all the indulgences that could be acquired in the Holy City. Their wide distribution, both in Latin and in the various vernaculars, indicates that they shaped late medieval piety in a manner that would be hard to overestimate. They not only listed all the treasures of mercy assembled in Rome, but also promised the effects of mercy provided by the Roman churches to those who could not travel to the city personally. Because of these promises the "Indulgentiae" then found their way into the most diverse private prayer books. Taken as a whole, these prayer books were a significant medium for the dissemination of indulgences.[87] They not only promised the individual indulgences for particular prayers; the calendars that opened the prayer books not infrequently listed in precise detail the indulgences that could be obtained in particular churches on the various feast days.[88]

Apart from such informational written media, which documented the granting of indulgences and mentioned which works of piety were needed to gain indulgence, other forms of written documents served the concrete granting of indulgences: these were, above all, dimissory letters and letters of indulgence, which had to be acquired before the receipt of the indulgence itself. Early printing was to have a particularly great impact on distribution in the fifteenth century. Letters of indulgence could now be printed and produced in editions of many thousands.[89] Blank forms developed, on which only the recipient's first and last name and the date and place of issue remained to be filled in. The list of written media for the granting and distribution of indulgences could be extended,[90] but the examples cited here already demonstrate the highly complex bond between the written word and counting in the system of indulgences. The written word was used to ensure that people knew the extent of the promises of grace that had been granted and received and, at the same time, to record which religious acts could lead to the acquisition of which gifts of grace. By bringing together money and the acquisition of letters of indulgence, this association between the written word and the counting of acts of piety then also assumed an economic, cultural, and social significance[91] which, to be sure, would already attract critics in the late Middle Ages.[92]

On the whole, this complex interplay between the written word and the counting of piety demonstrates that writing could indeed have a rationalizing effect on religious life and serve the utilitarian benefit analysis of securing salvation. The written word, after all, made a substantial contribution to perfecting the system of counting piety. In this sense modern processes of recording and reproduction could be placed in the service of a piety trapped in a commercial mentality. The same kind of written records long shaped and used by merchants were deployed equally in the practice of piety. The new forms of religious writing could not only cover "devotional costs" but also record prayer performance in bookkeeper's style. To this extent merchant bookkeeping and celestial bookkeeping entered into a fruitful alliance. For Christianity, however much it may be a religion of the book, this alliance was not wholly unproblematic, though. After all, the Holy Scripture admonished individuals to look to the inner motives for their behavior and change their ways from within. Recording external achievements could have a deep and systematically destructive effect on the demand for introspection. Despite its evident rationalizing effect, this shows that—at least in the realm of religion—the increasing significance of the written word for coping with everyday life by no means necessarily led to growing introspection and internalization.

Ambivalences and Critiques

However strongly counting may have penetrated late medieval piety, it did not fail to inspire criticism. Meister Eckhart, writing at the beginning of the four-teenth century, was its most vehement critic: "One Ave Maria, spoken in this spirit [without individual volition], whereby the person renounces himself, is of more use than one thousand psalters read without it; indeed, to take one step in it would be better than to cross the sea without it."[93] Eckhart argued quite tradi-tionally here, following in the footsteps of Augustine: "Just as, in the words of Augustine, 'the single prayer of an obedient man, however short, is better than ten thousand prayers of a scoffer' and a single deed performed out of greater love is better than all the deeds in the world if the love therein be less—for number, size, length, breadth, height, and depth add nothing to goodness and merit."[94]

The primacy of the *recta intentio* over any kind of arithmetic or quantifica-tion is characteristic of Eckhart's devotional doctrine as a whole. Not the multi-plicity of spiritual exercises was decisive, but rather a life in which one's will was at one with God.[95] The only number the Meister recognized was one. From it everything else arose; all further numbers led to multiplicity and separated the human being from God.[96] Indeed, those who produced too many words ul-timately treated God like "a goat, which one feeds with leaves."[97] Eckhart accord-ingly branded as fools those persons who fasted and prayed frequently, but refused to change their ways.[98] God cared only for the proper attitude: "For God does not regard the works, but only what love and devotion and spirit are in the works. What matters to Him are not our works, but rather the spirit in all our works and our love for Him in all things."[99] Everything else counted for nothing, and to judge the goodness of works by their number was a fallacy: "For every-thing which falls under numbers thereby drops out of the concept of the morally good, and conversely everything that is morally good drops out of the concept of numbers and cannot be counted."[100]

Eckhart's position arose from his ethics, which were strictly grounded in theonomy. From the fact that "in God, there is neither number nor multiplicity nor negation"[101] he inferred human moral action: "God is neither [made] good nor better by time, number, mass, or size; similarly, God's work in us is not increased by the time, number, mass, or size of the outward act."[102] By calling into question works of external piety, and legality more generally, Eckhart came to unmask the logic of counting piety as a commercial mentality. "Look, all of these men are merchants who shun gross sins and would like to be good men and perform their good works in honor of God, such as fasting, vigils, praying, and the like, every sort of good work, and yet do it so that our Lord may give them something in return or do something that would please them: they are all merchants."[103] Eckhart sought completely to overcome the notion of barter with God. He who gave God something in the hope of receiving something in return was "cheated in such an exchange."[104] The Meister's *sacrum commercium* took quite another direction: "It is an equal exchange and a just trade: as far as you step out of all things so does God go in with all of His, no less and no more, as long as you completely renounce what is yours in all things."[105]

It is questionable, however, whether such critiques had much effect on the practice of piety, and we cannot be cautious enough in our assessments. "The surviving evidence shows," Joachim Wollasch has noted for the "quantifying mentality" in the realm of caring for the dead, "that fourteenth-century developments could not be held back by the warnings of theologians."[106] The theological critique of arithmetical piety was not merely without consequences for the practice of piety. It was also nowhere formulated so clearly as in the works of the mystic Eckhart. Where he opposed any notion of merit and all legality, the fifteenth-century reform theologians adopted a much more moderate approach in their critiques. Jean Gerson, for example, vehemently opposed the accumulation of indulgences and the quantification of the effects of the Mass, but he called into question neither meritorious works nor the Mass as an instrument for imparting grace.[107]

The sources of the critique of arithmetical piety have by no means been sufficiently studied. What does seem clear, however, is that such critiques were quite widespread. They became most popular in series of maxims which were being produced by the late thirteenth century and would reach the high point of their dissemination in the fifteenth century. They have survived in various vernaculars as the so-called Proverbs of the Five Masters,[108] the Proverbs of the Twelve Masters of Paris[109] and the *Novem puncta* or the Proverbs of St. Albert, which have been erroneously attributed to Albertus Magnus.[110] We need further study both of their transmission and their theological tradition.[111] As a rule, the sayings are structured antithetically, as in the writings of Meister Eckhart, which state that "one Paternoster spoken in days of sickness is better than three Psalters spoken in health," "that in only one hour of suffering he washes away more sins than in thirty years in purgatory";[112] "the man who thinks of his lost time and his sin is more pleasing to God and more useful to man than a thousand of the Psalms of David; God will remit thirty years in purgatory to the man who wishes to be better than he is now."[113] With their antitheses, the *Novem puncta* became a virtual antitype of contemporary piety and its fundamental focus on performance and computability: they set exercises in virtue and inner attitude against exercises of indulgence and instruments for preparing for the afterlife. An example are the aphorisms which Alfons Auer lists in an ideal-typical summary:[114]

1. The maxim that a penny (spent on alms) during one's lifetime was better than a golden column reaching to heaven after one's death. [= against testamentary donations]
2. Better to withstand harsh words than to beat a rod against one's back. [= against scourging]
3. Better to humble oneself than to make a pilgrimage to the ends of the earth. [= against pilgrimages]
4. Constant peace of mind is better than running from one end of the earth to another. [= against pilgrimages]
5. Better to shed one tear out of honest love than tears of pain. [= inner attitude over corporal asceticism]
6. It is better to go to God oneself than to have someone else ask for one. [= against stipends, etc.]
7. Not to judge is better than to shed blood seven hours every day. [= corporal asceticism]
8. Patience is better than rapture in third Heaven. [= against the search for external experiences of grace][115]
9. Compassion is better than feeding the sick. [= inner attitude against the corporal works of mercy as a means of gaining indulgence].

This critique took a different direction from Meister Eckhart's: the proverbs continued the practice of bookkeeping and never questioned the merit of pious works. They merely called for an emphasis on inner attitude rather than a quantification of external works: attitude replaced external works and could match their effects; repentance, for example, compensated for one thousand psalters, and the mere wish to mend one's ways effected a remission of thirty years in purgatory.[116] While Meister Eckhart stressed a conception of grace rooted in theonomy and ultimately saw the *recta intentio* in the renunciation of all self-will, here the *recta intentio* consisted of virtuous works and *compassio*. In the proverbs both virtues and *compassio* merely took the place of the external exercises of indulgence (prayer, pilgrimage, tears, alms, donations, etc.). Inner attitude itself now became an act for obtaining indulgence. How greatly this position differed from that espoused by Meister Eckhart is revealed above all by the last maxim in the *Novem puncta*: *compassio*—compassion with Christ—is given precedence here over caring for the sick. Eckhart, in contrast, gave caring for the sick precedence over any kind of religious experience: "Even if one were as enraptured as Saint Paul, and knew of a sick man who was in need of a bowl of soup, I would deem it far better for you to leave off your raptures out of love and serve the needy in greater love."[117]

The proverbs thus represent a second variety of possible critique of arithmetical piety: external works were to be replaced by virtues. This form of critique was wholly under the influence of a moralizing tendency such as has often been noted in late medieval piety.[118] Reform preachers, for example, warned against the idea that prayers could produce garments for the saints, who would then protect those who prayed, and admonished the beholder to virtue: The raiment of the saints comes not from much praying, from the Paternoster, rather it means that you should practice virtue, which will then be signified by the flower.[119] It was in the spirit of this moralizing that the Proverbs of St. Albert demanded a form of piety that shifted its attention from preparing for the hereafter to a Christian way of life in this world. The proverbs expressed this in ideal-typical form:

> Give a penny now, when you could still enjoy it, that is more pleasing to me [God] than if you were to give a great heap of gold after your death.
>
> If you are angry with your neighbor, or he with you, for God's sake avoid having words when you are wronged. That is of more use to you than all the priests of a bishopric reading a Mass for your soul after your death.[120]

According to the proverbs, our well-being in the hereafter is decided not by precautionary or posthumous works of piety, but solely by works of mercy and charity performed during our lifetime. Here one's own lifetime, as opposed to the afterlife, comes into focus with a clarity that mirrors that "emergence of a marked temporal ethic"[121] which has recently been described for the late medieval experience of time. Heartfelt piety and a Christian mode of living in this world thus increasingly came to compete with arithmetical piety and its quantification of the external act.

Elaborating the Inner Human Being by Numbers and Counting

If we reduce the late medieval practice of piety to the dichotomy of counting, on the one hand, and heartfelt piety, on the other, we would not be doing it justice; indeed we would be ignoring important gradations between the two. Numbers and counting were also used as techniques for cultivating the inner human being. The most important example of this is, once again, the rosary. As much as it quantified and recorded devotional performance, the persons praying were supposed, at the same time, by means of repeated serial prayers, to immerse themselves in the secrets of salvation and even to express these in their life practice by striving after virtue. This complex interplay leaves many questions open: which use of repeated prayers was historically older—the rosary as a meritorious work against which Luther directed his polemic, or the meditative prayer of immersion? Might one even locate different milieus of piety that gave precedence to one or the other function of prayer, and do these correspond to the division between "educated" and "uneducated"? Or must we seek another boundary line here, one that points more to the differences in access to the Christian mysteries of salvation and does not necessarily presuppose social distinctions? To put it more pointedly: in the light of the apparent duality in the use of the rosary, must we not radically question the dichotomies between "heartfelt piety" and "merit," "legality" and "grace," "inwardness" and "outwardness"? Should we not expect a type of piety so shaped by calculability that introspection was still trained and expressed through numbers? Indeed, were the contrasts between inside and outside that we imagine we perceive nowadays experienced that way at all by the pious people of the late Middle Ages, or might they not have united the two in a way alien to us today? Whatever answers we may find to these questions, late medieval piety was by no means uniform, and its multifaceted quality resists any hasty synthesis.

The use of counting for the development of the inner human being as well as his or her instruction in Christian concepts of faith and morality was one of these many facets. The counting, enumeration, division, and addition of material can be found above all in the realm of catechesis. Dieter Harmening sees a dual thrust at work here, whose objectives were "to provide an all-encompassing picture of belief and behavior in conformity with the norm on the one hand, and didactic and practicable texts for instruction on the other."[122] In the manuscripts, the individual articles were strung together almost endlessly; thus for example a manuscript from the monastery of the Augustinian Canons at Indersdorf[123] assembles the following articles one after another over ten sheets: seven cardinal sins; ten commandments; nine other people's sins; six sins against the Holy Spirit; four heinous sins; twelve articles of faith, whereby the Apostolicum is divided into five articles of the divinity and seven articles of the humanity of Christ; seven works of corporal mercy; six works of spiritual mercy; seven sacraments; seven gifts of the Holy Spirit; eight beatitudes; five senses.[124] The very arrangement of the catechism tables reveals the will to enumerate and make lists.[125] For example, in the listing of the seven deadly sins it begins with an enumeration of the individual sins, which are contrasted with the corresponding virtues:

The seven deadly sins:

1 Pride		Humility
2 Avarice		Generosity
3 Lust		Chastity
4 Anger	its opposite is	Love
5 Gluttony		Temperance
6 Envy		Gentleness
7 Sloth		Industry[126]

Then the individual mortal sins, beginning with pride, are further analyzed according to their "daughters and helpers":

The daughters and helpers of pride:

 1 inner pride
 2 outer pride
 3 boastfulness
 4 arrogance
 5 vainglory
 6 new sins
 7 sumptuous dress
 8 dancing, parading, jousting
 9 self-confidence
10 ingratitude
11 ambition, striving for honors
12 war or strife
13 curiosity
14 splendor or luxury
15 overextending by undertaking great things
16 the protection of sin
17 unruliness, stubbornness
18 the freedom to sin
19 the habit of sin[127]

Only after this enumeration are the individual sins strung together, prefaced in each case by the word "Item," and commented on in a brief sentence. Where this form of enumeration came from requires further elucidation. It is quite likely, though, that the arrangement and formal method of the catechism tables stems from the same milieu as their content and language, namely, the German reception of scholasticism.[128] Whatever future research may bring to light in this matter, numbering and listing did not serve as mere organizational principles here. Rather, they were intended to assist in the transmission of catechetical knowledge and to render it as comprehensible and learnable as possible.[129]

For the contemplation of the Passion, such forms of dissection were virtually demanded and deployed as a technique to strengthen the imagination of the beholder, further move his emotions to compassion, and thus guide him in the *imitatio Christi*. These connections are made crystal clear in a "Weekly Devotion on the Seven Occasions When Christ Shed His Blood."[130] The text begins by assigning each day of the week an occasion when the blood of Christ was shed: Sunday was the day of his circumcision, Monday the day when he sweated blood on the Mount of Olives, Tuesday the day of scourging, Wednesday the day when he was crowned with thorns, Thursday the day when he was disrobed twice and his wounds torn open, Friday the day of the Crucifixion, and Saturday the opening of the wound on his side. Each individual shedding of blood was then assigned a precisely fixed number of points of contemplation (*stücke, puncta*); thus, for example, in the case of the circumcision: "the first [shedding of blood] is the circumcision. There you find seven individual points."[131] Then the individual points of contemplation are listed. The first is "contemplate the bitter pains of the tender young child," the second, "furthermore he shed his pure child's blood for our sake," the third, "the hot tears he wept there."[132] The precise naming of the points was intended to ensure that the events contemplated would be grasped in their precise detail.

The theoreticians of methods of meditation consciously demanded this division of events into portions. They considered the provision of precisely fixed points of meditation essential for successful religious exercises. Thus in his "Meditatorium," John Mauburnus, one of the most important proponents of methodical meditation, described having fixed points (*determinata puncta habere*) as one of the foremost *necessaria meditanti*.[133] Only the knowledge of the certain and exactly fixed points of the different objects of contemplation— as described in the chapter "De punctis determinatis necessariis meditanti"— ensured human meditation before the face of God.[134]

Yet, these fixed points were not the end of the matter. The points of contemplation were constantly being extended, subdivided, and interlaced; thus, for example, the fifth point in the circumcision of Christ was divided into a further four subpoints: "the fifth point: you should also contemplate why he wished to be circumcised and to shed his young blood and these are four things."[135] Ul-

timately, these subdivisions could be continued ad infinitum. Arnold of Bru-
dericks even expressed the purpose of such dissections in mnemonic verse:

> Sectio luminat, eminet, explicat, attrahit, offert.
>
> Distinguit, numerat, mentem juvat, intrat, abundat.[136]

The psychological effect that such dissections were supposed to achieve is obvious: to allow the contemplator to see the individual events of the Passion as
vividly as possible in his mind's eye. In addition, the subdivision and fixing of the
points of contemplation were supposed to help engrave the sacred more strongly
on the mind and heart of the meditator.[137] Those, in contrast, who did not
adhere to the predetermined number of points of contemplation might find their
hearts beginning to wander.[138] Finally, dissection was intended to multiply the
spiritual nourishment of contemplation and, when the faithful grew weary, to
offer further points that refreshed their devotions.[139] Ultimately, it was believed,
the collection of an overabundance of points of contemplation would make
people firmer in their meditations and more quickly inflamed by enthusiasm.[140]

The effect of such a dissection on meditations on the Passion was that the
narrative context of the Gospel accounts was completely dissolved. Instead of telling the story of the Passion, the contemplations faithfully enumerated the details.
The events of the Passion were even embellished with incidents not to be found in
the Bible. Theoreticians of meditation on the Passion, such as Ludolph of Saxony,
had justifications for this as well: no detail was to be lost, since the more minutely
the person meditating recalled the details of biblical events, the more vivid they
promised to become in his mind's eye. In order to inspire greater devotions,
Ludolph wrote, he also recounted what the Gospels left out and embellished it
with imaginative representations (*imaginativas repraesentationes*).[141]

Numbers were, in turn, introduced into meditations for the purposes of
embellishment. Thus the author of the meditations on the occasions when Christ
shed his blood knew the exact number of lashings, hammer blows, and wounds
inflicted along with the number of Christ's tormenters and the length of the
stream of blood that flowed from his body. These figures were intended to make
the contemplated events appear as dramatic and realistic as possible. This, it was
hoped, would so arouse the emotions that the person meditating would achieve
the required inner attitude of *compassio*. But this was still not enough: this
affective restructuring through imagination was ultimately intended to inspire
the beholder to adopt a virtuous mode of living. The meditation on the third
occasion of bloodshed, the scourging, is arranged accordingly. The anonymous
author gives the length of the stream of blood that flowed from Christ's body
during the scourging as fifteen feet. After this figure is named, the beholder is
called upon to "contemplate his innocent humanity, so that you may be moved to

compassion."[142] He is then enjoined to practice "deep humility following His example," in order that he may be released from the sins of anger and impatience through contemplation of the humility of Christ. Numbers were provided in order to stage within the contemplator a reality intended not merely to fire his imagination but also to inspire him to emulate Christ in his own way of life.

How important concrete counting, too, was for such contemplations of and exercises in the virtues is revealed by the widely disseminated "Sixty-Five Articles of the Passion of Christ" by Jordan of Quedlinburg.[143] Jordan distributed the individual stations of the Passion over the daily canonical hours. During the hours one was supposed to meditate on the individual stations of the Passion in a three-step process. The *theorema*, the respective central points of an article in the form of a prayer, were followed by the *documenta*, the moral consequences and instruction for one's mode of living. Then the beholder was to use various exercises (*conformatio*) to adapt himself to the contemplated events.[144] During such meditations one virtually counted off the individual points. Abbot Garcia Cisernos of Montserrat, for example, developed a methodical psalmody meditation which was to be practiced during the hours.[145] Those at prayer were to count off the events of the Passion on their fingers. One station of the Passion was assigned to each finger segment. During the hours the left thumb was used to count the segments of the other fingers. During matins, for example, one finger segment was contemplated with one station of the Passion for each of the twelve Psalms.[146] The hand, frequently used as an instrument for counting, here becomes a mnemonic device for the contemplation of the Passion.[147]

In the late Middle Ages, symbolic numbers increasingly came to play a new role both in such methodical meditations and in the training of the virtues. They were introduced into catechesis for mnemotechnical reasons.[148] "Catechism allegories on the number seven are particularly numerous."[149] They were often based on the seven petitions of the Lord's Prayer, which were then combined with the various septenaries (the deadly sins, virtues and vices, gifts of the Holy Spirit, and so forth) and juxtaposed as mirror images according to the model of sickness (sins and vices), remedies (the petitions of the Lord's Prayer), and health (the gifts of the Holy Spirit). Such a combination of septenaries was already known to the ancient church.[150] Within the literary traditions of late antiquity and the early Middle Ages, the applications, for example, of the vice schema ranged "from a functional element in esoteric spirituality to a mnemonic aid in catechesis."[151] A significant shift in usage did occur, though. In the ancient church, for example in the works of Origen and Evagrius, the septenary or octonary of vices and virtues "was placed entirely in the service of developing a monastic spirituality and way of life"[152] and, as a schema of advancement, was intended to show monks the path to perfection. At the latest in the work of John Cassian, and increasingly in the early Middle Ages, the schemas were detached from this context and used largely for purposes of moral instruction. Only with the reorientation of theology in the twelfth century would the "psychology of the vice schema"[153] experience a new flowering.

Late medieval authors adopted such combinations of various septenaries in order to devise a methodical meditation that aimed at training in the virtues. The most important step in this direction was the combination of the septenary and the day of the week.[154] A large number of weekly devotional exercises emerged, which enjoined the persons praying to practice the virtues. The most prominent such exercise was one that Jean Gerson sent to his sisters in a letter,[155] which probably provided the model for one of the most important vernacular weekly exercises, Johannes Geiler von Kayserberg's "Sermon with a Prayer for the Seven Days of the Week."[156] There were much less well known forms as well. A weekly devotional exercise for Holy Week known as "Spiritual Knighthood"[157] incorporated the schema of vice and virtue into a method of meditation with the greatest consistency. In it, one of the seven instruments of Christ's torture is contemplated daily from Palm Sunday to Holy Saturday. Each of the instruments of torture is paired with one vice and one virtue; the crown of thorns, for example, with the vice of pride and its counterpart, the virtue of humility. The individual days are methodically structured. The morning prayer introduces the instrument of torture to be contemplated, then the person praying is told which vice is to be combated on that day. The struggle is conducted by exercising the corresponding virtue over the course of the day. The day also ends with a prayer; following the number of Christ's wounds, five Paternosters are said in different bodily attitudes. The instrument of torture, the virtue aimed at, and the attitude assumed by the body all corresponded to each other. Thus when contemplating the crown of thorns, for example, the hands of the person praying were to be crossed over his or her head as a sign of humility. Apparently, the attitude assumed by the body was intended to intensify the exercise of virtue once again at the close of the day. Johan Huizinga still regarded such combinations of numerical schemas and the use of symbolic numbers for practical moral life as a rigid formalization of number symbolism into mere "arithmetical exercises" and "decadence."[158] Viewed against the background of the history of the development of arithmetical piety, however, the methodical application of number symbolism appears in a different light: number symbolism was not simply assigned a practical moral value here. Rather, it was also applied as a method for training in the virtues.

It is in this sense that we may place the use of counting as an aid to the practice of virtue and to the training of the inner human being alongside Norbert Elias's instruments of civilization. After all, counting served here to regulate the emotions (such as *compassio*) and aid in the practice of self-discipline and self-regulation (humility, controlling anger and impatience, etc.), all in the name of acquiring virtues. In contrast to the use of numbers and counting in order to quantify religious acts, in this methodical and moral use both appear to be media with whose help religious life in the late Middle Ages was to be ethically rationalized. Numbers did not serve merely as a means of quantification. They also provided the individual with a controlled procedure for practicing Christian ideals of virtue.

Outlook

We are left with the question of which historical processes allowed counting to become a fundamental logic of medieval piety and which led to changes, intensifications, and also to a process of distancing. In the history of religion and more specifically of Christianity, what first comes to mind is the religious change which is often referred to as the axial period.[159] A step toward internalization was taken here, which was characterized by a shift from the slaughter of sacrificial animals to self-sacrifice for truth, ethos, and human society and, in the treatment of guilt and punishment, by the shift from responsibility for one's acts to responsibility for one's intentions. For Greek philosophical religion with its *thysia logike*, as for the prophets of Israel with their critical view of sacrifice, only the ethos of truth, the willingness to serve God, and justice counted, but not the flesh of the sacrifice. The New Testament represents the same religious logic. Jesus of Nazareth even said that brotherliness and reconciliation were the necessary preconditions for having one's prayers answered (Mt. 5:23–24). He also preached the father's readiness to forgive in opposition to the notion of retribution and gave precedence to the human readiness to change one's ways over expiatory punishment. For the development of arithmetical piety in the early Middle Ages, this meant that the understanding of the Mass as a sacrifice, as well as tariffed penance, point to a certain rearchaization. Both the sacrificial character of the Mass and the tariffing of penance would become the driving forces behind the counting of acts of piety throughout the Middle Ages and into the modern period, and, in the face of ecclesiastical practice, would confront theologians with scarcely solvable problems well into the twentieth century.

From the point of view of the history of development, however, changes also appear for which the connection between religious practice and cultural change requires further elucidation. Thus, for example, the late Middle Ages shows us different faces: on the one hand, the accumulation of religious acts with which it continued and heightened early medieval practices, and on the other, the increase in the late Middle Ages not only in critiques of counting, but also of the deployment of counting as an exercise for achieving greater inwardness. It remains the task of further discussion to explore the extent to which the development of veritable bookkeeping methods in piety was influenced by social transformations in the cities of the high and late Middle Ages, particularly in commerce, and a stronger inclusion of the laity in religious performance. A look at the written word would seem to confirm this. To be sure, computation relied from the beginning on the written word and in many cases inspired new forms of writing.[160] Only when the culture of writing had taken hold of large segments of everyday life could the counting of piety also become intensified and perfected. In regard to critiques of counting and also to counting as an exercise in internalization, we will also need to ask to what extent the often described process of interiorization, which began in the twelfth century, was at work here. High and late medieval changes in the culture of writing were doubtless also not insignificant for the shift in the valuation and use of computation. The emergence of new written media, the increase in reading proficiency, and also new and more elaborated methods of structuring texts[161] meant that counting within piety could also participate in the growing intersection between self-edification and the written word.[162]

In light of the value judgments often made in the literature against counting in religion, let us recall the following: first, the categories of the Mass understood as sacrifice and the notion of penance open up a horizon of comprehension for practices that have become alien to us today. Putting aside justifications and value judgments, counting may be viewed, against the background of a religious logic so oriented toward settling accounts, as a technique that people used to take care of themselves. Within the logic of this piety, both counting and recording one's performance represented forms of extreme rationalization and relief. For the conception of God this even meant that, by counting, people could cast their spell on a God described—by the nominalists, for example—as arbitrary, and assuage his wrath. To this extent counting and the notion of settling accounts also bound God to justice and balance.

Even when used as a method for structuring the inner human being, counting proved itself a technique for taking care of oneself. Before human beings developed an elaborate vocabulary of introspection with which they could speak of their inner selves and change them through techniques of self-observation and self-description—so the thesis goes—they used ritualized forms such as counting to change and express those inner selves. With the Reformation, such a notion of counting as a method of developing the inner human being was erased from western Christianity. Counting became denominationalized and was understood narrowly from the perspective of merit. While adherents to the new faith abandoned their rosaries and Luther described the rosary wholly from the perspective of legality, orthodox Catholics fixed rosaries like protective amulets to the banners with which they marched off to the wars of religion.[163] What the late Middle Ages had gained—namely, the insight that repetitive exercises were necessary in order to penetrate the secrets of faith as well as the inner self—was now lost. Ultimately, the complete secularization of counting was left to the modern age. However much the faith in arithmetical piety may have disappeared, counting itself has become a technique central to a secular comprehension of the world. Wilhelm Dilthey took it upon himself to admonish us not to grasp the world and humanity in statistical terms. In a spirit of Mephistophelian mockery, he penned the following rhyme deriding our excessive faith in statistics:

> Stick to numbers, and you shall see
> Through pangs of doubt you will walk free
> Into the peace of certainty.[164]

Notes

This chapter, with Chapter 1, is slightly abridged from Arnold Angenendt, Thomas Braucks, Rolf Busch, Hubertus Lutterbach, and Thomas Lentes, "Gezählte Frömmigkeit," *Frühmittelalterliche Studien* 29 (1995): 1–71.

1. French scholars have coined such terms as "la comptabilité de l'au-delà"; see Jacques Chiffoleau, *La comptabilité de l'au-delà. Les hommes, la mort et la religion dans la région d'Avignon à la fin du moyen âge (vers 1320–vers 1480)*, Collection de l'école française de Rome 47 (Rome, 1980) and "La religion flamboyante (v. 1320–v. 1520)," in *Du christianisme flamboyant à l'aube des Lumières (XIVe–XVIIIe)*, Histoire de la France religieuse, vol. 2 (Paris, 1988), 11–183, esp. 140–49 ("Multiplications flamboyantes"). Following Chiffoleau, Catherine Vincent has more recently spoken of a "mathématique du salut" ("Y a-t-il une mathématique du salut dans les diocèses du nord de la France à la veille de la réforme?" *Revue d'histoire de l'église de France* 77 [1991]: 137–49). Neither, however, actually demonstrates the presence of bookkeeping let alone mathematics. Instead, they more traditionally attribute to late medieval piety the characteristics of "frequency," "quantification," and "accumulation."

2. In response to Chiffoleau's work, Joachim Wollasch ("Die Hoffnungen der Menschen in der Zeit der Pest," *Historisches Jahrbuch* 110 [1990]: 23–51) and Franz Neiske ("Frömmigkeit als Leistung. Überlegungen zu großen Zahlen im mittelalterlichen Totengedenken," *Zeitschrift für Literaturwissenschaft und Linguistik* 21 [1991]: 21–30) have rightly emphasized that the massive increases in the commemoration of the dead in the late Middle Ages probably had more to do with the inclusion of new, particularly lay, social groups than with a completely new approach involving a bookkeeping mentality. Despite the fact that the system of counting piety was perfected in the late Middle Ages, we must not ignore the lines of tradition stretching back to the early Middle Ages.

3. See Gislind Ritz, *Die christliche Gebetszählschnur. Ihre Geschichte, ihre Erscheinung, ihre Funktion*, Ph.D. diss., Munich, 1955; on the different forms of prayer, see 34–36;

on the different forms of counting strings for prayer, which Ritz refers to as *Gebets-zählschnur*, see 37–71.

4. On the imagery of the rosary, see Gislind Ritz, "Der Rosenkranz," in *500 Jahre Rosenkranz (1475–1975)*, Ausstellung im Erzbischöflichen Diözesan-Museum Köln, 25 October 1975–15 January 1976 (Cologne, 1975), 51–101, 57–60.

5. See, for example, Gerard Achten and Hermann Knaus, *Deutsche und Niederländische Gebetbuchhandschriften der Hessischen Landes- und Hochschulbibliothek Darmstadt*, Die Handschriften der Hessischen Landes- und Hochschulbibliothek (Darmstadt, 1959), index entry "Rosenkranz."

6. On the individual objects see the examples under their respective keywords in Achten and Knaus, *Deutsche und Niederländische Gebetbuchhandschriften*; on the practice of such serial prayers in fifteenth-century Dominican convents, see Francis Rapp, "La prière dans les monastères des Dominicaines observantes en Alsace au XVe siècle," in *La mystique rhénane. Colloque de Strasbourg 16–19 mai 1961* (Paris, 1963), 207–18.

7. On this whole area see Thomas Lentes, "Die Gewänder der Heiligen. Ein Diskussionsbeitrag zum Verhältnis von Gebet, Bild und Imagination," in Gottfried Kerscher (ed.), *Hagiographie und Kunst. Der Heiligenkult in Schrift, Bild und Architektur* (Berlin, 1993), 120–51, esp. 121–29.

8. *Das Leben der Schwestern zu Töß beschrieben von Elsbet Stagel*, ed. Ferdinand Vetter, Deutsche Texte des Mittelalters 6 (Berlin, 1906), 84–85.

9. Colmar, Bibliothèque municipale, Ms. 267bis, fol. 68r f.

10. Cologne, Historisches Archiv, GB 8° 133, fol. 21r. The number of verses of the Te Deum (40,000 times 29 equals 1,160,000) that were to be spoken here corresponds almost exactly to the number of drops of blood. On the correspondence between the number of prayers and the venerated object, see at n. 24.

11. Berlin, SBPK, Ms. germ. oct. 53, fol. 105v f.

12. Berlin, SBPK, Ms. germ. oct. 18, fol. 69r f.

13. Nikolaus Paulus, *Geschichte des Ablasses im Mittelalter*, vol. 3 (Paderborn, 1923), 301–2 (on criticisms of prayer books), and 516–33 (opponents of indulgences).

14. Franz Xaver Haimerl, *Mittelalterliche Frömmigkeit im Spiegel der Gebetbuchliteratur Süddeutschlands*, Münchener Theologische Studien I.4 (Munich, 1952), 128.

15. Haimerl, *Mittelalterliche Frömmigkeit*, 57.

16. See the section "Penance and Counting" in Chapter 1.

17. "Lehrgespräch über das Fegefeuer," Colmar, Bibliothèque municipale, ms. 269, fol. 37r–46r; in the enumeration of the six ways in which people depart from this life, the author distinguishes three kinds of reasons why people end up in purgatory (fol. 39r f.).

18. *Die Offenbarungen der Margaretha Ebner und der Adelheid Langmann*, ed. Philipp Strauch, trans. Josef Prestel, Mystiker des Abendlandes (Weimar, 1939), 116.

19. See the examples in Siegfried Ringler, *Viten- und Offenbarungsliteratur in Frauenklöstern des Mittelalters. Quellen und Studien*, Münchener Texte und Untersuchungen zur deutschen Literatur des Mittelalters, 72 (Munich and Zurich, 1980), 195–98.

20. Ringler, *Viten- und Offenbarungsliteratur*, 197.

21. Gertrude of Helfta, *Legatus divinae pietatis* III. 9.1, ed. Pierre Doyère, Sources chrétiennes, 143 (Paris, 1968), 36[20]: "Ad quod Dominus: 'Dona distribuo.' His verbis intellexit Dominum orationes Congregationis distribuentem in remedium animarum . . . Tunc addidit Dominus dicens: 'Numquid et tu lucrum meriti tui mihi offere vis in augmentum hujus mei donationis?'"

22. Cologne, Historisches Archiv, GB 8° 133, fol. 19r–24r.

23. Ibid., fol. 19r.

24. Ibid., fol. 19r f.

25. See the examples in Ringler, *Viten- und Offenbarungsliteratur*, 140ff., along with further figures on the wounds and other sufferings of Christ.

26. The history of how these prayers on the wounds of Christ were handed down has not yet been written. The most important work remains Maria Meertens, *De Godsvrucht in de Nederlanden*, vol. II: *Lijdensdevoties* (Antwerp, 1931), 13–24; see also A. Stracke, "De origineele tekst der XV Pater noster op het lijden des Heeren en diens latere lotgevallen," *Ons Geestelijk Erf*, 17 (1943): 71–140. I discuss the different forms and the dissemination of such serial prayers in more detail in my dissertation on late medieval prayer books, *Gebetbuch und Gebärde. Studien zum religiösen Ansdruchsverhalten (1300–1550)*. Publications of the Max-Planck-Institut für Geschichte, forthcoming, 2001.

27. Ludolph of Saxony, *Vita Jesu Christi* pars II c. 58.4, ed. L.-M. Rigollot, Ludolphus de Saxonia, *Vita Jesu Christi* 4 (Paris and Rome, 1870), 458: "Cuidam etiam seni matronae reclusae multitudinem et numerum omnium vulnerum Christi scire cupienti, et pro hac re flebiliter Deum oranti, vox coelica missa dixit: Quinque millia quadringenta nonaginta vulnera mei corporis exstiterunt; quae si venerari volueris, orationem Dominicam cum salutatione Angelica quindecies quotidie in memoria Passionis meae replicabis, sicque anno revoluto unumquodque vulnus venerabiliter salutabis."

28. Ludolph of Saxony, *Vita Jesu Christi*: "Et accipitur hic numerus secundum annum bissextilem, ut semper sufficere possit; quia minor numerus quem quidam ponunt, scilicet quinque millia quadringenta septuaginta quinque, aliis annis tantum, sed non hoc sufficit."

29. Ibid. "Mittitur, ut legitur, olim, vox coelica lenis / Cor refovendo senis flebilis, ut sequitur: / D. duc undecies, X. dempta simplice, Christi / Unde revixisti, vulnera cuncta scies."

30. Berlin, SBPK, Ms. germ. oct. 31, fol. 218v.

31. Colmar, Bibliothèque municipale, Ms. 273, fol. 189r.

32. On the doctrine of the fruits of the Mass see Adolph Franz, *Die Messe im deutschen Mittelalter. Beiträge zur Geschichte der Liturgie und des religiösen Volkslebens* (Freiburg i. Br., 1902), 36–72; on the entire discussion see Erwin Iserloh, "Der Wert der Messe in der Diskussion der Theologen vom Mittelalter bis zum 16. Jahrhundert," in Iserloh, *Kirche—Ereignis und Institution. Aufsätze und Vorträge*, vol. 2: *Geschichte und Theologie der Reformation* (Münster, 1985), 373–413; Hans Bernhard Meyer, *Luther und die Messe. Eine liturgiewissenschaftliche Untersuchung über das Verhältnis Luthers zum Meßwesen des späten Mittelalters*, Konfessionskundliche und kontroverstheologische Studien, 11 (Paderborn, 1965), esp. 148–56.

33. Franz, *Die Messe im deutschen Mittelalter*, 61 with n. 4.

34. Franz, *Die Messe im deutschen Mittelalter*, 312; Meyer, *Luther und die Messe*, 155; Iserloh, "Der Wert der Messe," 400–401.

35. We need more research on the pre-Reformation critique of these ideas that limited the efficacy of the Mass. On early and high medieval critiques see Chapter 1. Iserloh ("Der Wert der Messe," 401–2) mentions the Carmelite Michael Aiguani of Bologna (d. 1400) as the only critic known to him. The bitter critique contained in the "earliest German interpretation of the Mass as a whole" (first edition ca. 1480, ed. Franz Rudolf Reichert, Corpus Catholicorum, 29, Münster, 1967) appears to have been unique

in the German-speaking region. This text expressly forbids the practice of praying only for the donor, to the exclusion of the prayer for all of the faithful (p. 135).

36. Iserloh, "Der Wert der Messe," 390–401.

37. Gertrude of Helfta, *Legatus divinae pietatis* III.18, 102–3: "Post hoc vero promissum, cum ad sumptum Sacramentum desideraret, ut sibi Dominus de Purgatorio tot animas praestaret, in quot partibus hostia in ore ipsius divideretur, et inde conaretur illam in plures partes dividere, Dominus dixit ad eam: 'Ut intelligas quoniam miserationes meae sunt super omnia opera mea et quia non sit abyssum pietatis meae possit exhaurire, ecce praesto ut per pretium istius vivifici Sacramenti multo plus accipias quam orare praesumis.' "

38. On the sources of the communitary commemorative prayer in Dominican convents, see Felix Heinzer, "*Dis liset man, so ein swester hinzuht.* Sondergut in der Sterbeliturgie der elsässischen Dominikanerinnenklöster," *Archives de l'église d'Alsace* N.F. 32, (1985): 337–42.

39. I quote here from the manuscript which comes from St. Nicholas in undis in Strasbourg, and is now in Freiburg im Breisgau. Augustinermuseum, Inv. M 29/5, fol. 78r f.

40. Gabriel Biel, *Canonis Misse Expositio* II, ed. Heiko A. Oberman and William J. Courtenay, Veröffentlichungen des Instituts für europäische Geschichte Mainz. Abteilung für abendländische Religionsgeschichte, 32 (Wiesbaden, 1965), 329–30.

41. Thomas à Kempis, *Oratio ad Christum*, ed. Michael Joseph Pohl, in Thomas à Kempis, *Opera omnia*, vol. 3 (Freiburg i. Br., 1904), 347.

42. Thomas à Kempis, *Sermones de vita et passione Domini* in Thomas à Kempis, *Opera omnia*, vol. 3, 225–28: "Numera si potes omnia verbera, omnia vulnera, omnes plagas, omnia improperia, omnia inquinamenta, a multis sibi inflicta: et compatere corde compassivo, omnia ista aequanimiter patienti . . . Ecce iam audisti quanta et a quantis passus est Christus: cui merito compati debet omnis christianus . . . Est autem passio Christi thesaurus ecclesiae qui non potest exhauriri nec consumi: sed est infinitae virtutis et dignatis. Per hanc quippe omne debitum solvitur: omne peccatum dimittitur; et paenitentibus regnum caelorum promittitur ac donatur: quod per multa milia annorum clausum tenebatur."

43. Thomas à Kempis, *Oratio ad Christum*, 347: "Quae etsi evangelistae non recitant, quibusdam tamen devotis fuisse revelatum multi affirmant, sicut his duobus versibus confinetur."

44. Gabriel Biel, *Canonis Misse Expositio*, 329: "Unde si quis per singulos dies integri anni diceret quindecies dominicam orationem, pro singulo vulnere unam orationem obtulisset, quod patet multiplicando numerum dierum anni scilicet ccclxv per xv resultabit numerus supra dictus."

45. See, for example, the serial prayers in the prayer book of Queen Agnes of Hungary. For examples see Haimerl, *Mittelalterliche Frömmigkeit*, 28ff.

46. See the examples in Haimerl, *Mittelalterliche Frömmigkeit*, 54ff. (Sebastian Brant), 119ff. (Hartmann Schedel), 123ff. (Sebastian Brant and Jakob Wimpfeling), which, alongside immensely high promises of indulgences all contain the most diverse forms of serial and repeated prayers.

47. *Zimmerische Chronik* IV, ed. Paul Hermann (Meersburg and Leipzig, 1932), 99–100.

48. Norbert Schindler, *Widerspenstige Leute. Studien zur Volkskultur in der frühen Neuzeit* (Frankfurt am Main, 1992), 76; it is, however, questionable whether a "degree of

privatization and 'internalization' of religiosity revealed itself [herein], which was no longer entirely congruent with the collective public rites of the old Church" (74). Public rites of preparation for the hereafter are transferred to the private sphere here, but these may well have been approved by the Church.

49. See Wolfgang Behringer, *Conrad Stoeckhlin und die Nachtschar. Eine Geschichte aus der frühen Neuzeit* (Munich and Zurich, 1994).

50. Quoted in Behringer, *Conrad Stoeckhlin*, 19.

51. Quoted in Behringer, *Conrad Stoeckhlin*, 20.

52. Quoted in Behringer, *Conrad Stoeckhlin*, 26.

53. To be sure, 30,000 Aves recited by four persons (Stoeckhlin, his wife, and their two children) over a period of three months can hardly be considered a "truly superhuman pious achievement" or a "well-nigh unattainable demand" as Behringer refers to it (*Conrad Stoeckhlin*, 27). Taking as our basis today's usual rosary of fifty Aves and one Paternoster after every ten Aves, this would amount to not quite two full rosaries a day, quite a common daily prayer quota.

54. See Lentes, "Die Gewänder der Heiligen," 139ff.

55. I have used the edition prepared by André Schnyder, *Die Ursulabruderschaften des Spätmittelalters. Ein Beitrag zur Erforschung der deutschsprachigen religiösen Literatur des 15. Jahrhunderts*, Sprache und Dichtung 34 (Berne and Stuttgart, 1986), 175–242.

56. Similar examples of group-specific prayer behavior can be found in Klaus Schreiner, "Gebildete Analphabeten? Spätmittelalterliche Laienbrüder als Leser und Schreiber wissensvermittelnder und frömmigkeitsbildender Literatur," in *Wissensliteratur im Mittelalter und in der frühen Neuzeit*, ed. Horst Brunner and Norbert Richard Wolf (Wiesbaden, 1992), 317–18.

57. Schnyder, *Die Ursulabruderschaften des Spätmittelalters*, 232.

58. Ibid., 233.

59. Ibid., 205.

60. On the development of the doctrine of the spiritual treasury of the Church, see Paulus, *Geschichte des Ablasses im Mittelalter*, 184–206.

61. One must distinguish between this and the notion that one effected indulgences through membership in a confraternity and thereby participated in the general spiritual treasury of the church (see the examples in Paulus, *Geschichte des Ablasses im Mittelalter*, 154–55). In the case of the confraternity of St. Ursula the members collected the "treasures" and then used them for the benefit of others, both living and dead. On the ecclesiological place of the confraternities, see Schnyder, *Die Ursulabruderschaften des Spätmittelalters*, 383–400).

62. Schnyder, *Die Ursulabruderschaften des Spätmittelalters*, 210.

63. Thus, Wollasch ("Die Hoffnungen der Menschen in der Zeit der Pest," 43), for example, notes that "the laity, deeply unsettled by the crises of the fourteenth century and above all by the Plague and its consequences, could [adopt] as their own hopes which, in an earlier time, had been placed in the practice of caring for the dead particularly by monastic communities."

64. Ritz, *Die christliche Gebetszählschnur*.

65. Strasbourg, Archives municipales, II 39/24; the text is printed in Schnyder, *Die Ursulabruderschaften des Spätmittelalters*, 507.

66. Ibid.: "I, F. Fridericus Pergamenus Wesaliensis . . . intend firstly to hear or read privately 100 sacrificia missae yearly beyond the duty of my order, and secondly to recite

the 11,000 Pater noster et Ave maria, once every two years as long as I live, and thirdly, as soon as I can, to transcribe the statuta of this confraternity and the tractatum on spiritual navigation in Latin according to my limited ability and alongside it the German in even letters, newly corrected."

67. Schnyder, *Die Ursulabruderschaften des Spätmittelalters*, 213.

68. Cf. n. 66 above.

69. Colmar, Bibliothèque Municipale, ms. 270.

70. On the "Gertrudenbüchlein" see Margot Schmidt, "Mechthild von Hackeborn," in *Deutsche Literatur des Mittelalters. Verfasserlexikon*, vol. 6, 2nd ed. (1987), 251–60, 258–59; I have examined the two seventeenth-century copies in the "Prälat-Schreiberschen-Andachtsbuch-Sammlung" of the ULB Münster: 1 E 2052 und 1 E 10855. I quote from 1 E 10855, which bears the title *Gertruden=Buch/oder Außerlesenes/geistreiches und andaechtiges Gebett=Buch: Darinn Das wahre Marck der andaechtigsten von Christo und der Mutter Gottes selbsten gemachten/und den zweyen H H. Closter=Jungfrauen und leiblichen Schwestern/Gertruden und Mechtilden/Theils muendlich/theils durch den H. Geist offenbarter Gebettlein/begriffen seynd. . . . Erstens getruckt zu Coelln. Anjetzo aber getruckt und verlegt in der Hochfl: Bischoefl: Haupt=und Residentz=Statt Aychstaett/bey Francisco Strauß/Hochfl: Bischoefl: Hof=Buchtruck: und Handler* [1668].

71. Münster, ULB, 1 E 10855, 146ff.

72. Ibid., 147.

73. I have examined the copies with the call numbers 1 E 2219 and 1 E 10896.

74. Münster, ULB, 1 E 2219: *Cum Licentia Orp.* [*sic*] *Cens. ibid. An. 1647 impress.*; ULB Münster 1 E 10896: *Cum. Lic. Ord. Cens. Trev. ibidem Anno Anno* [*sic*] *1647.*

75. *Geistlicher Schild gegen geist-/und lebliche Gefährlichkeiten allzeit bei sich zu tragen; darin sehr kräftige Segen und Gebete . . . zum Trost aller Christglaubigen, sonderlich deren so zu Wasser oder Land reisen, damit sie durch die Kraft dieses bei sich tragenden Schilds vor vielen Gefahren erhalten werden.* Münster, ULB, 1 E 10896, title page.

76. Münster, ULB, 1 E 2219, 20–21.

77. Ibid., 96.

78. Ibid., 97–98.

79. Karlheinz Frankl, "Papstschisma und Frömmigkeit. Die 'Ad instar-Ablässe,' " *Römische Quartalschrift*, 72 (1977): 57–124, and 184–247, here 101.

80. Ibid.

81. Ibid., 111–12.

82. Of the rich source material, which has scarcely been used up until now, I will mention only the example of the indulgence and consecration book from the Swiss Dominican convent at Töss (Staatsarchiv Zürich C II 13, 365), which informs us about which kinds of indulgences could be procured in Töss. Such books apparently record the only letters of indulgence accorded to the convent.

83. See Hartmut Boockmann, "Über Ablaß-'Medien'," *Geschichte in Wissenschaft und Unterricht*, 34 (1983): 709–21, 711–12.

84. See, for example, the scribe's note on a promise of indulgence in a prayer book from St. Nicholas in undis (Berlin, SBPK, Ms. germ. oct. 18, fol. 70r).

85. See the examples in Boockmann, "Über Ablaß-'Medien'," 713ff.

86. Volker Honemann, " 'Mirabilia Romae,' " in *Deutsche Literatur des Mittelalters. Verfasserlexikon*, vol. 6, 2nd ed. (1987), 602–6, on the "Indulgentiae," 603ff.; the Latin and vernacular tradition of the "Indulgentiae" is examined in Nine Robijntje Miedema, *Die*

"Mirabilia Romae." *Untersuchungen zu ihrer Überlieferung mit Edition der deutschen und niederländischen Texte*, Münchener Texte und Untersuchungen zur deutschen Literatur des Mittelalters, 108 (Tübingen, 1996).

87. Their (i.e., the prayer books') significance for the history of indulgences requires more thorough study, however. Paulus, *Geschichte des Ablasses im Mittelalter*, 3 (293–302) treats only printed prayer books, and Haimerl, *Mittelalterliche Frömmigkeit* (see above, nn. 14 and 15), with his negative assessments, overlooks the extent to which the promises of indulgence reflected late medieval people's concerns about salvation.

88. All of these forms come together in the above-mentioned Cologne prayer book (see n. 10). The book begins with a calendar, which not only records the individual saints' days but also offers figures on what indulgences could be acquired on that day in the convent church. At the same time it mentions which indulgences were distributed in which Roman church on each given day.

89. On the St. Peter's indulgence of 1515, for example, see Hans Volz, "Der St. Peter-Ablaß und das deutsche Druckgewerbe," *Gutenberg Jahrbuch* 41 (1966): 156–72.

90. One might mention the vernacular *summaria* of the indulgence bulls, the *Instructiones* on the granting of indulgences, and the *Instructiones Confessorum*.

91. On indulgences as a cultural factor see Paulus, *Geschichte des Ablasses im Mittelalter*, 3 (226–64); in conclusion he notes, with apologetic undertones (264) that "One may quite rightly claim that state society owed countless benefits to the much-reproached indulgence."

92. See the examples in Paulus, *Geschichte des Ablasses im Mittelalter*, 3 (450–69) (indulgences as a source of money), and 470–500 (abuses in the practice of indulgences).

93. Meister Eckhart, *Reden der Unterweisung* c. 11, ed. Josef Quint, in *Meister Eckehart. Deutsche Predigten und Traktate* (Munich, 1963), 69.

94. Meister Eckhart, *Expositio libri Genesis* n. 130, ed. Konrad Weiß, in *Meister Eckhart. Die lateinischen Werke* vol. 1 (Stuttgart, 1964), 284[1]: "Sicut ergo melior est, ut ait Augustinus, 'unica' quantumvis brevis 'oratio oboedientis quam decem milia contemnentis' et melior est actus unicus quilibet in maiori caritate omnibus actibus mundi minoris caritatis, eo quod numerus, magnitudo, longitudo, latitudo, sublimitas et profundum nihil adiciunt bonitatis et meriti, sed sola caritas mensura."

95. On Eckhart's critique of external works, see Otto Langer, *Mystische Erfahrung und spirituelle Theologie. Zu Meister Eckharts Auseinandersetzung mit der Frauenfrömmigkeit seiner Zeit*, Münchener Texte und Untersuchungen zur deutschen Literatur des Mittelalters, 91 (Munich and Zurich, 1987), 168–70.

96. Meister Eckhart, *Expositio libri sapientiae* n. 300, ed. Heribert Fischer, Josef Koch, and Konrad Weiß, in *Meister Eckhart. Die lateinischen Werke* vol. 2 (Stuttgart, 1992), 633[1]: "Secundum est notandum quod sola multitudo et numerus separat a deo."

97. Meister Eckhart, *Expositio sancti evangelii secundum Iohannem* n. 378, ed. Karl Christ et al., in *Meister Eckhart. Die lateinischen Werke*, vol. 3 (Stuttgart, 1994), 322[4]: "notandum primo quod hic percutiuntur qui in multiloquio verborum orantes confidunt, Matth. 6: 'orantes nolite multum loqui sicut ethnici; putat enim quod in multiloquio suo exaudiantur. Nolite ergo assimilari eis.' . . . Tales faciunt de deo capram quae foliis pascitur."

98. Meister Eckhart, Sermon 33 ("Sancti per fidem vicerunt regna"), ed. Josef Quint, in *Meister Eckhart. Die deutschen Werke*, vol. 2 (Stuttgart, 1971), 154[6]f.: "It is a great

foolishness, that many a man fasts and prays and does great works and is always alone . . . and is restless and angry."

99. Meister Eckhart, *Reden der Unterweisung* c. 16, 77.

100. Meister Eckhart, *Expositio libri Sapientiae* n. 110, 446[1]: "Omne enim quod cadit in numero, hoc ipso cadit extra rationem honesti, et e converso omne quod est honestum, cadit extra rationem numeri et est innumerabile."

101. Ibid. n. 112, 449[1]: "In deo autem nec cadit numerus nec multitudo nec negatio."

102. *Expositio sancti evangelii secundum Iohannem* n. 584, 512[2]: "deus non est bonus nec melior tempore, numero nec mole aut magnitudine; sic nec opus divinum in nobis augetur tempore, numero, nec mole sive magnitudine actus exterioris."

103. Meister Eckhart, Sermon 1, in *Meister Eckhart. Die deutschen Werke*, vol. 2: 153–54.

104. Ibid.

105. Meister Eckhart, *Reden der Unterweisung* c. 4, 57.

106. Wollasch, "Die Hoffnungen der Menschen in der Zeit der Pest," 39–40.

107. On the ambiguity of Gerson's position in regard to the fruits of the Mass, see Iserloh, "Der Wert der Messe," 395ff.; on his view on indulgences, see Paulus, *Geschichte des Ablasses im Mittelalter*, 6ff., on his critique, see Paulus, 301–2.

108. Betty C. Bushey, " 'Sprüche der fünf Lesemeister' I und II und verwandte Texte," in *Deutsche Literatur des Mittelalters. Verfasserlexikon*, vol. 9, 2nd ed. (1993), 192–95.

109. Alfons Auer, *Leidenstheologie im Spätmittelalter*, Kirchengeschichtliche Quellen und Studien, 2 (St. Ottilien, 1952), 72–97; Volker Honemann (with materials by Hardo Hilg), "Sprüche der zwölf Meister zu Paris," in *Deutsche Literatur des Mittelalters. Verfasserlexikon*, vol. 9 (1993), 201–5.

110. Auer, *Leidenstheologie im Spätmittelalter*, 98–135.

111. The question of the intellectual environment, in particular, needs to be examined anew. Thus Auer, for example, still attributes the proverbs wholly to the mystical tradition of the fourteenth century: "Still wholly mystical, these ideas are like petrels that herald new intellectual storms" (*Leidenstheologie im Spätmittelalter*, 129). On the whole, the proverbs represent for him a "first pre-Reformation tendency" (ibid., 124). Auer could only arrive at this interpretation, however, because he glossed over the significant changes that had occurred between the proverbs and Meister Eckhart or Tauler, whom he regards as their models. This came about because, in light of the similar antithetical structure of the proverbs and Eckhart's statements, he assumes that both arose in a similar intellectual environment; in so doing, however, he overlooks the differences in content. While Meister Eckhart denied legality as such, the proverbs merely put inner dispositions in the place of outer works of piety, in order to regard inner disposition as a meritorious work.

112. Quoted in Auer, *Leidenstheologie in Spätmittelalter*, 88.

113. Ibid., 102.

114. Ibid., 100–101; the glosses on individual works of piety were added by the present author.

115. On critiques of the fourteenth-century mania for visionary experience see Otto Langer, *Mystische Erfahrung und spirituelle Theologie*, 212–38.

116. Auer, *Leidenstheologie im Spätmittelalter*. See text above at n. 13.

117. Meister Eckhart, *Reden der Unterweisung* c. 10, 67.

118. Thus Kurt Ruh, for example, asserted that late medieval tracts on the Passion

were increasingly interpreted in a moralizing manner. Ruh, "Zur Theologie des mittelalterlichen Passionstraktats," *Theologische Zeitschrift* 5 (1950): 17–39, 29. In regard
to fifteenth-century reform efforts, Dietrich Schmidtke (*Studien zur dingallegorischen
Erbauungsliteratur des Spätmittelalters. Am Beispiel der Gartenallegorie*, Hermaea 43,
Tübingen, 1982, 257–67) even speaks of a "concentration on the virtues of the individual"
and an increasing emergence of a "moral sensibility," "which was a factor in the development of the Reformation." Berndt Hamm ("Frömmigkeit als Gegenstand theologiege-
schichtlicher Forschung. Methodisch-historische Überlegungen am Beispiel von Spätmittelalter und Reformation," *Zeitschrift für Theologie und Kirche* 74 [1977]: 464–97) goes even
further, asserting that in "no era of church history was . . . dogmatics so deeply imbued
with ethics as in the period between the late-fourteenth and mid-sixteenth century" (477).

119. The quotation comes from the "Karlsruher Rosengarten" (Karlsruhe, Badische
Landesbibliothek, Cod. St. Georgen 98, fol. 57r–139v), fol. 118r.

120. Auer, *Leidenstheologie im Spätmittelalter*, 120.

121. Klaus Schreiner, " 'Diversitas temporum'. Zeiterfahrung und Epochengliederung
im späten Mittelalter," in *Epochenschwelle und Epochenbewußtsein*, ed. Reinhart Herzog
and Reinhart Koselleck, Poetik und Hermeneutik, 12 (Munich, 1987), 381–428, 385.

122. Dieter Harmening, "Katechismusliteratur. Grundlagen religiöser Laienbildung
im Spätmittelalter," in *Wissensorganisierende und wissensvermittelnde Literatur im Mittelalter. Perspektiven ihrer Erforschung*, ed. Norbert Richard Wolf, Wissensliteratur im
Mittelalter, 1 (Wiesbaden, 1987), 91–102, 94.

123. Bayerische Staatsbibliothek, cgm 110; on the manuscript, see Egino Weidenhiller, *Untersuchungen zur deutschsprachigen katechetischen Literatur des späten Mittelalters*, Münchener Texte und Untersuchungen zur deutschen Literatur des Mittelalters, 10
(Munich, 1965), 25ff.

124. Fol. 231v–241r; cf. the enumeration in Weidenhiller, *Untersuchungen*, 26.

125. A good example is "Eine gute peicht" from the Staatsbibliothek München, cgm
866; see Weidenhiller, *Untersuchungen*, 52–83.

126. Weidenhiller, *Untersuchungen*, 58.

127. Ibid., 58–59.

128. On the localization of language and content in the milieu of the German
reception of scholasticism, see Weidenhiller, *Untersuchungen*, 204–12; when it comes to
the system of organization, we should also keep in mind the form of *divisio*, which was
adopted from rhetoric and played an important role in the *ars praedicandi*. It appears (but
this needs further investigation) that numerical analysis became increasingly prevalent
in the late Middle Ages; on this see the references in Herbert Kraume, *Die Gerson-
Übersetzungen Geilers von Kaysersberg. Studien zur deutschsprachigen Gerson-Rezeption*,
Münchener Texte und Untersuchungen zur deutschen Literatur des Mittelalters, 71 (Munich and Zurich, 1980), 198ff.

129. See Kraume, *Die Gerson-Übersetzungen*.

130. Berlin, SBPK, Ms. germ. oct. 31, fol. 167r–182v.

131. Ibid., fol. 167r.

132. Ibid.

133. *Rosetum*, fol. CXXIII. We still lack a reliable edition of the *Rosetum* of Johannes
Mauburnus. Since no printed edition was available to me, I quote from Henri Watrigant,
"La méditation méthodique et Jean Mauburnus," *Revue d'ascétique et de mystique* 4 (1923):
13–29, 20–21.

134. Henri Watrigant, "La méditation méthodique," 21: "Qui semper meditationem suam in Dei conspectu esse volet, huic nulla tam industria conducibilis, quam certa et determinata de variis materiis habere puncta."

135. Berlin, SBPK, Ms. germ. oct. 31, fol. 167v.

136. Quoted in Watrigant, "La méditation méthodique," 21.

137. See, for example, *Rosetum*, fol. CXXIII (quoted in Watrigant, "La méditation méthodique," 21): "Hinc Cassianus suadet, ut aliquod sacrum fixe infigatur menti, quod semper inspiciat et intendat, quotiesque ab illo se videat elongari, doleat, et aciem mentis reflectat ad illud, satagens in cordem permanere."

138. Ibid.: "Alioquin facile cor quibuslibet occurentibus adhaeret, si certis non sit quibusdam punctis affixum."

139. Ibid.: "Hinc docet auctor triplici via, et suadet spiritualia fercula multiplicare, ut sic sint promptuaria plena eructantia ex hoc illud, ne numquam nauseat super aliquo cibo, ex ejusdem continua aut diuturniore replicatione, sed mox cum se in uno devotionis exercitio sentit lassari ad aliud devotionale se covertat, ut si in divinitatis contemplatione jugiter figi non valet jam de Christi vita et coeli gloria aut alia meditanda assumat."

140. Ibid.: "Oportet ergo, ut de certis et devotis materiis quisque provideat sibi, quas ubi habuerit, oportet ut super singulis puncta sibi aggreget et multiplicet, ut sic singulis immorari possit et semper, quae circa singula meditari debeat, noscat. Et hoc Magister Nyder docet in suo Alphabeto amoris, allegans Cancellarium Parisiensem Joannem Gerson, scilicet, qui suasit abundantiam colligere punctorum, per que se semper homo, et in meditatione stabilire et inflammare possit."

141. Ludolph of Saxony, *Vita Jesu Christi* pars I, Proæmium 11, 8: "Nec credas quod omnia quae Christum dixisse vel fecisse meditari possumus scripta sunt, sed ad majorem impressionem ea tbi sic narrabo prout contigerunt, vel contigisse pie credi possunt, secundum quasdam imaginativas repraesentationes, quas animus diversimode percipit."

142. Berlin, SBPK, Ms. germ. oct. 31, fol. 171v.

143. On Jordan of Quedlinburg see Adolar Zumkeller, "Jordan von Quedlinburg (Jordanus de Saxonia)," in *Deutsche Literatur des Mittelalters. Verfasserlexikon*, vol. 4, 2nd ed. (1983), 853–61; J. M. Willmeumier-Schalij, "De LXV artikelen van de Passie van Jordanus van Quedlinburg in middelnederlandse handschriften," *Ons Geestelijk Erf* 53 (1979), 15–35.

144. See the overview in Walter Baier, *Untersuchungen zu den Passionsbetrachtungen in der "Vita Christi" des Ludolph von Sachsen*, vol. 2, Analecta Cartusiana, 44 (Salzburg, 1977), 309–14.

145. See Stephanus Hilpisch, "Chorgebet und Frömmigkeit im Spätmittelalter," in *Heilige Überlieferung. Ausschnitte aus der Geschichte des Mönchtums und des heiligen Kultes, Festgabe zum Silbernen Abtsjubiläum von Ildefons Herwegen*, ed. Odo Casel (Münster, 1938), 263–84, 277–81.

146. Hilpisch, "Chorgebet und Frömmigkeit," 277.

147. The significance of the association between numbers and body parts for mnemonic techniques as well as spiritual contemplation has gone largely unrecognized. Horst Wenzel has shown how important this can be, using the sermons of Berthold of Regensburg as an example. See Wenzel's essay "An fünf Fingern abzulesen. Schriftlichkeit und Mnemotechnik in den Predigten Bertholds von Regensburg," in *Von Aufbruch und Utopie. Perspektiven einer neuen Gesellschaftsgeschichte des Mittelalters. Für und mit Ferdinand*

Seibt aus Anlaß seines 65. Geburtstages, ed. Bea Lundt and Helma Reimöller (Cologne, Weimar, and Vienna, 1992), 235–47.

148. Harmening, "Katechismusliteratur," 99.

149. Ibid.

150. On the history of the schemata of vice and virtue, see Rainer Jehl, "Die Geschichte des Lasterschemas und seiner Funktion. Von der Väterzeit bis zur karolingischen Erneuerung," *Franziskanische Studien* 64 (1982): 261–359; Birgitta Stoll, *De virtute in virtutem. Zur Auslegungs- und Wirkungsgeschichte der Bergpredigt in Kommentaren, Predigten und hagiographischer Literatur von der Merowingerzeit bis um 1200*, Beiträge zur Geschichte der biblischen Exegese, 30 (Tübingen, 1988).

151. Jehl, "Die Geschichte des Lasterschemas," 358.

152. Ibid., 357.

153. Ibid., 358.

154. To be sure, Rupert of Deutz already recognized a connection between the septenary and the day of the week in the twelfth century (cf. Stoll, *De virtute in virtutem*, 148ff.), but he provided no concrete instructions in the sense of a methodical meditation.

155. E. Vansteenberghe, "Quelques écrits de Jean Gerson. Textes inédits et études," *Revue des sciences religieuses* 14 (1934): 375–86.

156. On the text and its later history, see Christel Matheis-Rebaud, " 'Die Predigt mit dem Gebet für die sieben Tage der Woche' von Johannes Geiler von Kaysersberg (1445–1510). Ein Beispiel für die religiöse und spirituelle Unterweisung von Klosterfrauen am Ende des Mittelalters," *Revue Mabillon* N.F. 2 [= 63] (1991): 207–39; on his dependence on Gerson see ibid., 213–14.

157. See Medard Barth, "Die Haltung beim Gebet in elsässischen Dominikanerinnenklöstern des 15. und 16. Jahrhunderts," *Archiv für elsässische Kirchengeschichte* 13 (1938): 141–48, 144–47. The history of this devotional exercise is still obscure. The only textual evidence Barth could cite was the Berlin manuscript, SBPK, Ms. germ. oct. 31, fol. 64r–73v; in the meantime I have found two other versions: a copy of the same edition in Zurich ZB C 162, fol. 143r–147r; and a significantly more detailed version in Strasbourg, BNU, Ms. 2139, fol. 144r–259r. All three manuscripts came from Dominican convents. It might thus be rather hasty to base an assumption about an origin in the milieu of the *devotio moderna* on a single piece of evidence (Heidelberg, Cod. Pal. Germ. 438), as Fritz Oskar Schuppisser does in his essay "Schauen mit den Augen des Herzens. Zur Methodik der spätmittelalterlichen Passionsmeditation, besonders in der Devotio Moderna und bei den Augustinern," in *Die Passion Christi in Literatur und Kunst des Spätmittelalters*, ed. Walter Haug and Burghart Wachinger, Fortuna Vitrea, 12 (Tübingen, 1993), 169–210, 191.

158. Johan Huizinga, *The Waning of the Middle Ages: A Study of the Forms of Life, Thought and Art in France and the Netherlands in the Dawn of the Renaissance* (Garden City, N.Y., 1954), 207, 208.

159. Karl Jaspers, *Vom Ursprung und Ziel der Geschichte* (Munich, 1949), 19–42. English: *The Origin and Goal of History*, trans. Michael Bullock (New Haven, 1953).

160. We may expect important insights, for example in regard to the inception of letters of indulgence, to emerge from the research project (Project N) directed by Volker Honemann on "Texted Broadsheets in the German Empire Before 1500 as an Expression of Pragmatic Literacy" (Medieval Center Münster: Literacy in the Middle Ages).

161. The above-mentioned Project N is studying the connections between the newly

emerging medium, cultural change, and purposive action using the example of the broadsheet.

162. The connections among self-education, control, and writing techniques that reinforced behavioral norms are being studied for the *devotio moderna* in the research project (Project I) "Pragmatic Literacy in the Devotio Moderna" under the direction of Nikolaus Staubach (Medieval Center Münster: Literacy in the Middle Ages); see Staubach's "Pragmatische Schriftlichkeit im Bereich der Devotio moderna," *Frühmittelalterliche Studien* 25 (1991): 418–61.

163. See Ritz, *Die christliche Gebetszählschnur*, 101.

164. "Im Ganzen haltet Euch an Zahlen, / So geht ihr durch des Zweifels Qualen / Zur Ruhe der Gewißheit ein." Wilhelm Dilthey, "Der Mensch und die Zahlen," in *Gesammelte Schriften*, vol. 16, ed. Ulrich Herrmann (Göttingen, 1972), 134–37, 136.

THREE

Perceiving Social Reality in the Early and High Middle Ages

A Contribution to a History of Social Knowledge

Otto Gerhard Oexle

On the Concept of a "History of Social Knowledge"

This essay will examine the relationship between "reality" and "knowledge," between the societies of past epochs and how they were perceived and interpreted.[1] Apart from the rather rare great treatises on the social order (*ordo* or "estate") by church fathers such as Augustine[2] or the very influential Pseudo-Dionysius the Areopagite,[3] and the systematic social teachings of the thirteenth-century theologians,[4] we mainly encounter two forms of perceiving and interpreting social reality in the Middle Ages—social metaphors and interpretive schemes.[5] Metaphors are definitions "by means of images."[6] Thus, authors used the metaphor of the human body and its members,[7] or of the militia, to describe the social order.[8] In comparison to such social metaphors, interpretive schemes are more explicit terminological constructs intended to name, organize, and interpret social phenomena.[9] One of these interpretive schemes is the "trifunctional scheme," that is, the assumption that society consists of three orders or estates (*ordines*): those who pray (*oratores*), those who fight (*bellatores, pugnatores*), and those who work (*laboratores, agricultores*).[10] In the years around 1000 and during the first half of the eleventh century this scheme was discussed with particular intensity.[11] The most impressive testimony of this discussion can probably be found in Bishop Adalbero of Laon's poem,[12] composed around 1025, which is generally known as the "Carmen ad Rodbertum regem."[13]

The medieval view of the world, society, and humanity has been considered static, particularly in regard to estate. An impressive study on the *Categories of Medieval Culture* proposes that the "medieval consciousness is static," and "medieval man" virtually unable "to apprehend the world and society as being in a process of development." Similarly, failing "to comprehend his own inner being in terms of development," the medieval person did not possess individuality in the true sense of the word: "the individual strove to correspond as closely as possible to the type in which he was cast, and to do his duty before God."[14] Certainly, people in the Middle Ages had no access to the categories of individuality and development in the modern sense. After all, these concepts required the influence of modern historicism in order to become points of departure for interpretations of the world, society, and the human being. This very fact ought to encourage us to address questions regarding the typicality and stasis of medieval thought, since the terms "stasis" and "typicality," as mere counterconcepts to the categories of "development" and "individuality" in the modern sense, may not be wholly apt.[15]

We know, to be sure, that actual social conditions in the Middle Ages were by no means static. On the contrary, throughout the centuries of what we think of as the Middle Ages, reality was characterized by a dizzying dynamism and mobility. Because of the contrast to the assumed stasis of perceptions of social reality in social teachings, interpretive schemes, and social metaphors, scholars have frequently drawn the conclusion that these static interpretations were nothing but stereotypes devoid of content, or that they merely sought to further the preservation of the status quo, and thus bore the mark of the ideological. Medieval reflections on the social whole and its individual parts and elements were seen as mere ideology, a mode of thinking that was not always removed from reality, but often also reality-distorting, interest driven, and manipulative,[16] and tantamount to a "theoretical sanctioning of societal forms of domination."[17]

These observations bring us to the two fundamental questions that recur in any examination of medieval interpretive schemes: (1) the question of the relationship of such schemes to reality, and (2) the problem of ideology. These two questions are closely intertwined. The problem of the relationship between reality and its perception in the Middle Ages is directly tied to the question of our modes of perception: how we as human beings living in the modern age decide to name, order, and interpret these medieval interpretations of reality. We must take into account three levels of reflection: the social reality of medieval society, its perception and interpretation by the people of those past centuries, and, finally, our own perceptions and interpretations of that reality and those interpretations.[18]

Let us begin by acknowledging that these questions have no simple idealist, materialist, or positivist answers, and that we cannot clear them up with dichotomous juxtapositions of base and superstructure or reality and ideal.[19] The dichotomy between the real and the ideal, which we so often encounter in the works of historians, is not very helpful[20] when it comes to recognizing what the legal historian K. Kroeschell has abstractly but aptly called the "complicated interrelationship between social structures and their notion of themselves."[21]

Georges Duby has vividly described this "complicated interrelationship" from the perspective of social history, in his observation that human beings do not orient their behavior toward real events and circumstances, but rather toward their image of them, which is never a faithful reflection of those circumstances.[22] Instead, people seek to orient their behavior around patterns of conduct which, in the course of history, they adapt, after a fashion, to material and real circumstances.[23] Duby's remark thus tells us that in order to understand the interrelationship between social structures and their "notion of themselves," we must account for three circumstances: (1) the given social reality, (2) the image people have of it, and (3) the behavior of people that results from this image, which in turn creates and shapes reality.[24]

This continually self-renewing process has been astutely analyzed from the perspective of the social sciences and the sociology of knowledge by Peter L. Berger and Thomas Luckmann, who describe the individual moments of this process as internalization, externalization, and objectivation.[25] Social reality can be described only in the "fundamental relationship of these three dialectical moments" and only when the mutual influence of all three is taken into account, namely, when we understand that society is just as much a human product as an objective reality, but that the human being, too, is "a social product."[26]

Externalization is the ongoing outpouring of human being into the world, both in the physical and the mental activity of men. Objectivation is the attainment by the products of this activity (again both physical and mental) of a reality that confronts its original producers as a facticity external to and other than themselves. Internalization is the reappropriation by men of this same reality, transforming it once again from structures of the objective world into structures of the subjective consciousness. It is through externalization that society is a human product. It is through objectivation that society becomes a reality sui generis. It is through internalization that man is a product of society.[27]

Knowledge is at the center of this "fundamental dialectic of society": "It 'programs' the channels in which externalization produces an objective world. It objectifies this world through language and the cognitive apparatus based on language, that is, it orders it into objects to be apprehended as reality. It is internalized again as objectively valid truth in the course of socialization. Knowledge about society is thus a *realization* in the double sense of the word, in the sense of apprehending the objectivated social reality, and in the sense of ongoingly producing this reality."[28]

The interpretive schemes of social reality should be understood in this way:

on the one hand they are "schemes of experience" which allow us to grasp social reality; on the other, they are "schemes of interpretation" to the extent that what we experience becomes imbued with meaning. This opens up the possibility of action.[29] The relationship of such schemes to reality is thus a dual one here as well. Such schemes contain reality because they attempt to perceive and interpret it. Naturally, it is never possible to understand, let alone represent or reflect reality absolutely. This by no means excludes the possibility of a partial or aspectual grasp of what is "real"; such a partial understanding of "reality" is doubtless always present in some form or other. At the same time, such schemes create and produce reality because, by conveying a sense of reality, they can enable and teach us to take action. Writing on early medieval thinking about estates, H. Fichtenau has rightly emphasized "the great extent to which it was rooted in reality, and helped to shape part of this reality."[30]

In its basic assumptions, this attempt to grasp the interpretive schemes of social reality as elements of social knowledge and to describe them as part of a history of social knowledge coincides with Marc Bloch's insight that all social phenomena are, at bottom, mental phenomena.[31] Proceeding from this insight, we may understand all social history—indeed all history—as the history of mentalities,[32] and conversely, one could claim that all histories of mentalities are, ultimately, "histoire totale."[33] In this broad sense, the following remarks may be understood as a contribution to the history of mentalities. Nevertheless, in what follows we will dispense altogether with the use of this term and the word mentality. There are several reasons for this.

If one is basically convinced that all social phenomena are essentially mental phenomena, then the term "mentality" appears superfluous, as H. Fichtenau has properly observed.[34] The use of the term also appears problematic from another, more pragmatic vantage point as well. For one thing, the term "mentality" is extremely difficult to define precisely in either historical or systematic terms,[35] and—despite more penetrating and thorough attempts at an ultimate definition[36]—it is generally applied quite vaguely and also differently by different authors. It is perhaps for this reason that French social historians—who are generally regarded as the originators of the history of mentalities—began some time ago to distance themselves from the term. "I now recognize that this term is ambiguous, much too vague, and has been employed as a sort of catchall," writes Georges Duby, without questioning the usefulness of the term in an earlier—but now distant—research situation.[37]

A second difficulty is that the history of mentalities is generally no longer understood—as Marc Bloch's concept of the "mental" suggested—as an all-encompassing aspect of a total history, but rather only as defining a certain sector, a delimited area with particular social historical objects, a historical sub-discipline.[38] Such authors even regard the history of mentalities as defined by particular methods or the use of particular historical sources.[39] In the light of such sectoral views of the history of mentalities, we may wonder whether the interpretive schemes of social reality belong to the realm of mentalities at all,[40] whether they have any "relevance for the history of mentalities."[41]

Any use of the term "mentality" poses a third problem as well, one of the history of concepts. The concept of mentality is entangled and apparently inextricably linked with the problem of the modern concept of ideology, which was mentioned above.[42] This may also help to explain the notorious and much lamented vagueness of the concept of mentality. A. I. Gurevich's assertion that "the actual concept of *mentalité* remains fairly imprecise" goes in this direction, and he asks, "Cannot this ambiguity be explained by the fact that the concept of 'mentality' is not always clearly enough separated from the concept of 'ideology'?"[43]

A history of knowledge in the sense indicated above aims at the notions and conceptions of reality—we could also say it seeks to grasp the images of reality, whether of the world[44] or of society, whereby such images may be expressed not only in texts but also in actual pictorial representations,[45] as can be observed particularly in the case of the trifunctional scheme.[46] Viewed in this way, the interpretive schemes approach the realm of what Jacques Le Goff has called "l'imaginaire médiéval."[47] In French scholarship, the concept of a "histoire de l'imaginaire" has even joined the older "histoire des mentalités," although the relationship between the two approaches remains unclear.[48] To be sure, the concept of the imaginary is ambiguous and has already given rise to a good deal of controversy in this context, such that the approach of a "histoire de l'imaginaire" remains an imprecise one, at least for the time being.[49]

In contrast to the concepts of mentality and the imaginary, the concept of (social) knowledge, as defined by Peter Berger and Thomas Luckmann from the perspective of the sociology of knowledge, has the advantage of being relatively simple and straightforward, and thus appears more suitable. To be sure, the insight that concepts "only gradually acquire greater precision through use," and that even the most suitable and "sharpest" conceptual systems are nothing more than "groping attempts . . . to find our way around limited areas of reality" applies in this case as well.[50] If knowledge is defined as the certainty that the phenomena of reality are "real and possess definable qualities," then the advantage of this concept and its utility for historical research lies in the circumstance that "knowledge" so defined encompasses both commonplace everyday knowledge and the "theoretical" knowledge of theology, philosophy, or any branch of scholarship.[51] Knowledge in this sense is the totality of the cognitive and normative knowledge of particular epochs, societies, groups, and individuals. It is generally pretheoretical but also encompasses, in the form of theories, those particular edifices of knowledge that contain "the body of 'official' interpretations" belonging to an era or society.[52]

Modern Interpretations of Medieval Interpretive Schemes

The first section sought to explain how the interpretive schemes of the early and high Middle Ages will be discussed in what follows. This preliminary explanation was necessary because the scholarship on the interpretive schemes of the Middle Ages is frequently characterized by an uncertainty about how to judge the relationship of such schemes to reality, both in general and in particular. This will be illustrated using the example of the discussion of the trifunctional scheme in the late tenth and early eleventh centuries.

Most scholars take the view that this interpretive scheme had no connection to reality or that it was at any rate highly debatable. Trifunctionalism is a social theory, which must "not be confused with reality." It is "not a representation of reality, but rather a theoretical concept,"[53] an "ideal type," which corresponded "in no way to the social structure of that time,"[54] an "abstract scheme" whose aim was not to describe "a true assignment of social functions."[55] The scheme was virtually "unreal" and "for that reason [!] ideological,"[56] an ideology whose purpose was to "sacralize" social structures, thus rendering them immutable:[57] "It is, first of all, a weapon, an ideological weapon."[58] Trifunctionalism should not be interpreted as a "reflex . . . of societal differentiation," nor as a "reflection of concrete social conditions." Rather, the scheme is "antiquated," indeed "archaic," and thus essentially ruled by tradition; furthermore, it "conceals" "social tensions" and was, ultimately, a mere "instrument for consolidating monarchichal rule."[59]

We could cite a number of other, similar, quotations, above all from Georges Duby's important 1978 monograph on functional tripartition.[60] They offer a plethora of those modern patterns of perception about which we spoke more generally in the first section: the dichotomous distinction between the ideal and reality; the distrust of ideology, the characterization of such schemes of interpretation as commonplaces or topoi in the banal sense of the word, that is, traditional but empty phrases passed on merely for the sake of convention. By broadening the materials examined, this second section will illustrate how problematic such patterns of perception can be.

It is helpful to begin by realizing that the interpretive schemes of the early and high Middle Ages represent modes of grasping and interpreting reality that were not restricted to the Middle Ages. This becomes immediately apparent if we incorporate the ancient version of functional tripartition into our considerations. Functional tripartition is the basis of the social order in Plato's state in which, to be sure, all men are brothers, but God, by admixing gold, silver, or iron at birth, has made some of them rulers, some of them auxiliaries, and some of them peasants, artisans, and laborers. The metaphor of the different metals underlines the hierarchy of these three classes or estates and their economic, guardian, and advisory functions,[61] in which the economic class must produce the subsistence for the two others. Plato combines an explanation of the (later so named) four cardinal virtues of wisdom, courage, discipline, and justice with this transcendently and metaphysically ordained social order. Wisdom and courage were attributed to the first two estates as a norm. Discipline as self-control and moderation of the appetites should be qualities of all estates in the polis, because they created unity; self-discipline is insight into the nature of the hierarchical social order and the differences and different worth of the estates. But precisely for that reason, self-discipline was the social norm assigned to and appropriate for the third, laboring estate.[62] Justice, finally, is realized when each member of each estate does "one job, the job he was most naturally suited for." Thus, the all-encompassing norm which applied to "each individual—child or woman, slave, free man or artisan, ruler or subject—[was] to get on with his own job and not interfere with other people."[63]

Many questions regarding the appearance of functional tripartition in Plato's *Republic*—the scheme is, incidentally, of central importance for the entire text[64]—cannot be addressed further here.[65] As far as we know, Plato's text also had no direct influence on early medieval discussions of this topic. The *Republic* is cited here because it permits insights into the structure of thinking about estate more generally, such as formed the foundation of medieval social metaphors and interpretive schemes. This basic structure of thinking about estate is thus by no means specifically, nor "genuinely," medieval.

Reflection about estates, about the proper order of society, is reflection about order more generally, about the world as a whole, about how the many and varied elements of existence are unified and shaped into a totality or "cosmos." Reflection on estates is thus rooted in, and part of, metaphysics. It proceeds from the assumption that the world is a whole fortunately ordered by God, whose individual parts, in their reciprocal relations, differ by degrees, and are thus unequal and yet—or precisely because of this—combine to form a harmonious unity. The principle of the world (and of the social order contained within it) is thus that of harmony through inequality. In the words of Augustine, "the orderly arrangement of creatures [*ordo creaturarum*] extends all the way from the highest to the lowest according to certain just gradations."[66] This produces the definition of *ordo* in the sense of both "order" and "estate," or, in Augustine's famous formulation, "Ordo est parium dispariumque rerum sua cuique loca tribuens dispositio," that is, "Order is the classification of things equal and unequal, that assigns to each its proper position." The "peace of all things is a tranquillity of order" (*pax omnium rerum tranquillitas ordinis*). Peace is the "ordered agreement" (*concordia*) of the parts.[67] This applies to the world as well as to human coexistence. The principle of "harmony through inequality" also applies to the social order. And this order of the world contains at the same time the preconditions for a true knowledge of this order. For that reason we derive the maxims of right conduct from knowledge—the knowledge of order requires us to bind our actions to it and in this way limits human beings to the order of their own lives and estates. We may demonstrate the influence of this attitude in individual epochs down to the details of concrete ways of life.[68]

The same basic ideas can be found in other authors of antiquity. They form the foundation of the many uses of the concept of *ordo* in Roman thought,[69] and we also encounter them in early Christianity, which both formulated a rejection of all notions of estate and at the same time took up antique reflection on estate, as Paul's epistles demonstrate.[70] Building on the ideas on estate of both antiquity and early Christianity, the church fathers further developed the metaphysics of *ordo* and *ordines*, thus creating the basis for medieval reflection on *ordo*. Let us return for a moment to the writings of the author known as Pseudo-Dionysius the Areopagite (ca. 500), and above all to Augustine and his early work *De ordine* (386).[71] Augustine's *De ordine* was the first systematic text on this subject, and no work of similar length appeared in the centuries that followed. The basic ideas on *ordo* and *ordines* which Augustine set out became a point of departure for all later reflections on estate; they retained their binding quality and are thus also representative for the subsequent centuries, as scholars have shown.[72] This topic would take us too far afield, but we should note that the metaphysical justification of the social order is a constitutive trait of corporative societies. The fact that the key concept of estate (*ordo*) is a metaphysical one may be considered a central characteristic of such societies. This moment is ignored in Max Weber's oft-cited definition of *Stand* (estate) and the *ständische Lage* (estate or corporative situation). We can say, however, that the elements of the corporative (*Ständische*) emphasized in Weber's definition ("privileged social esteem," "honor"), which are justified by a specific way of life, formal education, or the prestige of descent or profession,[73] only become understandable when viewed against the background of their metaphysical justification. The definition of estate (*ordo, ordre*) as a metaphysical concept may also be found in early modern treatises on estate, for example in the work of the jurist Charles Loyseau.[74]

The basic principles of estate thinking sketched here in reference to Plato and Augustine, which have their roots in metaphysics and thus also imply an epistemology and an ethics of the system of estates, are naturally no new discovery. What interests us here, however, is how to use this information to acquire criteria for an appropriate assessment of the interpretive schemes of social reality, which scholars have previously neglected. These schemes may be summarized in three points:

1. In the modern age, reflection on society no longer has a metaphysical character.[75] It thus can no longer claim to describe reality "in itself" or as it "actually" or "essentially" is. For that reason, it also can no longer provide undisputed and universally valid norms of behavior. Modern statements about society are purely descriptive. This very descriptive quality was peripheral to medieval interpretive schemes, even if it was by no means absent from them. As Otto Brunner puts it, "The medieval literature on estate involves the ethics of individual groups, whereby the type of group is of no consequence. . . . It presents us with the ethos of the individual 'status.'" Thus this reflection does not simply mirror "the inner structure of this world" in the sense of a description. This does not mean that it was "without any relationship to medieval reality," however.[76] We could say that medieval reflections on estate were at once normative and based in reality, and that it is herein that they contradict the basic assumptions of modern thought. For this reason, though, these medieval modes of understanding social reality cannot be grasped using the modern opposition between "ideal" and "reality."[77] To put it another way, the fact that the interpretive schemes "must not be confused with social reality," that they are "not a reflection of reality" nor a "mirror-image of concrete social conditions"[78] is too self-evident to dispute. That they therefore "in no way" corresponded to the social circumstances of the time[79] is surely a misplaced claim, however, since it does not so much focus on the medieval interpretive schemes as orient itself unreflectively toward modern attitudes. The alternative, that interpretive schemes either have a representational or reflective character or no connection whatsoever to reality and are thus unreal, seems to be one of the anachronisms or projections of modern thinking against which Lucien Febvre warned us, because of their disadvantageous effects on historical knowledge.[80] Our task here is thus to move beyond the unpromising alternatives of the representation (reflection) of social reality and unreality (ideal) and ask how interpretive schemes partially grasped individual aspects and elements of reality. We must assume such a partial and aspectual relationship to reality, if only because the elaboration of such schemes would have made no sense otherwise. We thus need to inquire into the elements of reality for each scheme and each phase in its history. In order to avoid misunderstandings, let us recall that no scheme implies a total connection to reality.[81] There were, naturally, always numerous elements of reality which a given era's interpretive schemes did not encompass. Nevertheless each scheme could, in its own way, and

perhaps with different emphases in the various phases of its history, render a piece of social reality comprehensible and express a behavioral maxim within these elements of experience and interpretation of the world and society.

2. Whether in Plato, Augustine, or Adalbero of Laon, all interpretive schemes are rooted in the same metaphysical presuppositions and formulate the same practical instructions and behavioral norms. Interpretive schemes thus also convey the impression of a continual return of the same. Under the circumstances, it might appear logical to define medieval interpretative schemes as topoi in the banal sense of the word, that is, as archaic, traditional, empty, hackneyed phrases. This might appear logical, but it would not be justified. Instead, it should be our aim in studying medieval interpretive schemes to distinguish between the metaphysical and ethical statements underlying all schemes and what was intended when a particular scheme was used in a particular political situation and in the light of particular social circumstances. To put it another way, scholars must learn to distinguish between the characteristics of the genre and those of a specific instance. This has rarely been the case up until now.[82] In his book on functional tripartition, Georges Duby defines the purpose of this interpretive scheme as expressing the inequality of the three estates while at the same time calling upon them to cooperate with and support each other. Duby regards this "ideology of unity" as typical of the trifunctional scheme.[83] This invocation of harmony in inequality was, however, as we saw above, the quintessence of all estate thinking from Plato until well into the early modern period. For that reason it can be found in the evidence and uses of functional tripartition, but it cannot therefore be considered typical of and specific to this particular scheme.

3. The basic assumptions of modern social thought are in every respect inimical to the basic idea of antique, medieval, and to some extent early modern corporative thinking: the notion of "harmony through inequality."[84] Those who, like Plato, Augustine, or Adalbero of Laon, promoted harmony through inequality as a social norm already fulfilled the prerequisites of ideological thinking in the modern sense: the concept of harmony through inequality must necessarily appear as a "tendency to harmonize social opposites."[85] But this perception, too, rests on an anachronism, in Febvre's sense.[86] We could doubtless direct the accusation of ideology to the numerous proponents of corporative thinking in the modern period.[87] This accusation is, however, precisely not applicable to antique and medieval reflections on estate.[88] I will return to this issue in the final section of this essay. Just because we have questioned the usefulness of the concept of ideology in this context certainly does not mean that the "ideological"— that is, the attachment of thinking to interests and a justification of existing social conditions with an eye to concealment—was absent in the Middle Ages, or that

there was no sociopolitical functionalization of ideas in that period.[89] What we need to test, rather, is the correctness of the assumption that this moment of the ideological was always present and always significant, and can thus serve as a basis for a defining characterization of interpretive schemes as ideologies.

Potential Relationships Between Interpretive Schemes and Reality

After the above remarks on the question of modern perceptions of medieval interpretive schemes and how to characterize them, the sections that follow will address the relationship between interpretive schemes and reality in individual instances. Using the example of functional tripartition, I showed how differently scholars have assessed the ability of these schemes to grasp reality. It is no less remarkable, however, that no one has as yet even begun to undertake a comparative analysis of various schemes from this vantage point. We are left with the strange finding that although most scholars categorically deny that the trifunctional scheme had any connection to reality, they have not even asked whether this was the case for other schemes, whose relationship to reality is considered self-evident.

Thus, for example, the division of society according to the two *ordines* of clergy and laity is treated as a reality—and indeed it appears to be so in the texts which medievalists study. But medievalists know that the clergy and laity did not always exist as separate *ordines*, but rather that they only emerged at a particular time in history. And even if we take into consideration the early appearance of this distinction and of the clerical estate, which possessed extraordinary significance for the creation of all later estates,[90] the fluidity of the lines between the clerical and lay elements of early and high medieval society[91] remains surprising, as does the enormous intellectual and spiritual effort required to stabilize this division in social, ecclesiastical, and political terms and to shape sociopolitical reality accordingly,[92] although, or precisely because, the two realms were continually intermingling in both thought and reality.[93] Thus we may be permitted to ask how real the distinction between clergy and laity in individual centuries actually was, and whether the clergy and the laity as estates always existed in the same way, as the terminology would appear to suggest. The distinction between *clericus* and *monachus* was also not an objective reality in the sense of being valid once and for all. Rather, from late antiquity onward there were repeated and heated controversies about the lines between these *ordines* and the criteria that should be used to define them. This was already a problem for the early church,[94] and it would be posed periodically, and variously resolved, in later epochs as well.[95] Comparable conflicts arose over the definitions of *monachus* and *ca-*

nonicus in the era of Charlemagne,[96] or in the efforts to define and delimit the estate of the regular canons in the eleventh and twelfth centuries.[97] And then there was the problem, which arose in the twelfth century, of defining the appropriate norms and way of life for members of the newly founded military-religious orders, who combined the lifestyle of monks with that of knights and thus aroused all manner of suspicion and hostility.[98] At any rate, we will discover that the assessment that reality was far more complex than the scheme could express, which is repeatedly emphasized in regard to functional tripartition, also applies to the schemes associated with the terms *clericus, laicus, monachus, canonicus* and the like.[99] Formulating this fact in the form of a principle, we can take up where Marc Bloch's above-mentioned insight—that all social phenomena are of a mental or psychic nature—left off.[100] What Bloch expressed using the example of the distinction between "freedom" and "bondage" in regard to the concept of "class" doubtless applies to all types of classification of classes, strata, estates, and the like. They are "collective notions," mental classifications of reality: "Given that human institutions are realities of a psychological nature, a class never exists outside of the idea which we have of it. To write the history of serfdom is, above all, to retrace, in the complex and changing curve of its development, the history of a collective notion—that of the loss of freedom."[101] And "it seems to me that many historians have made the mistake of attributing a sort of independent existence to classes. But what is a social classification but the idea—at once mutable and terribly difficult to translate into language—that men in society conceive about their own hierarchy?"[102] This view of the relationship between reality and knowledge thus clearly applies both to the apprehension of social structures in history and to the historian's ways of knowing.

I have two intentions in sketching the following comparison of interpretive schemes from the perspective of their relationship to reality: on the one hand to elucidate this question in a more complex manner than has often been the case up until now, and on the other, to suggest a typology of various forms of relationships to reality. If we observe how interpretive schemes are used to experience, interpret, and produce social reality,[103] we encounter several different versions. The distinction between clergy and laity shows particularly clearly the extent to which schemes are capable of producing reality. How schemes can follow reality because it requires interpretation may be observed using the example of the *tria genera hominum* or *tres ordines ecclesiae*.

1. As we know, the religions of antiquity had no clergy. The Greeks and Romans represent "a completely lay world" (J. Burckhardt); [104] the distinction between clergy and laity is thus specifically Christian. Christianity, however, also began without a clergy, as we know from the New Testament, where the word "clergy" is used as a term referring to all of the baptized.[105] In the New Testament,

the Greek interpretation of the "layman," *idiótes* (in the sense of a private individual, a simple citizen without public office or particular professional knowledge, one who is ignorant in comparison to an expert or knowledgeable person), as well as the Latin word *idiota* (ignorant or uneducated person), does not refer to distinctions within the congregation, but rather—with a positive flavor—to preachers of the gospel, including the Apostles, to the extent that they confronted the scribes as *homines sine litteris et idiotae* (Acts 4:13).[106] Elsewhere, for example in Paul's epistles, many duties and services in the congregation are mentioned, including administrative duties, but the New Testament makes no distinction between those who hold office and those who do not—the majority, in other words.[107] This distinction appears only at the end of the first century, in the First Epistle of Clement, which repeatedly emphasizes the duty of each member of the congregation within his estate,[108] and refers to all those not entrusted with an office as "laymen," contrasting them, in this negative exclusion, with the collectivity of officeholders.[109] This distinction was already established in the third-century writings of Tertullian, Cyprian, and Origen.[110] A century later Eusebius defined two different "ways of life" within the church: one of them was consecrated to the service of God and thus kept aloof from the common worldly modes of behavior and activities—marriage, trade, and property—while the other was involved in all of these and thus occupied a subordinate rank within the church.[111] Gratian followed in this tradition in the twelfth century with his famous definition of the two "estates" (*genera*) in the church: "There are two types of Christians. The ones are destined for the service of God, for contemplation, and prayer, and above all must abandon the din of the world, and these are the clerics and monks, who have undergone a *conversio*. . . . The others are laymen. . . . They may possess worldly property . . . may marry women, cultivate land, sit in judgment, pursue lawsuits, place offerings on the altar, tithe, and thus achieve salvation if they do good and avoid sin."[112]

As we know, in the course of the fourth century the clergy as an estate was accorded political, legal, and economic privileges, thereby acquiring, in its separate and special position, an extraordinary consistency, which was additionally intensified from that time forward by the development of its own corporate ethic influenced by the demand for celibacy.[113] The clergy thereby became "the model for all privileged estates" in Europe,[114] a process of far-reaching significance and complex consequences. We must ask what motive forces initiated this development, which not only produced something new, but also in many respects contradicted the original elements of the Christian gospel. A. von Harnack has pointed out that this process began with a purely spiritual and religious justification for the special status of the clergy. Thus, however many elements may have played a role, the entire development was actually set in motion by a few brief maxims.[115] One of these was the Deutero-Pauline proposition that "no soldier of the Lord becomes involved in secular pursuits" ("Nemo militans Deo implicat se negotiis saecularibus," 2 Tim. 2:4) and the other the Pauline demand that those who serve in the *militia Christi* have a claim on the financial support of others (1 Cor. 9:7; 2 Cor. 11:8). As Harnack writes, obedience to these maxims "permeated the nature of the entire society and changed its signature."[116] Both maxims, incidentally, had a shared origin in the New Testament view of Christian life as that of a *militia*. In both cases the analogy to the profane *militia* was transformed into a metaphor and offered as its proof. The two maxims supplement each other and are at the same time polar opposites; and for that very reason, as Harnack once again rightly notes, they encompass "an entire corporative order within themselves."[117]

We could write a history of the Christian clergy and its separation from the laity that proceeds from Harnack's suggestion—a history of modes of thinking about and apprehending reality, which in turn produce reality. As already indicated, this "mental" aspect was, certainly, not the sole factor in the emergence of a clergy and of the social dichotomy between clergy and laity, but it was an important one. A look at the contribution of Augustine illuminates the significance of this aspect of the emergence of the clerical estate, its development, and the changes it underwent over the many centuries of its history. In his *De opere monachorum* (ca. 400), Augustine both justified and explained monks' duty to perform manual labor. Indeed, he wrote, work was what characterized a true monk. Clerics, in contrast, were exempted from the duty to perform physical labor and more generally from the duty to earn their own living.[118] Nobody is likely to dispute the fact that Augustine's justification of his position, and the biblical evidence he offers for the form taken by the clergy and monasticism were no less significant than the real historical privileges of the fourth century or the actual fifth-century conflicts over the position of monks in the church and their relationship with the clergy and the bishops.[119]

2. Monasticism, which arose over the course of the fourth century and soon spread throughout the West,[120] at first had no place in the distinction between clergy and laity. Monasticism was, after all, originally and for quite some time a movement of laymen. Because of their special way of life, in groups who lived apart from the rest of society and followed the norm of the *Vita communis*, monks were clearly distinct from other laymen. The older division of society into two estates or "ways of life" had thus in a sense become obsolete. The new situation called for a new interpretation, and once again it was Augustine who rose to the occasion.[121] Through the allegorical interpretation of biblical texts he determined that there were three estates, *tria genera hominum*, thereby creating a new interpretive scheme. These three estates were the holders of ecclesiastical

office, the monks, and the laity. Augustine knew full well that he had discovered something new, and for that reason he declared that he did not wish to impose his interpretation on anyone. At the same time, he believed that the division of human beings into these three *genera* was something natural and as such not really subject to dispute.[122] In fact, Augustine's idea was everywhere rapidly disseminated and established. For Pope Gregory the Great, who repeatedly referred to it in his own writings, these *tria genera homines* or, as he called them, *tres ordines ecclesiae*, were already absolutely self-evident. And so they remained in the centuries that followed, in which we find numerous discussions of this scheme, albeit without any new elements.[123]

Now that I have sketched the forms of relationship between interpretive schemes and reality, particularly during the period of the transition from antiquity to the Middle Ages, the following sections will map out other forms such as we find in the early and high Middle Ages: interpretive schemes could focus processes of social reality and get to the heart of the matter ("The Trifunctional Scheme and Early Eleventh-Century Realities"); the concepts of an old scheme could be used to grasp a new reality ("New Estates in the Twelfth Century and Their Interpretation"); and interpretive schemes could also be pushed aside to make room for a new reality ("Challenges to Interpretations of Reality in the High Middle Ages").

The Trifunctional Scheme and Early Eleventh-Century Realities

The creation of estates in the West by no means ended with the separation between clergy and laity and the emergence of monasticism. At the beginning of the eleventh century, interpretive schemes reveal a new phase in the creation of estates. With this assertion we return once again to the trifunctional scheme. Hints of this scheme already reappear in the texts of the ninth century, without— so far as we can tell—any inspiration from rediscovered antique texts.[124] Explicit discussions of the scheme began to appear in the final years of the tenth[125] and the early years of the eleventh century both in England and on the Continent; at this time the scheme was a pivotal point in reflections on estate. Since the scheme had no biblical background,[126] and a reception of the antique literature is unlikely here, attention has focused on the historical moment of its appearance around the year 1000 and the decades that followed, on the sociopolitical conditions surrounding this "breakthrough" of functional tripartition in western thinking about estate.[127]

Like all interpretive schemes, functional tripartition contains the ethical injunction to cooperation, since *oratores*, *bellatores*, and *laboratores* all depended on the specific services offered by the other *ordines*. Here too, though, the meaning of the scheme transcended its ethical message. Rather, all statements on this subject from the period around 1000 onward were also concerned with understanding, interpreting, and evaluating particular real processes and at the same with expressing opinions on specific events and issues of the day. The appearance of the trifunctional scheme around the year 1000 and the intensive discussion of it, above all in texts of the first half of the eleventh century, provides an excellent case study—from the perspective of a history of knowledge—of the relationship between interpretive schemes and the political, social, economic, intellectual, spiritual, and religious processes of "reality." The extensive discussion of this scheme and its (albeit generally disputed) connection to reality, particularly in the past twenty years, thus proves a useful one.[128] This debate also indicates that discussions of the scheme involve fundamental questions of knowledge and of the assessment of interpretive schemes more generally.

In the case of functional tripartition, the question of the relationship between reality and knowledge may be discussed from three perspectives: First, in the context of sociopolitical processes typical of the history of England and France or the former western Frankish kingdom—external threats and internal security, which raised the issue of how to protect those who could not, or were not permitted to, bear arms, and were thus defenseless. This question was treated within the framework of reflections on estate, on *ordo* and *ordines* (but not only there), and in the form of reflections on the separation and blending of estates such as we already find in Plato.[129] The scheme as it appeared in this context was also combined with reflections on *militia* based in particular on the Pauline epistles.[130] Reflections on the new scheme thus had strong connections to tradition. Second, the scheme encompassed newly emerging estates at the same time—the knightly and peasant estates, which were reflected upon for the first time in relation to each other. The creation of both estates stretched back to the Carolingian period, to the eighth and ninth centuries. Nevertheless, they apparently became particularly visible and recognizable for contemporaries at the beginning of the eleventh century. Third, for that reason we also find assessments of the two new estates of knights and peasants, and statements on the significance of their activities for the social whole, in discussions of functional tripartition at that period. These three aspects will be briefly sketched here.[131]

1. The (re)appearance of functional tripartition was preceded by that functional bipartition of society which Pope Gelasius I mentioned for the first time around 500 in his description of the cooperation between episcopal (papal) and royal (imperial) authority in the functional classification of two estates (*ordines*), offices (*officia*), functions (*actiones*), and dignities (*dignitates*).[132] The division of society, frequent in the Carolingian period, into *orantes* and *bellantes*, *in-*

tercessores and *defensores, ordo ecclesiasticus* and *ordo militaris, militia Christi* and *militia saecularis* rested on this functional bipartition. K. Leyser has underscored the estate-creating effect of bearing arms and the constitution of this *militia saecularis* in the Carolingian period.[133] The third function, manual labor, however, was mentioned as early as the ninth century, and *agricultores* named alongside the *sacerdotes* and *milites*, both on the Continent and in the Anglo-Saxon lands.[134]

In contrast, we have as yet no evidence of a clear and explicit discussion of functional tripartition in the tenth century.[135] Discussion of the social order from the perspective of functional tripartition began only in the final years of the tenth century,[136] at first in England, in texts by the monk and abbot Ælfric and his close associate Archbishop Wulfstan (II) of York.[137] After having treated the question "Qui sunt oratores, laboratores, bellatores?" in his *Lives of the Saints* (ca. 995),[138] Ælfric was asked around 1003–5 by his archbishop, Wulfstan, for his opinion on various pastoral issues and questions of canon law. One of the questions Wulfstan posed was whether monks and clerics should be allowed to bear arms, and it had a highly topical and specific background—the Danish invasions of the Anglo-Saxon kingdom at the time of King Ethelred (978–1016).[139] This dangerous situation which, as we know, led to the conquest of the Anglo-Saxon kingdom, called for the clarification of two questions: first, how to protect and defend those who could not or were not allowed to bear arms, and second, who should be permitted to use weapons, and under what circumstances the bearing of arms was religiously justified. Ælfric answered the archbishop's questions in detail with his remarks on functional tripartition. "As is well known," he writes, there are three *ordines* within the church: *laboratores, bellatores*, and *oratores*. He then proceeds to elucidate this tripartition from the perspective of the specific duties and functions of each estate.

The estate of *laboratores* provides us with the means of subsistence, and the estate of the *bellatores* must defend our land (*patriam nostram*) from the incursion of enemies, and the estate of *oratores*, that is, the clerics, monks, and bishops, who are elected to fight with the weapons of the spirit (*ad spiritualem militiam*), must pray for all and proclaim the true faith and provide the faithful with the holy sacraments. And everyone who is ordained for this *militia*, even if he previously bore worldly arms, must lay down those arms at the moment of ordination and take up the weapons of the spirit: the armor of justice and the shield of faith and the helmet of salvation and the sword of the spirit, which is God's word, and he must fight manfully the spirits of evil. Whoever belongs to this *militia* and nonetheless bears worldly arms against earthly foes—is he not an apostate, who has deserted the divine for the worldly militia? For that reason one may not fight in both militias at the same time, because the hand that sheds human blood is not fit to offer the Lord's chalice.[140]

Ælfric answered both of the questions involved in the problem of canon law within the framework of a distinction between the *ordines* and their functions. The use of weapons by *oratores*, that is, monks, clerics, and bishops, involved a blending of estates and was thus unlawful. The opinion was, of course, determined by tradition; it corresponds to the tradition of corporative thinking as we already find it in Plato.[141] Ælfric also underscores his viewpoint by referring to the equally traditional, Pauline, distinction between the two *militiae*: the *militia spiritualis* (*militia Dei*) and *arma spiritualia*, and the *militia saecularis* and *arma saecularia*. For this reason he also extensively cites Ephesians 6:10ff.[142] Ælfric's main point, as his earlier discussion of functional tripartition already demonstrated, was that monk, cleric, and bishop "cannot belong to both militias at the same time."[143]

We should add that in the twelfth century—in deliberate contrast to Ælfric's position—Bernard of Clairvaux justified the new way of life of the so-called knight's orders as a new type of militia (*novum militiae genus*) by making the daring claim, which was diametrically opposed to the opinion of the Apostle, that the very same people were engaged here in a dual struggle (*gemino pariter conflictu*) simultaneously using two kinds of weapons (*utrisque armis*): "against both 'flesh and blood' and 'the spiritual hosts of wickedness in the realm of the invisible'" (cf. Eph. 6:12). This new *genus militiae* was indeed something previously unheard-of and unseen (*saeculis inexpertum*), as Bernard aptly noted.[144] Ælfric took quite a different view: for him, it was precisely—and only—the sharp distinction between the two *militiae* that provided the religious justification for the use of arms by the *bellatores* who made up the *militia saecularis*. For, just as the *oratores* prayed "for all," the *bellatores* fought for all three estates together: they fought against "our enemies," defended "our cities" (*ure burga*) and "our land" (*urne eard*, *patriam nostram*).[145] Or, as Ælfric puts it in a reformulation of Romans 13:4 on the *bellator*, whom he also refers to as *miles* and *cniht*: "Non sine causa portat miles gladium."[146] In another version of this idea Ælfric later wrote in his treatise *On the Old and New Testament* (1007–8) that the royal throne stands "upon these three [columns or] pillars: *laboratores, bellatores, oratores.*" This applied especially in perilous times, when it was particularly important to observe the strict distinctions between functions in order to ward off danger.[147]

Until now, the scholarly controversies surrounding this interpretive scheme have paid too little attention to the early Anglo-Saxon evidence on functional tripartition. This is unfortunate, since these Anglo-Saxon texts address the relationship to reality in a manner that is as clear as it is specific. If we take this into account, the similarity to the political and social situation that we also encounter in the earliest continental documents on functional tripartition is obvious. The situation was one of disorder, which led in the nascent France of the period around 1000 to the emergence and rapid spread of the so-called Peace of God movement.[148] The goals of the two famous and much discussed texts on functional tripartition—Adalbero of Laon's "Carmen" (ca. 1025) and the sermon of Bishop Gerard (I) of Cambrai, probably composed in 1036, which relates the history of the episcopate of that city—intersect at many points.[149]

Gerard of Cambrai is regarded in the literature as an opponent of the Peace of God movement.[150] On closer inspection, however, this view appears problematic. Gerard opposed not the Peace of God movement as a whole, but rather the procedure, which was propagated and enforced by certain of his brother bishops, of setting up armed episcopal militias to enforce peace agreements and combat those who broke them.[151]

We thus encounter the same context for the discussion of functional tripartition here as in the works of Ælfric and Wulfstan, and for that reason also the same basic assumptions and norms that were at the heart of those English discussions of the scheme: the strict distinction between and separation of the three *ordines* and their functions, combined with the theme of the distinction between the two *militiae*.

It was in this spirit that Adalbero of Laon prefaced his remarks *de ordine* with the famous satirical poem on the Cluniacs.[152] He accuses them of "meddling in the activities and circumstances of other estates and deviating from that which was appropriate to the clergy,"[153] or, as Adalbero himself puts it, the Cluniacs undertook a *transformatio ordinis*. Adalbero caricatures this transformation in the figure of a monk (*monachus*) turned knight (*miles*) on horseback and wearing full armor who introduces himself as a member of the new *bellicus ordo monachorum*, a new militia, in which he now fights (*militat*) under the command of the *princeps militiae*, "King" Odilo of Cluny.[154] What makes this satire so effective and so scathing is that, by invoking the new militia, the *bellicus ordo monachorum*, Adalbero deliberately plays on monks' traditional understanding of themselves as a *militia spiritualis*, and on the corresponding autobiographical accounts of the Cluniacs as well as other orders.[155] How realistic was this satire, and what actual occasion did Adalbero have to portray the Cluniacs as "knights" or a "warrior estate"? Following C. Erdmann, we may point to the influence that the Cluniacs indeed exercised on the nascent lay knighthood, their contributions to "reshaping the lay world," to "the development that led to the orders of knights," and to the "run-up to the age of the Crusades," and their "role in the rise of a new ethic of war."[156] And we will agree with Erdmann's remark that "seen in this light . . . Adalbero took a proper view of things."[157] Other possible reasons for such a critique of Cluny, which relate to the accusation of an unwarranted blending of estates and functions, would take us too far afield here.[158]

Similar criticisms could have been levied at the same period against the militias set up by bishops, the most famous of which was perhaps that founded by Archbishop Aimo of Bourges around 1038, in which hundreds of clerics, together with many others, fought and ultimately met their deaths.[159] In the first half of the eleventh century, these *militiae*, too, represented a novel[160] alteration of the *ordo*, one impermissible according to the ecclesiastical and canon law tradition. The canon law tradition, which had developed following the Deutero-Pauline dictum in 2 Timothy 2:4 ("Nemo militans Deo implicat se negotiis saecularibus"), forbade the clergy to carry weapons.[161] In 1023, the bishops of Soissons and Beauvais called upon their brother Bishop Gerard of Cambrai to form such an "episcopal task force for the maintenance of peace."[162] Gerard, to be sure, considered this a "dangerous enterprise" which would overthrow the "order of the church" (*sanctae ecclesiae status*) if—as the bishop remarked in the spirit of the Gelasian idea of the dual nature of Christ[163]—the roles assigned to the "two persons" or "functions," *regali videlicet ac sacerdotali*, were to be exercised by one and the same person.[164] This explanation inspired his fellow bishops to the timeless maxim that "he who does not agree with those who desire peace is no friend of peace."[165] In the 1030s, Gerard promoted the same political and intellectual objectives in the face of the peace movement led by his fellow bishops, now using functional tripartition as his justification and arguing that "the human race was from the very beginning" divided into three estates—*oratores*, *pugnatores*, and *agricultores*.[166]

It is worth noting here that the militia, as both a fact and a concept, represents one of the central phenomena of the eleventh century, a sort of core around which numerous decisive processes of intellectual, political, ecclesiastical, and social life revolved, as C. Erdmann demonstrates in his still unsurpassed 1935 study of the emergence of the idea of the crusade.[167] From the mid-eleventh century on, beginning with Leo IX, who raised and led a militia against the Normans in 1053, the reform papacy followed the example of the episcopal militias.[168] Gregory VII was even referred to as "the most warlike pope who ever sat on the throne of St. Peter." As archdeacon of the Roman church he had already conceived and realized the idea of a true *Militia Sancti Petri*,[169] and at the beginning of his pontificate he had even propagated the plan that he, as *dux ac pontifex*, should hurry to the aid of the Byzantine East at the head of an armed contingent of Christians, marching on to the Holy Sepulchre in Jerusalem.[170] In so doing, Gregory VII popularized the idea of the crusade, just as the *Militia Sancti Petri*, which was largely his creation, promoted the emergence of the idea and reality of knighthood.[171] All this is characteristic of an epoch shaped by the problems of the intermingling and separation of the spiritual and the secular, the sacred and the profane, the clergy and the laity, and by mighty struggles over *ordo*—the proper order of society and the world (G. Tellenbach).[172]

We might say that these great conflicts and debates on fundamental questions at the beginning of the eleventh century were already hinted at in the discussions of functional tripartition. It had its roots in the Gelasian division of functions, which Gregory VII then pushed aside or, rather, reinterpreted, in the form of super- and subordination.[173] Although from about the year 1000 onward the proponents of the idea of functional tripartition held other, quite opposite views in regard to the separation of functions and to the militia, their interpretive scheme also contributed to shaping the idea and reality of knighthood.

2. The trifunctional scheme was used not only to discuss current issues of the day but also to grasp the new formation of closely related estates. J. Fleckenstein, in particular, has drawn our attention to this process of estate formation, which involved the distinction and reciprocal distancing between peasant and knight, *rusticus* and *miles*. The two terms, as Fleckenstein has aptly stated, were "apparently assigned to different forms of existence" and at the same time corresponded "with each other historically in a suggestive manner. . . . The increasing use of both terms, which one may observe since the twilight of the Carolingian period, thus indicates nothing more than the progressive differentiation into two separate occupations of previously undifferentiated agricultural and military activities. . . . Indeed, one could say that peasants and knights only truly began to take shape when they sought to distance themselves from each other."[174] We may quite rightly attribute world-historical significance to this process of a division of occupation and labor.[175]

The distinctions among the peasant population according to their legal status of freedom, half-freedom, and servitude, which we find in Carolingian manorial records, had apparently leveled out by this point:[176] "The various groups in the manorial system—from the dependent farm servants (*unfreie Hofknechte*) and servile villeins (*leibeigene Hufenbauern*) to the better-placed free peasants who paid tithes (*Zinsbauern*)" had "gradually grown into an internally stratified peasantry of serfs." The "old differentiation, based on birth, between *liber* and *servus* was gradually replaced, by the eleventh century, by the new functional distinction between *rusticus* and *miles*, peasant and knight" (W. Rösener). The peasant appeared for the first time as a historical and social figure, along with the newly emerging peasant estate. Whereas previously legal distinctions had been most relevant, now the similar economic activities of those who did physical labor moved to the forefront, and were perceived in this light. At the same time, in a process that had already begun in the eighth and ninth centuries, the mounted warrior in heavy armor gradually became established, pushing back the armed peasant contingents. A class of professional warriors arose, bringing together various strata for military service: noble soldiers and freemen, who were soon joined by the ministerials who managed through this function to rise out of servitude.[177]

Was the temporal coincidence of these processes with the (re)appearance of the trifunctional scheme at the beginning of the eleventh century a mere accident? It is more likely that there was some connection between the two, that is, that the statements about peasants (*laboratores, agricultores*) and knights (*bellatores, pugnatores, milites*)[178] that emphasize their differences and the significance of their reciprocal duties and functions reflect this sociohistorical process of a division of occupation and labor; we could then say that the trifunctional scheme was the first to grasp this process in its context.

The trifunctional scheme's inclusion of both clerics and monks in the same *ordo*—that of the *oratores*—also has an unmistakable connection with reality.[179] After all, this inclusion of both marks a change in the shape of monasticism, that is, its growing similarity with the clergy, a process in the history of monasticism and social history more generally that emerged gradually and for the first time during the Carolingian period. By placing itself at the service of the king, Frankish monasticism allowed the original monastic obligation to perform manual labor to retreat more and more in favor of spiritual and pastoral duties. This reorientation may already be observed, down to the quantitative details, in the Frankish monasteries of the eighth and ninth centuries, when the number of lay brothers decreased and the number of ordained monks increased correspondingly.[180] This clericalization of monasticism had two sides, then; it encompassed the process of combination with the duties of the clergy and, at the same time, that of a separation of functions in regard to manual labor. This process reached a high point during the tenth and eleventh centuries in Cluniac monasticism, of which it could rightly be said that its "essence" was defined by the liturgy, the celebration of the Mass, reading texts and prayer.[181] In his decree, Gratian, too (as already indicated above) recognized only one *genus Christianiorum* other than the laity, that of the *clerici*, which encompassed both clerics in the stricter sense of the word and monks (*Deo deuoti, uidelicet conuersi*) and whose members were all equally characterized by the duties of the *diuinum offitium, contemplatio,* and *oratio*.[182]

3. In this way the trifunctional scheme may be considered an indicator of social processes—it focused them and got to the heart of the matter. At the same time, though, we may also regard the scheme as a factor that intensified and promoted these processes because it suggested a particular image of reality. The best measure of this effect of the trifunctional scheme is the fact that it formulated and propagated corporative norms for both knight (*bellator, pugnator,*

miles) and peasant (*laborator, agricultor*). In other words, from about the year 1000 onward the trifunctional scheme both formulated particular elements of knightly ethics and introduced a new valuation of manual labor.

When Bishop Bonizo of Sutri laid down a code of conduct for knights (*miles*) in his *Liber de vita christiana* (1090–95), he included the injunctions "to fight to the death for the good of the *respublica*" and "to defend paupers, widows, and orphans."[183] Both life norms have a long prehistory[184] not directly connected with the trifunctional scheme. Yet we cannot overlook the fact that both norms were repeatedly expressed from the period around 1000 onward. We find them in Ælfric's above-cited remarks on the *bellator*, the "worldly soldier" (*woruld-cempa*), whose task it was to defend "our soil," "our towns," and "our country" against "the enemy": "ordo bellatorum debet armis patriam nostram ab incursibus hostium defendere."[185] Adalbero of Laon referred to the *bellatores* as *tutores aecclesiarum* and explained: "They defend the great and small among the people (*vulgus*)/all of them, and they protect themselves in the same way."[186] The correspondence between the ideas of the trifunctional scheme and the aims of the Peace of God movement become evident here once again. We might describe the latter's fundamental and central objective as the protection of the church, and of those who serve it, that is, clerics, monks, and nuns, but also of all defenseless persons: "Defenselessness was always the criterion for protection."[187] Let us recall that the *bellatores* derived their justification for bearing arms, including their religious justification, from the fact that they performed their duties "for all," as Ælfric had explained.[188] All three *ordines* needed each other, as Adalbero of Laon and Gerard of Cambrai repeatedly emphasized, following the reasoning of all theories of estate from time immemorial. This was the underlying purpose of the tripartition of humanity. In Adalbero's words, "The house of God, of which we believe that it is one, is tripartite: / The ones pray, the others fight, and yet others work. / These three are one and admit of no separation, / The service [*officium*] of the one makes possible the work of the other two, / all mutually help all."[189] Each of the three estates required the activities of the other two in order to fulfill its own duties. Or, as Gerard of Cambrai wrote, "they help each other."[190] This was a case of genuine mutuality, which served to justify each of the three functions, including the use of weapons. Gerard of Cambrai expresses this very idea with particular succinctness when he writes of the *pugnatores* that "the task [*officium*] entails no guilt if there is no sinful intention."[191] This sentence has been called a "remarkable statement" which "boldly [anticipates] the solution of a problem . . . that would exercise minds throughout the entire eleventh century."[192] The "boldness" of this sentence is indeed remarkable; it corresponds to an idea expressed by Augustine, while at the same time running counter to the tenor of early medieval canon law, particularly the statements made by canonists of the early eleventh century (Fulbert of Chartres, Burchard of Worms).[193] Gerard's view is, however, virtually a natural outgrowth of the trifunctional scheme.

The objectives of the Peace of God movement included not only the protection of the church and the defenseless but also the "guarantee of nourishment" and with it the protection of all those who supplied it to others, the peasants and their "labor essential for life."[194] Again we see the trifunctional scheme in concord with the goals of the Peace of God movement. If all three *ordines* performed their tasks "for all," then manual labor had a significance similar to the other functions, which signaled a new valuation of physical labor.[195] The *laboratores* ensure "our subsistence" (*urne bigleofan*), writes Ælfric ("ordo laboratorum adquirit nobis uictum");[196] the *laboratores* were *weormen*, "who are supposed to produce that from which the whole people [*theodscipe*] live."[197] In the words of Gerard of Cambrai, the estate of the *oratores* was beholden to the "*agricultores* because their labor produces nourishment for the body. . . . In the same way the *pugnatores* are . . . fed by the fruits of the fields."[198] It was above all Adalbero of Laon who emphasized the new valuation of manual labor implicit in the basic assumptions of the trifunctional scheme. Those who work (*qui laborant*)— Adalbero refers to them as *servi*—were a *genus afflictum*, "a wretched estate," whose unhappy lives were dominated by labor and toil (*labor*).[199] Adalbero underscores the indispensability of this work in a dialectical understanding of master and servant that was unusual for its time.[200] Taking up a sentence of Augustine's on the Christian household, according to which "those who give orders serve those over whom they appear to rule,"[201] Adalbero shows that "all" are nourished by the work of the *servi*, that the master (*dominus*) is supported by his servant (*servus*), although he believes that it is the other way around ("Pascitur a servo dominus quem pascere sperat"), and that therefore kings and bishops too are not the masters, but rather the "servants of their servants" (*servis servire videntur*).[202]

These assertions reveal Adalbero's opposition to the teachings of the church fathers, particularly Gregory the Great and Isidore of Seville, who preferred to regard human difference (*diversitas*) as a consequence of sin,[203] and therefore asserted that the domination of some and the servitude of others was justified, because bondage must be considered a punishment for sin imposed by God in his mercy: "So that the freedom of servants to do evil might be restricted by the power of their masters."[204] The functional interpretation of manual labor as a vitally necessary service performed on behalf of all those others who do not work dismisses the transcendental interpretation of servitude, and the labor associated with it, as a punishment.[205] This was something new, indeed epoch-making, although we cannot discuss it in more detail here. In the history of thinking about the meaning and value of manual labor, which was always closely tied to the notion of estates,[206] the trifunctional scheme represented a discovery, which, in the light of the value placed on labor by early Christianity, must be called a rediscovery:[207] "the promotion of labor as a value."[208] This was to remain a characteristic of the trifunctional scheme until the beginning of the modern period.[209]

Naturally, when we consider the interpretation and valuation of the activities of knights and peasants that was peculiar to the trifunctional scheme, we must keep in mind that those who made these pronouncements were monks and bishops, that is, members of the *ordo* of *oratores*. The *laboratores* remain voiceless for us, and the *bellatores* also do not speak for themselves in the sources. For this reason it might appear plausible to borrow from the modern concept of ideology[210] and portray the eleventh-century *bellatores* and *milites* as objects of clerical interpretation or even manipulation.[211] In a similar way, Jacques Le Goff has noted that the trifunctional scheme of the early eleventh century revealed a new valuation of labor, to be sure, but that this occurred "against the actual will of the originators."[212] As a contrast to such assumptions, which owe much to the modern problem of ideology, we might point to some thoughts expressed by A. I. Gurevich on the subject of the trifunctional scheme.[213] Responding to the sharp distinction that scholars have drawn between "popular culture" and "clerical culture," Gurevich urges us to consider whether these truly were always "two cultural traditions, so different in both origin and composition" or whether there might not be much to be said for the idea that in the early and high Middle Ages "learned and popular cultures represented different traditions within the context of one culture." And he adds the suggestion, which is indeed plausible, "that the dialogue-conflict of both traditions, which were constantly interacting and opposing one another, formed the basis of the cultural and religious development of the West in that period; they can only be properly understood in correlation to one another."[214] What this means for the assessment of the trifunctional scheme and the monastic and clerical evidence we have of it, however, is that it must be placed in a broader framework. "The idea that a part is organically included in a whole, that each individual social rank is included in a society which is an indissoluble unity, a kind of 'body,' all the members of which mutually supplement and support each other and are vitally important to the whole, was undoubtedly exploited by the clergy. But this idea was scarcely the property or creation of the theoreticians of the Middle Ages alone, rather it had been broadcast universally in all categories of collective consciousness."[215] We could also say that the body of ideas about estate represented a "world of meanings" in the early and high Middle Ages, which was, in a certain sense, "inhabited" by everyone.[216] This certainly does not mean that we can exclude the possibility that estate thinking and its schemes and metaphors were used to further the interests of a single group and its representatives, namely the clergy.[217] The point here is that this capacity for ideological deployment should not be presumed from the outset, and in general, to be the only possible use for such schemes. Rather, we should also consider whether people outside the clergy might not also have recognized themselves in such schemes, and whether the trifunctional scheme might not have expressed elements of the self-interpretations and historical and social self-image of *bellatores* and *laboratores*.[218]

New Estates in the Twelfth Century and Their Interpretation

The above observations are intended to illuminate various aspects of the question of the relationship between "reality" and "knowledge": the production of reality through the schemes used to interpret it; the creation of schemes because an existing reality was in need of interpretation; and the condensation and underscoring of elements of perceived reality in the schemes employed to interpret it. The early history of the trifunctional scheme also reveals how interpretive schemes were deployed as arguments in sociopolitical controversies.[219] We may trace the efficacy of the trifunctional scheme in another context as well. Thus, in his apologia for the religious-military orders (*De laude novae militiae*, written shortly before 1136) Bernard of Clairvaux had to confront the fact that the way of life of the Knights Templar met with disapproval because it brought together "chivalric and monastic elements," and thus blurred the distinctions between the spiritual and profane militia, between *oratores* and *bellatores*, which, "according to the conceptions of his contemporaries," violated all order.[220] We could add further examples to demonstrate the efficacy and reality of interpretive schemes in this sense, because groups defined themselves and clarified their aims and intentions by appropriating or questioning interpretive schemes, confronting other people's schemes with their own, or using such schemes to criticize the behavior of others. It was a worthwhile exercise to present a summary account of the extent to which intellectual and social conflicts in the Middle Ages were conducted as disputes over schemes for interpreting social reality. Let us recall that the conflict over lay preaching in the late twelfth and thirteenth centuries was sparked by older interpretations of the *ordo laicorum*,[221] and that the mendicant dispute of the 1250s and 1260s, which involved the mendicant orders' right to preach and engage in pastoral activities, was also conducted as a dispute over the estates and the doctrine of hierarchy propounded by Pseudo-Dionysius the Areopagite.[222]

The two sections that follow, however, will be concerned with the fact that new social realities were not always expressed in new schemes. Indeed, even widely accepted schemes could, ultimately, be ignored in order to allow a new reality to come into being.

The trifunctional scheme became widely disseminated beginning in the second half of the eleventh century and was expressed in a number of written versions.[223] As is well known, though, complex intellectual, social, and economic changes sparked the creation of new estates in the course of the eleventh and twelfth centuries. One of these new phenomena was the emergence of a stratum of persons who lived in the towns and whose existence was defined by manual labor: the collectivity of the town-dwelling artisans and merchants, the "citizens," whose sociopolitical form became that of the urban, "burgher" community.[224] The other was the emergence in the twelfth century of a stratum of learned, formally educated men or intellectuals whose appearance is associated with the beginning of the European university.[225]

In the twelfth century (and later as well) repeated attempts were made to incorporate the new urban burgher stratum of artisans and merchants into the trifunctional scheme, and to place the *negotiatores* and the various groups of *operarii* alongside the *milites* and *agricolae*,[226] thus transforming the tripartition into a functional quadripartition. The details, particular circumstances and types of such attempts have been little studied.[227] Such efforts to define the new town dwellers—the merchants and artisans characterized by the status of free labor—as an estate in their own right were largely unsuccessful. The future, too, belonged to the trifunctional scheme, whose wide dissemination in the literature of the late Middle Ages and the early modern period was yet to come.[228] In the visual arts, the scheme only became truly widespread in the sixteenth century,[229] and the high point of its social and constitutional influence, the emergence of a "third estate," in the sense of the formation of political estates, also lay in the future.[230] Although the trifunctional scheme thus persisted despite the rise of an urban burgher class, we should emphasize that the combination of peasants and town dwellers into one estate, which later came to be known in France as the "third estate,"[231] was neither devoid of meaning nor divorced from reality. Rather, it expressed something quite real—the presence of a stratum of the population whose social and economic existence was defined by work. This was something new in the history of the West.[232]

Equally typical of the twelfth century is the appearance of the sociohistorical figure of the scholar and the university-educated man, the professional academic and the academically trained practitioner. A discussion of the preconditions for this emergence would take us too far afield here; it will suffice to ask whether and how the men in question and their contemporaries perceived this new phenomenon. Here, too, attempts were made to add a fourth estate to the older tripartition, but not until the early modern period were the three estates of the Reformation, the *ordo* or *status ecclesiasticus*, *politicus* and *oeconomicus*,[233] joined by an *ordo* or *status scholasticus*.[234] Twelfth-century authors adopted a different approach. At that time, the new scholars and academically trained men were already understood as a phenomenon in their own right, a separate stratum or estate, and were referred to collectively using a single term. This group was juxtaposed to the rest of society, which was neither learned nor educated, and which was referred to by its own counterterm. No neologisms were created for this purpose, however. Instead, the older, familiar terms *clericus* and *laicus* were adapted to the new purpose. Beginning in the twelfth century, *clericus* was no longer used to refer only to the holder of ecclesiastical office, who was distinguished from the layman by ordination, but also to the *valenter litteratus*, a man who had studied hard, regardless of his estate (*ordo*) or way of life (*habitus*).[235] The background to this change in the meaning of *clericus* was a dual one; of course, the clerics, alongside the monks—or, to be more precise, the estate of *clerici*, which included the monks[236]—had always represented the literate part of society. In addition, with the growing regional mobility of students in the twelfth century, the status of cleric offered that minimum of protection which students and scholars, as outsiders in the towns, so sorely needed.

Nevertheless, the simple equation of the learned *clericus* with the cleric was already no longer possible by the twelfth century, and, together with its new meaning, the word *clericus* immediately gained a significance in its own right. In the twelfth century, the concept of the "layman" was also redefined accordingly: *laicus* now also referred to someone who was not an expert, who lacked specific training or education.[237] These new meanings of *clericus* and *laicus*, which arose in the twelfth century, are still with us today.[238] It is also remarkable how, once again as early as the twelfth century, the new *clerici* came into competition with the older estates, the priests and knights.[239] The attitude that *arma* and *litterae* represented areas of life of equal worth, because the *litteralis scientia* "ennobled," became established.[240] The new *clerici* were, in a certain sense, at odds with the older *ordines* because any man, whether noble or pauper, could become a scholar or at least study at a university. Nevertheless, the definition of the new *clerici* as an estate is evident not merely because of the adoption of the older corporative terms of the *duo genera Christianorum*, but also in regard to social reality: through the marked self-awareness of these scholars and university graduates, their characteristic habitus and forms of behavior and, not least, their new and specific mode of thinking and writing, "Scholasticism," which lent its name to an entire epoch in the history of European learning.[241] The contemporaries of these scholars did not merely note these developments but also acknowledged them, sharing the value they placed on the new intellectual and scientific work and permitting the new type of *clericus* to become a social model.

Challenges to Interpretations of Reality in the High Middle Ages

At the same time, the movement of voluntary, religiously motivated poverty called into question all thinking on estates and with it all interpretative schemes. The much cited correspondence between the little-known Tenxwind of Andernach and her famous contemporary Hildegard of Bingen in the years around 1150 illustrates in exemplary form this collision between opposing views of the order of the world, society, and the duties of the individual.[242] Tenxwind's criticism of the social exclusivity of Hildegard's convent, which refused to accept nonnoble (*ignobiles*) or less wealthy women (*minus ditati*), was respectful in tone but uncompromising in substance. Tenxwind reminded Hildegard that Christ had chosen his Apostles from among "fishermen, the lowly and the poor," that God had chosen not those who were "powerful and of noble birth," but rather the "low and despised" (1 Cor. 1:26ff.), and that God shows no partiality (Rom. 2:11; see Acts 10:34).[243] The reply she received was absolutely in keeping with corporative thinking and the tradition of the church fathers. God had decided that the lower estate was not to raise itself above the higher one ("quod minor ordo super superiorem non ascendat"), as Satan and the first man had done; and the order of Creation was an articulated and stratified one, as was demonstrated by the animal kingdom. ("Who puts his entire herd—oxen, asses, sheep, goats—in a single barn, so that they are indistinguishable from each other?") This order of Creation was obeyed by the hierarchies of angels as well as the *ordines* of human society: "Thus there must be a distinction, so that the different people, united in one herd, do not dissolve in arrogance and disgrace, and above all, so that the honorableness of the ways of life (*honestas morum*) is not destroyed when they tear each other apart in hatred, when, namely, the higher estate attacks the lower, and when the lower reaches up to the higher. For God distinguishes among his people, on earth as in heaven, namely among angels, archangels, thrones, dominations, cherubim and seraphim." God loves all, "even if they do not have equal names." This was the meaning and purpose of *ordo*, that each recognized his or her own limitations: "It is good that man does not occupy the mountain, which he cannot move, but rather remains down below and learns gradually that which he can understand."[244]

Indeed, as the editor A. Haverkamp has remarked, the correspondence juxtaposes two "world-views with extremely different religious and social roots."[245] Following Haverkamp, we may define them more closely in terms of a contrast between a mode of thinking rooted in the New Testament and "a line of thinking that was still grounded in the Old Testament"—the image of God as a *deus potens*, the central social ideas of "fear and reverence, service and obedience," and of domination and submission.[246] We could also define the contrast in terms of the juxtaposition of New Testament thought and its questioning of any estate order on the one hand, and antique reflections on *ordo* on the other, as they were conveyed in the Middle Ages through the works of Augustine, Pseudo-Dionysius the Areopagite, Gregory the Great, and Isidore of Seville.[247] Hildegard of Bingen's reply offers a virtual compendium of this antique and patristic perspective on the stratified world of estate and its justification.

The validity of this perspective was called into question ever more radically as the poverty movement of the high Middle Ages grew and developed. This was, nevertheless, not self-evident. In his impressive study of St. Francis of Assisi, Raoul Manselli has shown very vividly how difficult it was for Francis to find a new way of life *secundum formam sancti Evangelii*, his own way of life, that is, which had long remained but a dim inkling, and to live it in opposition to the ruling interpretations of the society, according to which he could live only as a priest and cleric or a monk or layman.[248] In fact, only if we keep in mind the traditional interpretations of the world and society, which were regarded as binding, can we truly appreciate Francis's intellectual and spiritual strength as revealed in his testament, in that sentence that defines the breakthrough to the new way of life (*forma vivendi*) for which he was destined: "nobody showed me what to do."[249] The power that the schemes of corporative thinking exerted over the individual becomes very clear here, as does the strength required to resist them. The consequence of Francis's new orientation in life was always to be a "minor man" (*minor*) and thus to undermine any estate order from the very beginning. "Let them be the least and lower than all those who are in the same house," Francis commanded his brothers,[250] and, once again looking back in his *Testament*, he said of them and himself, "and we relinquished the power and rank that education, knowledge, and intelligence can provide, and we were less than all others."[251] This is the most succinct summary of his life maxim. In freely accepting the role of the "idiot," that is, of a man who refused to exercise the power and rank that education and intelligence might afford him, Francis particularly called into question the new estate of scholars and academically trained men who were active at the recently established universities.[252] The power of this questioning of estate norms and the authenticity of its orientation toward New Testament norms is also demonstrated by the fact that Francis did not, however, oppose the estate order as such, but instead accepted the existence of every type of estate:[253] all *ordines* of the clergy, all monks, "poor men, kings and princes, laborers and peasants, servants and masters, all virgins and people who live in chastity and married people," all *laici*, and so forth, as is stated in the *Regula non bullata*, which also offers a compendium of older interpretive schemes.[254] The *fratres minores* confronted all of these *ordines* not as a new estate, but rather as a way of life that fundamentally undercut and called into question the very nature of estates.

The life of Elisabeth of Thuringia, a contemporary of St. Francis, demonstrates how a voluntary identification with those who were not poor by choice could catapult a person out of the estate order, making her an "idiot," and even subjecting her to accusations of madness. We know that after her husband's death Elisabeth's relatives declared that she was not in her right mind. They disapproved of her way of life, which was unbecoming to her noble rank, and of her devotion to the poor, and having paid her compensation, banished her to Marburg. This way of life was, in the truest sense of the word, *unanständig* (indecent, from the same root as *Stand* or estate) and Elisabeth would continually have compromised her kin and the entire court of the landgrave had she remained in Thuringia.[255]

Such ways of thinking and living as we encounter in the cases of Tenxwind, Francis, and Elisabeth draw our attention to the polar tensions between thinking within the estate order and the rejection of these interpretations of society, which have become so important for the history of the Middle Ages. It is highly significant that this polarity, as was mentioned above, can already be found in the New Testament. It took up important elements of antique ideas on estate, for example the above-mentioned metaphor of the *militia* or the metaphor of the body, which Paul used for his interpretation of the Christian congregation (1 Cor. 12:12ff), on the one hand. On the other, we also find fundamental rejections of the corporative norms of Greco-Roman antiquity and of estate thinking altogether:[256] in the radical condemnation of property ownership and the high value placed on poverty as well as manual labor; in the choice of fishermen as Apostles and the blessing of paupers, prostitutes, and tax collectors; in the emphasis on the vocation of each individual, regardless of rank;[257] in the significance thereby given to even the most mundane and lowliest occupations, estates, places, and ways of life;[258] in the at once "hidden and real"—that is, sacramentally and eschatologically real—abolition of all classifications, including the "natural" one of male and female, as Paul noted in his Epistle to the Galatians.[259] This polar tension, present in the New Testament itself, continued to define social thought in ever new ways in the centuries that followed. It was additionally accentuated by the reception of antique thinking on estate and the idea of *ordo* in the patristic literature and again in the reception of Aristotelian philosophy in the twelfth and thirteenth centuries, but that is another subject.

In summary, however, I should point to another such polar tension, whose beginnings are to be found in a later period than that examined here, but which is nevertheless significant for our topic in several ways. It is the contrast between "realist" and "nominalist" thinking in the late Middle Ages.[260]

Late Medieval Nominalism and Its Consequences for the History of Interpretive Schemes and Their Interpretations

The so-called nominalism of the late Middle Ages,[261] which appeared in the fourteenth and fifteenth centuries in the form of the *via moderna*, was "to be sure, not itself modern in character," but it was "the essential precondition" for a new and modern mode of thought and for the thought of modernity. It was, at the same time, "in a sense the gate through which the transition to a new age was made possible,"[262] by virtue of the fact that it was still wholly defined by metaphysical questions, but answered them in a manner that ultimately led to the demise of metaphysical thinking. William of Ockham[263] laid the foundation for the new thinking with his heightened understanding of God and the idea of divine omnipotence. At the same time, however, Ockham's justification for the notion of the omnipotence of God "necessarily led to the abandonment of this very idea of God . . . as modern philosophy demonstrates. . . . The new questions that emerged from this process ultimately destroyed the very premises that had made them possible."[264] It is precisely this fact that makes it so difficult for us to grasp the so-called nominalism of the Middle Ages and its epochal significance even today. This remains the case whether we perceive only the destructive consequences of this approach and feel compelled to lament them,[265] or resist the idea that modern thought had significant roots in medieval theology, which would contradict the widespread view of modern thought as a liberation from heteronymous traditions, an emancipation from the tutelage of theology[266]— because, after all, the emergence of modern scholarship cannot be understood as "a process of empirical data," but "rather above all and fundamentally" as "a metaphysical event."[267] Moving beyond these versions of the devaluation or disdainful neglect of late-medieval nominalism, we can agree with H. Rombach's assessment that it represents "perhaps the most radical upheaval in the history of philosophy since Plato."[268]

We should keep this verdict in mind, particularly from a historical viewpoint, and in the light both of estate thinking in antiquity and the kindred reflections on estate in the early and High Middle Ages. William of Ockham's thesis that the intellect can only apprehend individual things (*singulare intelligitur*)[269] ushered in the end of cosmological thinking. This thesis led to the abandonment of the assumption that the world and its order (*ordo*) as such could be apprehended in reality, as well as to the accompanying disintegration of the unity of knowledge and ethics within the framework of a metaphysically based perception of the *ordo*—that unity which, since Plato (and once again since Augustine),[270] had determined reflections on the position of human beings in the world and in the multiplicity of individual *ordines*. Ockham's thesis pulled the rug out from under interpretations of knowledge as a knowledge of essences, that is, as an agreement between the intellect and the thing.[271] His emphasis on the individual and contingent nature of knowledge signaled "the abandonment of an intelligible world order, in which both the apprehending person and reality participate."[272] This required an altogether new kind of knowledge as a basis, and also a new mode of scholarly thinking—a scholarship, in other words, which could no longer claim the ability to make statements about the real shape of the world, but which, instead, ultimately came to understand itself as a mere ordered system of coherent propositions about phenomena, whose essence must however remain hidden. The thing perceived was now a mere product of the mind, but this product of the mind is the "actual object of apprehension."[273] This idea paved the way for the modern question of the relationship of cognition and reality, of reality and knowledge.[274]

This phenomenon of late medieval nominalism is implicated on several levels in the approach and subject of the present essay, which has addressed the question of the relationship between reality and knowledge.

1. On the one hand, the dissolution of the unity of metaphysics, epistemology, and ethics, that unity which perceived the world as a stratified order and thereby derived the maxims for the life and conduct of individuals, groups, and estates, completely undermined estate thinking and with it all social metaphors and interpretive schemes. Ockham's new approach "meant the end of the medieval idea of order" because "order as a characteristic of reality [presupposes] an absolute rationality," "in which the intelligibility of reality is ultimately grounded."[275] We know little, however, about the individual phases and course of this process from the fourteenth century on, as Ernst Troeltsch pointed out in his famous 1922 study of the social teachings of the Christian churches. In so doing he set social historians a task that still lies before us: to analyze the correspondence between "the metaphysics of the natural-supernatural graduated structure of the cosmos" and a "quantitatively graduated morality of the individual estates in relation to the absolute ideal" and, at the same time, to study how all of this disintegrated. For "it was not only dogma, but also, and above all, social ethics that became dissolved in nominalism."[276] To observe this process would doubtless be not merely instructive but also fascinating, because "nominalist" thinking has by no means spread and established itself uniformly since the fourteenth century. Instead, particularly

since the sixteenth century, "realist" interpretations of the world and society returned to the foreground and initially managed to assert themselves time and again.[277] Within the context of social teachings and the history of the schemes used to interpret social reality, this may be observed in the renewal and updating of high medieval social teachings in the Catholic Reform and Counter-Reformation.[278] We also find it, however, in the fact that Martin Luther, despite the nominalist tendencies of his own theology,[279] followed the tradition of antique and high medieval reflections on estate and understood the proper order of society in "realistic" terms as a tripartition: *ordo ecclesiasticus*, *ordo politicus*, and *ordo oeconomicus*.[280]

2. On the other hand, we must also deal with the consequences of late medieval nominalism in regard to the cognitive mode of the scholarly disciplines, that is, historical knowledge, and to the problem of ideology and the concept of ideology, which we treated at the beginning of this essay.[281] After all, the results of the breakdown of metaphysics, and with it of the idea of *ordo* and reflection on estate encompass modern scholarship as research[282] as well as the modern problem of ideology as it emerged in the eighteenth century.[283] Here, too, we see the results of the fact that since the advent of nominalism, scholarly knowledge can no longer be understood as "true" knowledge, the "agreement between the mind and the thing." In scholarship as in life, the one, ultimately always attainable, true interpretation of the world and society has been replaced, once and for all, by a multiplicity of propositions about the world and society. These propositions were and are rivals, and thus subject to occasional mutual accusations of pretensions to exclusivity and suspicions of ideology.

This is the situation in which historians interested in studying medieval, metaphysically based interpretive schemes (or anything else, for that matter) find ourselves. In this case, too, we must always be aware that historical scholarship does not simply describe history "in itself" or as it "actually" was in its "real existence" or "core," but that it seeks to grasp historical phenomena with the help of questions and methods, schemes of perception, and interpretation, which are relative and aspectual not least because they are themselves historically mediated.[284] This should encourage us to subject our own interpretive schemes and terminology to constant and thorough scrutiny. Max Weber, Otto Hintze, and Otto Brunner were the main founders and promoters of the decidedly "nominalist" mode of modern scholarship.[285] We also find this tendency (by way of the epistemology of Émile Durkheim)[286] in the basic premises of French social history;[287] its ways of looking at things and its findings have frequently been used in this essay. Here, too, the question of realism and nominalism in historical knowledge refuses to die—and is answered in a nominalist spirit.[288] Or, to end with a genuinely nominalist dictum of Marc Bloch, "true realism in history is knowing that human reality is multiple."[289]

Notes

This chapter is based on Otto Gerhard Oexle, "Deutungsschemata der sozialen Wirklichkeit im frühen und hohen Mittelalter: Ein Beitrag zur Geschichte des Wissens," in *Mentalitäten im Mittelalter: Methodische und inhaltliche Probleme*, ed. Frantisek Graus, Vorträge und Forschungen 35 (Sigmaringen, 1987), 65–117. This essay was written at the same time as another entitled "Die funktionale Dreiteilung als Deutungsschema der sozialen Wirklichkeit in der ständischen Gesellschaft des Mittelalters," printed in *Ständische Gesellschaft und Mobilität*, ed. W. Schulze, Schriften des Historischen Kollegs München, Kolloquien, 12 (Munich, 1988), 19–51. Both publications are based on conference lectures, which pursued different aims according to the conference theme and participants. Nevertheless, the two essays contain similar trains of thought. This is intentional.

1. On this see O. G. Oexle, "Die funktionale Dreiteilung der 'Gesellschaft' bei Adalbero von Laon. Deutungsschemata der sozialen Wirklichkeit im früheren Mittelalter," *Frühmittelalterliche Studien* 12 (1978), 1–54, esp. 5ff. (hereafter "Die funktionale Dreiteilung"); and Oexle, "Die 'Wirklichkeit' und das 'Wissen'. Ein Blick auf das sozialgeschichtliche Oeuvre von Georges Duby," *Historische Zeitschrift* 232 (1981): 61–91.

2. One could mention Augustine's text *De ordine* from the year 386, CSEL 3 (1922), 121ff. The term "society" will be used in what follows in the general sense of the social whole, although, and because, no such term existed in the Middle Ages. See Oexle, "Die funktionale Dreiteilung," 3. The term "estate" (German *Stand*) will be used in the sense of the medieval concept of *ordo*; see Oexle, "Die funktionale Dreiteilung," 3–4; and Oexle, "Stand, Klasse (Antike und Mittelalter)," in *Geschichtliche Grundbegriffe*, vol. 6, ed. Otto Brunner, Werner Conze, and Reinhard Koselleck (Stuttgart, 1990), 155–200, introduction ("Zum Problem des Begriffs Stand"). On the meaning of the term stratum (*Schicht*), which will be used here occasionally, see Oexle, "Die funktionale Dreiteilung," 47 and n. 284.

3. See R. Roques, *L'univers dionysien*, 1954; and introduction to Denys l'Aréopagite, *La hiérarchie céleste*, Sources chrétiennes 58bis, 2nd ed. (1970), Vff.; G. O'Daly, "Dionysius Areopagita," in *Theologische Realenzyklopädie* 8 (1981), 772ff.

4. Ernst Troeltsch, *Die Soziallehren der christlichen Kirchen und Gruppen* (Tübingen, 1912, reprint 1965), 252ff. and 286ff. (on Thomas Aquinas). The book was translated into English as *The Social Teaching of the Christian Churches*, trans. Olive Wyon (London and New York, 1931); see also O. Schilling, *Die christlichen Soziallehren* (Munich, 1926), 121ff.; R. Linhardt, *Die Sozialprinzipien des heiligen Thomas von Aquin* (Freiburg, 1932); W. Dettloff, "Himmlische und irdische Hierarchie bei Bonaventura," *Miscellanea Mediaevalia* 12/1 (Berlin, 1979): 41ff.

5. Oexle, "Stand, Klasse (Antike und Mittelalter)." The material is also collected in W. Kölmel, *Soziale Reflexion im Mittelalter* (Essen, 1985).

6. H. Friedrich, *Epochen der italienischen Lyrik* (Frankfurt a. M., 1964), 648.

7. T. Struve, *Die Entwicklung der organologischen Staatsauffassung im Mittelalter*, Monographien zur Geschichte des Mittelalters, 16 (Stuttgart, 1978).

8. A. von Harnack, *Militia Christi* (Tübingen, 1905; reprint, 1963); A. Wang, *Der "Miles Christianus" im 16. und 17. Jahrhundert und seine mittelalterliche Tradition*, Mikrokosmos, 1 (Leipzig, 1975).

9. On this term see Oexle, "Die funktionale Dreiteilung," 7.

10. See the following titles, which have appeared in the past twenty years alone, G. Duby, *Les trois ordres ou l'imaginaire du féodalisme* (Paris, 1978); Oexle, "Die funktionale Dreiteilung"; D. Dubuisson, "Le roi indo-européen et la synthèse des trois fonctions," *Annales* 33 (1978): 21–34; C. Carozzi, "Les fondements de la tripartition sociale chez Adalbéron de Laon," *Annales* 33 (1978): 683–702, and "La tripartition sociale et l'idée de paix au XIe siècle" in *La guerre et la paix. Frontières et violences au moyen âge*, Actes du 101e Congrès National des Sociétés Savantes, Lille 1976 (1978), 9–22; J. Batany, "Du *bellator* au *chevalier* dans le schéma des 'Trois ordres' (Étude sémantique)," in ibid., 23–34; O. Niccoli, *I sacerdoti, i guerrieri, i contadini. Storia di un'immagine della società*, Saggi, 607 (1979); J. Le Goff, "Les trois fonctions indo-européennes, l'historien et l'Europe féodale," *Annales É.S.C.* 34 (1979): 1187–215; H. Fichtenau, "Soziale Mobilität in Quellen des 10. und frühen 11. Jahrhunderts," in *Wirtschafts- und sozialhistorische Beiträge. Festschrift für Alfred Hoffmann* (Vienna, 1979), 11–29; M. Rouche, "De l'Orient à l'Occident: Les origines de la tripartition fonctionelle et les causes de son adoption par l'Europe chrétienne à la fin du Xe siècle," in *Occident et Orient au Xe siècle*, Publications de l'Université de Dijon, 57 (Paris, 1979), 31–55; J.-P. Poly and E. Bournazel, *La mutation féodale, Xe–XIIe siècles*, Nouvelle Clio 16 (1980), 220ff.; J. H. Grisward, *Archéologie de l'épopée médiévale: Structures trifonctionnelles et mythes indo-européens dans le cycle des Narbonnais* (Paris, 1981); A. Vauchez, "Naissance d'une chrétienté, milieu Xe–fin XIe siècle," in *Le Moyen Age*, vol. 2: *L'éveil de l'Europe* ed. R. Fossier (Paris, 1982), 79–116, 89ff.; R. Fossier, *Enfance de l'Europe. Aspects économiques et sociaux* vol. 1, Nouvelle Clio 17 (1982), 78ff. and vol. 2, Nouvelle Clio 17 bis (1982), 884ff.; C. Carozzi, "D'Adalbéron de Laon à Humbert de Moyenmoutier: La désacralisation de la royauté," in *La cristianità dei secoli XI e XII in Occidente: coscienza e strutture di una società*, Miscellanea del Centro di Studi Medioevali 10 (1983), 67–84; Flori, *L'idéologie du glaive*, 121ff. and 158ff.

11. See below, "The Trifunctional Scheme and Early Eleventh-Century Realities."

12. Most recently edited by C. Carozzi, *Adalbéron de Laon, Poème au roi Robert*, Les classiques de l'histoire de France au Moyen Age 32 (Paris, 1979). This edition cannot, however, be regarded as a successful one. See O. G. Oexle, "Adalbero von Laon und sein 'Carmen ad Rodbertum regem'. Bemerkungen zu einer neuen Edition," *Francia* 8 (1980): 629–38. On the dating "ca. 1025," see Oexle, "Die funktionale Dreiteilung," 20.

13. The poem was given its title by A. de Valois in his 1663 edition of the text. See G. A. Hückel, *Les poèmes satiriques d'Adalbéron*, Université de Paris, Bibliothèque de la Faculté des Lettres, 13 (1901), 49–184, here 123 and n. 388. A better title might be "De ordine," borrowed from the text of the same name by Augustine (see above, n. 2); Adalbero mentions Augustine, along with Gregory the Great and Pseudo-Dionysius the Areopagite, as one of his sources and predecessors in reflecting on *ordo* and *ordines*.

14. Aron Iakovlevich Gurevich, *Categories of Medieval Culture*, trans. George L. Campbell (London, 1985), 170, 132–33.

15. O. G. Oexle, "Memoria und Memorialbild," in *Memoria. Der geschichtliche Zeugniswert des liturgischen Gedenkens im Mittelalter*, ed. K. Schmid and J. Wollasch, Münstersche Mittelalter-Schriften, 48 (Munich, 1984), 384–440, esp. 436ff.

16. This is the core of the modern concept of ideology.

17. See K. Lenk, "Problemgeschichtliche Einleitung," in *Ideologie*, ed. K. Lenk, 4th ed. (Neuwied, 1970), 17; which provides a good introduction to the history of ideologies and of concepts of ideology.

18. On this central problem in social history see (based on the work of Otto Brunner) O. G. Oexle, "Sozialgeschichte—Begriffsgeschichte—Wissenschaftsgeschichte. Anmerkungen zum Werk Otto Brunners," *Vierteljahrsschrift für Sozial- und Wirtschaftsgeschichte* 71 (1984): 305–41.

19. We touch here on the central question of the German sociology of knowledge in the period up until 1933, for which Marx's distinction between base and superstructure became the most important impetus, but also on the problem of historicism, i.e., the fact of the relativity and historical nature of all thought. For a succinct account of the genesis of the sociology of knowledge and its main problems see the introduction to Peter L. Berger and Thomas Luckmann, *The Social Construction of Reality: A Treatise in the Sociology of Knowledge* (New York, 1966).

20. See also N. Monzel's apt critique of the "metaphors of pressure that became common after Hegel and Marx in both idealist and materialist theories of history," quoted in W. Schwer, *Stand und Ständeordnung im Weltbild des Mittelalters*, Görres-Gesellschaft. Veröffentlichungen der Sektion für Wirtschafts- und Sozialwissenschaft, 7 (Paderborn, 1952; reprint, 1970), 96ff., quotation on 98.

21. K. Kroeschell, *Haus und Herrschaft im frühen deutschen Recht*, Göttinger rechtswissenschaftliche Studien, 70 (Göttingen, 1968), 51.

22. Georges Duby, "Histoire sociale et idéologie des sociétés," in *Faire de l'histoire*, vol. 1, ed. J. Le Goff and P. Nora (1974), 147–68, 148. See, from a philosophical viewpoint, the stimulating essay by G. Lardreau, "Georges Duby, ou la nouvelle positivité de l'histoire," in *Dialogues*, ed. G. Duby and G. Lardreau (1980), 5–35, as well as Oexle, "Die 'Wirklichkeit' und das 'Wissen.'"

23. The social process thus appears as a fabric of the most diverse factors and events and their effects. We must thus relinquish the definition of unambiguous and unidirectional cause-and-effect processes, the "dichotomy" between causes and effects (Marc Bloch).

24. Duby thus stands in the tradition of French epistemology and its definition of the "social," particularly as represented by Émile Durkheim, who remarked "that social life [is] wholly made up of representations"; see É. Durkheim, *Les règles de la méthode sociologique*, 20th ed. (Paris, 1981), xi. The same may be said of Marc Bloch with his assertion that "Historical facts are, by their very nature, psychological facts. It is, accordingly, in other psychological facts that they normally have their origins." Marc Bloch, *Apologie pour l'histoire ou métier d'historien*, 7th ed. (Paris, 1974), 157–58; see also the quotation below, n. 31. See Carlo Ginzburg, "A proposito della raccolta dei saggi storici di Marc Bloch," *Studi medievali* 3, no. 6 (1965): 335–53, and particularly S. Jöckel, *"Nouvelle histoire" und Literaturwissenschaft*, 2 vols., Romanistik, 44, 2nd ed. (1985), which especially focuses on the ties between the social history of Marc Bloch and Lucien Febvre and the sociology of Émile Durkheim and his school. See the discussion of Durkheim's epistemology on 20ff., 28ff., and 89ff.; on M. Bloch, see 58ff. and esp. 85ff. Max Weber's suggestion that "the 'images of the world' created by ideas . . . [have] quite frequently set the course in which the dynamic of interests moved action forward" follows in the same epistemological tradition. Max Weber, *Gesammelte Aufsätze zur Religionssoziologie*, vol. 1, 7th ed. (Tübingen, 1978), 252.

25. Berger and Luckmann, *The Social Construction of Reality*.

26. Ibid., 57–58.

27. Peter L. Berger, *The Social Reality of Religion* (Harmondsworth, 1973), 14.

28. Berger and Luckmann, *The Social Construction of Reality*, 62.

29. On this, see Schütz, *Der sinnhafte Aufbau der sozialen Welt* (Vienna, 1932; new ed. 1974), 105ff. and 111ff. I have borrowed the term "interpretive scheme" (*Deutungsschema*) from his work. Cf. Oexle, "Die funktionale Dreiteilung," 7 and n. 30.

30. H. Fichtenau, *Lebensordnungen des 10. Jahrhunderts*, vol. 1, Monographien zur Geschichte des Mittelalters, 30/1 (Stuttgart, 1984), 4.

31. M. Bloch, *Apologie pour l'histoire*, 158, on "conditions sociales—donc, dans leur nature profonde, mentales."

32. As Fichtenau aptly notes in *Lebensordnungen des 10. Jahrhunderts*, "Ultimately, all history is also the history of mentalities" (p. 3).

33. J. Glénisson, "Tendances, méthodes et techniques nouvelles de l'histoire médiévale," in *Actes du 100ᵉ Congrès National des Sociétés Savantes*, vol. 1, *Tendances, perspectives et méthodes de l'histoire médiévale* (1977), 7–30, 21: "The history of mentalities appears, in short, as a total history and ultimate explanation."

34. See above, n. 32.

35. Of the now vast literature on the concept of mentality and the "histoire des mentalités," the following deserve particular mention: Georges Duby, "Histoire des mentalités," in C. Samaran (ed.), *L'histoire et ses méthodes* (Paris, 1961), 937–66; Jacques Le Goff, "Les mentalités: une histoire ambiguë," in J. Le Goff and P. Nora (eds.), *Faire de l'histoire*, vol. 3 (Paris, 1974), 76–94; G. Tellenbach, "Mentalität," in *Geschichte, Wirtschaft, Gesellschaft. Festschrift für Clemens Bauer* (Berlin, 1974), 11–30.

36. See Frantisek Graus, "Mentalität—Versuch einer Begriffsbestimmung und Methoden der Untersuchung," in *Mentalitäten im Mittelalter. Methodische und inhaltliche Probleme*, ed. F. Graus, Vorträge und Forschungen, 35 (Sigmaringen, 1987), 9–48.

37. G. Duby, "La rencontre avec Robert Mandrou et l'élaboration de la notion d'histoire des mentalités," in *Histoire sociale, sensibilités collectives et mentalités: Mélanges Robert Mandrou* (Paris, 1985), 31–35, 34.

38. For a French perspective, see Philippe Ariès, "L'histoire des mentalités," in *La nouvelle histoire*, ed. Jacques Le Goff (Paris, 1978), 402–23. For views from the German side, see Rolf Reichardt, "Histoire des Mentalités," *Internationales Archiv für Sozialgeschichte der deutschen Literatur* 3 (1978): 130–66; Ernst Hinrichs, "Zum Stand der historischen Mentalitätsforschung in Deutschland," *Ethnologia Europaea* 11 (1979–80): 226–33; the quotation in the text comes from H. Schulze, "Mentalitätsgeschichte—Chancen und Grenzen eines Paradigmas der französischen Geschichtswissenschaft," *Geschichte in Wissenschaft und Unterricht*, 36 (1985): 247–70, 258.

39. J.-M. Thiriet, "Methoden der Mentalitätsforschung in der französischen Sozialgeschichte," *Ethnologia Europaea* 11 (1979–80): 208–25.

40. If we follow Frantisek Graus in his understanding of "mentality" as the "common tonus of the long-lasting forms of conduct and opinions of individuals within groups," which, as a "tonus" of thought and behavior "in a sense, 'underlies' both areas," in contrast to "ideologies, doctrines, and dogmas," which "exist only when formulated," whereas mentalities "are not formulated by the participants (insiders)," are also not "directly conveyed by a formulated [oral] tradition," and cannot be taught, then interpretive schemes and social metaphors cannot be the objects of a history of mentalities. Graus, "Mentalität," 17.

41. In his summary of the conference on mentalities organized by the Konstanzer

Arbeitskreis für Mittelalterliche Geschichte, Reinhard Schneider chose to follow Graus. "Protokoll über die Arbeitstagung vom 26.–29. März 1985," no. 277, 112. The French "histoire des mentalités," however, also counts as "mentalities" conscious thought content of a collective nature.

42. See Oexle, "Die funktionale Dreiteilung," 52 and n. 315.

43. Aron Iakovlevich Gurevich, "Medieval Culture and Mentality According to the New French Historiography," 186, *Archives européennes de sociologie*, 24 (1983): 167–95, who refers to Jacques Le Goff, "Les mentalités: une histoire ambiguë."

44. See also Gurevich, *Categories of Medieval Culture*, and "Medieval Culture and Mentality," 193–94, and Y. Congar's remarks on medieval "images de l'Église" in *L'ecclé-siologie du haut moyen âge* (Paris, 1968), 98ff.

45. See F. Niehoff, "Ordo et Artes. Wirklichkeiten und Imaginationen im Hohen Mittelalter," in *Ornamenta Ecclesiae. Kunst und Künstler der Romanik*, vol. 1 (Cologne, 1985), 33–48.

46. See Niccoli, *I sacerdoti, i guerrieri, i contadini*.

47. J. Le Goff, *Pour un autre Moyen Age* (Paris, 1977), 15. In his study, *Les trois ordres ou l'imaginaire du féodalisme*, Duby describes the history of the trifunctional scheme as an "image de l'ordre social" (15–16).

48. See the literature cited in nn. 37, 44, and 47. E. Patlagean attempts an overview in the article "L'histoire de l'imaginaire," in *La nouvelle histoire*, ed. Jacques Le Goff et al. (Paris, 1978), 249–69. While Patlagean defines the "histoire de l'imaginaire" as part of an "histoire des mentalités" (251), in Le Goff's view the history of mentalities has developed further into an "histoire de l'imaginaire" ("Les trois fonctions," 1196). Le Goff defines his concept of the "histoire de l'imaginaire" in *L'imaginaire médiéval* (Paris, 1985), esp. i–xxi (preface).

49. While Patlagean defines the imaginary in opposition to the real ("the totality of representations which extend beyond the limits imposed by the facts of experience and the deductive sequences which they permit"; "L'histoire de l'imaginaire," 249), Le Goff defines it in opposition to ideology and would have it restricted to the realm of the aesthetic, that is, to literature and art. See "Les trois fonctions," 1208.

50. W. Heisenberg, "Die Einheit des naturwissenschaftlichen Weltbildes" (1941, re-printed in Heisenberg, *Wandlungen in den Grundlagen der Naturwissenschaft*, 11th ed., Stuttgart, 1980), 107–28, 128.

51. Berger and Luckmann, *The Social Construction of Reality*, 1. See also H. Plessner's introduction in ibid., ix–xvi.

52. Berger, *The Social Reality of Religion*, 30.

53. W. Rösener, "Bauer, Bauerntum," in *Lexikon des Mittelalters*, vol. 1 (Munich, 1980), 1564, and K. F. Werner, "Adel," in ibid., 119. On the trifunctional scheme as "theory" see Fossier, *Enfance de l'Europe*, vol. 1, 78ff. and vol. 2, 884ff.

54. Rouche, *De l'Orient à l'Occident*, 43.

55. Poly and Bournazel, *La mutation féodale*, 233, 229.

56. C. Carozzi (discussion contribution) in Rouche, *De l'Orient à l'Occident*, 51. See Carozzi, "Les fondements de la tripartition sociale" (cited above, n. 10). Accord-ing to Carozzi, the trifunctional scheme was an "ensemble de fantasmes" in Adalbero of Laon's work (701), "hopelessly insufficient, it is a frame with cracks everywhere" (698), because "reality is indeed quadripartite" (ibid.)! For this reason the trifunctional scheme was an "ideology" (693) whose purpose was to "brutally harden social barriers" (695).

57. Vauchez, "Naissance d'une chrétienté," 90; similarly, P. Bonnassie, "Idéologie tripartite et révolution féodale," *Le Moyen Age* 86 (1980): 251–73.

58. Le Goff, "Les trois fonctions," 1208.

59. T. Struve, "Pedes rei publicae. Die dienenden Stände im Verständnis des Mittelalters," *Historische Zeitschrift* 236 (1983): 1–48, 16ff. and 35. On the trifunctional scheme as an ideology that bolstered the monarchy see also Le Goff, "Les trois fonctions," 1208–9.

60. Duby, *Les trois ordres*, 17, 19ff., 39ff., 77ff. and passim.

61. Plato, *The Republic*, trans. Desmond Lee, 2nd rev. ed. (Harmondsworth, 1987), 415a–d; 434b–c; cf. 543c and 547a.

62. Ibid., 427d–432e; cf. 434b–c.

63. Ibid., 433a, 433d.

64. The three "classes" of the polis correspond to the three elements of the mind or soul: reason, desire or appetite, and enterprise or pugnacity (438d–441c), that is, the forms of activity of the mind that occur in each individual and thus influence the shape of the community (435c, 441a; cf. 580d–581c). The same hierarchy applies here (442a). The five forms of constitution mentioned in book 4 of the *Republic* (445c–d) and explained in more detail in book 8 (543a–569c) may also be assigned to three classes. See also the discussion of functional tripartition (priests; warriors; artisans, peasants, shepherds) in the *Timaeus* (17c; 24a–b).

65. B. Sergent, "Les trois fonctions des Indo-Européens dans la Grèce ancienne: bilan critique," *Annales* 34 (1979): 1155–86.

66. Augustine, *De libero arbitrio* III, 9, 24, Migne, PL 32, 1283; English trans. *The Free Choice of the Will*, trans. Robert P. Russell, The Fathers of the Church: A New Translation, vol. 59 (Washington, D.C., 1968), 63–241, 187.

67. Augustine, *De civitate Dei/The City of God Against the Pagans*, XIX, 13, trans. William Chase Greene, 7 vols. (London and Cambridge, Mass., 1960), 6:174–75.

68. See H. Fichtenau's vivid portrayal of tenth-century society and the seven strata and groups that made it up from the perspective of "order as rank." *Lebensordnungen des 10. Jahrhunderts*, vol. 1, 11ff.

69. Oexle, "Stand, Klasse (Antike und Mittelalter)," section 3, 4.

70. Ibid., section 4.

71. See above, nn. 2 and 3; Oexle, "Stand, Klasse (Antike und Mittelalter)," section 5.

72. J. Rief, *Der Ordobegriff des jungen Augustinus* (Paderborn, 1962); H. Häring, *Die Macht des Bösen. Das Erbe Augustins*, Ökumenische Theologie, 3 (Zurich, 1979), 73ff., 105ff.

73. M. Weber, *Wirtschaft und Gesellschaft*. Studienausgabe, 5th ed. (Tübingen, 1972), 179–80, 534–35.

74. C. Loyseau, *Traité des ordres et simples dignitez* (Paris, 1613), "Avant-propos," 5ff.

75. Otto Brunner, "Das Zeitalter der Ideologien: Anfang und Ende," and "Das 'Ganze Haus' und die alteuropäische 'Ökonomik,'" in his *Neue Wege der Verfassungs- und Sozialgeschichte*, 2nd ed. (Göttingen, 1968), 45–63 and 103–27.

76. Otto Brunner, *Land und Herrschaft*, 5th ed. (Vienna, 1965), 400; *Land and Lordship: Structures of Governance in Medieval Austria*, trans. Howard Kaminsky and James V. Melton (Philadelphia, 1992).

77. Struve's suggestion that we should understand functional tripartition "less as a reflection of concrete social relations than as a mirror for the society of the time" clearly expresses this juxtaposition. See his "Pedes rei publicae" (cited above, n. 59), 19.

78. See the quotations at nn. 53 and 59 above.

79. See the quotation at n. 54 above.

80. Lucien Febvre, *Le problème de l'incroyance au XVIe siècle. La religion de Rabelais* (1942, reprint Paris, 1968), 15.

81. See above, p. 95. There is probably a general consensus among historians that the concepts of social historical scholarship do not, and cannot, achieve a total picture of historical reality. In regard to the viewpoint that the trifunctional scheme is "empty" by virtue of its tripartite form (Protokoll no. 277, as cited in note 41, 24), one should point out that social historians also use tripartite conceptual schemes (e.g., the upper, middle, and lower classes), without anyone claiming that this is a mere scheme with no connection to reality or an "empty tripartite scheme" (ibid.).

82. See Oexle, "Die 'Wirklichkeit' und das 'Wissen,' " 76ff.

83. Duby, *Les trois ordres*, 141ff., 329, and passim.

84. On the "new revolutionary concept of equality" since the second half of the eighteenth century in the context of the "new, revolutionary phase" of development of the European middle classes, see Otto Dann, "Gleichheit," in *Geschichtliche Grundbegriffe*, vol. 2, ed. Otto Brunner, Werner Conze, and Reinhard Koselleck (Stuttgart, 1975), 1014–15.

85. See Struve, "Pedes rei publicae," 19, on functional tripartition. At the core of this assessment is the modern concept of ideology. See above, n. 17.

86. Febvre, *Le problème de l'incroyance*, 15.

87. See R. H. Bowen, *German Theories of the Corporative State with Special Reference to the Period 1870–1919* (New York, 1947); K. Sontheimer, *Antidemokratisches Denken in der Weimarer Republik* (Munich, 1978); M. H. Elbow, *French Corporative Theory, 1789–1948* (New York, 1953).

88. See Oexle, "Die 'Wirklichkeit' und das 'Wissen,' " 80ff.

89. W. Eberhard, "Ansätze zur Bewältigung ideologischer Pluralität im 12. Jahrhundert: Pierre Abélard und Anselm von Havelberg," *Historisches Jahrbuch*, 105 (1985): 353–87.

90. On this, see Otto Hintze, "Weltgeschichtliche Bedingungen der Repräsentativverfassung" (1931) reprinted in *Staat und Verfassung, Gesammelte Abhandlungen*, vol. 1, 3rd ed. (Göttingen, 1970), 140–85, esp. 173–74.

91. See Fichtenau, *Lebensordnungen des 10. Jahrhunderts*, vol. 1, 293ff., and J. Fleckenstein, "Problematik und Gestalt der ottonisch-salischen Reichskirche," in *Reich und Kirche vor dem Investiturstreit*, ed. K. Schmid (Sigmaringen, 1985), 83–98. See also below 109–12.

92. G. Tellenbach, *Libertas. Kirche und Weltordnung im Zeitalter des Investiturstreites*, Forschungen zur Kirchen- und Geistesgeschichte, 7 (1936); and "Gregorianische Reform. Kritische Besinnungen," in Schmid, *Reich und Kirche*, 99–113.

93. See below, the section titled "The Trifunctional Scheme and Early Eleventh-Century Realities."

94. L. Ueding, "Die Kanones von Chalkedon in ihrer Bedeutung für Mönchtum und Klerus," in *Das Konzil von Chalkedon*, vol. 2, ed. A. Grillmeier and H. Bacht (Würzburg, 1953), 569–676; A. Zumkeller, *Das Mönchtum des heiligen Augustinus*, Cassiciacum, 11, 2nd ed. (Würzburg, 1968).

95. See below, "The Trifunctional Scheme."

96. Otto Gerhard Oexle, *Forschungen zu monastischen und geistlichen Gemeinschaften im westfränkischen Bereich*, Münstersche Mittelalter-Schriften, 31 (Munich, 1978), 120ff.

97. H. Fuhrmann, *Papst Urban II. und der Stand der Regularkanoniker*, Bayerische

Akademie der Wissenschaften, Phil.-hist. Kl., Sitzungsberichte, Jahrgang 1984, Heft 2 (1984).

98. J. Fleckenstein, "Die Rechtfertigung der geistlichen Ritterorden nach der Schrift "De laude novae militiae" Bernhards von Clairvaux," in *Die geistlichen Ritterorden Europas*, ed. J. Fleckenstein and M. Hellmann, Vorträge und Forschungen, 26 (Sigmaringen, 1980), 9–22.

99. See the statements cited above in the section, "Modern Interpretations of Medieval Interpretive Systems."

100. See above, nn. 24 and 31.

101. Marc Bloch, "Liberté et servitude personnelles au Moyen Age, particulièrement en France: contribution à une étude des classes" (1933), reprinted in M. Bloch, *Mélanges historiques*, vol. 1 (Paris, 1983), 286–355, here 355.

102. Marc Bloch, "Féodalité, Vassalité, Seigneurie: à propos de quelques travaux récents," *Annales d'Histoire Économique et Sociale* 3 (1931): 246–60, 253.

103. See above, "On the Concept of a 'History of Social Knowledge.' "

104. J. Burckhardt, *Über das Studium der Geschichte*, ed. P. Ganz (Munich, 1982), 198. On what follows see Y. Congar, "Laïc et laïcat," in *Dictionnaire de spiritualité*, vol. 9 (1975), 79ff; Oexle, "Stand, Klasse (Antike und Mittelalter)," section V/1.

105. See 1 Pet. 5:3 and Ignatius of Antioch, Eph. 11:2; J. A. Fischer, *Die apostolischen Väter*, Schriften des Urchristentums, 1 (Darmstadt, 1964), 150.

106. Thus Paul, too, refers to himself as an "idiot": in speech, not in knowledge (2 Cor. 11:6). See H. Schlier, "idiotes," in G. Kittel, *Theologisches Wörterbuch zum Neuen Testament*, vol. 3 (1938), 215–17; I. Schneider, "Das Wort idiota im antiken Latein," in *Untersuchungen ausgewählter altgriechischer sozialer Typenbegriffe und ihr Fortleben in Antike und Mittelalter*, ed. E. C. Welskopf, Soziale Typenbegriffe im alten Griechenland und ihr Fortleben in den Sprachen der Welt, 4 (Berlin, 1981), 111–31; J. Schneider, "Das Wort idiota im mittelalterlichen Latein," in Welskopf, *Untersuchungen ausgewählter altgriechischer sozialer Typenbegriffe*, 132–57.

107. R. Zerfass, *Der Streit um die Laienpredigt*, Untersuchungen zur praktischen Theologie, 2 (Freiburg i. Br., 1974), 179ff.

108. Epistle of Clement, 37, 1 and 41, 1; Fischer, *Die apostolischen Väter*, 72 and 76. The *militia* metaphor is evoked here, which is grounded in the Bible (Christian life as a kind of spiritual military service: 2 Cor. 10:3–4; cf. Eph. 6:10ff.), but also had antique roots: H. Emonds, "Geistlicher Kriegsdienst. Der Topos der *militia spiritualis* in der antiken Philosophie" (Tübingen, 1938), reprinted in the 1963 edition of A. von Harnack's 1905 *Militia Christi*, 131ff.

109. Epistle of Clement, 40, 5; Fischer, *Die apostolischen Väter*, 76.

110. See esp. P. van Beneden, "Ordo. Über den Ursprung einer kirchlichen Terminologie," *Vigiliae Christianae* 3 (1969): 161–76.

111. Demonstratio evangelica 1, 8 Migne PG 22, Sp. 76f.

112. C. 12 q. 1 c. 7; E. Friedberg (ed.), *Corpus iuris canonici*, 1 (Leipzig, reprint 1959), 678.

113. K. L. Noethlichs, "Zur Einflußnahme des Staates auf die Entwicklung eines christlichen Klerikerstandes," *Jahrbuch für Antike und Christentum* 15 (1972), 136–53; B. Kötting, *Der Zölibat in der Alten Kirche* (Münster, 1970).

114. Hintze, "Weltgeschichtliche Bedingungen der Repräsentativverfassung," 174.

115. Harnack, *Militia Christi*, 8ff.

116. Ibid., 16.

117. Ibid., 17.

118. *De opere monachorum* XIII, 14ff. CSEL 41, 554ff. On the significance of the text see the remarks by R. Arbesmann in his German translation, 1972, xivff., and Zumkeller, *Das Mönchtum des heiligen Augustinus*, 229ff.

119. See above, nn. 94 and 113.

120. K. S. Frank, *Grundzüge der Geschichte des christlichen Mönchtums*, 3rd ed. (Darmstadt, 1979); C. H. Lawrence, *Medieval Monasticism* (London, 1984).

121. On what follows, see Otto Gerhard Oexle, "Tria genera hominum. Zur Geschichte eines Deutungsschemas der sozialen Wirklichkeit in Antike und Mittelalter," in *Institutionen, Kultur und Gesellschaft im Mittelalter, Festschrift für Josef Flechenstein zu seinem 65. Geburtstag*, ed. L. Fenske, W. Rösener, and T. Zotz (Sigmaringen, 1984), 483–500.

122. Ibid., 490.

123. Ibid., 490ff.

124. See below, n. 134. This is not the place to describe the controversies over the genesis and origins of the scheme; see Oexle, "Die funktionale Dreiteilung," 33ff. G. Dumézil has traced the spread of the scheme throughout the Indo-European region; see ibid., 14 (with literature). D. Dubuisson argues for Irish-Celtic origins in "L'Irlande et la théorie médiévale des 'trois ordres,'" *Revue de l'histoire des religions* 188 (1975): 35–63, and "Le roi indo-européen et la synthèse des trois fonctions"; Niccoli, *I sacerdoti, i guerrieri, i contadini*, 9ff.

125. On (purported) documents from the 990s, see above, n. 10.

126. G. Dumézil, "L'idéologie tripartie des Indo-Européens et la Bible," *Kratylos* 4 (1959): 97–118.

127. See Le Goff, "Les trois fonctions," 1205.

128. See the titles mentioned above in nn. 10 and 124.

129. See above, "Modern Interpretations of Medieval Interpretive Schemes."

130. See above, nn. 8 and 108.

131. On the following, see Oexle, "Die funktionale Dreiteilung" and "Die 'Wirklichkeit' und das 'Wissen'."

132. Tract. IV "Ne forte quod solent" c. 11, quoted in C. Mirbt, *Quellen zur Geschichte des Papsttums und des römischen Katholizismus*, 5th ed. (Tübingen, 1934), 85–86, no. 188.

133. K. Leyser, "Early Medieval Canon Law and the Beginnings of Knighthood," in *Institutionen, Kultur und Gesellschaft im Mittelalter* (Sigmaringen, 1984), 549–66.

134. Let us recall the following texts: (1) the distinction among the imperial monasteries' services (*servitia*) to the king according to *dona*, *militia*, and *orationes*, from the time of Louis the Pious (*Corpus Consuetudinum Monasticarum* 1, 1963, 493ff.); (2) the distinction among *sacerdotes*, *milites*, and *agricultores* in the mid-ninth-century commentary to Revelation attributed to Haimo of Auxerre, in Migne, PL 117, 953 (on Rev. 1:9), which is pointed out by Duby in *Les trois ordres*, 138–39; (3) the distinction among *oratores*, *bellatores* (*nobiliores cum inferioribus*), and *inbelle vulgus* (*imbelles, pauperes*) in the *Miracula Sancti Bertini* (after 891), c. 7, in MGH SS 15.1, 513; (4) the distinction among the three groups or strata (*geferscipas*) of *gebedmen*, *fyrdmen*, and *weorcmen* in *King Alfred's* [871–99] *Old English Version of Boethius*, c. 17, ed. W. J. Sedgefield (1899), 40; (5) D. Iogna-Prat has drawn our attention to further evidence from the second half of the ninth century (Heiric of Auxerre's *Miracula S. Germani*) in his essay "Le 'baptême' du

schéma des trois ordres fonctionnels: L'apport de l'école d'Auxerre dans la seconde moitié du IXe siècle," *Annales É.S.C.* 41 (1986): 101–26. This text distinguishes among *belligerantes*, *agricolantes*, and *tertius ordo* with their functions of *militia*, *labor*, *orationes*, *et officium* (ibid., 106). This distinction was quoted at the beginning of the eleventh century at Cluny in the "Sermo de beato Maiolo" (ibid., 118). See D. Iogna-Prat, "Continence et virginité dans la conception clunisienne de l'ordre du monde autour de l'an mil," in *Académie des Inscriptions et Belles-Lettres: Comptes rendus des séances de l'année 1985* (Paris, 1985), 127–46, 131.

135. The titles mentioned above in n. 10 also discuss various tenth-century texts.

136. In his "Liber apologeticus" (994), Abbo of Fleury demonstrates his knowledge of the trifunctional scheme. He divides the church into *tres ordines, ac si tres gradus*, each according to female (*conjugatae/continentes vel viduae/virgines vel sanctimoniales*) and male (*laici* or *conjugati/clerici/monachi*). He organizes the laity into the groups of *agricolae* and *agonistae*, and the clerics into *diaconi*, *presbyteri*, and *episcopi* (Migne, PL 139, 463–64). In this case, trifunctional partition is wholly embedded in the older scheme of the "tres ordines ecclesiae." See Oexle, "Tria genera hominum," 494–95. Abbo may have become familiar with the trifunctional scheme in England. Oexle, "Die funktionale Dreiteilung," 41–42.

137. On Ælfric and Wulfstan see M. McC. Gatch, *Preaching and Theology in Anglo-Saxon England: Ælfric and Wulfstan* (Toronto, 1977); E. John, "The World of Abbot Ælfric," in *Ideal and Reality in Frankish and Anglo-Saxon Society. Studies presented to J. M. Wallace-Hadrill*, 300–16. Cf. Flori, *L'idéologie du glaive*, 123ff.

138. *Ælfric's Lives of the Saints*, ed. W. W. Skeat, vol. 2, Early English Text Society 94 (London, 1890), 120ff.

139. See F. M. Stenton, "The Decline of the Old English Monarchy," in *The Oxford History of England*, vol. 2, *Anglo-Saxon England*, 3rd ed. (Oxford, 1971), 364ff.; D. P. Kirby, *The Making of Early England* (1967), 115ff. The discussion of the trifunctional scheme in the *Miracula Sancti Bertini* and in Alfred the Great (see above, n. 136) has a similar background, see Oexle, "Die funktionale Dreiteilung," 33, 38–39.

140. B. Fehr, *Die Hirtenbriefe Ælfrics in altenglischer und lateinischer Fassung*, Bibliothek der angelsächsischen Prosa 9 (1914), 225 no. 2a c. 14.

141. See above, "Modern Interpretations of Medieval Interpretive Schemes."

142. See above, n. 108. On the patristic and Carolingian prehistory of the distinction between the two *militiae*, see text to nn. 130 and 131.

143. *Ælfric's Lives of the Saints*, 122f. v. 827ff.

144. *De laude novae militiae*, c. 1, Migne, PL 182, 921.

145. See also Ælfric's *Lives of the Saints*, 122 v. 817–18, as well as *On the Old and New Testament*, ed. S. J. Crawford, *The Old English Version of the Heptateuch*, Early English Text Society, 160 (London, 1922), 72 l. 1212 and 71 ll. 1204ff.

146. Ælfric, *On the Old and New Testament*, 72.

147. Ibid., 71 ll. 1204ff. One finds the same formulation in the "Institutes of Polity" attributed to Wulfstan (various versions) in *Die "Institutes of Polity, Civil and Ecclesiastical," ein Werk Erzbischof Wulfstans von York*, ed. K. Jost, Schweizer Anglistische Arbeiten, 47 (1959), 55ff. On further documents, see Oexle, "Die funktionale Dreiteilung," 41 with nn. 246 and 248. These formulations take up the version of the scheme presented in Alfred the Great's work. See Oexle, ibid., 33.

148. Oexle, "Die funktionale Dreiteilung," 41ff. The fact that no comparable condi-

tions of disorder prevailed in Germany at the time may well be the explanation for the much later appearance there of the trifunctional scheme. Ibid., 50.

149. See above, n. 12, and *Gesta episcoporum Cameracensium* III, 52 in MGH SS 7, S. 485. On the dating of Gerard's sermon, see Oexle, "Die funktionale Dreiteilung," 44 with n. 264a, and "Die 'Wirklichkeit' und das 'Wissen,'" 74f.

150. B. Töpfer, *Volk und Kirche zur Zeit der beginnenden Gottesfriedensbewegung in Frankreich*, Neue Beiträge zur Geschichtswissenschaft 1 (Berlin, 1957), 103; H. Hoffmann, *Gottesfriede und Treuga Dei*, Schriften der MGH, 20 (Stuttgart, 1964), 57ff.

151. See Oexle, "Die funktionale Dreiteilung," 42ff., and below, text to nn. 159–72.

152. On the structure of Adalbero's poem see Oexle, "Die funktionale Dreiteilung," 20ff.

153. C. Erdmann, *Die Entstehung des Kreuzzugsgedankens*, Forschungen zur Kirchen- und Geistesgeschichte, 6 (Stuttgart, 1935, reprint 1955), 343.

154. *Transformatio ordinis*: v. 36, Carozzi, *Adalbéron de Laon, Poème au roi Robert*, 4. The other passages cited are at v. 112ff. and 155–56, ibid., 8 and 12. The way in which monks are equipped with the attributes of knights but—and herein lies the caustic point—not only with these (v. 92ff., ibid., 8), deserves detailed analysis.

155. For the details, see Oexle, "Die funktionale Dreiteilung," 22f.

156. Erdmann, *Die Entstehung des Kreuzzugsgedankens*, 62ff.

157. Erdmann, *Die Entstehung des Kreuzzugsgedankens*, 64. On the limitations of the assessment of Adalbero as a "traitor," "conservative," and "reactionary," see Oexle, "Die funktionale Dreiteilung," 16ff., esp. 18–19.

158. Oexle, "Die funktionale Dreiteilung," 23.

159. Töpfer, *Volk und Kirche zur Zeit der beginnenden Gottesfriedensbewegung*, 91ff.; Hoffmann, *Gottesfriede und Treuga Dei*, 104ff.; J. Semmler, "Facti sunt milites domni Ildebrandi omnibus . . . in stuporem," in *Das Ritterbild in Mittelalter und Renaissance*, Studia humaniora. Düsseldorfer Studien zu Mittelalter und Renaissance, 1 (Düsseldorf, 1985), 11–35, esp. 26ff.

160. This is emphasized by Semmler in "Facti sunt milites," 26–27.

161. Ambrose, *De officiis ministrorum* I, 35, ed. A. Cavasin (Turin, 1938), 171.

162. Semmler, "Facti sunt milites," 28.

163. See above, text to n. 132. The same view was expressed by Bishop Fulbert of Chartres. Oexle, "Die funktionale Dreiteilung," 45–46.

164. *Gesta episcoporum Cameracensium* III, 27, in MGH SS 7, 474, with the explanation: "Huic enim orare, illi vero pugnare tribuitur. Igitur regum esse, seditiones virtute compescere, bella sedare, pacis commercia dilatare; episcoporum vero, reges ut viriliter pro salute patriae pugnent monere, ut vincant orare."

165. Ibid., 474.

166. See above, n. 149.

167. Erdmann, *Die Entstehung des Kreuzzugsgedankens*.

168. On Leo IX, the "first pope to derive his wars from religion on principle," who had already commanded a militia as bishop of Toul, see Erdmann, *Die Entstehung des Kreuzzugsgedankens*, 107ff. (quotation on 108), and Semmler, "Facti sunt milites," 22ff. and 26ff.

169. Erdmann, *Die Entstehung des Kreuzzugsgedankens*, 134ff. (quotation on 161) and 185ff.; see also Semmler, "Facti sunt milites."

170. E. Caspar (ed.), *Das Register Gregors VII.*, vol. 1, 2nd ed. (Berlin, 1955), 166 (II, 31), see also II, 37, in ibid., 173.

171. Erdmann, *Die Entstehung des Kreuzzugsgedankens*, 165 and 188ff.

172. Tellenbach, *Libertas. Kirche und Weltordnung im Zeitalter des Investiturstreits*, 151ff. ("The struggle for proper order in the Christian world").

173. Ibid., 187. The central evidence here is Gregory's programmatic letter of 1081 to Bishop Hermann of Metz. Caspar (ed.), *Das Register Gregors VII.*, VIII, 21, vol. 2, 544ff.

174. J. Fleckenstein, "Zur Frage der Abgrenzung von Bauer und Ritter," in *Wort und Begriff "Bauer*," ed. R. Wenskus, H. Jankuhn, and K. Grinda, Abhandlungen der Akademie der Wissenschaften in Göttingen, Phil.-hist. Kl., Dritte Folge, 89 (Göttingen, 1975), 246–53, 246. See also J. Fleckenstein, "Adel und Kriegertum und ihre Wandlung im Karolingerreich," in *Nascità dell'Europa ed Europa carolingia: un'equazione da verificare*, Settimane di Studio del Centro Italiano di Studi sull'Alto Medioevo, 27 (Spoleto, 1981), 67–94; and W. Rösener, "Bauer und Ritter im Hochmittelalter. Aspekte ihrer Lebensform, Standesbildung und sozialen Differenzierung im 12. und 13. Jahrhundert," in *Institutionen, Kultur und Gesellschaft im Mittelalter* (Sigmaringen, 1984), 665–92.

175. Otto Hintze, "Staatverfassung und Heeresverfassung" (Dresden, 1906), reprinted in Hintze, *Staat und Verfassung*, 52–83, 62.

176. For an overview see W. Rösener, *Bauern im Mittelalter* (Munich, 1985), 18ff., esp. 27ff.; the quotations that follow are on 29–30.

177. See the summary by J. Fleckenstein, "Über Ritter und Rittertum: Zur Erforschung einer mittelalterlichen Lebensform," in *Mittelalterforschung*, Forschung und Information, 29 (Berlin, 1981), 104–14, esp. 108ff.

178. Just as the terms *laborator* and *agricultor* refer to "peasants," the terms *bellator* and *pugnator* may be applied to the "knights" (*miles*). The distinction frequently made in the literature, in view of the trifunctional scheme, between "warriors" and "knights" proves untenable in the light of the texts themselves; see the remarks made by Ælfric (see above, nn. 140 and 146). For Adalbero of Laon and Gerard of Cambrai, too, the *bellator/pugnator* is neither merely identical to kings and princes (see below, n. 189), nor do the terms refer only to warriors. The portrayal of the monk as a knight (*miles*) (see above, n. 154) shows that by Adalbero's day the transformation of the warrior into a knight (in the sense of a horseman in heavy armor) was complete; see Fleckenstein, "Über Ritter und Rittertum," 106f.

179. Oexle, "Die funktionale Dreiteilung," 49; and "Tria genera hominum," 498f. On what follows, see J. Semmler, "Karl der Große und das fränkische Mönchtum," in *Das geistige Leben* (Karl der Große 2), ed. B. Bischoff, 2nd ed. (Düsseldorf, 1966), 255–89; A. A. Häußling, *Mönchskonvent und Eucharistiefeier*, Liturgiewissenschaftliche Quellen und Forschungen, 58 (Münster, 1973); A. Angenendt, "Pirmin und Bonifatius," in *Mönchtum, Episkopat und Adel zur Gründungszeit des Klosters Reichenau*, ed. A. Borst, Vorträge und Forschungen, 20 (Sigmaringen, 1974), 251–304, 252ff. and 290ff.

180. Oexle, *Forschungen zu monastischen und geistlichen Gemeinschaften*, 101ff. and 110f.

181. G. Tellenbach, "Zum Wesen der Cluniacenser," *Saeculum* 9 (1958): 370–78, esp. 376.

182. See text at n. 112 above.

183. Bonizo, *Liber de vita christiana* VII, 28, ed. E. Perels, Texte zur Geschichte des

römischen und kanonischen Rechts im Mittelalter, 1 (Berlin, 1930), 248–49. See Erdmann, *Die Entstehung des Kreuzzugsgedanken*, 235ff.

184. The idea of commitment to the *respublica* is of Roman origin (Erdmann, *Die Entstehung des Kreuzzugsgedanken*, 236), while the idea of the *defensio* of the *pauperes* comes from early medieval monarchical and aristocratic ethics. See Oexle, "Die funktionale Dreiteilung," 37.

185. See above, text to n. 140. Abbo of Fleury (see above, n. 136) writes of the "agonistae: . . . contenti stipendiis militiae, non se collidunt in utero matris suae (sc. Ecclesiae), verum omni sagacitate expugnant adversarios sanctae Dei Ecclesiae," in Migne, PL 139, 464.

186. V. 282ff., Carozzi, ed., Adalbéron de Laon, *Poème au roi Robert*, 20.

187. H.-W. Goetz, "Kirchenschutz, Rechtswahrung und Reform. Zu den Zielen und zum Wesen der frühen Gottesfriedensbewegung in Frankreich," *Francia* 11 (1983): 193–239, 209ff.; quotation on 214.

188. See the text by Ælfric cited above, n. 140.

189. Quoted here according to the manuscript. See Oexle, "Die funktionale Dreiteilung," 24.

190. *Gesta episcoporum Cameracensium* III, 52, in MGH SS 7, 485: "Oratorum a saeculi vacans negotiis dum ad Deum vadit intentio, pugnatoribus debet, quod sancto secura vacat otio; agricultoribus, quod eorum laboribus corporali pascitur cibo. Nihilominus agricultores ad Deum levantur oratorum precibus, et vectigalium solatiantur armorumque delicta piorum quos tuentur expiat precatio sancta, foventur ut dictum est mutuo. Quibus—dum Abraham et Iosue et David ex voce Domini arma tulisse in prelium vetus ostendit pagina, et sacerdotes gladio accingunt reges, regnante gratia in nostra matre aecclesia Dei sponsa—officium non est in culpa, si deest peccatum in conscientia."

191. See above, n. 190.

192. Hoffmann, *Gottesfriede und Treuga Dei*, 60. Like Ælfric before him (see above, n. 146), Gerard uses Rom. 13:4 ("Hos [sc. pugnatores] et apostolus ministros Dei appellat, ita dicens: 'Minister enim Dei est, vindex in iram,' subinferens: 'Non enim sine causa gladium portat'") to justify the *pugnatores*. Hoffmann, 485–86.

193. J. Flori, *L'idéologie du glaive*, 17 and 18–19.

194. Goetz, "Kirchenschutz, Rechtswahrung und Reform," 215 and 217.

195. I refer the reader to my discussion in "Die funktionale Dreiteilung" (27ff.) and "Die 'Wirklichkeit' und das 'Wissen'" (83–84). For full references see n. 1 above.

196. *Ælfric's Lives of the Saints*, v. 815 and 819, 120ff.; *Die Hirtenbriefe Ælfrics*, 1. 21, 225; "On the Old and New Testament," l. 1208, 71. Cf. Abbo of Fleury's *Liber apologeticus*: "agricolae quidem insudant agriculturae et diversis artibus in opere rustico, unde sustenatur totius Ecclesiae multitudo." Migne, PL 139, 463–64.

197. In the "Institutes of Polity, Civil and Ecclesiastical" attributed to Wulfstan, 56. See above, n. 147.

198. See above, n. 190.

199. On the connotations of *labor*, see Oexle, "Die funktionale Dreiteilung," 30 with nn. 182 and 183.

200. On this subject in antiquity and the modern period, see K. Rothe, "Herrschaft und Knechtschaft," in *Historisches Wörterbuch der Philosophie*, vol. 3 (1974), 1088–96; H. Mayer, "Herrschaft und Knechtschaft. Hegels Deutung, ihre literarischen Ursprünge und Folgen," *Jahrbuch der Deutschen Schillergesellschaft* 15 (1971): 251–79, esp. 256ff.

201. Augustine, *De civitate Dei* XIX, 14, 399. On some early medieval echoes (Boethius, Odilo of Cluny), see Oexle, "Die funktionale Dreiteilung," 31.

202. Quoted here according to the manuscript. See Oexle, "Die funktionale Dreiteilung," 30.

203. Gregory the Great, *Moralia* 21, 15, 22, Migne, PL 76, 203; see also the *Regula pastoralis* II, 6 in ibid., 77, 34.

204. Isidore, *Sententiarum libri tres* III, 47, Migne PL 83, 717. On the antique background to this attitude, see Rothe, "Herrschaft und Knechtschaft," 1088ff.

205. This is already noted in Oexle, "Die funktionale Dreiteilung," 27ff. The objections to this raised by J. Fried in "Über den Universalismus der Freiheit im Mittelalter," *Historische Zeitschrift* 240 (1985): 324 n. 42, are based on misunderstandings. In subjecting the life of the two lay estates to the *lex humana* (Carmen v. 276–77, Carozzi, 20) Adalbero naturally does not deny that the social order was established by God; this was, after all, the precondition for all corporative thinking. He does, however, deny that the inequality of *nobilis* (*dominus*) and *servus* is a consequence of divine punishment.

206. On Plato, see above, "Modern Interpretations of Medieval Interpretive Schemes." Cf. Oexle, "Stand, Klasse (Antike und Mittelalter)," sections 3/3, 4/1, 5/4.

207. Ibid., section 4/1.

208. Le Goff, "Les trois fonctions," 1204.

209. Ibid., 1206 and 1208.

210. See above, "On the Concept of a 'History of Social Knowledge'" and "Modern Interpretations of Medieval Interpretive Schemes."

211. It is in this sense that scholars have proposed that the idea of knighthood (*Rittertum*) was an "ecclesiastical" ideology, the result of "ecclesiastical access to those who bore arms," a "massive ideologization," and "the exercise of heteronomy over those who bear arms . . . by ecclesiastical forces." Gerd Althoff, "Nunc fiant Christi milites, qui dudum extiterunt raptores. Zur Entstehung von Rittertum und Ritterethos," *Saeculum* 32 (1981): 317–33, 331–32.

212. Le Goff, "Les trois fonctions," 1204.

213. Gurevich, "Medieval Culture and Mentality," 183ff., in which he grapples with the interpretation of the history of the trifunctional scheme in Georges Duby's *Les trois ordres*.

214. Gurevich, "Medieval Culture and Mentality," 185. One can also understand the findings in Jacques Le Goff's book *La naissance du Purgatoire* (Paris, 1981) in this sense.

215. Gurevich, "Medieval Culture and Mentality," 186. The remark is directed against Duby's assessment of functional tripartition: "And if we concur with this view, then perhaps some of the assertions in Duby's book about the link between the trifunctional scheme and the feudal revolution and the need for the ruling class to keep the masses in check should be formulated in a more guarded and hypothetical form; for, if such a link did exist, then it was scarcely so direct and immediate" (Duby, *Les trois ordres*).

216. See Berger and Luckmann, *The Social Construction of Reality*, 123ff.

217. See above, text to nn. 42, 84–89.

218. The question of the dissemination of the trifunctional scheme (e.g., in polemics and sermons) cannot be discussed here. See Oexle, "Die funktionale Dreiteilung," 49 with n. 298, and "Adalbero von Laon," 635ff.

219. See above, "The Trifunctional Scheme and Early Eleventh-Century Realities," on Adalbero of Laon's polemic against the Cluniacs and Gerard of Cambrai's treatment of the problem of the militias raised and commanded by bishops.

220. Fleckenstein, "Die Rechtfertigung der geistlichen Ritterorden nach der Schrift 'De laude novae militiae' Bernhards von Clairvaux," 17. See the text at n. 144 above.

221. Zerfass, *Der Streit um die Laienpredigt*, esp. 178ff.

222. Y. Congar, "Aspects ecclésiologiques de la querelle entre mendiants et séculiers dans la seconde moitié du XIIIᵉ siècle et le début du XIVᵉ," *Archives d'histoire doctrinale et littéraire du Moyen Age* 36 (1961): 35–151; Zerfass, *Der Streit um die Laienpredigt*, 321ff. and 328ff.

223. Oexle, "Die funktionale Dreiteilung," 49–50.

224. See Otto Brunner, "Stadt und Bürgertum in der europäischen Geschichte," in O. Brunner, *Neue Wege der Verfassungs- und Sozialgeschichte*, 213–24; E. Ennen, *Die europäische Stadt des Mittelalters*, 2nd ed. (Göttingen, 1975).

225. J. Le Goff, *Les intellectuels au Moyen Age* (Paris, 1957); A. B. Cobban, *The Medieval Universities: Their Development and Organization* (London, 1975); P. Weimar (ed.), *Die Renaissance der Wissenschaften im 12. Jahrhundert*, Züricher Hochschulforum, 2 (Zurich, 1981); Otto Gerhard Oexle, "Alteuropäische Voraussetzungen des Bildungs-bürgertums—Universitäten, Gelehrte und Studierte," in *Bildungsbürgertum im 19. Jahrhundert*, vol. 1, ed. Werner Conze and Jürgen Kocka, Industrielle Welt, 38 (Stuttgart, 1985), 29–78.

226. An early example is Bernard of Clairvaux's sermon to the clergy of Cologne (1147), in Gaufrid of Auxerre, *Declamationes* c. 10, in Migne, PL 184, 443. A pseudo-Bedan text, "De quatuor ordinibus," which distinguishes among and defines *oratores*, *defensores* (*milites*), *mercatores*, and *laboratores* (in ibid., 94, cols. 556–57), was probably also written in the twelfth century.

227. See Le Goff, "Les trois fonctions," 1209–10, with references to (then) recent scholarly approaches and controversies.

228. R. Mohl's *The Three Estates in Medieval and Renaissance Literature* (New York, 1933) provides rich material that has not yet been fully exploited; see also Niccoli, *I sacerdoti, i guerrieri, i contadini*, 23ff., 35ff., 44ff.

229. See Niccoli's *I sacerdoti, i guerrieri, i contadini*, and the contribution by T. und R. Wohlfeil in Schulze, *Ständische Gesellschaft und Mobilität* (see unnumbered note).

230. See Oexle, "Stand, Klasse (Antike und Mittelalter)," section 5 and the literature listed there.

231. On the *tres status totius regni* in France as well as the term "third estate" (*tiers état, tiers membre*), which we find since the beginning of the fifteenth century, see Oexle, "Stand, Klasse (Antike und Mittelalter)," and "Die funktionale Dreiteilung als Deutungsschemata."

232. This is emphasized by Hintze in "Weltgeschichtliche Bedingungen der Repräsentativverfassung," 173.

233. This division of the estates goes back to Martin Luther. See W. Maurer, *Luthers Lehre von den drei Hierarchien und ihr mittelalterlicher Hintergrund*, Bayer. Akad. der Wiss., Phil.-hist. Kl., Sitzungsberichte, 4 (Munich, 1970); R. Schwarz, "Luthers Lehre von den drei Ständen und die drei Dimensionen der Ethik," *Lutherjahrbuch* 45 (1978): 15–34, and "Ecclesia, oeconomia, politia. Sozialgeschichtliche und fundamentalethische Aspekte der protestantischen Drei-Stände-Theorie," in H. Renz and F. W. Graf (eds), *Troeltsch-Studien* 3 (1984): 78–88.

234. U. Engelhardt, *"Bildungsbürgertum." Begriffs- und Dogmengeschichte eines Etiketts*, Industrielle Welt, 43 (Stuttgart, 1986), 44ff.

235. The term was already used in 1115 by Rupert of Deutz. See Migne, PL 169, 203–4. On this subject more generally see P. Classen, "Die Hohen Schulen und die Gesellschaft im 12. Jahrhundert," *Archiv für Kulturgeschichte* 48 (1966): 155–80, 171ff.; I. Schneider, "Das Wort idiota im mittelalterlichen Latein"; K. Schreiner, "Laienbildung als Herausforderung für Kirche und Gesellschaft," *Zeitschrift für Historische Forchung* 11 (1984): 257–354, 327ff.

236. See the quotation from the "Decree" above, at n. 112.

237. Oexle, "Alteuropäische Voraussetzungen des Bildungsbürgertums," 76ff.

238. See the corresponding meanings of the French words *clerc* (*lettré, savant, expert, intellectuel*; also of *employé* in the sense of *secrétaire*) and the English *clerk*.

239. In the twelfth century, jurists were referred to as "priests of the law" (*iuris interpretes iuris sacerdotes*), Ernst H. Kantorowicz, *The King's Two Bodies* (Princeton, 1957), 118 with n. 89.

240. Philip of Harvengt (d. 1183), ep. 16, in Migne, PL 203, 149.

241. Oexle, "Alteuropäische Voraussetzungen des Bildungsbürgertums," 40ff., 66ff.

242. A. Haverkamp, "Tenxwind von Andernach und Hildegard von Bingen. Zwei 'Weltanschauungen' in der Mitte des 12. Jahrhunderts," in *Institutionen, Kultur und Gesellschaft im Mittelalter* (Sigmaringen, 1984), 515–48, with an edition of the texts on 543ff.

243. Ibid., 544–45.

244. Ibid., 547–48.

245. Ibid., 539.

246. Ibid., 540–51.

247. See above, nn. 3, 4, 205, and 206. See also Oexle, "Stand, Klasse (Antike und Mittelalter)," sections 4 and 5.

248. Raoul Manselli, *San Francesco*, 3rd rev. ed. (Rome, 1982), esp. 45ff., 66ff., and 74ff.

249. *Testament*, 14/15, ed. C. Esser, in *Opuscula sancti patris Francisci Assisiensis*, Bibliotheca franciscana ascetica Medii Aevi, 12 (Grottaferrata and Rome, 1978), 310.

250. *Regula non bullata* c. 7, 2, in ibid., 253.

251. *Testament*, 19, in ibid., 311.

252. On this, see O. G. Oexle, "Armut und Armenfürsoge um 1200. Ein Beitrag zum Verständnis der freiwilligen Armut bei Elisabeth von Tübingen," in *Sankt Elisabeth, Fürstin—Dienerin—Heilige* (Sigmaringen, 1981), 78–100, 80–81.

253. On the dialectic between the abolition of all estates, the norm of "remaining in one's place" and the justification for new estates in the New Testament, see Oexle, "Stand, Klasse (Antike und Mittelalter)," section 4.

254. *Regula non bullata* c. 23, 7, 290f.

255. M. Werner, "Die Heilige Elisabeth und die Anfänge des Deutschen Ordens in Marburg," in *Marburger Geschichte*, ed. E. Dettmering and R. Grenz (1980), 121–64, 122ff.; Oexle, "Armut und Armenfürsoge um 1200," 80f.

256. Oexle, "Stand, Klasse (Antike und Mittelalter)," section 4.

257. The central text here is the vocation of the "tax collector" (*homo sedens in teloneo*; Matthew in Mt. 9:9); compare the condemnation of the occupation of tax collector (*portitor*) and its classification under the base occupations (*artificia et quaestus sordidi*) by Cicero, *De off.* I, 42 (150).

258. E. Auerbach's *Mimesis: The Representation of Reality in Western Literature*, trans. Willard R. Trask (Princeton, 1953) (esp. 41ff.), remains the best and clearest account.

259. Gal. 3:28: "non est Iudaeus neque Graecus, non est servus neque liber, non est masculus et femina; omnes enim vos unus estis in Christo Iesu." On this, see H. Schlier, *Der Brief an die Galater*, 4th ed. (Göttingen, 1965), quotation on 174–75.

260. On the possibilities of bringing together the two polar opposites, see T. Boman, *Das hebräische Denken im Vergleich mit dem griechischen*, 7th ed. (Göttingen, 1983).

261. The term "nominalism" is frequently considered problematic. See F. Hoffmann's (largely unsatisfactory) discussion in the article "Nominalismus I" in *Historisches Wörterbuch der Philosophie*, vol. 6 (1984), 874–84. For a stimulating and varied introduction, see R. Imbach (ed)., *Wilhelm von Ockham, Texte zur Theorie der Erkenntis und der Wissenschaft* (Stuttgart, 1984). See also the thorough accounts by W. Vossenkuhl, "Wilhelm von Ockham—Gestalt und Werk," in *Wilhelm von Ockham. Das Risiko modern zu denken*, ed. O. Aicher, G. Greindl, and W. Vossenkuhl (Munich, 1986), 97–179, esp. 117ff. and 141ff.; and K. Flasch, *Das philosophische Denken im Mittelalter von Augustin zu Machiavelli* (Stuttgart, 1986), 441ff.

262. H. Rombach, *Substanz, System, Struktur, Die Ontologie des Funktionalismus und der philosophische Hintergrund der modernen Wissenschaft*, vol. 1, 2nd ed. (Freiburg, 1981), 80.

263. Rombach, *Substanz, System, Struktur*, vol. 1, 78ff.; J. Miethke, *Ockhams Weg zur Sozialphilosophie* (Berlin, 1969); G. Leff, *William of Ockham: The Metamorphosis of Scholastic Discourse* (Manchester, 1975). Imbach provides a very good annotated bibliography in *Wilhelm von Ockham, Texte zur Theorie der Erkenntnis und der Wissenschaft*, 240ff.

264. Imbach, *Wilhelm von Ockham*, 134–35.

265. On nominalism as a mere destruction of metaphysics, see R. Guardini, *Das Ende der Neuzeit* (Basel, 1950), esp. 39ff. ("The Emergence of the Modern Conception of the World") and G. Siewerth, *Das Schicksal der Metaphysik von Thomas zu Heidegger*, Horizonte, 6 (Einsiedln, 1959), 87ff., esp. 114ff. On similar, although of course differently justified, Protestant assessments, see C. T. Davis, "Ockham and the Zeitgeist," in *The Pursuit of Holiness in Late Medieval and Renaissance Religion*, ed. Heiko A. Oberman, Studies in Medieval and Reformation Thought 10 (Leiden, 1974), 59–65, 60.

266. This is H. Blumenberg's thesis in *Die Legitimität der Neuzeit* (1966, expanded and revised edition in four parts, 1973–76, 3rd ed. 1984). Here, too, modern "mentalities" (see above, n. 80) have had the effect of rendering religion and science conceivable only as antagonists. See also W. Pannenberg, "Die christliche Legitimität der Neuzeit," in his *Gottesgedanke und menschliche Freiheit* (Göttingen, 1972), 114–28.

267. Rombach, *Substanz, System, Struktur*, vol. 1, 112. See also Imbach's apt observation that Ockham's "conservative motivation, whose intention was more to restrict than to liberate philosophical reason," and which "drew its strength from an unshakeable Christian faith" and produced such "emancipatory effects and awakened late medieval thought from its dogmatic slumber," represents one of the "most instructive paradoxes in the history of philosophy" (*Wilhelm von Ockham*, 9).

268. Rombach, *Substanz, System, Struktur*, vol. 1, 340.

269. William of Ockham, *Scriptum in librum primum Sententiarum*, dist. 3, q. VI, ed. S. Brown and G. Gäl, *Guillelmi de Ockham opera philosophica et theologica*, vol. 2 (St. Bonaventure, N.Y., 1970), 492ff. On Ockham's epistemology, see H. Boeder, *Topologie der Metaphysik*, Orbis Academicus, Sonderband 5 (Freiburg, 1980), 313ff.

270. See above, "Modern Interpretations of Medieval Interpretive Schemes."

271. On true knowledge (*veritas*) as *adaequatio* (*conformitas*) *intellectus et rei*, see

Thomas Aquinas, *Summa theol.* I q. 16 art. 1 and 2, *Sancti Thomae Aquinatis opera omnia,* vol. 4, 1888, 206ff., and *De veritate* I, in ibid., vol. 3 (1980), 1ff.

272. Imbach, *Wilhelm von Ockham,* 97–98.

273. Rombach, *Substanz, System, Struktur,* vol. 1, 86ff. and 90; quotation on 90.

274. Ibid., 92–93.

275. Imbach, *Wilhelm von Ockham,* 7.

276. Troeltsch, *Die Soziallehren der christlichen Kirchen und Gruppen,* 283–84.

277. Looking back at the history of European scholarship, we find the same conflict in the initial persistence of Aristotelean science during the early modern period.

278. Troeltsch, *Die Soziallehren der christlichen Kirchen und Gruppen,* 286ff.; cf. E. Iserloh, J. Glazik, and H. Jedin, *Reformation, katholische Reform und Gegenreformation,* Handbuch der Kirchengeschichte, vol. 4 (1967), 561ff., 573ff.

279. Heiko A. Oberman, *Luther* (Berlin, 1981), 119ff.

280. See above, n. 233.

281. See above, "On the Concept of a 'History of Social Knowledge'" and "Modern Interpretations of Medieval Interpretive Schemes."

282. Cf. Otto Gerhard Oexle, "Die Geschichtswissenschaft im Zeichen des Historismus. Bemerkungen zum Standort der Geschichtsforschung," *Historische Zeitschrift* 238 (1984): 17–55, esp. 19–20, 30ff., and 44ff., and "Alteuropäische Voraussetzungen des Bildungsbürgertums," 66ff.

283. See above, 93 with nn. 16–18. On the genesis of the modern phenomenon of ideology, see also H. Rombach, *Die Gegenwart der Philosophie* (Freiburg, 1962), 88ff.

284. Oexle, "Die Geschichtswissenschaft im Zeichen des Historismus," 30ff., 41ff., 53ff.

285. Ibid., and Oexle, "Sozialgeschichte—Begriffsgeschichte—Wissenschaftsgeschichte," 329ff., 337ff.; H. Schulze, "Otto Hintzes Geschichtstheorie," in *Otto Hintze und die moderne Geschichtswissenschaft,* ed. O. Büsch and M. Erbe, Einzelveröffentlichungen der Historischen Kommission zu Berlin, 38 (Berlin, 1983), 125–33, 131–32.

286. Oexle, "Die Geschichtswissenschaft im Zeichen des Historismus," 45 with n. 114.

287. See the references in nn. 24, 31, 101, and 102 above. Cf. H. Schulze, "Mentalitätsgeschichte—Chancen und Grenzen eines Paradigmas der französischen Geschichtswissenschaft," 259–60.

288. See G. Lardreau's essay "Georges Duby, ou la nouvelle positivité de l'histoire," 9ff.

289. Marc Bloch, "Technique et évolution sociale: réflexions d'un historien," in M. Bloch, *Mélanges historiques,* vol. 2 (Paris, 1983), 833–38, 838.

PART II

TRANSFORMING

FOUR

Liturgy and Legitimation, or How the Gallo-Romans Ended the Roman Empire

Bernhard Jussen

The Aristocrat Becomes a Bishop: Perspectives on the Recasting of the Political and Social Order

In the year 587, when the historian Georgius Florentius Gregorius occupied the office of Bishop of Tours, there appeared in the city a figure whose aspect and actions were immediately familiar to contemporaries: "He wore a tunic and a hood of goat's hair, and in public practised abstinence in the matter of food and drink." The people understood the man's appearance and behavior at once, and brought him large numbers of the blind and sick, expecting them to be healed. But the bishop's men also understood immediately—and made short work of the interloper: "he was taken by our people [*nostri*], and was expelled from the territory of the city."[1]

The sixth-century historian took this episode from the year 587 as an opportunity to tell another, similar story. Another such figure was said to have appeared in the city a few years earlier: "He was clad in a long sleeveless tunic, over which was a fine linen mantle, and wore a cross from which hung a number of little flasks containing, as he said, holy oil." He had said that he came from Spain, bearing relics of Saint Vincent and Saint Felix.[2] Up to this point the tale resembled the first one, and the outcome would also prove similar. Before ending the story, though, the chronicler would introduce a few conflict-filled interludes.

Having arrived at the church of St. Martin, the peculiar man sent word to the bishop asking him to "Come forth to greet the sacred relics." The bishop refused, for which he offered the readers of his *History* an exceptionally weak excuse: it was already evening and he was at table. Thus he had asked the wanderer to wait until the next day, at which point he would go out to meet the relics (*mane procedemus ad occursum*). The bishop and chronicler describes the events of the next day as an admission of his own helplessness, as if the ascetic had led him around by the nose. The ascetic "entered" (*advenit*) before Gregory could prepare the reception of the relics, and stopped first at Gregory's house. Gregory, to be sure, presents himself to his readers (and to the ascetic) as an innocent, asking in mock surprise "what his conduct meant," but the ascetic knew what he was doing when he complained that it "was thy duty to receive (*occursus*) us with more respect." With these words he left the bishop standing where he was and went alone into the church, where he performed the necessary liturgy without Gregory, raised his cross from time to time, and finally ended his completely unhindered entrance and was on his way (*abiit*).[3]

For the bishop and chronicler Gregory this peripatetic charismatic, who obviously managed to get the better of him, was virtually an apocalyptic sign. He associated the appearance of this person—who staged his disregard (*me post-posito*) for the local ruler and bishop so provocatively in the middle of the city—with the Scripture of Matthew 24:24 about the last days: "false Christs and false prophets will arise and show great signs and wonders, so as to lead astray, if possible, even the elect." The man who scorned episcopal authority signaled the end of the world—the classic pseudoprophet. Even the dating of the occurrence within the *History* followed the rhythm of the apocalyptic numbers: the episode occurred seven years before the appearance of a second charismatic.[4]

Gregory imbedded his apocalyptic message to the reader within the story of a mutual provocation. The bishop respected the foreign relics, and also wished to give them their due, without, however, doing any *honor* to the ascetic. The ascetic, for his part, recognized the bishop's sovereignty over the city's churches, but refused to bow to his schedule. With astonishing plainness the chronicler translates the conventional turn of phrase "to receive the relics" into a naked clash over social status. When Gregory did not meet the request "to receive *the relics*" the ascetic soon protested openly, "You should have prepared *us* a better reception."

This excerpt from a long and instructive account in Gregory's *History* describes from the perspective of one of the parties a conflict of authority that is familiar to us from many other examples throughout the Middle Ages: the conflict between the standardized authority of the episcopate and the extraordinary authority of ascetic charisma. If we read this story to the end we encounter a solution to the conflict that is no less familiar. The officeholder asserted himself, and, after a few further provocations, the ascetic challenger to episcopal authority found himself in prison.[5] This was, however, only the superficial and temporary solution to an everyday constellation that proved itself all but impossible to master.

GAUL BETWEEN 400 AND 600: A TEST CASE FOR
THE STUDY OF CULTURAL TRANSFORMATIONS

If we use an account of an apocalyptic "pseudoprophet" from Gregory's *History* as an introduction to a study of processes of political and social change here, there is a simple reason for this. The conflictual constellation that the chronicler Gregory formulated from his own viewpoint around the year 600, and which would recur during the centuries that followed, had scarcely been visible even in outline two hundred years before. It was the product of an unusually all-encompassing political and social transformation: the transformation of Gallia from the Roman *imperium* to the Frankish *regnum*. Within a period of two hundred years (400–600), a single region of the disintegrating empire experienced a reordering of the forms of rule, legitimation, and representation, and indeed of the entire cultural semantics. Gregory's tale of the apocalyptic wanderer is a comparatively entertaining vantage point from which to examine the basic lines of this transformation.

Let us begin with the commonsense version of things: we can easily agree that the constellation in Gregory's account is particularly significant for the mind-set of the early and high Middle Ages. A bishop ruled not only over the souls of believers, but also over the city's prisons. The political authority of the bishops over the cities is regarded as a central and particularly stable form of political and social order in the Middle Ages, and also as the first elaborated form of order in the new empire more generally. The view that the role of the Merovingian bishops "anticipates that of the Carolingian or Ottonian-Salian 'imperial bishop' " is not particularly controversial.[6] The presence of ascetics was a lasting and perhaps *the* central challenge to this form of rule. The relationship between ascetics and the bishops who were political rulers by virtue of their office was characterized by a tenuous balance, a temporary solution that, no sooner had it become stabilized, was challenged anew. "Columbanus" is scholarly shorthand for the first great challenge to this equilibrium at the beginning of the seventh century.[7] This constellation was the product of those very transformations that are at issue here. In order to understand the "typically medieval" conflict situation in Gregory's story of the pseudoprophet we need to return to the changes that had been under way since about 400. Around that time the lines of conflict between itinerant ascetics and episcopal rulers were scarcely visible, even in outline, although ascetics roamed and bishops ruled everywhere.

From the standpoint of institutional history, it is methodologically tempting to investigate the transformations in Gaul between antiquity and the Middle Ages, since in this case a study of the law clearly does not get us very far. One of the fundamental medieval forms of rule, rule by bishops, was conceived neither by the antique emperors nor by the early medieval kings. The historical evidence can be sketched in a few sentences, and it forces us to abandon the juridical viewpoint: around 400 the emperors disappeared from Gaul and soon all of the imperial coordinates and techniques for distinguishing social hierarchy lost their context and hence their authority.[8] At this time, around 400, no bishop was yet ruler of a city and scarcely an aristocrat was interested in episcopal office. One hundred years later, around 500, the aristocrats occupied the episcopal sees and as bishops also ruled in the cities.[9] By around 600 the aristocrats had clearly established their new political and religious local authority as a central element in the new Merovingian regional rule.[10]

The new local form of rule was consequently—and this is what will interest us here—established in Gaul (and only there) by means of a multiplicity of activities of local self-help at the very time in which the leading families of Gaul found themselves without a point of reference for the legitimacy of their power. They could no longer depend on the legitimation of a Roman emperor, and not yet on a royal family in Paris. When, beginning around 500, the Merovingian kings established a stable regional power base in the north of Gaul, they already found themselves confronted in the cities with that form of local aristocratic rule for whose legitimation the coordinates of the empire remained important, but were no longer the central point of reference.[11]

How did this happen—how was the structure of rule transformed and by whom? How did Gaul become "medieval"? Gregory's tale of the apocalyptic vagabond, of the demands for and refusal of the reception of the relics, of putting off the ascetic and disregarding the bishop, of bizarre clothing, of respect for relics, and of a provocative liturgy, points to the direction our search will take: liturgy and legitimation.

The Scholarly View: Representations of Legitimate Rule

The reshaping of early Christian episcopal office into an office of local political rule in Gaul is particularly interesting because it was the central medium for reshaping the entirety of political and social semantics. The sections that follow represent an attempt at grasping some of the procedures involved in this mental and practical reorganization. A few brief theses at the outset will suffice to distinguish the approach used here from some dominant, particularly juridical, interpretations.[12]

The Juridical View: Delegation or Usurpation?

Scholars generally discuss whether episcopal authority was delegated by the emperors or usurped by the bishops themselves. This discussion, however, remains within the mental framework of imperial definitions of what was legitimate or illegitimate for a region in which the emperor's authority was disappearing. It thus retains the very mental framework whose disappearance led to episcopal rule in the first place.

Equally widespread is the explanation that episcopal office enjoyed *prestige* and *power*. For this reason, the argument goes, with the disappearance of the emperors the episcopate, for lack of alternatives, simply grew into a political role. Such explanations do not take us very far, however. They do not explain, first, why *imperial* aristocrats were interested in a *local* office which heretofore had interested local elites, at most. Second, the *power* of this office did not rest on the same model of authority as the power of the older forms of office. It did not rest on imperial delegation, but rather on access to the sacred. This model of authority, however, generally benefited those very people whose concept of a good bishop failed to survive, namely the ascetic charismatics. Why, then, was it precisely those who thought in terms of political careers who succeeded in redefining episcopal office? Third, *prestige*, too, is a matter of definition. The radically aristocratic Sidonius Apollinaris (d. after 486) considered completely different aspects to be conducive to prestige than the radically ascetic Sulpicius Severus (d. ca. 420). The reference to prestige is thus not an explanation; indeed it takes us to the heart of the conflict. What prestige was ultimately associated with episcopal office, who enforced this, and by what means?

An Alternative View: Reordering the Matrix of Political and Social Orientation

In the early imperial period the senators, as an imperial aristocracy, represented and shared out power and wealth at the imperial court as a central site of competition. From about the year 300 onward the outlines of this system of political and social distinction became increasingly blurred, and after 400, Gallic senators had scant opportunity to pursue political careers outside of Gaul. A regional, for example Gallic, field of competition did not exist, however. The aristocrats had power on the local level, to be sure, but little interest in holding office. Consequently, when the imperial court was no longer available as the central field of competition they found themselves without both a point of reference and a political and social semantics for their claims to authority.[13] Naturally, this does not mean that they suddenly ceased to argue in imperial terms. "Rome" remained a significant mental construct for those who no longer had an opportunity to make an actual career within the system of Rome. And we know the extent to which the Frankish rulers also sometimes sought to express their prestige within this construct—by erecting circuses, reforming the alphabet, or holding imperial (honorary) office. Nonetheless, the argument of Rome carried diminishing weight when one was trying to legitimate a claim to rule in Gaul, and we thus need to ask how it lost this weight and how another means of legitimation became established.

We may observe the fading of the mental framework of *imperium* in many

individual details. To be sure, the strongly tradition-conscious aristocrat Sidonius Apollinaris made fun of the Burgundians for dressing their hair with rancid
butter.[14] Many other Romans, however, apparently found barbarian customs
appealing and adopted them. We know this only because in the period around
400 several laws were promulgated that forbade the wearing of trousers and long
hair in the cities. Certain shoes of barbarian cut were also prohibited.[15] Sidonius
looked on in bewilderment as even the highly educated son of one of the most
distinguished families deigned to speak in the tongue of the "barbarians": "It
distressed me to see the ease with which you have acquired a knowledge of the
Germanic language . . . you, who are the grandson of a consul in the male line . . .
who are thus descended from the seed of a poet." He continued, "I ask you to tell
me why a foreign tongue suddenly lives in your breast."[16] A defender of things
Roman apparently saw signs of a "barbarization" of style everywhere, even
within his own ranks. For a tradition-conscious Roman this must have been a
highly unsettling experience, since it was unmistakable evidence that a pattern of
perception central to Roman identity had become irrevocably lost. It scarcely
made sense any more to mark the social boundaries of "inside" and "outside"
with the conceptual pair "Roman/barbarian." Sidonius's "mature" ideal reader
who "appreciates a somewhat old-fashioned style" had become a rarity.[17]

To take another example, Gregory of Tours—the last known instance from
the period around 600 of a Gallic identity before the change to a "Frankish"
self-conception—abandoned the Roman distinction between *civitas/urbs* and
castrum/oppidum. He referred to the *civitas* of Bordeaux as an *oppidum*, and he
would have preferred to call the locality (*locus, castrum*) of Dijon a *civitas* because of its massive fortifications: "Why it is not called a *civitas* I do not know."
One may interpret Gregory's modes of representation in certain cases as a political game (perhaps because the bishop of Bordeaux was more an enemy than an
ally), but we cannot overlook that he no longer used the basic categories of
Roman political geography in the Roman manner.[18] He no longer used the word
civitas to refer to a Roman administrative center. Yet another example: Gregory's
frame of reference was "Gallia," but the territory so designated was different from
what the Romans called Gallia; it was much larger, comparable to contemporary
France. Conversely, for him "Viennesis" was no longer a Roman province but
rather the territory of the *civitas* of Vienne.[19] Gregory apparently already understood the old terms differently, and no longer thought in Roman spatial
categories.

We can thus observe that beholders, but increasingly aristocrats as well, gradually lost their taste for the old imperial form of aristocratic self-representation. In
place of the old forms of social orientation we find new ones which naturally did

not simply arise but had to be fought out. This working and fighting out of new representations and legitimations was a process in which the "medieval" political order became established.

Gregory of Tours's accounts offer us not least the first glimpse of how, in urban reality, the juxtaposition "Christian/non-Christian" replaced the old contrast "Roman/barbarian" as an image central to the conception of political and social identity. Not only was Gaul virtually defined by religious orthodoxy in Gregory's manner of thinking, but what is also striking is that the first evidence we have of anti-Jewish riots is reported for the end of the sixth century, a signal that the conduct of solidarity groups was no longer being produced within the mental framework of the *imperium* but rather that of *ecclesia*.[20]

This shift from *imperium* to *ecclesia* as a mental point of reference is not a spectacular finding. But it also does no more than mark a basic trend of the era, which could have led to very different outcomes in individual cases. If we wish to examine the different options available to participants and the way in which they fought out these options, the development of the liturgy proves to be a particularly good vantage point.

The Material: The Establishment of the Liturgy as the Establishment of a Viewpoint

When Gallic aristocrats eager for a political career developed an interest in episcopal office, which they came to monopolize completely within fifty years, they were merely changing the framework for the legitimation of their rule. The only frame of reference that still existed and which was not—like the old Roman state religion—tied to the fate of the empire was *ecclesia*.[21] The entry of politically ambitious aristocrats into the mental framework of *ecclesia*, however, had consequences for the definition of political rule that would henceforth represent the fundamental conflicts of the Middle Ages. Aristocrats became involved in an area whose definition had been hotly contested for centuries and in which the usual political hierarchy had previously possessed no validity.

The Christian liturgy was the only possible field for the legitimate representation of an aristocracy whose traditional arenas of competition and representation had been rendered largely useless. It is no accident that the development of the liturgy in the fifth and sixth centuries coincided with the establishment of a new form of rule. The evolution of the liturgy was highly dependent upon who was developing it, that is, who occupied the episcopal sees. How the liturgy was organized in detail was a question of perspective and helped to set the terms for the representation of officeholders. The ecclesiastical liturgy encompassed texts and clothing, insignia, the rhythm of the day, week, and year, a local choreography and personnel, and finally the participating mass of laypersons. For the construction of new post-Roman machineries of rule all of this was not merely useful but virtually indispensable. It would doubtless be a worthwhile exercise to compare the development of the Eastern and Western liturgies from this perspective.

These references to the political and social development of Gallia between 400 and 600 already hint at some of the dominant conflicts of the period. Thus a conflict emerged over the definition of legitimate rule, for example in the struggles of the "political" bishops first with the old local authority of the *curia* and later with the new Frankish rulers. This will interest us here only in passing, especially since evidence of conflicts with the old authorities is scarce,[22] and relations with the new rulers have already been frequently studied.[23] Clear conflicts also emerged around the proper image for a bishop. Politically ambitious candidates for episcopal office repeatedly came into conflict with those who did not wish to see bishops turned into politicians.

The Bishop Becomes an Aristocrat: Styles, Qualifications, and Models of Authority

Assuming that episcopal office did not simply "grow into"[24] municipal authority "out of the necessity of the moment,"[25] and that it was redefined and recast by certain interested parties, our first task is to provide these interested parties and their opponents with historical contours, and to seek the linguistic forms with which they redefined the office and the means they used to assert themselves.

From this viewpoint, the ongoing battles over episcopal style are particularly striking. As early as the third century the Roman bishops were occupied with protest from Antioch. A synod had lodged a complaint in Rome against the clothing and behavior of a brother bishop. Centuries later Pope Zachary (d. 752) still considered the style of episcopal garments important enough to warrant detailed treatment in a letter on general principles to the *major domus* Pippin. The tenor of the discussion had changed in the intervening years, however. In the third century, the "Christian bishops of Italy and Rome" were on the side of those who sought to put an end to a luxurious style among bishops.[26] By the fifth century, however, the Roman bishops were calling for an end to an ostentatiously impoverished style, a position they maintained into the eighth century. This change of heart may be viewed as significant for the political and social transformations between antique and medieval Gaul. No bishop simply "grew into" his clothing, and no "necessity of the moment" relieved him of a choice of costume.

THE CULTURE OF APPEARANCE: IMPOSING A DOMINANT STYLE

Many years have passed since the "fathers" of the sociological gaze programmatically declared clothing a central form of cultural semantics, and consequently an urgent object of analysis. From the perspective of the sociologist, clothing is the most common and ubiquitous material for the "attainment and assertion of social distinction" and for the "collective construction of identity for social groups in a place."[27] Nevertheless, historians have rarely tried to place this material for a "culture of appearance" in past societies at the heart of their analyses. To the extent that "it did not become an operational field of fashion to any significant extent," clothing style was a particularly appropriate form of political symbolism.[28] "The legibility of clothing codes in the premodern period" is "scarcely controversial" in the literature. That the hierarchy of estate should be expressed in clothing was apparently an accepted principle "in the premodern period."[29]

Since the establishment of episcopal office, conflicts had arisen over how a bishop should dress and conduct himself. Those aristocrats who regarded episcopal office as the zenith of their political careers asserted their claim to the office primarily through debates over style. A comparison of three accounts, which were written down between the fourth and sixth centuries and which deal with events that allegedly occurred between the third and sixth centuries will furnish examples. The first account is a report by Eusebius (d. ca. 340) on Paul of Samosata (d. after 272), the second a tale by Sulpicius Severus (d. ca. 420) on the episcopal election of Saint Martin (d. 397), and the third Gregory of Tours's (d. 594) apocalyptic account of the pseudoprophet of his own day.

Questions of Dress: Looking Like a Bishop

The first story relates to a certain Paul who was bishop of Antioch from 260 until 272 at the latest, and who was said to have come from Samosata on the empire's eastern frontier. In his *Ecclesiastical History*, Eusebius himself devotes only a few lines to Paul, but quotes liberally from a synodal letter filled with vehement attacks on him. An Antiochan synod had composed the letter in the winter of 268–69 and sent it to the bishops of Rome and Antioch.

The assembled bishops had declared Paul to be a heretic and deposed him. This does not, however, appear to have greatly interested Eusebius; at any rate his excerpts from their resolutions scarcely tell us of which heresy the bishop had been judged guilty. Eusebius concentrates on another aspect of the letter altogether: the bishop's protest against Paul's episcopal style. The synod had protested against a type of bishop "who prefers to be called *ducenarius* rather than bishop, struts proudly in the marketplace, dictates letters while he walks in public and reads, surrounded by a large entourage walking before and behind him. He had a tribune built for him [for] ecclesiastical assemblies with a high throne. He also has a *secretum* and, like a secular ruler, refers to it as such. . . . He criticizes and chides those who do not applaud him and wave to him with handkerchiefs as in the theater, who do not follow his male and female hangers-on by cheering and jumping."[30] A cursory reading of the letter might lead us to assume that Paul's episcopal office entailed a secular office as well. If we are to believe the current trend among historians of antiquity, though, this was not what the bishops were trying to say. They were criticizing "a procuratorial understanding of episcopal office" (Brennecke) and with it the attempt to model episcopal style on that of senators and imperial officials.[31] He possessed a throne and an audience chamber (*secretarium*) and demanded the acclaim of the people. And, if we are to believe the Antiochan synod of winter 268, he was not alone in this behavior: "He also tolerates such conduct by the sycophantic bishops and priests of the neighboring villages and cities in their speeches before the people."[32]

The outrage of the assembled bishops led to Paul's formal dismissal, but this had no immediate effect. Not until the emperor was called in, an emergency measure unusual for the time, could the bishop actually be deposed in favor of a candidate whom the assembled bishops found more to their liking. Around the year 270, then, at least in Antioch, the opponents of an aristocratic style were in the majority among the episcopate, and they managed by dint of great effort to gain the upper hand over a brother bishop who was, we can say in retrospect, "the Christian bishop of the future."[33] And Eusebius wanted his readers to know that this synod had allies at that time among the "Christian bishops of Italy and Rome."[34]

A century later, the majority of bishops in Gaul and Spain reacted with equal aversion to the opposite extreme. Here the ascetic rigorists were in as difficult a position as a Paul of Samosata had been in Antioch or Italy. And once again style of dress was an issue. When around the year 400 the emperor ordered the persecution of followers of the "heretic" Priscillian in Spain, Gallic ascetics expressed fears that "a great number of ascetics [*sancti*] would also be destroyed in the process." Sulpicius Severus recorded this, adding the explanation that "scarcely any distinction was made between different sorts of persons. In those days one judged by appearances only, so that more than one man was considered a heretic more because of his paleness and attire than his opinions."[35] And Sulpicius left no doubt that this attitude was shared by the majority of Gallic bishops.[36]

Interventions from Rome: Celestine and Zachary

This hypersensitivity to questions of style also revealed itself a few decades after the persecution of the Priscillianists, when in 428 "a number of bishops" (*quos-*

dam sacerdotes) in southern Gaul were accused of emulating the ascetics and the laboring population by tying a belt around their hips. Since the occupants of episcopal office at this time did not have official vestments but rather wore their usual clothing, their social origins were easily recognizable.[37] The deliberately "poor" clothing style of some bishops, however, ruffled the social order and was apparently considered a provocation. The opponents of this behavior in Gaul found an ardent ally in the Roman bishop Celestine, who wrote a sharply worded letter attacking these belt wearers for visually setting themselves apart: "We must distinguish ourselves from the common people and others by our teachings, not our clothing; by conversation, not vestments; by purity of spirit, not ritual."[38] The signs of episcopal office, the message suggested, should not disturb the signs of the social order.

The problem was a fundamental one and could not simply be smoothed over. The constant demands for an ascetic lifestyle were all too obviously incompatible with the splendid attire that the aristocrats continued to wear when they assumed episcopal office. A good three hundred years later Pope Zachary (d. 752) sent a sort of basic ecclesiastical policy program to the then most powerful man in the Frankish kingdom, the *maior domus* Pippin. The letter indicates that the "poor" episcopal style remained a provocation. The pope began by citing instructions from his predecessor Leo (d. 461) in a sixth-century collection of canon law: "that metropolitan bishops . . . should observe in full the laws regarding dignity [*ius dignitatis*] prescribed for them in ancient times and that they should deviate from the established rules neither out of carelessness nor arrogance." Then the pope permitted himself to add (*subiungimus*) a more precise elaboration to his source in the papal archives: deviations were permitted "neither in clothing nor in behavior." Episcopal style became an issue once again: "A bishop must wear garments that correspond to his dignity [*dignitas*]."[39] Then the reader learns which style Zachary sought to defend the bishops' "dignity" against: "And if they wish to live the life of a monk, then they should at least give the sermon which they owe to the people entrusted to them wearing a splendid costume. Let them follow the precepts of their heart in private." Finally, he repeated in different words the argument that had been made by Celestine in the year 428: "For what recommends itself to us is not the honor of our clothing [*honor vestium*], but rather the splendor of our souls."[40]

Some scholars consider this an addition made with "little skill," "which has nothing substantive to do with the main theme of the chapter,"[41] yet the main subject of the chapter is the "honor" of the bishop or, in the pope's words, "how the metropolitan bishop should be honored by the suffragan bishops and parish priests."[42] The clothing question was indeed related to this topic, since it had for some time been at the center of discussions of episcopal *dignitas*. At the beginning of the Carolingian era, Zachary confirmed, in a letter of principles, the papal position in an old conflict. The question of *honor vestium* was not, as it might appear at first glance, an attack on episcopal "luxuriousness in dress."[43] The object of criticism was, on the contrary, the "honor" of deliberately poor clothing.

What appears at first glance to be a harmless call to the bishops to dress in a manner befitting the dignity of their office (*iuxta dignitatem suam*) proves on closer inspection to be an attempt to establish a particular definition of episcopal *dignitas* as the only valid one. The *honor* of the monastic style was not to apply to episcopal *dignitas*. Style was a weapon in the social struggle. It was, as we can easily see, the site on which a much broader conflict was fought. The clothing debate was one about what could be considered episcopal honor and dignity and what could not.

Behind the Style Question: Who Defined "Dignitas"?

In his account, written around the year 400, of Martin's election to the episcopate, Sulpicius Severus underlines particularly clearly that what the struggle over style was ultimately really about was which criteria should be applied to episcopal *dignitas*. In his day, the question of what should be regarded as episcopal honor and dignity and what should not was still an open one.

He has the opponents of Saint Martin, "a few laymen and particularly several bishops" remark that "a man of unsightly appearance, with shabby clothes and unkempt hair is unworthy [*indignus*] of the episcopate."[44] This party did not wish to see anyone occupying the episcopal see who rejected the very things by which one recognized the social order. Sulpicius has his hero's supporters appear and express the contrasting, "correct" opinion: "Martin is the most worthy [*dignissimus*] of the episcopate."[45] Although the model of the ascetic bishop triumphed in this case, in general it failed to assert itself against conceptions that defined the bishop in terms of the attributes of the existing social order, following the model of aristocratic *dignitas*.

The entire choreography of public appearance and conduct was open to debate, whereby differing notions of asceticism and *dignitas* were dramatized in a particularly concentrated form in the ritual of investiture. Around the middle of the fifth century, a certain Rusticus became bishop in Clermont by being "set on the bishop's throne [*in cathedra positus*]."[46] Gregory of Tours relates the following story from the year 479 about one of his own predecessors: "He rode in his pride through the whole city, and on the Sunday next after the saint's passing, he made ready a feast in the church house, and invited all the citizens. And slighting the senior among them, he reclined first upon the couch."[47] An elaborate choreography: a portable throne carried "through the whole city," with "all the citizens," a procession, feast, and seating plan. The evil and arrogant candidate was easily branded as a man who flouted the social order. The holy Bishop Martin, in contrast, was praised for the very same attribute of flouting the social order: "Never did he use the bishop's throne," indeed, "no one ever saw him seated in the church." Or: "He sat on a simple stool such as slaves use."[48] "Throne" and "stool" were controversial symbols in the struggle to define episcopal *dignitas*, elements in a concert of controversial signs: jewelry and clothing, hairstyle, personal hygiene, a belt worn around the hips.

Inheritance or Acquisition? The Assertion of a Type of Qualification

The politically and socially explosive nature of the varying conceptions of episcopal *dignitas* only becomes clear when we compare the conceptions with the logic of a society organized into estates. *Dignitas* in Martin's sense was something that one could only acquire by ones' own efforts, while according to the politically minded aristocrats *dignitas* was something one had to inherit. When the political elite fixed their ambitions on episcopal office and regarded it as the zenith of the *cursus honorum*, they were adapting the office to the mental categories of the Roman political and social order. It was customary that only aristocrats would be considered eligible for high office. They had a traditional claim to a monopoly on the *virtutes* necessary for rule; virtues were the hereditary characteristics of their *ordo*.[49] In short, the episcopate became caught up in the logic of the Roman system of estates.

The Gallo-Roman *nobiles* reinterpreted the necessary qualifications for episcopal candidates in an extremely radical manner, neutralizing a central concept of Christian doctrine. Christian thought rested on the idea of a strictly individual *conversio* as the only path to salvation. This idea was certainly present in aristocratic circles in Gallia in the fifth and sixth centuries.[50] As long as access to episcopal office was controlled through publicly visible *conversio*, the office could not be monopolized by one estate, since politically trained candidates were continually exposed to the competition of severe ascetics. It was at this point that those who regarded the episcopate as the potential crowning of a political career intervened. By making *nobilitas* a criterion for entry into the episcopate they asserted a nonindividual hereditary qualification, namely that which had for centuries been identical to the hereditary claim to political rule.

At first sight this scarcely appears a spectacular change, but rather the simple application of the familiar self-perception of the political elite to a new object of political desire. Nonetheless, what we are dealing with here is a decisive moment in the ecclesiastical and political order of the Middle Ages, when two late antique systems of order became intertwined: late Roman political thinking, that of a society of estates, became entrenched within patterns of ecclesiastical organization. The consequences for episcopal habitus are obvious: when qualification is based on a hereditary position, the officeholder must above all represent his inherited position, that is, the characteristics of the social order—from properly dressed hair to the appropriate attire, chairs, and education. The conflict over the episcopal style of public appearance and conduct thus takes on clearer outlines: the debate over style was one over two contrary types of qualification, only one of which—"inherited" qualification—was appropriate to aristocratic episcopal rule.[51]

Asceticism: Transgression or Attribute of the Social Order?

It would be hard to overlook the fact that asceticism continued to appear as a virtually standard feature of episcopal self-representation.[52] To be sure, since the fifth century, with the praise of *nobilitas,* the new, hereditary qualification for the episcopate came to dominate bishops' Lives and epitaphs, but we can always also find "at least traces of a 'stylisation ascétique.'"[53] Those candidates for episcopal office who had been groomed for political careers apparently did not simply pit the argument of *nobilitas* against that of asceticism. To be sure, they declared *nobilitas* to be the dominant criterion, but at the same time also claimed asceticism for themselves. Did this enable them to harmonize an inherited qualification with a strictly individual one, or were they referring to two irreconcilable types of qualification? A closer look at how politically ambitious candidates dealt with the attribute of "asceticism" yields another explanation: there were different modes of defining asceticism as an ideal way of life.

While the ascetic stylization of a Martin of Tours radically called into question the order of the "world" and with it the *dignitas* of political candidates, those who interpreted the episcopate as the zenith of their political careers treated asceticism differently. They interpreted asceticism not as a violation of the social order but as an element of noble education, of *paideia*. Asceticism was an attribute of *nobilitas,* an "expression of social distance" and "the exquisite condensation of hard-won skills of social living—the one, reliable code that governed the behavior of the powerful."[54] The Gallic imperial aristocrats thus contrasted asceticism as an unusual ability with an asceticism that, although it still demanded effort, was one of the basic virtues attributed to *nobilitas*. As interpreted by these politically minded *nobiles,* asceticism became a standardized, caste-specific quality and thus one conferred by birth.

The ideas and habitus of this asceticism supported and visually represented the social order in much the same way as did educated speech, tidy hair, the ancestral line, and so forth. In a process of reinterpretive appropriation, the imperial aristocrats in Gallia integrated the power of religious authority into

their accustomed model of authority. They counted asceticism, the central characteristic of religious authority, among the attributes of *nobilitas* and thus integrated a new source of social power into the old pattern of the claim to rule.

However, to anticipate a later argument, this explanation is not quite as
perfect as the choice of evidence cited up until now might lead us to believe. The
very same bishops who had worked hard to assert the symbols of the social order
in the ecclesiastical procedures propagated just the opposite in many situations.
Before taking a closer look at this institutional weakness of episcopal rule in the
cities, however, we need to address one of those reinterpretations that aristocrats
used to secure the episcopate for themselves.

The New Classification of "Types of Men": Asserting a Point of View

The appropriation of asceticism, which reinterpreted it and transformed it into
an everyday quality, was part of a much broader reinterpretation by means of
which the ascetic transgressors of the social order were reintegrated into that
order and, as candidates for episcopal office, rendered harmless. How were they
integrated into this order? A text by Sidonius Apollinaris is particularly helpful
for an examination of this question. Sidonius once intervened in an episcopal
election to push through the nomination of a certain Simplicius. In so doing he
claimed, in a quite striking manner, to represent common sense: "If I nominate a
monk there will be displeasure, even should he be able to make a particular claim,
and have lived the life of a hermit, even if he could be compared to a Paul,
Hilarion, Antony, or Macarius. People will say: 'This candidate does not fulfill the
requirements of a bishop, but rather that of an abbot; he is better suited to speak
on behalf of souls before the divine judge than of bodies before a secular one.' "[55]

Sidonius took it for granted, as part of a universally accepted social division
of labor, that souls were more the business of abbots, and bodies more that of
bishops. One might at first assume that the phrase about speaking on behalf of
bodies before a secular judge had nothing to do with a glorification of the office,
and even less with an aristocratic monopoly over the episcopate, but merely cited
the long established role of bishops as protectors of the poor and oppressed.
Sidonius however spoke quite plainly and recommended his own candidate
using appropriate arguments. He made no attempt to boast of his asceticism.
Instead, in traditional senatorial manner, he praised the man's career, ancestors,
and relatives by marriage. His candidate had been a *comes* and "his kinsmen were
either bishops or judges." His wife came of a distinguished family, whose members had occupied "chairs of learning" and "episcopal sees."[56] The qualifications
necessary for the protection of "bodies" as a bishop were the very same that had
always been required for political authority. What Sidonius presented as the

universal will (*murmur euerberat, inquiunt*) was an episcopate as political office and the domain of that hereditary class of *nobiles* who claimed a monopoly of political rule.

Sidonius assumed as quite self-evident a view of society that growing numbers of his contemporaries spoke of as the "three types of men." Abbots were—to translate Sidonius's argument into the language of his contemporaries—a different "type of man" (*genus hominum*) from bishops. Let us recall that the first evidence of this classification of types of men in Gallia appeared in the first half of the fifth century in a work by Eucherius of Lyon (d. between 449 and 455).[57] It was invented by Augustine. He was the first, in his doctrine of the "three types of men" (*tria genera hominum*), to develop the idea that the radical ascetic was a different type of man from the bishop.[58]

This notion was extremely helpful for the redefinition of episcopal *dignitas*. Augustine had shown his successors a way to separate the quality of individual conduct from the question of social organization. What was particularly clever about his argument was its imperceptible combination of two nonanalogous versions of the three types of men: sometimes he referred to the three types as "married men, abstinents, leaders" (*coniugati—continentes—rectores*), and sometimes "laymen, monks, clerics" (*laici—monachi—clerici*). As similar as these two versions of the three types of men may appear at first glance, they are very different indeed. They are neither subject to the same criteria of classification nor do they refer to the same number of persons. In one case, Augustine is classifying ways of life, and in the other ecclesiastical organization. In one case, he refers only to good men (*coniugati—continentes—rectores*), and in the other to all men (*laici—monachi—clerici*).[59]

This was the intellectual underpinning for the argument made by Sidonius. It reacted to an asceticism that had slipped beyond the grasp of the social order by modifying the social model of order. By declaring radical ascetics (*quieti, continentes, monachi*) and officeholders (*rectores, clerici*) to be completely different "types" (*genera*), one could oppose such forces as Sulpicius, who wished to see the habitus of the radical ascetic identified with the episcopate. Each of these types was, to be sure, subject to moral norms: "Some remain, the others fall."[60] The quality of conduct, however, had nothing to do with what type of person one was: "There are false monks, false clerics, and false believers. There are good and bad . . . among all three types."[61] Put another way, the particularly unpredictable, strictly personal criterion of holiness or *dignitas*, which each candidate had to acquire on his own, was decisively diluted. A new interpretation of society made it possible to ensure that in most cases ascetics would no longer be considered as candidates for the episcopate. The portrayal of society as *tria genera hominum* was admirably suited to efforts to marginalize the strictly personal qualification of demonstrative asceticism among candidates for the episcopate in favor of a hereditary qualification.

Radical figures such as Salvian of Marseilles may have protested loudly and vehemently, but on the whole the new image of the bishop triumphed within a short time. When Sidonius pushed through his aristocratic candidate in Bourges only "a few priests whispered in corners and holes, but they did not allow the slightest murmur of complaint to be heard in public."[62]

EXAMINING THE RELATIONSHIP BETWEEN CHARISMA AND OFFICE

If we trace the reshaping of episcopal office, for example in the works of Gregory of Tours, we immediately notice that the treatment of asceticism and of qualifications for the episcopate was not as unambiguous as my account up to this point might have made it appear. And Gregory may be considered symptomatic of a conflict that we find throughout the Middle Ages. Although the episcopal model proposed by Sulpicius Severus was the loser historically and the aristocratic style came to dominate, it was precisely Sulpicius's vita of Saint Martin that would serve as the model for saints' Lives in the centuries that followed. Aristocratic bishops with an aristocratic habitus, such as Gregory of Tours, continued to propagate a vita that precisely rejected the aristocratic style.

On the whole, by Gregory's day power relations between officeholders and charismatics had largely been settled in favor of the former. Nearly two hundred years after Sulpicius Severus, the episcopal rulers of cities were better armed against the authority of persons like Martin than his opponents had ever been. Inconvenient ascetics and itinerant charismatics of this type were expelled from the clergy on the spot[63] or, like Gregory's apocalyptic wanderer, ended up in prison.[64] An attention-getting stylite whose extreme asceticism gained him much renown in the Ardennes in Gregory's time was brought down from his pillar by the bishops with the striking argument "nor shalt thou, in thine obscurity, be compared to Simeon of Antioch, the Stylite." Then the bishop responsible summoned the ascetic to a remote place and, in his absence, had the pillar smashed without further ado. If Gregory's *History* casts a positive light on this charismatic, and quite a negative one on the bishops involved, this was not least because the chronicler turned this story into a veritable lesson in "proper" hierarchy. The ascetic had challenged the bishops' authority, the people flocked to him in droves and the man preached from atop his pillar. Then, however, "as ever in his spite he ['the Enemy'] striveth to harm those who seek God," the bishops had forced him down from his pillar. Gregory puts an argument in the bishops' mouths that nicely illustrates the competition between office and charisma, but expressly allowed them to go down in history as "evil," thus rendering the moral of the story all the more obvious: the ascetic obeyed the institution. He began by climbing down from the pillar "because it is imputed a sin not to render obedience to bishops." And when he returned to find the pillar reduced to rubble (*omnia dissipata*) the ascetic avoided conflict, as he tellingly explained, "for fear that I might be called refractory to the order of the bishops."

The hierarchy was as it should be, personal performance conformed to the office even when it was conducted in an "evil" manner, conflict was avoided, and from now on the extraordinary ascetic settled for an ordinary monastic existence. And so he went down in the *History* as a "good man" and as an example of proper obedience to hierarchy.[65] This tale highlights two problems. First, charismatics were dangerous competition for officeholders. Second, the chronicler found the question of proper hierarchy important, while he was willing to risk the suspicious bishops looking "evil" in relation to the "good" ascetic. Both aspects are connected with the establishment of episcopal rule, and there is more to be said here on both subjects.

A New Source of Conflict: Office Versus Charisma

The difficulties the bishop-rulers encountered in their exclusion of ascetic candidates can, in turn, be gleaned from Gregory's account of the apocalyptic pseudo-prophet. It was only the exclusion of ascetics from the episcopate that created the context for such a story. In order to make this clearer, let us quote once again from Gregory's description of this itinerant: "He was clad in a sleeveless tunic, over which was a fine linen mantle, and wore a cross." In the course of the account, Gregory added that he was "a man of uncultured speech" and that he was unkempt, and had a foul smell. These traits bore a striking similarity to descriptions of Martin of Tours and ascetics of the time. Martin's biographer Sulpicius attributed the following description to the holy man's enemies: "A man of unattractive appearance, with shabby clothes and unkempt hair." The charismatic from the period around 580 is described in terms very similar to those used for Martin a good two centuries earlier, and many others as well.[66] Like Martin he was a controversial figure, and like his famous predecessor he had many followers among the people and many enemies among the bishops.

The situation, however, differed in significant respects. The type of the radical ascetic who transgressed the social order was much more precisely positioned in that social order at the time of Gregory than at the time of Sulpicius. If around the year 400 this "Martinian" type of radical asceticism was one possible way of qualifying for the office of bishop, this function was largely lost once candidates had to display the inherited qualification of *nobilitas*. Gregory's late sixth-century account shows how the line of conflict had shifted. While at the time of Sulpicius the type of the radical ascetic had been a competitor *for* the episcopate, now that the contest had been decided in favor of the aristocratic type he represented competition *to* the episcopate.

There could only be a conflict between charisma and office when charisma was not the dominant criterion for access to the office of bishop. This basic medieval conflict between two forms of authority became established at this period, when inherited qualifications for the episcopate asserted themselves against strictly individual ones. The demonstrative ascetics were thus thrown back upon their original power, an ad hoc authority which the ruling institutions found it difficult to control.

Charisma as a Basis for and Challenge to Episcopal Office

For Gregory, to be sure, *nobilitas* was a self-evident precondition for entry into the episcopate.[67] This was, however, only one side of Gregory's accounts. With the very same conviction he told stories about radical ascetics in episcopal office, above all, of course, his predecessor Martin. Gregory and his fellow bishops disseminated countless stories about radical ascetics. This paradoxical behavior, of which Gregory is only one of many examples, deserves systematic scrutiny. Although politically ambitious candidates sought to defuse the risky criterion of ascetic conduct (through *nobilitas* as a hereditary criterion, their own definition of asceticism, and a new social classification) and thus avoid competition from the ascetics, in their sermons they continued to propagate the type of the un-worldly ascetic, who was sometimes a bishop. In order to provide a full explanation of this at first glance contradictory behavior one would need to place the self-stylization of the elite in relation to the expectations of their people, the faithful. I do not need to do that here.[68] A few indications should suffice to make clear the contribution of the aristocratic bishops and rulers to the fact that the apocalyptic figure in Gregory's chronicle was anything but an exception, and anything but powerless.

The chronicler particularly emphasizes that this man had assembled a large following and that there were many such men in Gaul (*multi enim sunt*).[69] The itinerant ascetic from the fifth Book of Gregory's *History* managed to mobilize the "crowd" because the symbols of the charismatic were standardized, from the clothing he wore to the cross he carried. To be sure, the aristocrats in the episcopal sees had repeatedly ensured that the symbols of the social order were also the symbols of the ecclesiastical hierarchy (personal hygiene, hairstyle, clothing, education, and so forth). At the same time, however, they were continually spreading stories in which these very symbols of cultivated *dignitas* were reviled. Gregory of Tours made a girl who had combed her hair on a Sunday into a negative example: "Because she had broken the Sunday commandment, the comb cut deeply into her hand, causing great pain." Only after she had gone to church and sought pardon could she remove the comb.[70] Venantius Fortunatus (d. after 600) told of a cleric who became lame after tying his shoes on a Sunday.[71] Moreover, a maiden, as Gregory preached, had endangered her very salvation with a similar mishap: "On Good Friday, the day, as we know, when our Lord suffered, I washed my face with water."[72] In regard to Sunday, the same bishops who had, in the course of a massive reinterpretation, turned the episcopate into a guarantor of the social order, had declared that some things that were veritable symbols of the culture were "not in keeping with this day."[73] Working in the fields and repairing fences were by no means the only things that were forbidden in order to mark the lord's day.[74] Tales of deformed children who had been conceived on a Sunday were also not merely about ritual cleanliness for the Mass.[75] When the rulers on the episcopal thrones forbade their flocks to wash and comb their hair on Sundays, the actions they used to mark Sunday ritually were the very symbols which the radical ascetics used to set themselves apart every day.[76]

This behavior on the part of the aristocratic bishops ultimately points to the basic institutional problem with attempts to turn episcopal office into an institution of political authority. The episcopate had been attractive for the Gallic imperial aristocracy because the office of bishop could mobilize a form of authority that did *not* depend upon rights delegated by the Emperor, and indeed, more importantly still, that did not appear in the official categories of political distinction and allocations of authority. On what, then, was this authority based? Jochen Martin has summarized the late antique transformation of forms of authority as follows: "Power tended . . . to become a phenomenon of the relationship between human beings and gods; social and political relationships were increasingly interpreted in religious terms."[77] To be sure, all those whose office placed them in proximity to the divine participated in this development, but it was the great hour of the charismatics in particular. The ruling bishops had to contend with this problem. As is well known, the bishops cemented their authority, in a sort of "late-Roman patron-client relationship," by participating in the authority of those heavenly helpers whose relics they possessed. Ambrose was the first to mobilize these invisible helpers by a translation of relics, and many others followed.[78] In other words: in order to promote the authority of their own episcopal sees, they had to propagate the radical charismatics. Thus as bishops they had to support the very people they sought to get out of the way when they filled posts. Worse still, as officeholders seeking to secure their own authority they had to propagate a type of authority that represented a permanent danger to them in the politics of the day: the charismatic authority of the radical ascetic.

Put another way, the authority of an episcopate monopolized by the *no-*

bilitas and equipped with municipal political power was constructed in such a way that it was continually recreating its own most dangerous challenge—the authority of individually acquired charisma. The bishops themselves kept the pattern of charismatic authority alive among the population by promoting their municipal cults. And it was in this way that extraordinary figures could arrive in the city and create cults out of the blue or gather flocks of followers, against whom the bishops often found themselves powerless. King Chlothar I's wife Radegunde established a cult at Poitiers which, as long as she lived, overshadowed the main local cult of Saint Hilary.[79] The biographer of Saint Genevieve also sought to portray his heroine as an ideal "handmaid of God" (*famula Dei*) and to legitimize her leading role in purely charismatic terms. He was extremely reticent about her social background and institutional integration in the city.[80] And if Gregory says that there "were many" in Gaul who could readily gather disciples and challenge the authority of the episcopate, the bishops had largely themselves to blame.

Nonetheless, even if the bishops were constantly creating new challengers for themselves—from Genevieve to the poverty movement and beyond—they ultimately succeeded in defending the authority of their office against charismatic authority. Even a crude sketch of this process would take us too far afield. I would like to close with a glimpse of how the aristocrats in the episcopal sees seized the production of cultural meaning, though, which will take us some way toward such an explanation. What is at stake here is the interpretation of time and space, access to the sacred, the truth, and the future. The design of processions was particularly important in this context, for it was in the processions that new rituals of consensus were created, and with them a central means of producing and reproducing cultural meaning which would persist for centuries.

Cultural Meaning: The Liturgy and the Establishment of Interpretive Monopolies

We will be better able to explain the logic of a number of specific political and social constellations of the Western Middle Ages if we turn our attention to that phase when, after late antique cultural semantics had lost its reality and authority, a new world of symbols, meanings, rituals, and so forth had to be produced. Although the phase in the fifth and sixth centuries, too, was one less of an invention than of a reorganization of the material of imagination, this phase in Gaul nevertheless remains, because of its particular disorder and the multiplicity of conceivable outcomes, a phase in which a comparatively large number of patterns of thought suddenly became repositioned.

If the first two sections showed how the old political and social elite on the one hand integrated episcopal office into their career ladders, and on the other adapted the episcopate to their ways of seeing things, an important initial question about the production of cultural meaning has already been answered: the question of the identity of the dominant producers. The dominant producers of cultural meaning in the newly established political and religious leadership functions deployed relatively homogeneous patterns of interpretation. The men at the height of their careers who, as bishops, tightly organized the clergy, whom they soon put in uniform (vestments, tonsure)[81] and turned into that "staff" (to use Max Weber's term) so necessary for any form of rule, were figures trained in secular rule who had often earned their spurs in secular office.

Expansive Liturgy: Semanticizing a Newly Ordered Society

At the moment of the development of the liturgy, that means of representation which remained central for many centuries, it was the old Roman aristocracy that pursued the bishops' liturgical conquest of space, time, and persons according to their own lights. A look at the history of the liturgy reveals enormous changes in the fifth and sixth centuries. To be sure, developments varied from city to city and from bishop to bishop, but there are clear trends all the same. Urban space became defined as liturgical space. The entire walled city with its surrounding countryside was celebrated as a single liturgical space. Time was organized liturgically: the whole day and sometimes the night as well was subjected to an all-encompassing liturgical rhythm.[82] Toward the end of the fifth century, persons who entered the service of the Church through ordination found themselves wholly absorbed by this service; they had to give up their professions and were increasingly supported financially by the bishops. This massive concentration of the liturgy in the sixth century was the decisive process in an extensive resemanticizing of social categories and spatial and temporal coordinates.

The intellectual underpinnings of the religious tracts, such as the assertion of the idea of the indelibility of ordination (*character indelebilis*) since Augustine,[83] were shared throughout the Mediterranean region, but liturgical development was not. The historically documented liturgical practices that we find in Gaul were not the necessary outcome of theological traditions, and the latter consequently do not provide a sufficient explanation for these practices. The development of the liturgy was a specifically Western phenomenon, in some cases even a specifically Gallic one. Scholars agree that Rome was anything but a motor of the new development in the West. "The Roman church" was, as Cyrille Vogel has put it, "more Oriental than Roman."[84] Liturgiologists have been unable to explain why this meticulously detailed and specific liturgy suddenly developed in Gaul in the fifth and sixth centuries, while Rome remained "Eastern" and the liturgical texts of the East "were not 'official liturgical texts' in the modern sense, but something more than the [oral] improvisations they were derived from."[85] In the East such texts had a local character well into the eighth century and could not be applied elsewhere.[86]

Theology offers no clear reasons for this. If, however, we understand liturgy as a central medium of cultural semanticization, then there is a plausible explanation for the sudden need for this liturgy. Unlike the East, where the empire, together with its entire framework of orientation, continued to exist for several centuries, in Gaul particularly, but to some extent in the West more generally, the fading of the image of *imperium* was increasingly associated with a loss of co-ordinates for fundamental orientations such as time and space, for the social categories, or the legitimation of political rule. Hair style, trousers or jewelry, the common language and its sophisticated usage, devotion to the emperor—nothing went unchallenged.

In this situation, with its acute need for semanticization, it was politically trained aristocrats in the episcopal sees (often with secular careers behind them) who used the liturgy to recoordinate space and time and who increasingly categorized society in visibly new ways. To be sure, classifications of society such as that using the "three types of men" were nothing new on the intellectual level, but it was only now that they reached the level of social conduct as dominant patterns of organization. The historiographic approach suggested here should not tempt us to suspect aristocratic interests behind every Christian ritualization during this transitional period. Conversely, it would be strange indeed if those who invented the rituals had not left their mark on them. After all, beginning in the mid-fifth century in Gaul a relatively homogeneous group, composed almost exclusively of aristocrats, was at work on the new rituals. We can expect that, as episcopal rulers, these aristocrats, using ritual, made their own social interpretations the basic patterns of the new society. It would seem a promising approach to examine the rituals for traces of these social interpretations.

Such traces can be sketched at least in outline, if we follow how the aristocrats in the episcopal sees liturgically imbued the cities, landscape, and social groups with their own "meanings." The evidence is, naturally, scarce and scattered. It suffices, however, to show how the bishops worked on the liturgy, at first individually, and then collectively through synods. What became condensed into different institutions later in the history of the liturgy—services around the stations of the cross, prayers at the canonical hours, or the Canonicate—initially always had the same effect: the religious, political, and social concepts of local rulers became established through the liturgy as the omnipresent official coordinates for the nascent society. The at once religious and secular elite portrayed its own position and that of all others in institutional terms. As new regional rulers, the Merovingians at first had scant opportunity to intervene in this structure. As masters of the liturgy, these municipal rulers were at the same time masters over spectacular local events.

New Rituals of Consensus: Processions, Social Order, and the Criteria of Group Solidarity

The *populus* had always played a significant role in the Roman Empire, whether in the popular assemblies of the republic[87] or in the circus. In the stands of the circus or the arena, the *populus* was an important participant in the Roman games, which current scholarship views not as a gigantic entertainment machinery but rather as "consensus rituals of the urban community" and "a medium of the most successful social disciplining [*Sozialdisziplinerung*] in the history of the world."[88] Each social group had its precisely assigned place in the stands. This gigantic consensus ritual disappeared in Gaul rather quickly along with all things "Roman." Even Salvian of Marseilles (d. after 467–69) had to admit that this was the case. The presbyter, who was particularly zealous in his attacks on the mania for games, found himself virtually forced to justify his critiques: "One might object that such goings-on do not occur in every Roman city. That is true. . . . It no longer occurs in the city of Mainz. But only because it has been destroyed and exterminated. It also no longer occurs in Cologne. But only because it is full of enemies. It no longer occurs in the brilliant city of Trier. But only because it languishes after being destroyed four times. Lastly, it no longer occurs in most Gallic and Spanish cities."[89]

Salvian continued his tirades, but the social system of games had apparently already been destroyed by the middle of the fifth century. Attempts at revival in the sixth century were doomed to failure, since the necessary context of a precise social ranking that could be reflected in the stands of the circus had long since disappeared.[90] These Roman games, however, consisted not only of plays, performances in the theater, chariot races in the circus or (already unusual in Salvian's day) gladiatorial contests in the arena. Games always began with a *pompa*, a procession, in which images of the gods were carried. The *pompa circensis* began at the forum and ended at the circus.[91] When, in the centuries that followed, Christian processions grew into the function of urban rituals of consensus, their entire meaning was changed, to be sure, but a practiced pattern of urban rituals was retained. Now, for example, one began in the main church and moved towards an oratory, holding aloft the new God and the bones of the saints. This observation does not, to be sure, take us very far. In order to explain these transformations we must deal with *how* the meaning was changed, how a ritual of consensus practiced by Roman urban society ended up as a ritual of consensus of Christian urban society. I would like to develop some initial observations using texts from the fifth to seventh centuries.

Whoever occupied the bishop's throne wielded the power to choreograph. In Clermont, for instance, the baptistry was outside the city so that those who wanted to have themselves or their children baptized at the proper time assembled at Easter with the bishop and the "whole people" before the city for the baptism and later returned to the cathedral.[92] The bishops staged such novel social events by means of which they brought people together in much the same way as the earlier games and their *pompae*.

Shortly after the year 500 Bishop Avitus of Vienne told a story central for understanding how processions were handled. He told of how one of his predecessors, Mamertus, "invented" (*concepit*) a procession around 470. This Mamertus apparently came from a powerful family of Gallic *Claudii*, and according to the little information we possess about him it would be no exaggeration to describe him as a "violent bishop" (Heinzelmann).[93] This man "composed the prayers of supplication" himself, "planned conversations in secret" and "determined" the course of events. The account indicates that the procession had to be carried out against the opposition of the defenders of the old political order: "Some at that time believed that the Senate of Vienne, whose *curia* was then flourishing through numerous illustrious men, could not be won over to innovations when it scarcely had any inclination for legitimate matters [*vix legitimis inclinari*]."[94] Mamertus could not help but "notice the anger aroused by the innovation [*fervor inchoationis*]."[95]

Here we see a second conflict alongside that over concepts of asceticism: the conflict over the legitimacy of rule. The aristocrat on the bishop's throne fought with his peers in the old institutions. The *illustres* in the *curia* sought out a debate on legitimacy and branded "inventions" (*inventa*) as illegitimate. To make a long story short, Mamertus won the conflict not through this debate but through skillful leadership of the *populus* and established his procession as an annual ritual. He became a model for many other aristocrats in the episcopate. Several immediately followed his example and, in 511, Mamertus's processions were introduced all over Gaul.[96]

In his account Avitus, himself the scion of a powerful family, displayed a far surer instinct and far more interest in the political significance of a procession than most authors of that transitional period in Gaul. With unusual clarity, he explained to his listeners that what had been at stake in the year 470 was municipal power politics and that the participants knew it. One of the apparently most powerful Gallo-Roman magnates had used episcopal office particularly deftly to strengthen his own position in the city. In so doing he had aroused anger in his city and caused a sensation throughout Gaul.

As an account of a struggle over the legitimacy of a ritual of consensus, Avitus's text remains an isolated example. The early medieval authors who repeatedly wrote about religious processions generally portrayed these events as affairs involving the entire city. They were very parsimonious, however, when it came to indicating the political and social stratification of religious processions. The accounts may be roughly divided into three categories. First there are the texts in which the participants are scarcely mentioned. Then there are those authors who write quite extensively about the participants in the event, but have nothing to say about the order of procession. These texts are particularly interesting. Finally, there are a few texts which offer at least small hints as to the actual order in which the participating persons walked.

Observers of the Processions: Processions Without Social Contours

Let us begin with the first group. Quite a few authors of the fifth to seventh centuries wrote of processions or solemn receptions without devoting more than a fleeting remark to the participants. When they mentioned that the bishops had mobilized the "sluggish people" (*tarda populi sequacitas*) for the procession in "a mighty mass," it was only to emphasize the outstanding position of the episcopate.[97] Or the focus was solely on the individual who was being greeted, as in the statement that "the majority of the people gathered to meet" Genevieve.[98] This lack of interest in the social stratification of processions may at first seem plausible in texts that propagated the model of individually acquired charisma. After all, the heroes of these texts represented disregard for social orders and their symbols. But even when episcopal lords described the arrival of other episcopal lords they were often no more precise: after his banishment Caesarius of Arles was met by the "entire community and both sexes." This was the description offered by his biographer, Bishop Cyprian of Toulon (d. ca. 545) and his assistants, Bishop Firminus of Uzès (d. ca. 552) and a certain Bishop Viventius.[99] Gregory of Tours was also frequently no more precise. In his book *Glory of the Martyrs* Gregory told of how in the mid-fifth century Bishop Namatius of Clermont turned the arrival of new relics into a public event: "In the morning he instructed the citizens, and with great piety hastened with candles and crucifixes to meet the holy relics."[100] Whether and how the citizens organized themselves interested him as little here as in many other accounts.[101]

A few authors—and this brings us to the second group of texts—are more forthcoming on the subject of the participants in processions. Victricius of

Rouen composed the most famous text on a procession in this disoriented period. But Constantius of Lyon, the biographers of Caesarius of Arles and the Abbess Rusticula, and not least Gregory of Tours also occasionally wrote detailed accounts of processions. These texts have led some historians to conclude that the population began to participate in processions in groups organized by estate as early as the late fourth century. The surviving texts in no way support this interpretation, to be sure, but it nevertheless rests on a correct observation: authors of the fifth to seventh centuries cited social categorizations with striking frequency when describing processions.

When Victricius of Rouen preached in detail about the translation of a relic in his "In Praise of the Saints" around the year 400, he went through and listed the most diverse possible social categories. The author had "priests and deacons," "monks" and "innocent children," "the mass of the chaste and widows," "maidens with the Cross," "the tears of the elderly" and "the *vota* of the mothers," virtually "every age" rejoice in praise of the saints.[102] Other authors also produced similar rhetorical lists of this type, if with differing categories. Constantius of Lyon offered his readers an eccentric classification of "types of men" when around 475/80 he related of the funeral procession of the holy Germanus of Auxerre in the city: "Every type of man [*hominum genus*] made haste to do him some other service [*diverso occurrit officio*]. Some repaired the streets . . . and bridges, some donated money [*expensas ingerunt*], others sang psalms and still others carried the bier."[103] If a clearer example is needed, the following list makes it plain that one need not read this division of types of men into those who prayed, those who paid, and those who paved as an order of procession.

Soon after the death of Bishop Caesarius of Arles in 543 his biographers described the funeral procession, once again using such a string of categories: "Good and bad, just and unjust, Christians and Jews, whether they walked before or behind the corpse, raised their voices."[104] A certain Florentius who composed a Life of the Abbess Rusticula of Arles (d. ca. 630) around 630 also allowed himself to be inspired by this prose style.[105] Once when the abbess had cleared her name after a slanderous accusation before the royal court she returned home with particular pomp: "People of every age, both sexes, religious and laity, nobles and commoners, rich and poor, natives and foreigners, hastened to meet her."[106]

We have no reason to believe that these authors were any more anxious to reveal anything about the protocol of the procession than the authors of the first group of texts, who mentioned only the "entire community" or a "mighty crowd." These lists tell us nothing about the order of procession. But what can we learn from them?

Before and After the Reordering Process: The Examples of Emperor Constantius
and Bishop Audoin

An interpretation becomes easier when we compare these texts of the fifth to
seventh centuries with an earlier example from the fourth and a later one from
the turn of the eighth century: the famous entry of Emperor Constantius into
Rome in 357, which Ammianus Marcellinus (d. shortly after 400) observed and
described, and the entry of Bishop Audoin (d. 684) into Rouen as described in his
Life (ca. 700).

Ammianus has left us a text that offers us a clear impression of the author's
view of the social order on the one hand and a number of hints as to the order of
the imperial procession into Rome on the other. The senate, Ammianus tells us,
set out to meet the emperor as a separate group from the *plebs*.[107] The patricians
among them distinguished themselves with a particularly traditional form of
self-representation. As at patrician funerals during the republic and the early
imperial period they carried the masks of their ancestors with them.[108] The
plebs, although described as diverse (*omne genus plebs*), were interesting only as
a mass (*celebritas*). During the entry outside the city the "men at arms" also
played a visible role as a guard of honor flanking the emperor. Within the city
itself, only the staging of civil hierarchy was of interest.[109] Through spatial as-
signments, Ammianus allocated places to the *plebs*, the senators, and the emperor: "He addressed the nobles in the senate-house and the populace from the
tribunal."[110]

Now let us turn to a text produced three hundred years later, which tells of
the reception of Bishop Audoin of Rouen. As the bishop approached the city, he
was met first by the common people (*suburbani cives et vulgi populus*). Thereupon (*exinde*), the text informs us, a messenger at the royal court (*aula regalis*)
announced the holy man's arrival. The king, queen, and nobles of the court
(*proceres palatii*) then enter the text applauding joyfully (*plaudentes manibus*).
The author then assigns the priests and monks their own song of praise (*canebant
laudes*), and, finally, describes the behavior of the poor as part of the ritual: "In
the meantime [*interdum*] the poor capered and called out."[111]

At first glance the differences between these texts of the late Imperial and
late Merovingian periods may be more striking than the similarities. It would be
hard to overlook the fact that the two authors were writing about fundamentally
dissimilar political and social worlds. Nonetheless, their perceptions of the events
do reveal something they shared and which a Victricius around 400 or a Florentius around 630 lacked. Where these texts spoke of social *ordines*, they sought at
the same time to illuminate ritual events and social positions. The positions of

participants in the procession, as in society, were described using the categories of estate. Ammianus mentioned the emperor, men at arms, senators, ancestral lines, and *plebs* and organized them according to spatial descriptions (outside or inside the city, the tribunal or the *curia*), various attributes (effigies, armor) or remarks on their habitus (the emperor's immobility). The author writing around 700 distinguished the king, queen, nobles, clergy, beggars, and the common people. He organized them spatially (*suburbia, palatium*), temporally (the people first, then the rulers; *interdum pauperes*), and through the assignment of significant tasks (*vulgi populus in occursum adgrediunt, rex etc. plaudentes manibus, sacerdotes canebant laudes, pauberes clamant*). In both cases, all of this did not combine to produce a precise description of the ritual. It may be that the king made his way from the palace to meet Audoin and that the "common people of the suburbs" applauded. What is more important here than the completeness of the description is the basic viewpoint of both authors. Ammianus, like Audoin's biographer, grasped the ritual events with the help of the vocabulary of estate. They were only able to do so because first, they had relatively clear notions of the basic forms of the social hierarchies they were describing, and second, these respective hierarchies were translated into the ritual of the *adventus*. It seems to have been perfectly natural for them to use the vocabulary of classification by estate as the vocabulary of a choreography.[112]

These two works should make it easier to understand those texts—from that written by Victricius around 400 to that composed by Florentius around 630— which contained more or less lengthy lists of social groups. These authors worked with social classifications, to be sure, but they could not use them to describe the orders of procession. It took several centuries after the disappearance of the Roman system of rank before the new, medieval patterns of classification were translated into the processions. This is not to say that people simply marched any which way in the fifth and sixth centuries. It does, however, point to the authors' insecurity in matters of social categorization. Authors writing in the period between the "antique" emperors and the "medieval" Carolingians did not bring their social categories together with the visible course of the processions.

To put it another way, the descriptions of a Victricius, Constantius, Cyprian, or Florentius are important evidence precisely because the vocabulary they used for the social strata of participants did *not* grasp the order of the processions. The texts did *not* function like the descriptions of the entries of rulers that we find in antiquity. This peculiarity makes the texts significant evidence of the extensive process of political and social reorganization that occurred during the transition from Roman to Frankish Gaul. By the year 400, the old patterns were already of no help anymore if one happened to be standing on the roadside in Rouen, trying to understand and describe the sociopolitical meaning of an order of procession.

Shapers of the Processions: Processions and Social Order

No protocol of Christian processions can be located in Gaul before the sixth century, let alone a potential social ordering of the participants. So much is clear from the texts that have been treated up until now.[113] Initial signs of a "translation" of the social order into the processions can be found, however, and that brings me to the third group of texts, in some accounts by Gregory of Tours. Particularly when writing about himself, he could at times go into greater detail. In his book *Glory of the Confessors* he told of how he established an oratory at Tours and filled it with relics. The relics were taken in a procession from the church of St. Martin to the new oratory. As in many other accounts the chronicler mentions crosses and candles, and naturally relics as well, but this time he also seems to have been interested in the order of the participants: "A great procession of priests and deacons in white clothing was there, as well as the excellent *ordo* of the *honorati* and a large number of people from the next *ordo* too."[114] Gregory's description of his own procession differs plainly enough from the lists offered by a Victricius, Constantius, or Florentius, who show no interest in the order of procession. Gregory, in contrast, provides a list of the participating *ordines*, which was actually translatable into a choreography.

The new Frankish elite, such as the evil *dux* Roccolen, also found an appropriate place in the ceremonial: "In the meantime came round the holy day of the Epiphany, and he was tormented with even greater pain. He then . . . came into the city. And when the procession issued, with chanting, from the great church [of St. Martin] on its way to the holy basilica, he rode upon his horse behind the cross, preceded by his banners." It is clear that the bishop afforded the *dux* a prominent place in the procession and ample room for self-representation.[115] The chronicler makes similar allusions when he relates the solemn reception given to Bishop Theodorus in Marseilles in the year 581: the bishop was met "with *signa* and *laudes* and various banners of the *honores*."[116] The identity of the *honores* who were represented by their banners remains unclear. One need not agree with the translators who have rendered them as "officials" or "guild associations"[117] in order to consider at least one thing clear: in mentioning the flags Gregory points to signs of inner-urban distinction that had become part of the procession and the *adventus* by his day.

In short, around the year 600 we find the first evidence of a "translation" of the social order into the processions. In his writings, Gregory occasionally has an eye, and words, for political and social symbols in the processions, and it appears that, in his own diocese, he also had a hand in organizing these symbols.

The Procession as a Ritual of Conflict: Anti-Jewish Pogroms, Battles over Office, and Duels over Authority

If we may regard Gregory as typical, then the processions increasingly reflected the social hierarchies of a society in formation. They also provided a ritual form for expressing what was inside and outside the "new" society, that is, for something that one might call a "Gallic" identity. Where Gregory distinguished Gaul as a unit from other units, orthodoxy (*credulitas pura*) was a dominant criterion and "our religion" (*nostra religio*) a significant catchphrase.[118] The procession also proves to be a moment of condensation for this phenomenon.

At the Feast of the Ascension in 576 Avitus of Clermont organized a procession from the cathedral church to the basilica outside the city gates, with chanting of psalms and a large crowd of people (*multitudo . . . sequentium*). On the margins of the bishop's procession, however, "the whole multitude following him rushed upon the Jewish synagogue, destroyed it from the very foundations, and leveled it flat with the ground." At Easter—again during a procession—"all the people" had already sought to stone a Jew.[119] Such accounts, familiar as they are to us, may not sound particularly spectacular, were it not for the fact that they had no precedents.[120] These texts are the earliest evidence of pogroms against Jews in Gaul. They may therefore be interpreted as a sign that the identity and group solidarity of what was still largely an urban community were undergoing a redefinition and that the new processions were rituals for the creation and constant repetition of a new social consensus.

The biographers of Bishop Caesarius of Arles (d. 543) also describe the participants in his funeral procession using the categories not of the Roman Empire but of religious orthodoxy. They, too, used the category "Jew" as part of a negative contrast: "good and bad, just and unjust, Christians and Jews." Here the category "bad—unjust—Jew" is revealed as the main heir of that "illiterate barbarian" whose last great defender, Sidonius Apollinaris, had already been fighting a losing battle one century earlier.[121] If Gregory did not make up the pogrom (and we have no reason to believe that he did), then the civic society of sixth-century Clermont viewed itself in such a way that collective actions were oriented around the pair of opposites Christian/non-Christian.[122]

The pogroms that occurred on the fringes of processions that were at once religious and civic are just one of the indications of how the new consensus rituals served as means of exclusion and delimitation. Gregory relates another variant for the year 580. In that year, he writes, he was compelled to defend himself at court against the accusation of having insulted the king. He did so successfully, but during his absence from Tours another man had "entered the church house as if he were already bishop." This man had made an inventory of the items of value, taken everything into his possession and given gifts to the principal clergy. Gregory's very brief account gives the impression that the conflict was fought out in the form of Gregory's solemn *adventus* in Tours. The challengers avoided the event, as might be expected, but, according to Gregory's self-assessment, "the rest of the citizens" proved loyal and came out to greet him. The balance of power was thus clear for all to see; Gregory ordered the usurper's "removal" (*removeri praecipio*) to a monastery where he was kept "in close durance."[123]

We do not have many examples of this form of ritualized conflict, so that our interpretation of the episode must rely on analogies to examples of Roman papal installations. A collection of imperial and papal letters compiled around 600 in Rome, the so-called *Collectio Avellana*, contains a reference to the installation of the archdeacon Felix as bishop of Rome in 355. The clergy had made this decision on their own, and the source notes the reaction of the people: "This displeased the entire people, and they stayed away from the procession."[124] "The people" apparently used the same method a few years later, in 366, during the hotly contested installation of the deacon Damasus as Roman bishop, and they paid dearly for it: "Damasus began harshly to punish the Roman people who had refused to participate in a solemn procession with beatings and a great bloodbath."[125]

The story that most clearly illustrates a procession as a particularly effective choreography of dissent is, once again, the tale of the apocalyptic itinerant ascetic who has intruded into every section of the present paper. Let us refresh our memories: the itinerant ascetic had stopped before the gates of Tours and demanded a proper reception for his relics. Gregory had refused to submit to his demands and instead "offered" that the ascetic could himself submit to the episcopal liturgy. The ascetic thereupon entered the city alone, and was allowed to complete his rituals and go his way unhindered.[126]

This, however, is only the more harmless part of the story related in Gregory's *History*. The ascetic continued on from Tours to Paris, and it is only there that Gregory's tale reaches its narrative climax. The story becomes a prime example of the conflict over forms of authority. The charismatic's challenge to Bishop Ragnemod of Paris was even more audacious than that he had offered to Gregory. Much more effectively than in Tours, he timed his appearance in Paris to coincide with the three-day Rogations preceding Ascension Day that had become compulsory in all of Gaul in 511. "While Bishop Ragnemod was making the round of the holy places in procession with his flock, this man also came up with his cross, wearing a garment quite unfamiliar to the people."

Then the charismatic resorted to the bishops' own methods. He "formed a procession of his own [*chorus*] meaning to go around [*circuire*] the holy places with his private following [*multitudo*]."[127]

On the one hand we have the bishop with his splendid vestments and brilliant procession, equipped with the authority of office and a staff of clerics, and on the other the ostentatiously shabby and stinking itinerant ascetic whose charisma sufficed to lure away a large following from the bishop's flock and unite them on the spot into a rival procession.

In his account Gregory depicts the conflict between two models of authority in liturgical terms. In the short term, the only available solution in such situations was force, in this case prison for the itinerant ascetic. In the long term, however, officeholders managed to keep this danger under relatively tight control, largely because they succeeded in asserting a monopoly over central forms of the production of cultural meaning, particularly over access to the truth, the future, and the hereafter. This manner of dealing with prophetic qualities, another "expropriation of the soothsayers,"[128] will be sketched in the following section.

Standardizing the Extraordinary: Interpreting Signs and Proclaiming the Truth

Particularly in the fifth book of his *History*, Gregory claims prophetic qualities as an episcopal trait, and the interpreters of this work have offered a plausible and pithy phrase for the dominant motif of this fifth book: "The prophet before the godless king" (Heinzelmann). The chronicler portrays himself as the incarnation of the good bishop who, "in the tradition of the Old Testament prophets, was continually showing [the king] the right path" (Heinzelmann). Again and again, Gregory "assumed the mantle of the prophet" (Reydellet). Interpretations of this kind concentrate on the chronicler's interest "in the wielding of episcopal power" and definition of it in relation to the power of kings" (Breukelaar), and his claim to "the bishops' role as the spiritual advisers and partners of kings" (Heinzelmann).[129]

This is, on the whole, quite plausible. If bishops were searching for a model for resistance to a secular power, the Old Testament prophets provided them with a key. Nevertheless, if someone actually did claim the "tradition of the Old Testament prophets," this raises a further question. How did the bishops alter the "mantle of the prophet" to make it fit? After all, the great exemplary prophet figures such as Amos or Elijah went down in the Scriptures as charismatic, extraordinary individuals, and precisely not as officeholders, let alone priests.[130] How could a sixth-century bishop, perhaps one typical of the bishops of his day, claim this prophetic tradition as an attribute of his office? It would be surprising indeed had this claim been a silent and unnoticed appropriation. Too great was the contrast between the exemplary biblical figures and this claim, too important the access to truth in the struggle over the form Christian society should take. It is quite apparent that this appropriation by no means proceeded quietly. In Gregory of Tours's *History* we find a number of tales that deal with "right" and "wrong" forms of prophecy. The results of these conflicts provide an instructive analogy to the conflicts surrounding proper *dignitas* and proper asceticism.[131] They also suggest that, although the model of the prophet was important for the positioning of the bishops vis-à-vis the kings, the bishops' claim to holiness had first to be asserted on another battleground: in the struggle with those to whom masses of the faithful were only too willing to attribute holiness.

A Paradigmatic Tale: The Story of the False Prophet

The apocalyptic wanderer of Gregory's ninth book is, once again, a key figure, by means of whom the lines of conflict are unfolded with particular narrative breadth. Many a reader nowadays might concur with Gregory's assessment and refer to the itinerant charismatic as a "vagabond" or "magician."[132] Magic and vagabondage, however, like charisma, are socially ascribed qualities. If this man, with his odd behavior, could walk into a strange city and immediately mobilize a crowd, then in sociological terms he falls into the category of a charismatic, just like the holy Martin, the holy Genevieve, or any number of figures attacked by Gregory and—which is particularly important—like the prophets of the Old Testament.

The wanderer was not a vagabond, but was declared to be one; he was not a magician, but he was called one. This technique of ascription, whose efficacy may be measured not least by its continuing ability to influence present-day readers, is particularly interesting if we wish to understand the transformation of the "antique" political and social frame of reference into a "medieval" one. How did people like Gregory succeed in gaining the upper hand over these "many" (*multi enim erant*) charismatics who recruited their *multitudo* wherever they went as itinerant holy men? Naturally, there were a number of methods, and Gregory mentions several of them in passing. His account focuses, however, on the question of what characterizes a prophet.

Gregory begins by fighting down the authority of his challenger with two not especially spectacular arguments. First, he declares the man's supporters to be ignorant folk (*populus rusticus*), whores, and stupid women. Then he asserts that the man was formerly a *famulus*, an argument from the arsenal of patterns of qualification of a society of estates. Epithets such as *famulus* or "child of paupers" (*de pauperibus provocatus*) were more than mere weapons deployed to reserve episcopal office for the *nobiles*. They were general arguments of moral disqualification. In 580 an entire assembly of bishops maintained "that the evidence of an inferior might not be believed against a bishop."[133]

However casually Gregory may have invoked these two arguments, he devotes far more detail to describing a third—indeed weightier—weapon against the itinerant provocateur. The man had maneuvered the bishop of Paris into a very similar situation as that experienced by the chronicler himself in Tours. While in Tours he had demanded a solemn welcome, in Paris he organized a solemn procession himself. The reaction of the bishop in Paris also resembled that of Gregory in Tours: " 'If thou bearest holy relics, place them awhile in the church and celebrate the holy days with us.' " As before at Tours, in Paris the man was expected to submit to the bishop's rhythm. What is more, he was expected to set aside his relics and participate in the episcopal ritual. He was supposed to relinquish the guarantors of his authority and support the institutionalized authority of the bishop through his own person.

The chronicler now steers his account directly to the heart of the conflict. He has the man fall to "cursing and abusing the bishop."[134] We do not know what he said, but we do know how the chronicler interpreted his words. This man, who cursed the bishop, stood for many of his ilk, whom the chronicler views as the incarnation of the Apocalypse, "of whom, I think, the Lord Himself speaketh in the Gospel." The chronicler presents these itinerant figures to his readers as the "false prophets" (*pseudoprophetae*) of the last days.[135]

The story of the pseudoprophet shows the early contours of a complex medieval conflict, the lines of which can only be suggested here. Opposition arose to the wandering self-styled prophet of the Semitic type, who represented a danger to every institution and social order, and was of course familiar to Christians from the holy Scriptures. The stigma of the "false prophet" was apparently a standard weapon deployed against persons resembling the Semitic Old Testament prophet. We find this stigma even among the followers of these charismatics, if used in an opposite manner. The biographer of the charismatic leader Genevieve places the very argument that Gregory of Tours actually made against the charismatics of his day in the mouths of his heroine's enemies. Just as the wandering ascetic was the incarnation of the Apocalypse for Gregory, so Genevieve represented the same to her opponents: "They said that a false prophetess appeared in their days."[136]

This stigmatization of the itinerant ascetic as a false prophet in early medieval texts suggests how the bishops reacted to competition from the ascetic charismatics: they denied any prophetic gifts to those who, like the biblical figures, were charismatic loners, and claimed those gifts as an attribute of episcopal office.[137] This means that prophetic quality was treated in a very similar way to asceticism. Just as asceticism became tied to *nobilitas*, the prophetic gift became attached to episcopal office. Both reinterpretations followed the same principle: an extraordinary ability became one that was generally attributed to any member of the group.

Ex Officio: Divination by Scriptures and Visions

To be sure, this episcopal claim to prophecy was as old as the mistrust of wandering prophets.[138] But it was only since the bishops had become the rulers of cities and exhibited more *nobilitas* than asceticism that the conflict assumed a systematic form. It would certainly lend sharper contours to the logic of medieval governance if we were to pursue prophecy as the site of the conflict between office and charisma over the course of the Middle Ages. I cannot even begin to do this here, and will limit myself instead to a few remarks on Gregory of Tours.

The apocalyptic wanderer of the ninth book was not Gregory's only opportunity to explain his idea of a proper prophet. His fifth book has a seeress (*mulier habens spiritum phitonis; ariola*) presenting herself as competition to the prophetic authority of the bishop in 577. First he lets the seeress make a few predictions, including the following: " 'It shall come to pass that King Chilperic shall die this year, and [his son] Merovech shall shut out his brothers and possess himself of the whole kingdom.' "[139] For Gregory this prophecy was laughable at best, and it offered him an opportunity to clarify exactly who had access to the truth and who did not: "Of God alone are these things to be obtained." The chronicler contrasts the true prophet, namely himself, with this prophecy, which represented, in truth, "the promises of the Evil One." He, the bishop, prophesies another end for the house of Chilperich. In his sleep he had seen an angel flying over the church, who had proclaimed the downfall of Chilperich's sons: " 'Woe, woe. God hath stricken Chilperic and all his sons; nor shall one survive from among the issue of his loins." Thus did the bishop dream; the sons died; the seeress was unmasked, and the chronicler "perceived" that not the soothsayer but the bishop was the true prophet.[140]

In this tale, the chronicler employs a simple method to unmask the seeress as a false prophet. If a prophecy was not fulfilled the prophet lost. In other cases, however, the chronicler musters more complicated and less convincing evidence. In a particularly clumsy manner, he unmasks an exceedingly successful itinerant charismatic to whom "the country people flocked . . . in multitudes." "Those who saw him declared that if any one had spoken evil of him in secret and at a distance, he would reproach him in public with these words: 'Thou hast said this or that about me, defaming my holiness.'" As proof Gregory offers the question, "Now by what other means could he have known this save through familiar demons?"[141] In the second book of the *History* an attentive reader could indeed have found an answer to Gregory's rhetorical question. In that book the chronicler tells of a deacon of the holy Martin who had called the ascetic crazed (*delerus*) when he was far away from him. Soon thereafter the holy man confronted him: "[T]hou deemest me crazed? . . . Were not my ears at thy lips when thou saidst it all that distance away?"[142] The same extraordinary ability could guarantee access to the holy in one case and to evil spirits in another. Such proofs hint at the difficulties involved in asserting prophetic gifts as an episcopal quality and attribute of office.

In some accounts this claim is explicitly raised against an unusual charismatic. In some the bishops' privileged access to truth was expressed in other ways. King Chilperich once sought contact with the holy Martin by placing a blank piece of paper on his grave. The saint, however, left no notes on it, evidence enough that the king had no contact with the afterlife.[143] In another story, the chronicler relates a divination by scriptures he once performed for the king's son Merovech. Gregory had opened the book of Solomon at random and read out to Merovech the first sentence he chanced upon. The message, however, remained incomprehensible to the king's son and the two men reacted very differently: "Though he did not understand, I considered this text was prophetic."[144]

These observations remain very fragmentary, and are limited to texts written by Gregory of Tours. They do at least suggest the outlines of an aspect of political and social reorganization that deserves more extensive study. Even after the ascetics had ceased to compete for access to episcopal office, they remained a constant threat to its authority. The episcopate sought to defuse this threat by denying the charismatics a central element of their holiness and laying claim to it as a component of office. The bishops wanted to manage the future themselves, and they wanted to interpret the signs. Relying for the time being on Gregory's writings: they prophesied ex officio, interpreted the flights of birds, practiced scriptural divination, and pronounced their dreams to be visions[145]—all of this as representatives of an office who dissociated themselves from the quite numerous and successful charismatic individuals of their day.

Some Open Ends: New Conflicts, Alternative Cultures, and the Other Parts of the Empire

This contribution is an attempt to grasp institutional change by examining the semantics of events. At the end, at least, some qualifications may be in order; that is, that the view of the discourses, the semantic level, can grasp only a part of the logic of events. Force or violence, such as the imprisonment of the ascetic, was, to be sure, always also a cultural sign, but it was more than that. The Plague (and its victims), which was constantly provoking processions, could be culturally semanticized, but it was not culturally produced and, it scarcely needs to be said, was more than a discourse. It is conceivable that a systematic look at the logic of events beyond the semantic level would change the interpretation.[146] This essay has doubtless neglected alternative systems of signs and legitimation, such as those of the Frankish kingdoms, in which the logic of war and spoils were an all-too-obvious reality. It could indicate that the aristocratic bishops did not conduct their competition in a power vacuum.[147]

The focus here was thus only on a particular detail: how, at a moment of political and social disorder and disorientation, a conflict over the "proper" order was carried out as part of a struggle over cultural symbols. The question that interested me was how a particular viewpoint was expressed in visual terms, how symbols were deployed, interpreted, and asserted over other symbols and interpretations, how certain symbols and interpretations were repeated, rehearsed, and secured, and also how internally coherent the various figures of argumentation used by a party or person were.

How did the imperial aristocrats in Gallia react when their everyday perceptions corresponded ever less with their traditional self-interpretation, self-representation, and offices? The more Romans in the cities dressed and spoke like "barbarians," the more the signs of Romanness, especially the games, disappeared, and the more the Gallic imperial elite withdrew from careers on the imperial level, the less able the aristocrats were to legitimize their claims to authority within the categories of *imperium*.

Our look at the forms used to represent political rule makes it clear why politically ambitious imperial aristocrats turned to local episcopal office and which patterns of argumentation they used to reinterpret and appropriate it for their own needs. The conflicts over forms of representation for episcopal office show particularly clearly how and against whom they asserted their point of view. The "culture of appearance"—attributes, clothing, thrones, and so forth—was the form within which they confronted those who were not interested in episcopal office as part of a political career. These persons repeatedly tried to use episcopal office to disturb the signs of the social order. Viewed as a rung on the career ladder, however, episcopal office always had the task of representing the social order. Here two very different concepts of episcopal *dignitas* clashed, two concepts that stood for two conflicting models of qualification: the strictly individually acquired qualification of the ascetics, who were indifferent to the social order, and the inherited qualification of politically ambitious aristocrats, who derived their legitimation precisely from the social order—the society of estates with its hereditary virtues.

The victory of the politically ambitious aristocrats meant nothing less than translating into ecclesiastical organization the perception of society in terms of estates. This was particularly significant to the extent that the occupants of episcopal sees sat at the very pivotal point at which, with the demise of the old frames of reference, a new cultural semantics was being produced. It was these bishops, trained for secular careers, who designed the liturgy, such as the processions, which, as new rituals of consensus, may be regarded as heirs to the circus.

The fact that the ascetics had largely lost the battle over conceptualizations of episcopal office did not make them any less dangerous, though. The monopolization of episcopal office as an object of political ambitions shifted the conflict with representatives of radical asceticism to a new battlefield. Those ascetics who disregarded the signs of the social order now competed less *for* than *with* the office of bishop. The texts show us how bishops struggled with these unusual figures over the central instruments of power, prophetic quality, and access to the holy and to the truth. Judging by the examples discussed here, it seems that these extraordinary abilities of individual persons were claimed by the bishops—against the clear verdict of the Old Testament texts—as ordinary capacities belonging to episcopal office.

New Lines of Conflict and the Integration of Alternative Cultures

It goes without saying that these observations offer us a glimpse of only a small segment of the reordering process which Gallic society underwent between the Roman emperors and the Frankish Carolingians. A few additional aspects have been touched on briefly, but not pursued any further. Of these aspects at least one, which will be the subject of a further essay, should be brought out more clearly. The longevity of the new political institution of episcopal rule should be easier to understand in the light of its ability to deal with alternative cultures, either by integrating or criminalizing them. Such cultures flourished not only at the new royal courts, but also among the bishops' own staffs, the clergy. And they flourished particularly under those aristocrats, whether Frankish or Roman, who were not bishops. I will sketch four main aspects and then close with a panorama of the other parts of the empire.

1. In the sixth century, there were apparently powerful persons without episcopal office who took country clerics under their protection, much to the displeasure of the bishops.[148] Columbanus and other Irishmen finally gave these persons the opportunity to establish an alternative religious culture.[149] The challenge from the ascetics could be kept in check as long as they had no powerful

protectors. With the appearance of the Irish holy men, however, the defenders of spiritual and political rule by bishops were no longer confronted merely with ascetics, but also with their mighty protectors on whose lands the ascetics stayed. Gregory of Tours did not live long enough to see that his literary scenario of the apocalyptic ascetic followed only by prostitutes and stupid women had little success. A few decades after his death it was powerful lords who turned to such ascetics in strikingly large numbers. The new Irish challengers came from a land that had never belonged to the Roman Empire and in which the episcopate had never been shaped by aristocratic interpretations. Instead, the ascetics had won the day there and reduced episcopal office to the power of ordination. The ascetics regained their ascendancy at the very moment in history when the traces of the Gallo-Roman families become lost to historians, and consequently the profile of episcopal personalities changed, when the last literary witness of a Roman-Gallic identity died with Gregory, when the "Frankish" rulers were both becoming visible as points of reference for a new group identity and already had their best years behind them. The relationship between unusual charisma and office needed to be renegotiated.

2. In the sixth century, the new regional authority of the Merovingians had to be harmonized with the recently established local powers. How was this accomplished? The type of the bishop who was also a municipal lord became established in a period without an efficient regional authority. The emperor was far away, and the Frankish kings not yet in sight; army commanders and usurpers tried their luck here and there with varying degrees of success. With the establishment of the Merovingians as regional rulers the arena changed. Who divided up the spheres; who defined a "good" king, or bishop; how was the relationship of the new royal officials—the counts and dukes—to the only recently established local political organizations, or of the bishops to the kings, and vice versa, negotiated? Studies exist on many aspects of these questions. Recent interpretations of Gregory's *History* have made clear that it should be read particularly as an intervention in the struggle over the relationship between king and bishop, as an episcopal effort to conceptualize the king and the bishop. This sixth-century source, upon which almost all of what we know is based, was the attempt to find a place for the new authority of the Merovingian kings in relation to the only slightly older concept of episcopal local rule.[150]

Proceeding from these studies, it would be interesting to investigate situations in which the kings themselves attempted to produce "meaning." The chronicler attributes a whole series of obstinate attempts at active intervention in the production of cultural meaning not to the heroically portrayed King Gunthchramn but to his antihero Chilperich. These included the reconstruction of the circus at Paris and Soissons, corrections to the alphabet, and statements of opinion on theological questions. The chronicler did not approve of such high-handed royal interventions in the production of meaning. It is also in this context that we should understand references to tendencies among the Franks not to follow established cults but to create their own.[151] Thus, Saint Vincent's in Paris was also known as the "Church of the Holy Cross." Radegunde of Poitiers, who relied on the power of proximity to the king and who managed throughout her lifetime to overshadow the bishop, also promoted this cult of the holy cross.[152] These royal attempts were ultimately unsuccessful, but in other fields the kings succeeded in leading the way. One need only think of the victory of the practice of the Burgundian, Austrasian, and Neustrian synods over the former practice of the provincial synods.

3. A further challenge apparently threatened the bishops from their own staffs. Episcopal organization increasingly extended to the *civitates'* lands beyond the city walls. Country clerics, who were outside the system of face-to-face encounters, were much more difficult for bishops to control than their urban counterparts. Not surprisingly, the clerics began to organize themselves. A few scattered sixth-century synodal texts may best be interpreted as indicating that clerics in the countryside organized something like guilds, much to the displeasure of their urban superiors. The bishops sought to suppress these activities, but with only limited success. To be sure, the bishops appear to have gained the upper hand over the clerical guilds within a century or so, but the clerics soon found themselves in village guilds, no longer among themselves, but no more controllable from outside. The reference to the bishops in relationship to the guilds addresses a further area of conflict, which can be traced for large stretches of the Middle Ages.[153]

4. One also finds a further conflict in Gregory's texts, one whose effect on the social order is undisputed. Although in Gregory's work religious orthodoxy was the absolute yardstick for good and evil, there was one thing he valued even more highly: family solidarity. This was the moral of a story about the religiously orthodox king's son Herminegild, who, being threatened by his Arian father Leuvigild, hatched a plan against his progenitor. Gregory leaves no doubt about the hierarchy of values: "The unhappy [*miser*] prince knew not that the divine judgement impends over him who nurses such intent against his own sire, even if he be a heretic."[154] *Miser* is a term that Gregory reserves for the enemies of God and his order.[155] The struggle against the father violated the divine order, a verdict also passed upon the king's son Merovech: "Merovech made many charges against his father and his stepmother. These may have been partly true; but in my opinion it is not acceptable in God's sight that a son should publish such things abroad." A son was not permitted to speak against his father—not even the truth, not even against even a father like Chilperich, Gregory's literary epitome of the

notoriously evil king. To bolster this divine ordering principle he cites, rather freely, from the Book of Proverbs: "The eye that looketh a father in the face, may the crows of the valleys pick it out" (Prov. 30:17).[156]

The Rest of the Empire: Some Concluding Remarks

We cannot conclude without at least a brief survey of the other parts of the Roman Empire, those territories in which rule by bishops was nonexistent. In conjunction with such a survey, the Gallic development takes on clearer contours. The imperial aristocracy in other parts of the empire did not experience the need for legitimation felt by the imperial aristocrats in Gaul. In the East, as in central and southern Italy, the old mental categories and hierarchy of honor continued to function for many years. The nobility in the East also lacked the strong aristocratic consciousness of the western senators. In the East *nobilitas* was a much less widespread idea, so that it did not enter the discussion as a criterion of episcopal *dignitas*. Office and charisma could be "clearly kept apart" in the East, whereby "in conflicts between the two the institution generally emerged the loser."[157]

In other territories in which, as in Gaul, the Roman system disintegrated, Christianity offered no escape for the politically ambitious. The Vandal invasion ended any flirtation with Christianity in Africa, and in the Islamic kingdoms that followed, the old imperial aristocracy could expect no advantage from belonging to a minority religion.[158]

In the provinces in Africa Christianity had also developed in a manner that did not make it attractive for the politically ambitious. The episcopate in Gaul was differently organized from its African counterpart in two important respects. First, in Africa the *civitas* was not coterminous with the episcopal see; rather, episcopal sees greatly outnumbered *civitates*. Second, the episcopate in fourth-century Africa was a mass office. Beginning in the early fourth century, Roman Africa had at least a thousand bishops at any given time, evenly divided between the orthodox and the Donatists. For that reason alone the episcopate in Africa, unlike that in Gaul, was not calculated to whet political appetites. The African bishops came from all strata of the population and had nothing in common but episcopal office.[159] Thus, dogmatic questions gained much greater weight than they had in Gaul. Here the criteria of *dignitas* or *nobilitas* were doomed from the outset. Beginning in the mid-fifth century in Gaul, in contrast, the bishops were united by a far more stabilizing bond than office or dogma, namely by a common *habitus*, social origins, wealth, education, and so forth.

To be sure, texts were precisely fixed in Africa as well. It is quite apparent that the bishops in Roman Africa had concerns other than those in Gaul, though. In Africa, there was a proliferation of texts, which were insufficiently orthodox in the eyes of the synods. Thus, standardization was a kind of censorship, in a striking parallel to the development of the African veneration of saints. In the case of the liturgy, too, the bishops made restrictive interventions into an over-zealous practice. No such problems existed in Gaul. Here the liturgy could be shaped in relative freedom from the pressures of dogmatic debates and social differences in the episcopate.

Finally, let us recall that nowhere did the aristocrats have so much time to reorganize themselves after the waning of the old framework of orientation as in Gaul. The Gallo-Romans succeeded in putting an end to the Roman Empire as a system of reference before they found themselves confronted—in the far north of the empire—with a new and very differently organized regional hegemony.

Notes

This chapter is translated from Bernhard Jussen, "Liturgie und Legitimation, oder: Wie die Gallo-Romanen das Römische Reich beendeten," in *Institutionen und Ereignis. Über historische Praktiken und Vorstellungen gesellschaftlichen Ordnens*, ed. Reinhard Blänkner and Bernhard Jussen, Veröffentlichungen des Max-Planck-Instituts für Geschichte 138 (Göttingen, 1998), 75–136.

1. Gregory of Tours, *Libri Historiarum* (henceforth referred to as *LH*) IX, 6, ed. Bruno Krusch and Wilhelm Levison, MGH SS rer. Merov. 1, 1, 2nd ed. (Hanover, 1951), 417; Engl. translation, *History of the Franks* (henceforth referred to as *HF*), trans. O. M. Dalton (Oxford, 1927), vol. 1, 373. My reflections in this essay take up those I have published in " 'Bischofsherrschaften' und die Prozeduren politisch-sozialer Umordnung in Gallien zwischen 'Antike' und 'Mittelalter,' " *Historische Zeitschrift* 260 (1995), 673–718; the present text has benefited from the critical and encouragingly radicalizing comments of Peter Brown, Philippe Buc, Egon Flaig, and Jochen Martin, who have my warmest thanks.

2. *LH* IX, 6, 418; *HF* 2:373.

3. *LH*, 418; *HF*, 2:374.

4. *LH*, 420; the logic of the temporal intervals in Gregory's work has been examined by Adriaan Breukelaar, *Historiography and Episcopal Authority in Sixth-Century Gaul: The Histories of Gregory of Tours Interpreted in Their Historical Context*, Forschungen zur Kirchen- und Dogmengeschichte 75 (Göttingen, 1994), 158 and 52–53.

5. *LH*, 418–20.

6. Reinhold Kaiser, *Das Römische Erbe und das Merowingerreich*, Enzyklopädie deutscher Geschichte 26 (Munich, 1993), 103; Kaiser also provides a corresponding bibliography.

7. On the challenging aspects of the Columbian movement see Arnold Angenendt, *Das Frühmittelalter. Die abendländische Christenheit von 400–900* (Stuttgart, Berlin, and Cologne, 1990), 205–23.

8. See below, "An Alternative View."

9. Martin Heinzelmann, "Bischof und Herrschaft vom spätantiken Gallien bis zu den karolingischen Hausmeiern. Die institutionellen Grundlagen," in *Herrschaft und*

Kirche. Beiträge zur Entstehung und Wirkungsweise episkopaler und monastischer Organisationsformen, ed. Friedrich Prinz, Monographien zur Geschichte des Mittelalters 33 (Stuttgart, 1988), 23–82, esp. 28–30 and 57.

10. Reinhold Kaiser demonstrates this *civitas* by *civitas* in his monograph *Bischofsherrschaft zwischen Königtum und Fürstenmacht. Studien zur bischöflichen Stadtherrschaft im westfränkisch-französischen Reich im frühen und hohen Mittelalter,* Pariser historische Studien 17 (Bonn, 1981).

11. See the brief summary below, "An Alternative View."

12. For a more extensive discussion see Jussen, "Bischofsherrschaften."

13. See ibid., sections 1 and 2, esp. 686–91 and 710–12; on the regionalization of the aristocracy particularly in the West, see Henrik Löhken, *Ordines dignitatum. Untersuchungen zur formalen Konstituierung der spätantiken Führungsschicht,* Kölner historische Abhandlungen 30 (Cologne and Vienna, 1982), esp. 105–11; on the end of careers outside of Gaul see Ralph W. Mathisen, "Fifth-century Visitors to Italy: Business or Pleasure?" in *Fifth-century Gaul: A Crisis of Identity?* ed. John Drinkwater and Hugh Elton (Cambridge, 1992), 228–38, esp. 231–33; the best introduction to almost all of the scholarly debates around the questions relevant here may be found in Jochen Martin, *Spätantike und Völkerwanderung,* Oldenbourg Grundriß der Geschichte 4 (Munich, 1987).

14. See Sidonius Apollinaris, *Carmen* 12, 7, in Sidoine Apollinaire, vol. 1, *Poèmes,* ed. André Loyen (Paris, 1960), 103–4.

15. *Codex Theodosianus* 14, 10, 2 (a.397) and 14, 10, 3 (a.399), and 14, 10, 4 (a.416), ed. Theodor Mommsen and Paul Krüger (Dublin and Zurich, 1904), 788; on this see Jussen, "Bischofsherrschaften," 710–12.

16. Sidonius Apollinaris, Ep. 5, 5, 1, in Sidoine Apollinaire, vol. 2, *Lettres,* ed. André Loyen (Paris, 1970), 180; in ibid., 5, 5, 3, he refers to the Burgundians as barbarians.

17. Sidonius Apollinaris, Ep. 8, 16, 2 (in ibid., vol. 3, 127).

18. On Bishop Berthram of Bordeaux see Margarete Weidemann, *Kulturgeschichte der Merowingerzeit nach den Werken Gregors von Tours,* vol. 1, Römisch Germanisches Zentralmuseum, Monographien 3.1 (Mainz, 1982), 143–44.

19. Breukelaar, *Historiography and Episcopal Authority,* 199 (civitas, castrum), 210 (Viennensis), 224 (Gallic identity); LH III, 19, 120–21: "Qui cur non civitas dicta sit, ignoro"; see LH III, 19 on Dijon as a locus.

20. See below, 177; on the equation of Gallia with religious orthodoxy, see Breukelaar, *Historiography and Episcopal Authority,* 214–15, and Martin Heinzelmann, *Gregor von Tours. Zehn Bücher Geschichte. Historiographie und Gesellschaftskonzept im 6. Jahrhundert* (Darmstadt, 1994), 136, 4.

21. The Roman state religion, for example sacrifices to Jupiter, would have been inconceivable without the Roman state; on this see Egon Flaig, "Entscheidung und Konsens," in *Demokratie in Rom?* ed. Egon Flaig, Karl-Joachim Hölkeskamp, and Martin Jehne (Wiesbaden and Stuttgart, 1995), 77–127.

22. A particularly illustrative example is discussed below, 171–72.

23. This is a central theme of the detailed interpretations of Gregory's *History of the Franks,* Heinzelmann's *Gregor von Tours. Zehn Bücher Geschichte,* and Breukelaar's *Historiography and Episcopal Authority.*

24. Ernst Jerg, *Vir venerabilis. Untersuchungen zur Titulatur der Bischöfe in den außerkirchlichen Texten der Spätantike als Beitrag zur Deutung ihrer öffentlichen Stellung,* Wiener Beiträge zur Theologie 26 (Vienna, 1970), 64.

25. Georg Scheibelreiter, *Der Bischof in merowingischer Zeit,* Veröffentlichungen des

Instituts für österreichische Geschichtsforschung 27 (Vienna, Cologne, and Graz, 1983), 172–73.

26. Eusebius, *Kirchengeschichte* VII, 30, 18, ed. Gustave Bardy, Sources chrétiennes 41 (Paris, 1955), 214–19, quotation 219; on this subject see below, "Questions of Dress."

27. The quotations as well as the phrase "culture of appearance" come from the exemplary study by Hans Medick, "Eine Kultur des Ansehens. Kleider und ihre Farben in Laichingen 1750–1820," *Historische Anthropologie* 2 (1994): 193–212, quotations 194, which also discusses reflections by Simmel, Lévi-Strauss, and Febvre. Medick has found unusually good material for a virtually microscopic view of changes in the "culture of color" among the lower classes, whose clothing even methodologically skilled authors often interpret in purely "functionalist" terms (ibid., n. 4). Neithard Bulst too has gained particularly deep insights into the "culture of appearance" between distinction and solidarity through his studies of sumptuary laws; see his "Kleidung als sozialer Konfliktstoff. Probleme kleidergesetzlicher Normierung im sozialen Gefüge," *Saeculum* 44 (1993): 32–46. See also the other contributions to *Saeculum* 44, no. 1 (1993), a special issue devoted to "Clothing and Identity."

28. Egon Flaig, "Politisierte Lebensführung und ästhetische Kultur. Eine semiotische Untersuchung am römischen Adel," *Historische Anthropologie* 1 (1993): 193–217, quotation on 201; this study is a shining example of what a sociological analysis of clothing can accomplish even for periods of history for which material is scarce.

29. Bulst, "Kleidung als sozialer Konfliktstoff," 34, and quotation, 36.

30. Eusebius, *Kirchengeschichte* VII, 30, 8f., ed. Bardy, 216.

31. This, at least, has been the most widespread interpretation since the appearance of Fergus Millar's "Paul of Samosata, Zenobia and Aurelian: The Church, Local Culture and Political Allegiance in Third-century Syria," *Journal of Roman Studies* 61 (1971): 1–17, esp. 12–13. (here p. 11 on the chronology of the synods); the quotation is from Hanns Christof Brennecke, "Zum Prozeß gegen Paul von Samosata. Die Frage nach der Verurteilung des Homoousios," *Zeitschrift für die neutestamentliche Wissenschaft und die Kunde der älteren Kirche* 75 (1984): 270–90, 273 n. 14, in which Brenneke summarizes Wolfgang Wischmeier's thesis; the old position that Paul actually held secular office is, however, defended by Frederick W. Norris, "Paul of Samosata. Procurator Ducenarius," *Journal of Theological Studies* 35 (1984): 50–70; the interpretation of the contemporary notion of episcopal office is otherwise the same in both analyses.

32. Eusebius, *Kirchengeschichte* VII, 30, 10, ed. Bardy, 217.

33. Peter Brown, *The Body and Society: Men, Women and Sexual Renunciation in Early Christianity* (New York, 1988), 192.

34. Eusebius, *Kirchengeschichte* VII, 30, 10, 219.

35. Sulpicius Severus, *Dialogus* III, 11, wd. Karl Halm, CSEL 1 (Vienna, 1866), 209; similarly, Sulpicius Severus, *Chronik* II, 50, 3f, in ibid., 103, on the Priscillianist hunter Ithacius.

36. *Dialoge* III, 11f, in ibid., 208–210. The "distrust of asceticism" which was widespread in Southern Gaul in the fourth and fifth centuries (Stancliffe 292) is the topic of Clara Stancliffe's *St. Martin and his Hagiographer* (Oxford 1983), 265–96, quotation 292.

37. See the overview in Louis Trichet, *Le costume du clergé. Ses origines et son évolution en France d'après les règlements de l'église* (Paris, 1986), 21–35; on the belt, see 30.

38. Coelestin, Ep. 4, 2 in Migne PL 50, 430–31 (431: "amicti pallio, et lombos praecincti . . . Discernendi a plebe vel caeteris sumus doctrina, non veste; conversatione, non habitu; mentis puritate, non cultu"); for more on this letter, see Jussen, "Bischofsherrschaften," 703–4.

39. Zacharias, Letter to Pippin a. 747, in *Codex Carolinus* 3, ed. Wilhelm Gundlach, MGH Ep. 3 (Berlin, 1992), 479–87, 480; the model for the text was no. 32 of the Decreta Leonis Papae in the *Collectio decretorum Pontificum Romanorum* of Dionysius Exiguus (d. before 556), ed. Migne PL 67, 293.

40. Zacharias, Letter to Pippin a. 747, 481.

41. Reinhold Rau, *Briefe des Bonifatius, Willibalds Leben des Bonifatius nebst einigen zeitgenössischen Dokumenten* (Darmstadt, 1968), 420 n. 5.

42. Zacharias, Letter to Pippin a. 747, 480.

43. Rau (*Briefe des Bonifatius*, 421) translates the phrase *honor vestium* as "Pracht der Kleider" (luxuriousness in dress), thus turning the argument on its head.

44. Sulpicius Severus, *Vita sancti Martini* 9, 3, ed. Jacques Fontaine, Sources chrétiennes 133f (Paris, 1967), 272.

45. Ibid.

46. *LH* 2, 13, 63; *HF*, 2:57.

47. *LH* 2, 23, 68–69; *HF* 2:62–63.

48. Sulpicius Severus, *Dialoge* 2, 1, 180: "illud non praeteribo, quod in secretario sedens numquam cathedra usus est: nam in ecclesia nemo umquam illum sedere conspexit... sedentem uero Martinum in sellula rusticana, ut sunt istae in usibus seruulorum."

49. For a detailed account see Martin Heinzelmann, *Bischofsherrschaft in Gallien. Zur Kontinuität römischer Führungsschichten vom 4. bis zum 7. Jahrhundert. Soziale, prosopographische und bildungsgeschichtliche Aspekte*, Beihefte der Francia 5 (Zurich and Munich, 1976), esp. 33–40.

50. Heinzelmann, *Bischofsherrschaft in Gallien*, index, 278 s.v.

51. The Gallic episcopal dynasties worked according to the same principle in those cases where aristocrats competed with each other for episcopal office; the members of the episcopal dynasties believed they had an additional, inherited qualification.

52. This section and the one that follows largely follow my argumentation in "Bischofsherrschaften," 704–6; the earlier essay, however, did not subordinate the argumentation to the important observation that it was a new *type of qualification* for access to episcopal office which asserted itself in the fifth century.

53. Heinzelmann, *Bischofsherrschaft in Gallien*, 235.

54. Peter Brown, *Power and Persuasion in Late Antiquity: Towards a Christian Empire*, (Madison, Wis., 1992), 39 and 122; for an extensive treatment of the virtues see Heinzelmann, *Bischofsherrschaft in Gallien*, 200–211.

55. Sidonius Apollinaris, Ep. 7, 9, 9, ed. Loyen, 55.

56. Sidonius Apollinaris, Ep. 7, 9, 16, 57.

57. Eucherius, Instructiones 1, *De Ezechiele* 1, ed. Karl Wotke, Corpus scriptorum ecclesiasticorum latinorum 31 (Vienna, Prague, and Leipzig, 1894), 87: "In his tribus sanctis tria hominum genera siginificari uidentur... in Noe enim gubernatores ecclesiae praefigurantur, in Daniele sancti continentiamque sectantes, in Iob coniugati et iustitiam diligentes."

58. On this and on the history of the influence of the doctrine see Otto Gerhard Oexle, "Tria genera hominum. Zur Geschichte eines Deutungsschemas der sozialen Wirklichkeit in Antike und Mittelalter," in *Institutionen, Kultur und Gesellschaft im Mittelalter. Festschrift für Josef Fleckenstein zu seinem 65. Geburtstag*, ed. Lutz Fenske, Werner Rösener, and Thomas Zotz (Sigmaringen, 1984), 483–500, 483–90 on Augustine and 490 on Eucherius.

59. For a detailed account see Bernhard Jussen, "Der 'Name' der Witwe. Zur 'Konstruktion' eines Standes in Spätantike und Frühmittelalter," in *Veuves et veuvage dans le haut moyen âge*, ed. Michel Parisse (Paris, 1993), 137–74, here 168–71.

60. Augustine, *Quaestiones evangeliorum*, 2, 44, in Migne PL 31, 1357: "Et ex illis qui sunt in otio, et ex illis qui sunt in negotiis saeculi, et ex illis qui Deo ministrant in Ecclesia, aliqui permanent, aliqui cadunt."

61. Augustine, *Enarrationes in Ps.* 132, 4, ed. Eligius Dekkers and Johannes Fraipont in *Aurelii Augustini opera* 10, 3, Corpus Christianorum, Series Latina 40 (Turnhout, 1956), 1929–30. 1928: "Tam sunt enim monachi falsi, quam et clerici falsi, et fideles falsi. Omnia genera . . . habent bonos suos, habent malos suos."

62. Sidonius Ep. 7, 9, 3, 53.

63. *LH* IX, 6, 417: "a nostris depraehensa."

64. *LH* IX, 6, 419: "captusque ab archidiacono et catenis vinctus, iussus est costodire."

65. *LH* VIII, 15, 382–83.

66. Cf. Sulpicius Severus, *Vita sancti Martini*, 272 (on Martin); *LH* IX, 6, 418 (on the charismatic), on the man's smell and poor education, *LH* IX, 6, 418: "Erat enim ei et sermo rusticus et ipsius linguae latitudo turpis atque obscoena"; ibid., 419: "De quo tantus fetor egrediebatur, ut omnium cloacarum adque secessorum fetores fetor ille devinceret."

67. Heinzelmann, *Gregor von Tours. Zehn Bücher Geschichte*, 10.

68. The reader is directed to Peter Brown, *The Cult of the Saints: Its Rise and Function in Latin Christianity* (Chicago, 1981), and Arnold Angenendt, *Heilige und Reliquien. Die Geschichte ihres Kultes vom frühen Christentum bis zur Gegenwart* (Munich, 1994), on the expectation of the faithful see esp. chapters 4 (on the development of the basic figures), 5 (on asceticism and the renunciation of worldly things), and 6 (on the man of God).

69. *LH* IX, 6, 420.

70. Gregory of Tours, *Liber Vitae Patrum*, 7, 5, ed. Bruno Krusch, MGH SS rer. Merov. 1, 2 (Hanover, 1885), 240.

71. Venantius Fortunatus, *Vita Germani* 102, ed. Bruno Krusch, MGH AA 4, 2 (Berlin, 1885), 11–27, 19.

72. Gregory of Tours, *De Gloria Confessorum* 5, ed. Bruno Krusch, MGH SS rer. Merov. 1, 2, (Hanover, 1885), 301.

73. Gregory of Tours, *De virtutibus sancti Martini* 3, 55, ed. Bruno Krusch, MGH SS rer. Merov. 1, 2 (Hanover, 1885), 195: "quod huic diei esset incongruum."

74. Such tales exist as well; for examples see Raymond Van Dam, *Leadership and Community in Late Antique Gaul*, The Transformation of the Classical Heritage, 8 (Berkeley, 1985), 288.

75. Gregory of Tours, *De virtutibus sancti Martini*, 2, 24.

76. Van Dam assembles these examples in *Leadership and Community in Late Antique Gaul* and interprets them in rather eccentric fashion; according to him, what these prohibitions had in common was that they forbade everything that symbolized culture as opposed to the natural state; on Sunday people were supposed to live in accordance with nature (287). Van Dam believes that what is at work here is the opposition (popular among anthropologists) between "the raw and the cooked," or agricultural cultivation and natural growth. Whether this ideal of a life in harmony with nature was actually part of medieval ideas of asceticism and not a projection of modern health food notions backward in time remains to be demonstrated.

77. Jochen Martin, "Die Macht der Heiligen," in *Christentum und antike Gesellschaft*,

ed. J. Martin (Darmstadt, 1990), 440–74, quotation 461; Peter Brown, *The Making of Late Antiquity* (Cambridge, Mass., and London, 1978), esp. 64ff.

78. Bibliography and overview in Jussen, "Bischofsherrschaften," 689–91; quotation from Brown, *The Cult of the Saints*, 63.

79. Raymond Van Dam, *Saints and Their Miracles in Late Antique Gaul* (Princeton, 1993), 28–41, esp. 39–41.

80. For a detailed interpretation of the evidence see Martin Heinzelmann, "Vita sanctae Genovefae. Recherches sur les critères de datation d'un texte hagiographique," in *Les vies anciennes de sainte Geneviève de Paris. Etudes critiques*, M. Heinzelmann and Joseph-Claude Poulin (Paris, 1986), 1–111, here esp. 57–70 on the *famula Dei*, 80–91 on their origins, 91ff on her relationships to the municipal curia and her financial means; Susanne Wittern, *Frauen, Heiligkeit und Macht. Lateinische Frauenviten aus dem 4. bis 7. Jahrhundert*, Ergebnisse der Frauenforschung 33 (Stuttgart and Weimar, 1994), 87.

81. Canon 20 of the 506 Synod of Agde forbade clerics wearing secular clothing; cf. *Concilia Galliae a. 314–506*, ed. Charles Munier, Corpus Christianorum, Series Latina 148 (Turnhout, 1963), 202: "uestimenta uel calceamenta etiam eis nisi quae religionem deceant, uti uel habere non liceat."

82. Cf., for example, the Synod of Vannes a. 461/91 c. 14, in ibid., 155: "Clericus quem . . . a matutinis hymnis . . . inventus fuerit defuisse, septem diebus a communione habeatur extraneus"; Agde a. 506 c. 30 (ibid., 206): "ab episcopis uel presbyteris . . . hymnos matutinos uel uespertinos diebus omnibus decantari."

83. Hans Erich Feine, *Kirchliche Rechtsgeschichte. Die katholische Kirche*, 5th ed. (Cologne and Graz, 1972), 129.

84. Cyrille Vogel, *Medieval Liturgy: An Introduction to the Sources* (Washington, D.C., 1986), 34.

85. W. Jardine Grisbrooke, "Eastern Liturgical Books," in *Encyclopedia of the Early Church*, ed. Angelo Di Berardino, trans. Adrian Walford, 2 vols. (Cambridge, 1992), 1:501–2, quote 501.

86. Anton Baumstark, *Comparative Liturgy* (London, 1958), 18.

87. See Flaig, "Entscheidung und Konsens."

88. Egon Flaig, *Den Kaiser hersausfordern. Die Usurpation im Römischen Reich*, Historische Studien 7 (Frankfurt a.M., 1992), quotations 58–59; see 52–59 on scholarship that opposes the equation of games with pleasure and proposes instead that they were rituals of consensus.

89. Salvian of Marseilles, *De Gubernatione Dei* 6, 8, 39, ed. Georges Lagarrigue, Salvien de Marseille, *Oeuvres*, vol. 2, Sources Chrétiennes 220 (Paris, 1975), 388.

90. On the circus construction of the Merovingian Chilperich (d. 584) at Paris and Soissons, see *LH* V, 17, 216: "apud Sessionas atque Parisius circus aedificare praecepit, eosque populis spectaculum praebens."

91. For an extensive account see Franz Bömer, "Pompa," in *Realencyclopädie der classischen Altertumswissenschaften* 21 (1952), 1878–1994.

92. *LH* V, 11, 205–6 on a Jew baptized at Easter 576: "renatusque Deo per baptismi sacramentum, cum albatis reliquis in albis et ipse procedit. Ingredientibus autem populis portam civitatis . . ."; ibid. on a mass baptism of Jews at Whitsun 576: "Pontifex . . . ad baptistirio forasmoraneum egressus est"; the phrase "cunctus populus" is used for the reentry into the city (ibid., 205).

93. Heinzelmann, *Bischofsherrschaft in Gallien*, 226; Ralph Mathisen treats this figure

in detail; see his *Ecclesiastical Factionalism and Religious Controversy in Fifth-Century Gaul* (Washington, D.C., 1989), esp. 173–234.

94. Avitus of Vienne, *Homilia in Rogationibus*, ed. Otto Seeck, MGH AA 6, 2 (Berlin, 1883), 108–12, 110.

95. Ibid.

96. On emulation by other bishops, see ibid., 111: "Sequutae sunt succiduo tempore quaedam ecclesiae Galliarum rem tam probabilis exempli, sic tamen, quod hoc ipsum non apud omnes iisdem diebus, quibus penes nos institutum fuerat, celebraretur"; Synod of Orléans 511 c. 827, in *Concilia Galliae* 2 a.511–a.695, ed. Carlo De Clercq, Corpus Christianorum, Series Latina 148a (Turnhout, 1963), 11–12.

97. In the words of Avitus, writing about Mamertus; cf. Avitus, *Homilia in Rogationibus*, 110.

98. *Vita Genovefae virginis Parisiensis* c. 25, ed. Bruno Krusch, MGH SS rer. Merov. 3 (Hanover, 1896), 225; similarly ibid. 11, 219 (going to meet Germanus).

99. *Vita Caesarii* 1, 26 ed. Bruno Krusch, MGH SS rer. Merov. 3 (Hanover, 1896), 466; on the Vita and the authors, see William Klingshirn, *Caesarius of Arles: The Making of a Christian Community in Late Antique Gaul*, Cambridge Studies in Medieval Life and Thought 22 (Cambridge, 1994), 6–9.

100. Cf. Gregory of Tours, *Liber in gloria martyrum* 43, ed. Bruno Krusch, MGH SS rer. Merov. 1, 2 (Hanover, 1885), 67–68.

101. See, for example, Gregory of Tours, *Liber in gloria confessorum* 78, ed. Bruno Krusch, MGH SS rer. Merov. 1, 2 (Hanover, 1885), 346: citizens of Reims a. 543 against the Plague; *LH* III, 29, 125–26: a procession a. 542 in Zaragoza against a siege; *LH* VI, 11, 282: Theodorus of Marseilles "cum grandi est a civibus laude susceptus" (for this story see below at n. 116); *LH* X, 30, 525: in Tours and Nantes a. 591 against the Plague; *LH* IV, 5, 138 and Gregory of Tours, *Liber vitae patrum* 6, 6, ed. Bruno Krusch, MGH SS rer. Merov. 1, 2 (Hanover, 1885), 234: in Clermont a. 543 against the Plague; *LH* IV, 4, 226: under Quintianus of Rodez against a drought; similarly at burials, e.g., *LH* VII, 3, 238–39.

102. Victricius of Rouen, *De laude Sanctorum* 3, ed. René Herval, in his *Origines chrétiennes. De la IIe Lyonnaise gallo-romaine à la Normandie ducale* (Rouen and Paris, 1966), 108–53, 114–17; for a corrective to the tendency to claim this text as the main evidence for corporatively organized processions, see Jussen, "Bischofsherrschaften," 694–98.

103. Constance de Lyon, *Vie de Saint Germain d'Auxerre* 46, ed. René Borius, Sources Chrétiennes 112 (Paris, 1965), 202.

104. *Vita Caesarii* II, 49, 501; on this vita see Klingshirn, *Caesarius of Arles*, 6–9.

105. For more on the vita and its interpretation see Gisela Muschiol, *Famula Dei. Zur Liturgie in merowingischen Frauenklöstern*, Beiträge zur Geschichte des alten Mönchtums und des Benediktinerordens 41 (Münster, 1994), 27–28 (on the literature) and Index, s.v.; see also Wittern, *Frauen, Heiligkeit und Macht*, 90–107, and 176 n. 107 with analogies between the vitas of Caesarius and Rusticula.

106. *Vita Rusticulae* c. 17, ed. Bruno Krusch, MGH SS rer. Merov. 4 (Hanover and Leipzig, 1902): 347.

107. The reason for this was that the emperor could turn to face either the senators or the *plebs*; see Ammianus Marcellinus, *Roman History*, 16, 10, 6, trans. John C. Rolfe, 3 vols. (London and Cambridge, Mass., 1963), vol. 1, 244–45: "unde cum se uertisset ad plebem."

108. Ammianus Marcellinus, *Roman History*, 16, 10, 5, vol. 1, 244–45: "cumque urbi propinquaret, senatus officia reuerendasque patriciae stirpis effigies ore sereno contemplans." The mention of effigies in such a procession is bewildering and tends to be ignored in analyses of the text and glossed over in translations; while Rolfe's English translation refers to "the august likenesses of the patrician stock," the German translator Seyfarth speaks of "the venerable figures of patrician origin" (Ammianus Marcellinus, *Römische Geschichte*, trans. Wolfgang Seyfarth, Berlin, 1983, 174). The text makes no sense, however, if we understand the effigies as a metaphor; there is no reason not to believe that Ammianus meant actual effigies of the patricians, especially since we know that after the end of the effigies in the *pompa funebris*, the patricians tended the *imagines* of their ancestors; this observation of Ammianus's is overlooked, for example, in extensive analyses of the entry in Werner Hartke's *Römische Kinderkaiser. Eine Strukturanalyse Römischen Denkens und Daseins* (Berlin, 1951), 305ff and John Matthews's *The Roman Empire of Ammianus* (Baltimore, 1989), 231ff; for a discussion of the *pompa funebris* the reader is referred to Egon Flaig, "Die Pompa Funebris. Adlige Konkurrenz und annalistische Erinnerung in der Römischen Republik," in *Memoria als Kultur*, ed. Otto Gerhard Oexle, Veröffentlichungen des Max-Planck-Instituts für Geschichte 121 (Göttingen, 1995), 115–48.

109. Matthews, *The Roman Empire of Ammianus*, 231ff with n. 4 (discussion of the literature).

110. Ammianus Marcellinus, *Roman History*, 16, 10, 13, 248–49.

111. *Vita Audoini* 12, ed. Bruno Krusch, MGH SS. rer. Merov. 5 (Hanover and Leipzig, 1910), 560–61.

112. The *Vita Boniti* (MG SSRM 6) recounts that the bishop only set out on the *adventus* when the people and the nobility were already on their way; the author also describes the participation of the magnates with the following exclamation: "How many noble women and men ran out to meet him . . . !"; to interpret this as a "delegation of nobles" at the diocesan border renders the record much more precise in retrospect than the author made it at the time; see Martin Heinzelmann, *Translationsberichte und andere Quellen des Reliquienkultes*, Typologie des sources du moyen âge occidentale 33 (Turnhout, 1979), 73.

113. We also find nothing in regard to the liturgy of the convents in Muschiol, *Famula Dei. Zur Liturgie in merowingischen Frauenklöstern*, here 149–54.

114. According to Raymond Van Dam, the incident occurred in 573 or 574. See his edition of Gregory of Tours, *Glory of the Confessors* (Liverpool, 1988), 35 n. 24; Gregory of Tours, *Liber in Gloria confessorum* 20, ed. Bruno Krusch, MGH SS rer. Mer. 1.2, 309; linguistically, at least, the clerics were not seldom isolated; *Liber in Gloria Martyrum* 82, 94; *LH* VIII, 10, 377 (burial of Chlodovech in 585); *Vita Boniti* 40, ed. Bruno Krusch, MGH SS rer. Merov. 6 (Hanover and Leipzig, 1913), 138.

115. *LH* V, 4, 199; *HF* II:172. Cf. the following note.

116. *LH* VI, 11, 281; Giesebrecht (Gregor von Tours, *Fränkische Geschichte*, Leipzig, 1878), Rudolf Buchner (Gregor von Tours, *Zehn Bücher Geschichte*, vol. 2, Darmstadt, 1955) and Robert Latouche (Grégoire de Tours, *Histoire des Francs*, vol. 2, Paris, 1965) translate *signa* in this case as "bells" (*Glocken*), which corresponds to the linguistic usage of a number of later vitas; in the procession with *dux* Roccolen (see previous note) in contrast, they interpret the *signa* as banners (*Feldzeichen/bannières*, Giesebrecht and Latouche) or, less plausibly, as ecclesiastical banners (*Kirchenfahnen*, Buchner).

117. Both suggestions come from Buchner; Giesebrecht simply leaves the word out,

and Latouche interprets it quite differently: "avec divers drapeaux dèployés en leur hon-neur" (with various flags used in their honor).

118. Breukelaar, *Historiography and Episcopal Authority*, 207–24.

119. *LH* V, 11, 205; *HF* II: 178.

120. The earliest examples have been studied by Michel Rouche, "Les baptêmes forcés en Gaule mérovingienne et dans l'empire d'orient," in *De l'antijudaisme antique à l'antisemitisme contemporain*, ed. V. Nikiprowetzky (Lille, 1979), 105–24; naturally it is conceivable that such excesses occurred earlier as well, and that we know nothing of them only because no author was interested enough to record them; the interpretation would be the same, however; a growing interest among writers could also be interpreted as a sign of changing identities.

121. On Sidonius see above, n. 16; for the text from the *Vita Caesarii* see above n. 104.

122. A scholarly view of such pairs of opposites is conceptualized by Reinhart Ko-selleck in his 1975 essay "Zur historisch-politischen Semantik asymmetrischer Gegen-begriffe," which has been reprinted in his *Vergangene Zukunft* (Frankfurt am Main, 1979), 211–59.

123. *LH* V, 49, 262; *HF* II: 226.

124. *Collectio Avellana*, 1, 2, ed. Otto Guenther, Corpus Scriptorum Ecclesiasticorum Latinorum 35 (Prague, Vienna, and Leipzig, 1895), 2.

125. *Collectio Avellana*, I, 3 S. 3; on the uprising see Karl Suso Frank, "Damasus," in *Lexikon des Mittelalters*, vol. 3 (1986), 469–70; on these documents as possible evidence of the procession as a constitutive element of episcopal elections, see Nikolaus Gussone, *Thron und Inthronisation des Papstes von den Anfängen bis zum 12. Jahrhundert*, Bonner historische Forschungen 41 (Bonn, 1978), 140–41.

126. See above text to nn. 1–3.

127. *LH* IX, 6, 418; *HF* II:374.

128. In a monograph bearing this title (in German, *Die Enteignung der Wahrsager. Studien zum kaiserlichen Wissensmonopol in der Spätantike*, Frankfurt am Main, 1993) Marie Theres Fögen analyzes a sudden "radical attack by the emperor on seers, inter-preters and soothsayers" (13) in the fourth-century legal sources and interprets it as an all-encompassing imperial attempt to monopolize knowledge; outside of Roman *ius* the "total exclusion of any kind of intuitive mantic and the exclusivity of the inductive" (Flaig, *Den Kaiser herausfordern*, 71 n. 122) already had a tradition stretching back to the Re-public; see David Potter, *Prophets and Emperors: Human and Divine Authority from Au-gustus to Theodosius* (Cambridge, Mass., 1994).

129. Heinzelmann, *Gregor von Tours. Zehn Bücher Geschichte*, 42 and 44; Breukelaar, *Historiography and Episcopal Authority*, 242; Marc Reydellet, "La Bible miroir des princes du IVᵉ au VIIᵉ siècle," in *Le monde latin antique et la Bible*, ed. Jacques Fontaine and Charles Pietri, Bible de tous les temps 4 (Paris, 1984), 431–53, 448.

130. An excellent introduction is Klaus Koch, *Die Profeten*, vol. 1., 2nd ed. (Stuttgart, 1987), esp. 11–47.

131. See above, "Behind the Style Question" and "Asceticism."

132. Heinzelmann, *Gregor von Tours. Zehn Bücher Geschichte*, 87, and Breukelaar, *Historiography and Episcopal Authority*, 170.

133. *LH* V, 49, 261 (an assembly of bishops at the king's court): "Tunc cunctis dicentibus: 'Non potest persona inferior super sacerdotem credi' "; 262: "de pauperibus provocatus"; *HF* II:224. On the charismatic as a *famulus* see IX, 6, 420.

134. *LH* IX, 6, 418–19; *HF* II:374.

135. *LH* IX, 6, 418–19; *HF* II:375.

136. *Vita Genovefae* 12, 219.

137. See Breukelaar, *Historiography and Episcopal Authority*, 245–52.

138. The apostolic constitutions (II, 25, 7), for example, had conceptualized the bishops as prophets; cf. *Les constitutions apostoliques*, vol. 1, ed. Marcel Metzger, Sources chrétiennes 320 (Paris, 1985), 230–31; on the mistrust of wandering prophets in the first century see Brown, *The Body and Society*, 43.

139. *LH* V, 14, 210; *HF* II:181.

140. *LH* V, 14, 210: "Cujus ego irridens stultitiam, dixi: A Deo haec poscenda sunt; nam credi non debent quae diabolus repromittit . . . Denique quadam nocte vigiliis in basilica sancti antistitis celebratis, dum lectulo decubans obdormissem, vidi angelum per aera volantem. Cumque super sanctam basilicam praeteriret, voce magna ait: Heu heu! percussit Deus Chilpericum, et omnes filios ejus; nec superabit de his qui processerunt ex lumbis ejus . . . Cum autem haec in posterum impleta fuissent, tunc ad liquidum cognovi falsa esse quae promiserant harioli." *HF* II:181–82.

141. *LH* IX, 6, 417; *HF* II:373.

142. *LH* II, 1, 37; *HF* II:36.

143. *LH* V, 14, 211–12.

144. *LH* V, 14, 210; to be sure, not all stories can be fit into a simple pattern; in another account (also in chapter 5, 14) Merovech understands such an oracle quite well and begins to weep.

145. For more detail on all of this see Breukelaar, *Historiography and Episcopal Authority*, 245–54.

146. See the collection of essays *Herrschaft als soziale Praxis*, ed. Alf Lüdtke, Veröffentlichungen des Max-Planck-Instituts für Geschichte 96 (Göttingen, 1991); one also needs to take into account that the expansion of Merovingian rule rested on other systems of signs and legitimation, for example war, as well.

147. See Ian Wood, *The Merovingian Kingdoms: 450–751* (London and New York, 1994).

148. See Otto Gerhard Oexle, "Conjuratio und Gilde im frühen Mittelalter. Ein Beitrag zum Problem der sozialgeschichtlichen Kontinuität zwischen Antike und Mittelalter," in *Gilden und Zünfte. Kaufmännische und gewerbliche Genossenschaften im frühen und hohen Mittelalter*, ed. Berent Schwineköper, Vorträge und Forschungen 29 (Sigmaringen, 1985), 151–214, esp. 182–83; with reference to the synod of Narbonne in 589 c. 5, in *Concilia Galliae*, ed. De Clercq, 255[40–43]: "Secundum concilium Nycheni sanctissimi concinnabula uel coniurationes non fiant clericorum, quae sub patrocinio solebant fieri laicorum. Nec unusquisque de inferiora gradu seniorem sibi elatus aut increpet aut iniuret."

149. Here one could proceed from the discussions surrounding the nobility's "self-sanctification," which are, to be sure, more concerned with the opposition between king and nobility than with the constellation that interests us here; the fundamental work here is Friedrich Prinz, *Frühes Mönchtum im Frankenreich. Kultur und Gesellschaft in Gallien, den Rheinlanden und Bayern am Beispiel der monastischen Entwicklung (4. bis 8. Jahrhundert)* (Munich, 1965).

150. See Heinzelmann, *Gregor von Tours. Zehn Bücher Geschichte*, and Breukelaar, *Historiography and Episcopal Authority*; Breukelaar (229) insists that in the sixth century,

the lines of conflict ran not, as is usually asserted, between the Franks and the Gallo-Romans, but rather between local rulers (bishops) and regional ones (kings); Gregory enters this conflict on the side of the Christian-legitimated local rulers.

151. Van Dam, *Saints and Their Miracles*, chap. 1.

152. Van Dam, *Saints and Their Miracles*, 41; on Saint Vincent's as a church of the Holy Cross, see Venantius Fortunatus, *Vita Germani* 116, 20: "Item cum Parisius ad basilicam beatae crucis vir dei procederet."

153. See Oexle, "Conjuratio und Gilde im frühen Mittelalter."

154. *LH* VI, 43, 315; *HF* II:275. Breukelaar, *Historiography and Episcopal Authority*, 170.

155. Heinzelmann, *Gregor von Tours. Zehn Bücher Geschichte*, 221 n. 66 with examples from Gregory's *History of the Franks*.

156. *LH* 5, 14, 209; *HF* II:181.

157. Jochen Martin, "Die Macht der Heiligen," in *Christentum und Antike Gesellschaft*, ed. J. Martin and Barbara Quint (Darmstadt, 1990), 440–74, esp. 451–55, quotation 455.

158. Gothic Italy would doubtless be more difficult to describe; it would require a separate study of developments in the episcopal sees.

159. For a detailed account, see Werner Eck, "Der Episkopat im spätantiken Africa. Organisatorische Entwicklung, soziale Herkunft und öffentliche Funktion," *Historische Zeitschrift* 236 (1983): 265–95, esp. 281–85 on the numbers, and 286–91 on social composition.

FIVE

Inventing a Social Category

The Sociogenesis of the Nobility at the End of the Middle Ages

Joseph Morsel

I saw that there is no Nature
That Nature does not exist,
that there are mounts, valleys, plains,
that there are trees, flowers, herbs,
that there are rivers and stones,
but that there is no whole of which these are part,
that a real and true assembly
is nothing else than an illness of our mind.
                              Fernando Pessoa
             "O Guardador de rebanhos," 1914

Adel, roughly, "nobility," is one of those common terms that we have adopted from the Middle Ages and which—because they refer to social formations that have since disappeared from our republics—are increasingly used in a metaphorical sense, which leads to their increasing dehistoricization. Thus the term belongs to those classifications used by sociologists to describe complexes of social characteristics which are however independent of the language normally used to refer to them in their own time. We may also find such an unreflected use of the term "nobility" among historians whenever they treat a historical group of persons who exercised authority by virtue of their own power and more or less monopolized political or military functions in the state apparatus, however rudimentary.[1] The debate, (re)kindled by Heike Grahn-Hoek, over whether the Frankish magnates of the sixth century should be referred to as a "nobility" or an "upper class" has, to be sure, dealt on the one hand with the identification of concrete persons as nobles and on the other with the definition of the term "nobility." No one has yet attempted to examine the relationship between the nobles and the nobility, however,[2] as if the existence of the nobility were, implicitly, a simple consequence of the existence of nobles.[3]

My intention here is not to address the problem of the existence or nonexistence of nobles since the early Middle Ages. Rather, I would like to point out the fateful sociological and sociohistorical short circuit that proceeds from the observed existence of nobles to the existence of a social category, known in this case as "the nobility." Scholars have written as if the social grouping of noble persons were not a process of social production but rather a phenomenon of natural concentration, as if the creation of a social formation were a natural affair defined in terms of its contents or its essential characteristics, and also as if the category (the nobility) did not react to the individual elements (the nobles)—a portion of the qualities of the individual nobles being determined by their membership in the nobility—in short, as if the whole were only a sum of its parts.[4] Such implicit assumptions, which are never put to discussion, are rooted not least in the circumstance that the components (that is, the nobles) are themselves regarded as actual substances, although what we are really looking at are representations of social conditions. Social historians, like sociologists, must break through the "naturalizing" effect (quite welcome in commonsense thinking) of groups portraying themselves, and being perceived, as virtually natural phenomena.

Using the example of the late medieval Frankish nobility, I would like to present such an attempt to break down, in retrospect, the naturalizing effect in social productions. My thesis, to put it a bit provocatively, is that in Franconia— as an exemplary case—the nobility only emerged at the end of the Middle Ages, around the year 1400. What this means is that, although an aristocracy of sociopolitically dominant people existed who—irregularly, ambiguously, and not all of whom—may be referred to as *nobiles*,[5] they by no means constituted the social entity that was later called the "nobility." I am not interested here in juxtaposing a term with a social "reality" in order to see whether the label fits (as if a *word* pointed to a *fact*), but rather to draw our attention to the process of social production itself. The formation of the structure known as the nobility cannot, naturally, be separated from the sociohistorical phenomena that preceded it (such as the feudalization of dynasts and the knightly status of the ministerials), but a decisive and unmistakable turning point occurred on the threshold to the fifteenth century, which led to the constitution of the nobility as a social discourse and, consequently, as a social reality.

Like Swabia and the Upper Rhine (regions in which the knights constituted themselves as an imperial knighthood [*Reichsritterschaft*] in the sixteenth century), Franconia is, to be sure, a borderline case in the history of the sociopolitical development of the late medieval and modern empire. While this history was characterized by state formation within fairly self-contained territories, the three above-mentioned regions stagnated in a state of *territorii non clausi* shot through with noble dominions. But we can learn much about the alleged norm by examining historical constellations in which the old ground rules no longer functioned. The analysis of such special cases necessarily leads us to question the so-called norm: why did developments as they appear to us today take such a course that the norm appears to us to be the norm? Only an analysis of the special case removes the appearance of necessity from the apparent normal case and permits us to see that it is as much a social product as the special case.

The first distancing measure applied here will be lexical statistics.[6] An intensive computer-assisted study of several hundred sources of various kinds[7] has permitted me to undertake lexicometric and semantic analyses, yielding sometimes surprising results. Instead of the apparent but misleading familiarity with the social world under study, we are left with material that begs rational explanation.

The Transformations of a Terminological Field

I collected for computer analysis all of the terms belonging to the semantic field of the nobility, that is, all words or expressions that in some way (lexemically or semantically) mention the noble quality or membership of an individual or group. The words so collected can be seen on the left side of tables 1 and 2. The figures express not the frequency of mentions of the terms themselves, but rather the number of documents in which the searched terms were found. This method of computation was determined by the heterogeneity of the body of texts, since the variations in lexical frequencies from one text to another are often simply related to a change in the type or form of text, and since the types and forms of texts were not distributed evenly over the time period under investigation. The dangers of distortion inherent in this heterogeneity had to be removed by this method. The central finding of table 1 must thus be understood as "an ever greater number texts mention the nobility" and not "the texts mention the nobility ever more frequently," even if the two interpretations are surely closely related. (Table 2 shows that the texts, when they mention nobles at all, refer ever more frequently to the nobility.) The numbers in parentheses refer to the expressions given in parentheses; they are included in the numbers without parentheses. The following symbols are also used in the tables: (D) means that the term refers only to dynasts (titled nobles) and (A) that it refers to nobles (*Adlige*) of all ranks.

At first glance, the tables reveal a complete reversal of the frequency pyramid within one century, the fifteenth. One notices that the adjectives *nobilis* and *edel* were extended to include the entire group of nobles. In addition, one may note that adjectives (*nobilis, edel, unedel*), which characterize individuals, were replaced by nouns (*edelmann, ritterschaft, adel*), of which the most common

Table 1: Evolution of the Lexical-Textual Frequencies (Nominal Values)

	Before 1325	1326–1350	1351–1375	1376–1400	1401–1425	1426–1450	1451–1475	1476–1500	1501–1525	sum
nobilis (D)	4	2								6
edel (D)	1	2	2	5	11	9	12	7	3	52
edelknecht		3	7	3	1	1				15
edel (A)				1	3	6	2	8	8	28
nobilis (A)					1	1		1	4	7
edelmann/ -leute				2	1		4	10	10	27
unedel				1		4	1	1	2	9
ritterschaft (von/ aus der ritt.)				1	1	4	16 (2)	31 (12)	18 (7)	71 (21)
adelig						1		1		2
adel (vom/aus dem adel)							8 (6)	23 (11)	32 (25)	63 (42)
edler							1		1	2
Total	5	7	9	13	22	26	45	82	78	287

Table 2: Evolution of the Lexical-Textual Frequencies (Rounded Off Percentages per Time Period)

	Before 1325	1326–1350	1351–1375	1376–1400	1401–1450	1451–1475	1476–1500	1501–1525
nobilis (D)	80	28.5						
edel (D)	20	28.5	22	38.5	50	34.5	8.5	4
edelknecht		43	78	23	4.5	4		
edel (A)				7.5	14	23.5	10	10
nobilis (A)					4.5	4	1	5
edelmann/-leute				16	4.5		12	13
unedel				7.5		15	1	2.5
ritterschaft				7.5	4.5	15	38	23
zum schild geboren					18			
adelig						4	1	
adel							28.5	41
edler								1.5

(*ritterschaft* and *adel*) refer to structures of social belonging. One was more likely to be "of the nobility" (*vom adel*, alternately *des adels* or *aus dem adel*) than "a nobleman" (*Adliger*), and these forms represent the great majority of mentions of the word *adel*. Or one might have been "of the knighthood" (*aus der ritterschaft*, alternately *von der ritterschaft*), which however was only true of one third of the mentions of *ritterschaft*.

The Spread of the Terms "Nobilis" and "Edel"

Nobilis and *edel* originally referred only to persons of high rank: princes, counts, and free lords, that is, persons belonging to the first four degrees of the "shields of knighthood" (*Heerschild*);[8] they were not used to refer to simple knights and esquires for whom the terms *ritter*, *edelknechte*, *milites*, or *armigeri* were reserved. Since the end of the fourteenth century, however, the designations *nobilis* und *edel* were also granted to lesser bearers of authority,[9] whose only possible titles were knight or esquire and who appear in texts of the late fifteenth century as part of the "common nobility" (*gemeiner adel*). The result appears to have been that the higher aristocracy began to add the designation "high-born" or "well-born" (*hochgeboren, wohlgeboren*) in the early fifteenth century, and to have neglected the terms *edel* or *nobilis* in the second half of that century. It thus appears that the lower strata of the aristocracy tried to adopt the designation *edel* and, perhaps under the influence of socially mobile nobles, to erase the social distinction between themselves and the higher aristocrats.

This shift in the usage of the term *edel* might explain the gradual disappearance of the term *edelknecht*: the men so designated did not disappear, but rather came to be referred to simply as *knecht*, if they were given any appellation at all. It thus appears likely that their characterization as *edel* had become self-evident to contemporaries. This cannot have been a consequence of the unambiguous nature of the word *knecht*, since *knecht* could also be the male counterpart of *magd* (maidservant), and because the designation of the *edelknecht* simply as *knecht* does not appear systematically (in contrast to the consistent reference to knights as *ritter* and their title of "Sir," *herr*). If, then, the title *knecht* did not in itself provide evidence of noble quality, then it must have been a personal identity marked by the patronymic. The patronymic would thus have been an important classification and identification characteristic of the nobility. This does not, however, mean that the noble family was conceived of as a structure for integrating nobles into the nobility. Although we find a growing number of references to the expression "from/of the nobility" (*vom Adel*), we never encounter such expressions as "from a family of the nobility" (*von einem Geschlecht vom Adel*). The study of the evolution of aristocratic uses of patronymics would consequently not be a part of the history of the parental relationship, but rather of the socio-genesis of integrated social groups such as the nobility.

Lexical Groupings of Nobles

It is noteworthy that the new use of the title *edel* appeared at the same time as the earliest use of *ritterschaft* (knighthood) to refer to the collectivity of the counts, lords, and lesser nobles (in 1400).[10] Although the counts and lords were soon (by 1432, at the latest) to disappear from the *ritterschaft* once again, it must be noted that this collective term (note the suffix -*schaft* from the same root as the English -*ship*) defined a category that would include practically all nobles and which was, until around 1430, the only one to which the nobles definitely belonged. The term *adel* was not yet in use.

There is evidence that the shaping of the term *ritterschaft* was an attempt at classification undertaken by territorial rulers. This blanket use of the term tellingly appears in a document issued by the bishop of Würzburg, and it is interesting to note that the dividing line is drawn not between the high and low nobility (princes, counts, and lords on the one side, knights and *edelknechte* on the other), but rather between the territorial ruler and the nobles whom he regarded as his subjects. This attempt at classification apparently failed, since the counts and lords soon appeared outside the *ritterschaft*.

Another term did, however, succeed in subsuming the old and new *edel*-folk: *adel*. In the body of texts subjected to statistical analysis here, the word appears for the first time in 1462, but it is wholly absent from the published collections of medieval Franconian documents, which generally end around the year 1400.[11] The word's late appearance is substantiated by dictionaries,[12] the concordances to literary works[13] and Franconian town chronicles.[14] One may thus be relatively certain that *Adel* was not used as a collective term for nobles (from the prince to the *edelknecht*) until around 1400. The chronology of the word's usage after 1400 remains to be studied in more detail, but it appears to have undergone a fundamental change around 1430–40.[15] One thing is clear, at any rate: the word *adel* has only been used to refer to the nobility since the fifteenth century. The spread of this term cannot be regarded as the simple result of a sudden translation of the Latin word *nobilitas* in this period. The word *nobilitas* was used almost exclusively to refer to the noble quality of a person or action.[16] In addition, in most cases, the use of the term is merely one of numerous examples of the formal adoption of a Roman word (such as *libertas*, *adoptio*, *patria*, and the like) into medieval Latin without the full range of Roman Latin meanings.[17] All of this fits in well with a seemingly offhand observation by Robert Fossier, who has pointed out that the medieval Latin terminology surrounding nobility concentrates more on noble qualities than on "that *nobilitas* [as a category] which is almost never mentioned."[18]

From the fifteenth century on, then, people began to speak more frequently of the nobility (*adel*). The novelty here was not the use of a new word,[19] but rather the quite sudden and general use of a term that referred to a social category, from which noble identity was derived (they are "of the nobility," *vom adel*); an appellation that the nobles adopted for themselves and conceived of as referring to themselves collectively. The equation of *adel* on the one hand and counts/lords/knights/esquires on the other runs through the texts written by nobles (counts, lords, and knights or esquires) around 1500, whereby the knights and esquires are also referred to as the *ritterschaft* or *gemeine adel*. This *gemeine adel* clearly represents the social formation which present-day historians refer to as the "lower nobility."

To recapitulate, in the fifteenth century we may observe a thoroughgoing semantic and lexical transformation which may be interpreted as the discursive emergence of the nobility. At the end of the fifteenth century, the formation of a new social grouping asserted itself with the spread of the term *adel*. Membership in this new formation would henceforth determine the noble quality of those who belonged to it, who were generally referred to as *die vom adel* (those of the nobility).

Substance and Substantives

What is the sociohistorical significance of this linguistic development, and above all, what does it tell us about the existence of a nobility? To what extent does the appearance of a new word or word usage signify a new structuring of society? Are these innovations merely pointless fashions, reflections of social transformations, or even active participants in those transformations? Does the absence of the word *adel* mean that what it was later understood to signify did not yet exist? Does it mean that the nobility only began to exist on the day when it was first given a name of its own and instruments of representation (which, as we will see presently, arose at around the same time)? Or, to turn the question around, does the emergence of a word mean nothing in regard to the existence of the social formation?[20]

I should emphasize first of all that historians, to be sure, have to refer to those formations that existed before the lexicalization of the nobility, and they may do so by using graphic distancing measures (such as quotation marks or italics) or special expressions ("noble persons"[21] instead of "the nobility," or a collective noun—if it is absolutely necessary—such as *Nobilität* or even "pre-nobility"). But whatever method we choose, we must never forget that each of these methods is a component of a classification which as such aims to shape, order, and reify social groupings. Consequently, we cannot simply adopt one of these methods without running the risk of reifying a social order implicitly or defining it in terms of an apparently natural character. The substantive creates social substance—but faith in the identity between substance and substantive (which one could call "substantialism" or "realism") erases the social process of linguistic production. Words which appear merely to describe a social reality nevertheless contribute to its creation: every description is at the same time a prescription.

The rejection of realism does not necessarily lead to nominalism, that is, to the belief in a fundamental distinction between social reality and its designations. Social reality does not exist independent of its ideational and linguistic formalization, since all social relationships necessarily have an ideational side, not only in order to legitimate and reproduce them, but also because the ground rules of these relationships, at least, must (implicitly or not) be present in the minds of individuals in order for them to enter into a relationship with each other in the first place.

This means that individuals must conceive explicitly of at least fragments of their society (that is, the system of all social relationships) in order to be able to act within the context of society. A new ideational construction, such as arose with the discursive emergence of the nobility, for example, should thus be regarded as a genuine instrument of social action and consequently as a genuine component of the social system. Such a change in the explicit conceptions of the social world was thus not a random game, but rather an active element of social change.

Furthermore, the concept of the nobility, as we see it emerging in Franconia, may at first have been a purely ideological or strategic concept, but it later became a palpably self-evident conceptual framework, which guided behavior, values, emotions, and, in turn, ideology—similarly, for example, to the idea of the three estates or orders of the trifunctional scheme (*oratores, bellatores, laboratores*). Thus when we enquire into the emergence and existence of the nobility we should take to heart the demand, now self-evident among sociologists, that we drop the opposition between ideal and reality.[22]

A successful linguistic or written development therefore demonstrates that a fundamental social process has occurred. On the one hand, it is an element and symptom of this process. On the other, it has had massive reifying and objectivating consequences. Historians must be aware of these consequences, because if we forget the sociogenetic moment we will be led to assume an apparently natural presence or institutionalization of the grouping. Without this awareness, historians will contribute to the credibility of the permanence and continuity of the category (that is, of the social relations to which it corresponds).

The nobility was thus created in the sociopolitical imaginative world in which it became a category of perception and action. Although this process has been represented and perceived as if the formation, originally a silent aggregate, had merely acquired a form and a name, it was not a process of purely formal revelation of something preexisting. The linguistic construction must have been directly connected to other social developments, which it helped to focus, in order for the new terminology successfully to take root. This social process (of which the linguistic and written changes form a large component) will be analyzed in more detail from the perspective of its two inseparable and simultaneous creative aspects: the processes of composition and enforcement. The process of composition led to the inner constitution and discursive homogenization of the social group of the nobility. Inseparable from this was the process of enforcement, which led to the self-evident acceptance of the group as—to some degree—an "objective" and "natural" fact by all those who belonged to it, as well as by outsiders, with the result that the production and reproduction of the group was legitimized as the normal case.

The Process of Composition

Research on the South German nobility has long recognized the individual political signs of this process—the leagues (*Einungen*),[23] noble societies,[24] tournaments,[25] occasional assemblies,[26] and the holding of castles in coparcenary (*Ganerbschaft*)[27]—without, however, connecting them all, let alone from this single vantage point. These phenomena are so well known that they do not need to be dealt with in detail here, nor would the allotted space permit it.

THE SYNTHETIC EFFECTS OF CONVERGENT STRATEGIES

In Franconia the important turning point came in the period around 1400: the first of the noble societies, although peripheral, go back to the years 1379 and 1387. The most significant and long-lived Franconian society, that of the Fürspänger, was probably founded in 1392; the first league (*Einung*), locally very limited, was active in 1398, and the first large general Franconian league (*Einung*) appears in 1402.[28] At the same time, remarkably enough, we may note two discursive innovations: the first general use of the word *ritterschaft* (1400) and the introduction of a new principle of classification in the registers of fiefs and vassals of the bishops of Würzburg, namely, the distinction between noble and nonnoble vassals[29]—a principle that also appears in other feudal courts during the fifteenth century. All of these phenomena appeared at a time of great conflict between cities and "lords" in southern Germany and then between the territorial towns and the bishop in the principality of Würzburg. The conflicts were just reaching a high point in the year 1400 when the united towns of the principality were overthrown by episcopal troops. The separation of vassals in the register of fiefs and vassals of the new bishop, who a few months before had led the army as provost of the cathedral, may have been a response to the attempt at rebellion by the towns, which had hoped to escape the jurisdiction of the bishop by gaining free imperial status as a group. Henceforth the burgher and peasant fiefs were classified locally, that is, according to a spatial, territorial logic, while the noble vassals continued to be listed according to the date on which they had received the fief, that is, according to a personal, feudal logic.

The written distinction may also, however, have been a political, symbolic attempt by the new bishop to drive a wedge between noble and nonnoble vassals, since the rebellious towns had received very dangerous support from noble vassals, which the bishop had managed to counter only after long and hard struggles. Neither in Franconia nor elsewhere was there any well established sociopolitical split between nobles and nonnobles which the bishop might have utilized.[30] It thus had to be created, and it is from this perspective that we may interpret the new manner of registering fiefs, together with the contemporaneous universalizing introduction of the term *ritterschaft* in episcopal documents.

It would be wrong, however, to regard the new formal ties between nobles as a simple consequence of princely pressure. To do so would be to overlook the fact that nobles also regarded their connections in societies and leagues as necessary in the face of the newly emerged territorial rulers, and that the nobles proved themselves resistant to pressure (the Great League of 1402, the failure of the global use of *ritterschaft*). It would thus be more correct to interpret the new noble grouping less as the consequence of a conscious intention (to construct a nobility) than of the deployment of several strategies on the part of both princes and nobles, whose convergence in one and the same sociopolitical form had important synthetic effects. At the beginning of the fifteenth century, however, none of the strategies had yet produced any ultimate result: the bishop did not succeed in holding all of his vassals, nor in keeping them out of the towns; at the same time splits continued to exist among nobles, as indicated by the failure of the blanket use of *ritterschaft* to take hold and by persistent feuds, as witnessed by the omnipresent arbitration clauses in the founding and organizational texts of all Franconian leagues beginning in 1402.[31] Factors other than the sociopolitical strategies must have been at work in order for the fifteenth century nobility to emerge.

Princes and Noble Lineages

In his study of the Würzburg feudal court in the late Middle Ages, Hans-Peter Baum reaches two central conclusions. First, "that the feudalization of Lower Franconia undoubtedly made great strides in the fourteenth and fifteenth centuries," with feudalization defined as the enfeoffment of ever more towns by the bishops of Würzburg and the transformation by "families" of the lower nobility of ever more freeholds into fiefs of Würzburg (mainly held in the male line)— which also applied to other feudal lords. Second, that, in the light of the value of fiefs and the disappearance of urban noble "families," "the lower nobility was a more homogenous social stratum in 1500 than it had been in 1300."[32] The feudal court played a major role in this homogenization process, contributing to the distribution and, ultimately, concentration of important instruments of power within the lower noble stratum. In addition, it contributed to the ever growing distinction between noble and nonnoble vassals, not only by separate bookkeeping in the registers of fiefs and vassals, but also by introducing different inheritance structures for fiefs held in the male line.[33]

One may also assume that relations of service and appointments to the cathedral chapter also contributed to the homogenization of the noble stratum, since they led to a temporary and thus open distribution of certain positions of authority within the group of nobles as a whole.[34] As Kurt Andermann has firmly emphasized, members of the lesser nobility were enabled, thanks to positions in the princely service and chapter of canons, "to participate in political power that would otherwise have been closed [to them]; participation in governance, after all, offered not merely the above-mentioned material advantages, which should not be underestimated, but above all political influence and social prestige, and contributed decisively to the economic and social stabilization of the noble position."[35] The feudal law court, the court, and the administrative apparatus—the princely territory appears to have constituted itself as a particular efficient structure for the reproduction of noble power and authority.[36]

This reproduction of the feudal aristocracy on the level of the princely territory appears to have favored a specific dimension of discursive structuring, namely that of the noble "lineage" (*Geschlecht*), which was conceived of agnatically and, depending upon individual political, economic, and social circumstances, crystallized around landed property, courts, or castles, but in any case around a patronymic, a coat of arms, and a crest, often referred to in the fifteenth century as *geschlecht, helm, name und schild*.[37] The maintenance and inheritability of noble authority over the land and its inhabitants, which represented the chief aims of the dynastic-familial structuring process, also received significant support, willingly or not, from the princes and their administrations. This support included, for example, the introduction of a special inheritance for—and only for—noble fiefs held in the male line, or a real, albeit irregular, filling of an unchanging succession of territorial offices by members of the same families whenever these offices partially overlapped with their own territories, which served not merely to strengthen the noble family's geographical ties, but also the legitimacy of their authority. Let us also recall the support—so essential to the noble families—that the princes offered in suppressing peasant uprisings against their authority over the land and its inhabitants.

This princely support of the dynastic-familial structure, which clearly followed the usual pattern of personal relations, was the consequence of noble resistance, by means of leagues and multiple vassalage, to the striving for territorialization that followed the formation of a grouping of subjects.[38] It was also the result of a possible convergence of princely strategies. The princes were interested on the one hand in playing individual families against the emerging noble collectivity in order to hinder or weaken noble coalitions by fomenting conflicts of family interest. On the other hand, they were concerned to keep the nobles out of the towns, and pursued this policy by favoring nobles discursively and practically, and by maintaining the existing system of rule in the countryside. Finally, the princes were also anxious to safeguard their own family interests. Similar interests may have been pursued quite seriously by certain bishops of Würzburg, who came ever more frequently from the lower nobility and probably tended to favor their own family members.

Territorial principality thus appears as a global reproductive structure of the aristocracy—as a collectivity of those families whose members were considered noble. This does not mean, however, that economic equality between the individual nobles had been created: the differences became leveled between the various families in regard to the kinds of instruments of power, which helped constitute the collectivity of noble families as a structurally homogeneous ruling class. However greatly their territories may have differed in size, the sources of their authority (allods, fiefs, or offices) were basically equal. This does not mean that the members of the noble families were dependent upon the princely state, as can be observed for France; this difference was apparent even to the Franconian nobles of that time.[39] The Franconian nobles did not, to use Philippe Contamine's apt phrase, proceed "from power to privileges."[40] Leagues and later cantonal organization provided strong backing, as their successful resistance to an imperial tax, the *Gemeiner Pfennig*, in 1495 reveals. Perhaps it was also the fear of a coalition between the nobles and the towns, which nobles used as a threat and managed to realize in the fifteenth century (with the official support of King Sigismund in 1422), that gave them leverage against the princes. In the course of the appearance of the term *adel*, the noble families thus underwent a process in which their positions were relatively homogenized and preserved within the social process of the emergence of territorial rule. This social homogenization process was inseparably linked to a process of delimitation, which increasingly isolated nobles from nonnobles, particularly the urban strata.

THE NOBILITY AS A PRODUCT OF THE CONFLICT BETWEEN THE NOBLES AND THE TOWNS

The use of the term *adel* to refer to the nobles as a group only appears to have become common in Franconia, as in Swabia and the Upper Rhineland, after about 1430–40.[41] At the same time, the tensions between the cities on the one side and the princes and nobles on the other intensified. In both Swabia and Franconia, assaults by nobles on the towns and the territories under their jurisdiction increased. These tensions led to a revival of the Swabian league of towns on the one hand and to the (first) margrave's war (1449–53) on the other. The reasons for these tensions in Franconia, which are the only ones that interest us here, cannot be explained in detail. It must be emphasized, however, that explanations limited solely to Franconia are insufficient: they may help us to understand why Nuremberg, which originally preferred to remain outside the Swabian league of towns in order to preserve its own interests,[42] eventually entered the fray after all. They also, however, ignore the important background to the conflicts: the balance of power in the empire, between the king/emperor and the princes, nobles, cities and Swiss confederation,[43] peasants, and so forth.

What is important, however, is the simultaneity between these tensions and the incipient usage of *adel* to refer to nobles as a group. If we compare the semantic fields before and after 1440–50, we notice new oppositions arising alongside and, to an ever growing extent, also in place of the semantic opposition between towns on the one hand and princes, counts, lords, knights and esquires, or princes, counts, lords and noblemen, or simply lords, on the other—namely, the opposition between cities and the nobility (*der adel*) or those of the nobility (*die vom adel*).[44]

It seems that the appearance of a new usage (*adel* for the entire group of nobles) was intimately connected with the conflict between princes and nobles on the one hand and towns on the other, that is, with a relationship of social delimitation. The development of a new discursive polarization in which both sides must have participated was thus directly tied to what Klaus Graf has aptly referred to as a "Cold War" between the towns and the nobility in the years between 1430 and 1440.[45] This discursive polarization is the result of the pointed expression of new and discursively focused social developments—an expression which led to a new pattern of interpretation of social reality.[46]

One can thus observe a multifaceted process of composition in late medieval Franconia, which led to the inner constitution of a social formation referred to as the nobility. On the one hand we may observe the organization of those aristocrats who felt threatened by the leveling measures of the nascent territorial state and fought back by creating leagues, assemblies, tournaments, castles held in coparcenary (*Ganerbenburgen*), and comparable structures of joint action and self-assertion. On the other hand, we may observe a tendency to homogenization and stabilization of the positions of the lower nobility in Franconia, thanks mainly to the courts and administrations of the territorial rulers. At the same time, the Franconian princes attempted to keep the nobles away from the towns and probably also to sow dissension among them, on the one hand by putting an interpretive scheme (noble/nonnoble) into place in writing and feudal law, and on the other by seeking to bolster the noble families as a means of splitting the nobility. The rising tensions between the towns and the princes, particularly between Nuremberg and the Margrave of Brandenburg, were an additional factor that led to a confrontation between nobles and towns comparable to that which had occurred at the end of the fourteenth century. This time, however, the result was regarded as an antagonism not between the princes, counts, lords, knights, and esquires on the one side and cities on the other, but rather between the "nobility" and the towns. This drawing of a discursive boundary mainly constituted the towns as an antipole to the nobility, with urbanites referred to as nonnoble, thus keeping them out of the nobility. All of this means that the constitution of a new social reality cannot be regarded simply as an aggregation of passive components in a neutral environment: a particular dynamic had to be set in motion before older structures could be broken down and new ones could assert themselves.

The Process of Enforcement

In order for the formation, with its inner structure and its limits, to become visible within the network of social relationships, it had to be portrayed, and its own peculiar characteristics stylized, so that it might attain the collective conviction without which it could not gain social recognition. In fact, the stylization of a social formation's characteristics prevents both its absorption into larger complexes (such as the *populus*, the "Franconians," the feudal courts, the leagues of subjects, and so forth) in which it was no longer recognized as a specific social form, and its endless fragmentation, which might result from attention being trained on its inner differences (for example, the identity of the noble families). This stylization is the most important dimension of the process of enforcement, whereby we should recall that the stylized representation appeared not *after* the practical emergence of the social formation, in order to position it within the network of social constellation, but *at the same time*. Representation is an essential component of social production, not the visualization of something already given.

The "Lineage" (*Geschlecht*) Versus the Nobility

The noble quality of persons lay in their membership in the nobility: they were "of the nobility" (*vom adel*) and, as a consequence, noble (*adlig*). Alongside the nobles and the nobility (as already indicated above) there was also an increasingly significant discursive basic structure, the noble lineage. The sources only speak of people being of the nobility (*vom adel* or *des adels*), but never of being of a family of the nobility, (*von einem geschlecht vom adel* or *des adels*). In relation to the nobility, then, the *Geschlecht* was terminologically eliminated.

This silence of the sources appears to point to a difficulty in integrating the discourse on the *Geschlecht* within the nobility. This discourse, which portrays the noble *Geschlecht* as the normal, significant, and self-evident kinship structure, corresponds to a patrimonial strategy essentially dedicated to securing the inheritance of those goods and people regarded as patrimonial within a particular kin group. This strategy is based on several preconditions: the identification and simultaneous strict delimitation of the kin group as against others; the identification of the lands and people who belonged to this kin group; the mobilization of all of the kin group's forces to protect the patrimony; and the creation of appropriate procedures for the succession. The noble *Geschlecht* represents the discursive dimension in and through which all of these conditions were met, namely, by means of the fixation of the lineage's name and coat of arms,[47] of the agnatic succession to noble fiefs, of the maintenance of written records,[48] and above all by means of frequent feuds.[49]

The discourse on the noble *Geschlecht* could thus represent a substantial hindrance to the coordination of actions by nobles, and the cohesion of the nobility could be endangered by the respective interests of individual *Geschlechter*. The repeated emphasis on arbitration clauses in the founding texts and statutes of the leagues (and later also of the tournaments), which was already mentioned above, is thus evidence not only of the persistence of conflicts between noble kin groups—which is substantiated by case studies—but also of the attempt to regulate feuds rather than prohibit them altogether,[50] since they fulfilled an indispensable social function. These regulations were intended to help articulate two needs: the sociopolitical cooperation among nobles which was required in order to resist the leveling measures undertaken by territorial rulers, and the cohesion of kin groups which had developed for the purpose of patrimonial reproduction. Similarly, one finds innovations in the discourse on kinship in late medieval Franconia which also aimed to enable *Geschlechter* with often opposing but at any rate quite specific interests to form ties without sacrificing these interests in the name of cooperation. As a discourse about social integration, noble anthroponymy in particular was one of these innovations intended to promote the adaptation and articulation of the two discursive structures (the nobility and the noble *Geschlecht*).[51]

ANTHROPONYMY, GROUP FORMATION, AND GROUP DELIMITATION

The change in patronymic and sphragistic customs also reveals a discursive transformation of women's position in aristocratic society. Until the middle of the fourteenth century, women most often used the same seals as their husbands, whose patronymic, coat of arms, and crests they adopted. Unless the women were of a higher rank than their spouses, they were regularly referred to only by their husbands' patronymics and, in the charters, as the wife (or mother, sister, or daughter) of a man named in full. In the late fourteenth and early fifteenth centuries, however, women began to use their fathers' coat of arms and names on their seals, and texts frequently referred to them not only by their husbands' patronymics but by their fathers' as well, as in "Margaretha Truchseß, born Steinrückin."[52]

As for the anthroponymy of men, we find signs of a similar development beginning at the end of the fourteenth century. Alongside their own patronymics, men also began to use their mothers' names with the paratactic element "called," as in "Hans von Thüngen, called von Eisenbach," son of a Thüngen and an Elsbeth von Eisenbach. One encounters this pattern for a brief time only, though; by 1400 appellations already concentrated on the paternal name only.

For both men and women, this development reveals an emphasis on descent and may thus be regarded as an indicator of the heightened identity of the individual noble *Geschlechter*. It should also be emphasized, though, that these changes were largely *discursive* in nature. *Structurally* women remained the links between two kin groups, which thereby incurred obligations to each other. What was new was that the identity of the noble kin groups so connected was now to be made visible beyond their own kinship circles, and that it emphasized only one part, referred to as the *Geschlechter*: all other social actors were made aware of the tie through the written and sphragistic marking of women's origins.[53]

The triple naming of women now led to the *visible* weaving of a noble social fabric, which was conceived of not as the mere coexistence of noble kin groups, but as a network of *Geschlechter* structured by matrimony. It appears that women's social role was now the structural integration of the nobility (by linking the noble *Geschlechter* to each other), while men's was the reproduction of the patrimonially oriented structure of noble *Geschlechter*. The necessary harmonization of the emergence of the nobility with patrimonial interests appears to have led to a fundamental discursive separation between the patrimonial and matrimonial dimensions of the aristocratic social structure (that is, descent and alliance): on the one hand the patrilinear discourse was intensified, while on the other, and inextricably linked with it, the social fabric was understood in matrimonial terms. The fact that it was apparently women who selected (or excluded) the helmets and crests for the participants in knightly tournaments and rewarded the victors does not reflect some mere courtly gesture. It was, rather, a ritual expression of their integrative function.[54] The integration of the nobility, and incorporation into the nobility, were thus henceforth portrayed in matrimonial terms, a circumstance also expressed in the way in which membership in the nobility was measured. The reference to the four ancestors (two paternal and two maternal) demonstrates integration into a matrimonially structured formation, which is not the case when one pointed to the number of generations of one's *noble* ancestors (as for example in France). The reference to four ancestors also had a delimiting function, since it showed tacitly who belonged only by matrimony and was thus not integrated into the nobility. In this way a self-definition of group membership was achieved: the nobility was defined not as a community of descent but as a community by marriage.

On the level of the patronymic, but also of the first name,[55] naming thus appears to have been a site of the attempted articulation of two social discourses—that on the nobility and that on the noble family. The same might be said of the tournament.

The Knightly Tournament as a Site of Noble Self-Definition

Many historians have remarked upon the astonishing revival of the chivalric world at the end of the Middle Ages—as witnessed, among other things, by the popularity of knightly first names. Since there was a widespread belief in the existence of a late medieval crisis of the nobility, this revival of chivalric culture has been considered a sign of crisis, an attempt to escape into an ideal world free of princes and burghers. This view does not, however, apply to Franconia, and probably not to other regions as well. Since the observed phenomena were not part of a true chivalrization of the nobility (as measured by the frequency of knightings),[56] we need to examine them as intellectual or symbolic phenomena. And yet the intellectual or symbolic should not be regarded as merely random or as trivial games; as Durkheim was the first to teach us, the ideal does not stand outside of reality, so that thought reality is part of reality. We also know how important such concepts are for connecting separate individuals and creating a common action dynamic. The process of aggregation would be virtually inconceivable without the mobilizing force of such concepts. Since it referred to knights, this ideology contained a model of equality and of a specific mode of living which makes it logical to portray the nobility as homogeneous (knightly) and as corporatively specific.

The understanding of the nobility as the entirety of all nobles (from prince to esquire) appears most emphatic in the texts that describe the great tournaments of the late fifteenth century. This applies particularly to the earliest of these texts (the 1478 invitation to participate in a tournament,[57] the Würzburg jousting ordinance, and the sumptuary laws recorded on the occasion of this tournament in 1479), which aim to revive the chivalric tournament and are thus of a purely programmatic nature.[58] These texts point out that participation in the tournament was one of the most important signs of, and thus one of the most important conditions for, membership in the nobility. Thus a social boundary was set up which at once continued to rest on matrimonial integration and stressed participation in the social dramaturgy of the tournament.

Since the reproduction of the noble *Geschlecht* played an important role in the reproduction of the nobility itself, it was unavoidable that visible inequalities would exist among nobles, according to their (largely inherited) wealth and titles. In order to prevent these ineradicable inequalities from endangering the discursive homogeneity of the nobility, what was unavoidable had to be integrated. The sumptuary laws and jousting ordinances issued in Würzburg in 1479, Heidelberg in 1481, and Heilbronn in 1485 accordingly denied any economic differentiation: competition between nobles was banished from the tabooed field of luxury and implicitly restricted to the field of the tournament. In addition the princes, counts, lords, knights, and esquires, although in fact graduated according to permitted expenditure, were grouped together in the sumptuary laws, as if there were no differences of quality but only of degree (within a single social quality, that of being of the nobility). In a similar way the differences of rank and title were integrated as a simple hierarchy of dignities: the difference in rank between princes and nonprincely nobles was placed on the same plane as the difference between knights and esquires. Through this integration of descent, expenditure, and titles (that is, ultimately, of noble origins) among nobles who participated in tournaments, the nobility was portrayed as homogeneous and structured.

Since the letter of invitation to the tournaments of 1478 attributed the same origins ("praiseworthy origins") to princes as to other nobles, and consequently all tournament participants were equal, and since tournament practice was portrayed as the chivalric side of noble existence,[59] the princes too must have appeared in the eyes of lesser aristocrats as part of the world of the nobility. All tournaments were held in towns[60] and particularly in the princely residences, which makes clear the tournament's dramaturgical function: it was conceived of not only as a means of structuring the noble fabric, but also, and particularly, as a means of asserting the nobility's existence and self-determination both within and without. By integrating princes into the jousting nobility in regard to expenditure, title, and descent, the territorial rulers were placed on the same level as other noblemen. This contrasts sharply with the early modern idea of the state, which radically separated heads of state from their subjects and conceived of them as essentially distinct beings. Even those urban strata excluded from participating in the tournaments were witnesses to the equestrian prowess of the nobility and their discursively monopolistic exercise of legitimate violence, and thus to their superior power and also the essentially different quality of the nobility, which presented itself as a homogeneous and closed social formation with its own patterns of behavior. While in other regions (in France, for instance) the king or prince and in some cases the towns could determine judicially who was noble and who was not,[61] in Franconia the tournament enacted a self-definition and self-recruitment of the nobility, which it also asserted vis-à-vis other social and political forces.

By means of first names and tournaments the Franconian nobles had thus created a kinship and chivalric model which at once delimited and isolated the nobility. In so doing the nobility was represented as homogeneous—a homogeneity articulated in conjunction with the reproduction of noble *Geschlechter* such that the one would not be detrimental to the other. It is in this way that we must understand chivalry as an ideological discourse which not only created a discursive equality among the members of the nobility directly at the level of individual nobles, but also, indirectly at the level of the noble *Geschlechter*, produced a diminution of differences.[62]

Discourse and Counterdiscourse

We may also mention the critical discourses directed against the nobility as apparently paradoxical contributions to the growing currency of the word "nobility." These included urban discourses which attacked nobles as bandits, as well as those from various nonnoble quarters that called into question the nobility as such.

Scholars have frequently noted that the late medieval urban sources increasingly report highway robberies which were committed by noblemen against merchants as part of alleged feuds. For a long time, historians regarded the assaults on townspeople or even against the towns themselves as signs of a crisis of the late medieval nobility, and some continue to do so today. This view has proven problematic, however, and needs to be revised.[63]

In order to refute the still dominant thesis of a crisis of the late medieval nobility and of their growing impoverization, we need only point out that the leaders of and participants in feuds were not impoverished (and also not thoroughly antiprincely) noblemen.[64] According to the accounts of a Nuremberg spy (himself noble), Franconian noblemen regarded feuds against the towns as proofs of their strength and superiority. The French chronicler Commynes explained the feuds and assaults against cities and princes in the German empire in terms of political rather than economic motives. The feuds against the cities conducted by noblemen and the criminalization of noble feuds by the towns must thus be assessed from another perspective. The approach chosen here suggests that we interpret these feuds as the result of a clash between two discourses of self-assertion. Just as the terms "nobility" and "towns" cannot be separated, the two discourses (of "opposition to the cities" and "opposition to the nobles")[65] should not be analyzed in isolation from each other: the one determines the other.

Interestingly enough, the two conflicting positions—the accusation of robbery against the nobility on the one hand[66] and the view of the feud as proof of strength and superiority on the other—are defined around problems of the circulation of goods. This circulation obeyed two wholly different logics, depending upon whether one looked at it from the position of the nobles conducting the feud or the townspeople who criminalized that same behavior. On the one side we find a sociopolitical, traditional, and aristocratic logic (giving and taking as signs and instruments of power), and on the other an economic, new, and urban logic (buying and selling as signs and instruments of wealth).[67] By conducting a feud, nobles emphasized the social, political, and cultural boundary between themselves and the urban nonnobles, while by criminalizing noble behavior the cities emphasized a similar boundary between themselves and the nobility. It is thus quite possible that the creation of a noble identity which was largely organized around the distinction from nonnobles is the chief explanation for the acts of violence complained of by the towns, in particular, which was in turn inextricably linked to the creation of an urban identity. The urban criminalization of nobles emphasized particular social values, but above all helped foster closer ties within the urban communities, as they may be observed for the time in question in Shrovetide plays,[68] patrician donation practices,[69] or the commemoration of battles.[70] It would doubtless be wrong, however, to view the objective of such noble or urban discourses as the calculated assertion of one or the other (feudal or burgher) social logic: what we see at work here is, rather, a discursive concentration of conflicting interest groups around one or the other of the two logics that coexisted in the late medieval social system. The urban discourse should not be regarded as a deliberate response containing the seeds of social and economic progress: it was, instead, the most suitable strategy for defending the interests of the urban upper strata, who were thereby enabled to mobilize the various forces in the city.

The discourse of criminalization in the cities did not, however, lead to the calling into question of the existence of an aristocratic group, nor even to the rejection of nobles as such: instead, the equation of the nobility with bandits demonstrates the acknowledgment, albeit critical, of the existence of the nobility as the collectivity of nobles.

In other cases, in contrast, we encounter the complete denial that the group of nobles constituted a nobility. Here the distinction between a value and its negative realization is effaced. In fact we know of several attempts to represent the cities as reservoirs of antique *nobilitas*, as if the rural nobles were mere marginal figures.[71] Scholars have also noted that the fifteenth century witnessed a growing preoccupation with the issue of the nobility of birth and the nobility of virtue.[72] The traditional ecclesiastical discourse on virtue was at first mirrored and then superseded by a secular one. Two things are, nevertheless, striking here: first, the existence of a nobility was not in itself questioned. The cities promoted not equality but a reversal of the existing hierarchy. The aristocratic principle was retained, but there were hot debates over who embodied this principle. Second, the rejection of the nobility was clearly directly connected to the rejection of the urbanity of town dwellers by the nobles[73] as well as to the behavioral norms attributed to nobles as a group in the jousting ordinances, so that the hereditary nobility was at the same time the nobility of virtue. The reciprocal denial of status was, however, not merely a matter of precedence or prestige, but an ideological problem as well. The denial of the difference between burghers and peasants led discursively to a sociopolitical subjugation of both to the nobility, because the burghers could thereby be brought back into the framework of the rural system of authority. And the denial of the nobility of nobles was repeatedly marshaled as an argument against their ecclesiastical dominance.

The late medieval church has frequently been referred to as a "hospital for the nobility" (*Adelsspital*) and this bond between the nobility and the church has been viewed as a crisis phenomenon in the history of the nobility. One might begin by objecting that in the late Middle Ages all social groups and strata preferred to regard the church as their "hospital."[74] Furthermore, the Franconian nobles themselves used the hospital argument as means of legitimating their occupation of convents and monasteries,[75] which would already appear to work against the view that this argument was an expression of social weakness. A certain equivalence was also established between the filling of benefices in cathedral chapters and participation in tournaments.[76] The word *Adel* was thus the operative concept in the expression *Adelsspital*, and not *Spital* with its overtones of suffering. To the extent that the term was adopted, the category of the nobility was not called into question. Critics merely denied that the nobility, for whom the church was reserved, was represented by the hereditary aristocrats. Criticisms, which juxtaposed a *nobilitas spiritualis* with the *nobilitas carnis*, neither questioned the principle that positions in the church should be reserved for a particular elite (sometimes referred to as a "nobility"), nor the existence of a *nobilitas*. All that was at stake were the principles according to which people gained access to church office. Through this dramatization of the principle of nobility in the recruitment of the higher clergy, it came to replace knightly birth as a prerequisite. The construction of the term *Adelsspital* and the attempts to redefine (not to abolish) it led to a sort of discursive institutionalization of the existence of the nobility.

Like the terminological pair nobility/cities (*adel/städte*), these discourses, which constituted themselves in opposition to the noble discourse, cannot be separated from it, since the latter developed not least in opposition to these counterdiscourses. The production of a counterdiscourse also contributed to the belief in the existence of the nobility: the accumulation of various sometimes conflicting discourses, even if they are critical and deny the sociopolitical primacy of the nobility, leads to increased representations of the category and thus also favors the understanding of it as a "natural" fact.[77] The more we speak of a category, the more firmly anchored its existence becomes in the collective mind and common sense—and its survival in collective memory.

Memory that Creates Nobility

Memoria was a constitutive element of medieval group formation, not only of the liturgical commemoration of the dead, which tied the living to the dead,[78] but also of general "cultural memory,"[79] which presupposed and forged a bond among those who remembered a past event, from the death of an individual to God's work in the world. It is thus no wonder that we may also observe such a commemorative dimension in the integration of and incorporation into the nobility, whether in the liturgical form of commemorating the dead, which firmly ignored the boundaries of the noble *Geschlechter*[80] and was performed within the framework of open noble groups (tournament and noble societies,[81] joint inheritance),[82] or in a "cultural" form.

This cultural *memoria* took the form of two central tasks, writing and history. At bottom, medieval writing must be understood as a memorial practice. This means that the innovations of writing were particularly significant in regard to the social dynamic. Whether they succeeded or failed, they were in any case attempts to give memory a name—a substantive which could correspond to a social substance. For if memory creates community, every community must also create a memory for itself, which explains the fact that *memoria* could be understood in express terms as the responsibility of the various groups involved. In this sense the appearance after 1430 of the word *adel* to refer to the collectivity of nobles, as well as the other above-mentioned lexical innovations, must be interpreted as geometric points of several sometimes conflicting constructions of memory: a "positive" *memoria* among the nobles, who collectively wished to see themselves as "the nobility" and each individual as "one of the nobility"; then a "distancing" *memoria* among the princes[83] and sometimes also the counts and lords, who wished to appear to be above the nobility; and finally a "negative" *memoria* among the urban elites, who sought to develop an antinoble *memoria*.

The second element is the historicization of the existence of the nobility. Alongside the recollection of the present, which expressed itself in documents, letters, catalogues, and the like, efforts were also made to create a memory of the past. What was at stake here was not simply a projection of the accepted or desired existence of the nobility into the past—a projection, sometimes in the form of incorporations of the nobility into tangible historical monuments, rituals, or political objects, which contributed to a belief in the antiquity of the nobility, as if it had always existed.[84] It is in this context that we should place the biography of Wilwolt von Schaumberg, which was directed at young noblemen and embedded Wilwolt in a history of the nobility stretching far into the past. Similarly, the lists of tournament participants, which were compiled by heralds in the late fifteenth and early sixteenth centuries,[85] should be regarded as the secular equivalent of the lists of names in the *libri memoriales* and registers of prayer fraternities among monasteries (*Verbrüderungsbücher*). The continuity from the tenth to the fifteenth century, which was established in the tournament books,[86] allowed the nobility to be portrayed as a durable phenomenon, one marked at least by the unbroken practice of the tournament.

Created by terminology and historiography, the nobility was thus passed down to later generations as a self-evident quantity. This transmission was so successful that people finally forgot how recent a phenomenon the nobility was.

Conclusion

At the end of these deliberations I may thus establish that in Franconia, the nobility as the collectivity of nobles was only invented discursively in the fifteenth century, but portrayed itself as if it had always been there. This "invention" proceeded and articulated itself particularly through terminology, which was in turn part of a broader and more complex social process. On the one hand, from the final decades of the fourteenth century onward, the aristocrats took common action in order to counteract the measures of the territorially oriented princes, which appeared to endanger traditional social relations. Subsequent princely attempts to keep nobles out of the towns and to buy their loyalty by favoring the preservation of the interests of noble *Geschlechter* led to the development of the territorial state as a framework for the reproduction of the feudal aristocracy, which might help explain why this aristocracy remained so strong in Franconia: the reproduction of noble "lineages" with princely support contributed to the continuity of existing power relations, and may even have improved their political, economic, social, and religious efficacy. On the other hand, and as a sort of quid pro quo, the cementing of relations between the feudal aristocracy and the princes led to the creation of a common front against the towns, particularly the free imperial cities, chief among them Nuremberg. It was at the intersection of these two developments that the new designation of the noble-princely side as *adel* occurred, which ultimately replaced the traditional feudal expressions *fürsten, grafen, herren, ritter*, and *knechte*, which had long served as the counterpart to *die städte* (the towns).

Our chief concern here was neither to provide an exact date nor to attribute the first use of *adel* as a term referring to all nobles to any particular author (one finds scattered but not always clear references to the word before the years 1430–40,[87] and the word may have gone through a transition period when it retained several meanings at once). What appears much more significant is that the use of *adel* in this sense increased markedly beginning around this time and became common, so that the word becomes an important terminological pole around which the social imaginary organized itself. Thus a reproduction of noble authority, which was accomplished within the framework of the territorial state and of a discourse on noble families, became more firmly established in the wider sociopolitical culture through the conflicts of the mid-fifteenth century.

The integration of the two discourses on noble families and the nobility—as this appears to have been pursued anthroponymically (that is, ultimately, in one more specific terminological manner)—resulted on the one hand from the objectivation and representation of the existence of the nobility as a "natural" fact, a result of the competition among nobles, princes, and town dwellers over the term in the field of tension between discourses and counterdiscourses, during which the nobles largely succeeded in asserting their own definition, which they had gradually developed through the practice of tournaments. On the other hand, the recognition and institutionalization of noble families by the princely administrations and the church guaranteed their preservation, making the coalescence

of nobles into the nobility possible without leading to a disintegration of the
Geschlechter and their interests.

This leads us to the following conclusion: the lexical and semantic innovations which we may observe in several socially determined discursive configura-
tions actually correspond to an important sociogenetic turning point, which led
to the social construction ("sociogenesis") of the nobility in late medieval Franconia. From that point onward the social relations upon which the power of the
feudal aristocracy was based were regarded as relations of social selection, which
ensured the preservation of the power of the aristocracy—now known as the
nobility—within the framework of the territorial state. This moment of socio-
genesis had sociopolitical aspects, namely the resistance to incorporation in the
territorial state, which also sought to equalize, as subjects, the aristocrats and
towns of all kinds, and the forms taken by this princely attempt at incorporation
itself, which believed it could assert itself by dividing the local forces. The construction of this relationship of social selection is inseparable from the genesis of
the territorial state and from the urban counterdiscourse. This moment of socio-
genesis also had consequences, though, which were of an equally sociopolitical
nature: it created the nobility as a fundamental structure in the society and
political system of the modern age.

A particularly successful expression of the production of self-evidence in regard
to the existence of the nobility is a 1509 broadsheet which consists of a woodcut
by the Franconian Lucas Cranach the Elder,[88] a printed title (*The Nobility*), and a
printed verse commentary.[89] The woodcut depicts a horseman in splendid armor
with bushy ostrich plumes and an ornate shabrack, which is strongly reminiscent
of the jousting equipment portrayed in the 1512 *Triumph of Maximilian* by Hans
Burkmair the Elder—all that is missing here is the lance—and which may well
refer to the knight with the same motif (the letter *G*) on his horse-blanket who
appears in the foreground of two depictions of tournaments in other contemporary woodcuts by Cranach (1509). Here we have the self-evidence of the nobility:
the accompanying text[90] makes it clear that the nobility—whether through the
confrontation between nobility and nonnobility, or the implicit replacement of
the Pauline *militia* by the nobility, or the simple, self-explanatory use of the word
Adel—exists in the collective imagination (and is also justified theologically as the
ruling class). In addition the juxtaposition of the word *Adel* with a depiction of a
horseman who looks like a participant in a tournament establishes a certain
synonymity between the nobility and the tournament and a convertibility between the pictorial representation of a jouster and the lexical representation of
a nobleman—further evidence that the process of assertion described above
attained its high point in the tournament. The fact that the title reads "The

Der Adel.

EIn Sprichwort heiſt / iſt wol bekant
Durchaus im gantzen Deutſchenland:
Da Adam reut vnd Eua ſpan/
Wer war doch da ein Edelman?
Es iſt wol war / Doch weil gewis
Der Adel Gottes ordnung iſt/

Soln wir im ſein gebörlich ehr
Erzeigen/nach S. Pauli lehr /
Auch ſol der Adel dencken dran /
Wie Keiſer Maximilian:
Ich bin gleich wie ein ar der Man/
Nur das mir Gott die Ehre gan.

C. N. O.

Nobility" (*der Adel*) and not "The Noble" (*der Adlige*) or (as in the accompanying verses) "The Gentleman" (*Der Edelmann*), brings us to a third observation:
the stylization has gone so far that a single noble/man can represent the entire
nobility. Now, if one met "one of the nobility" one had met them all, so that the
nobility appeared at once ubiquitous and temporally unlimited, especially since
the group was embodied equally by a simple nobleman or Emperor Maximilian.
Thus a reciprocal relationship of interdependence was created: on the one hand
the nobleman ("one of the nobility") drew his identity (his "honor," according to
the accompanying verses) from his membership in the group, whose existence
became all the more certain as individual nobles became conceivable.

Assuming that the nobility and a noble identity arose in such a way, we must
evaluate various phenomena differently than has been done up until now. This
applies, for example, to the probably large number of feuds in Franconia which
appear as side effects and at the same time as instruments of this construction of
a noble identity. This also applies to the harsh criticisms made of the nobility.
These opposing discourses belong together in the social dynamic, which is, after
all, characterized by the fact that no change can affect one particular group alone:
after all, the social classifications correspond to social conditions, whose development cannot be conceived of in isolated and separate terms. The "invention" of
the nobility thus cannot be separated from other changes which led to the
"invention" of other social categories.

The study presented here is intended as a contribution to the history of
social classifications and nomenclature. The intention is less to present the invention of the nobility as the formation of the nobility into an estate (in Max Weber's
definition as a community characterized by its "honor," its mode of living, its
rejection of economic differences, and its material and matrimonial monopo-
lies)[91] than to demonstrate the power of discursive practices to construct social
phenomena. As interpretive schemes, they at once focus social relations and
supposedly describe these very relations, for which reason they are objectivated
and portrayed as "natural." The discourses are that very dimension of social
action that leads to the articulation of the inseparable ideal and material aspects
of social relations and the social dynamic. And social classifications, which appear merely to organize social reality, but in fact—with the social order—create
that reality in the first place, are revealed to be one of the most important
components of the social discourses. The case study of the Franconian nobility
shows how necessary it is to distinguish clearly between contemporary, overly
historicizing classifications and present-day scholarly systems of designation—
and not simply to adopt any of them as self-evident. Furthermore, the history of
classifications must be regarded as a genuine component of the history of the
social formations affected by them. After all, classifications are the product of the

inner structuring of these formations and their incorporation into the social system, and contribute to their objectivation, realization, and apparent "naturalness." The debate surrounding the broader or narrower definition of the word "nobility" thus appears to overlook perhaps the most important point, namely that at a certain period the feudal aristocracy—whose possible sociological or biological continuity is not at issue here—constituted itself or was constituted as a ruling and dominant social formation known as the "nobility." "The nobility" is thus a historically evolved term, not a scholarly term of sufficient clarity. Perhaps we should dispense with the term "nobility" in scholarly discourse, and find another word better suited at once to describing the relationship of authority and delimitation and to reminding us that the genesis and shape of a social formation is always tied to particular social relations. In this way we might be able to make it clear that "the nobility" is nothing more than a historically unique manifestation of seigneurial power relations.

Notes

The present essay is a much abridged version of Joseph Morsel, "Die Erfindung des Adels: Zur Soziogenese des Adels am Ende des Mittelalters—das Beispiel Frankens," which appeared in the volume *Nobilitas. Funktion und Repräsentation des Adels in Alteuropa*, ed. Otto Gerhard Oexle and Werner Paravicini, Veröffentlichungen des Max-Planck-Instituts für Geschichte 133 (Göttingen, 1996), 312–375. For that reason I will dispense here with detailed source references and bibliography.

1. See, for example, Klaus Schreiner, "Adel oder Oberschicht? Bemerkungen zur sozialen Schichtung der fränkischen Gesellschaft im 6. Jahrhundert," *Vierteljahreschrift für Sozial- und Wirtschaftsgeschichte* 68 (1981): 225–31, here 229, or Dietrich Claude, *Adel, Kirche und Königtum im Westgotenreich*, Vorträge und Forschungen, Sonderband 8 (Sigmaringen, 1971), 8. The process of dehistoricization (achieved mainly through a functionalist definition) thus also encompasses the term's spatial expansion to include all aristocrats on all continents, such as we find in John H. Kautsky, "Funktionen und Werte des Adels," in *Legitimationskrisen des deutschen Adels 1200–1900*, ed. Peter Uwe Hohendahl and Paul Michal Lützeler, Literaturwissenschaft und Sozialwissenschaft, 11 (Stuttgart, 1979), 1–16, or also Ludolf Kuchenbuch, "Adel," in *Geschichte*, ed. Richard van Dülmen, Fischer Lexikon, 4563 (Frankfurt am Main, 1990), 105–20.

2. Heike Grahn-Hoek, *Die fränkische Oberschicht im 6. Jahrhundert. Studien zu ihrer rechtlichen und politischen Stellung*, Vorträge und Forschungen, Sonderband 21 (Sigmaringen, 1976); Franz Irsigler, review in *Hessisches Jahrbuch für Landesgeschichte* 27 (1977): 279–84; Schreiner, "Adel oder Oberschicht?"; Thomas Zotz, "Adel, Oberschicht, Freie. Zur Terminologie der frühmittelalterlichen Sozialgeschichte," *Zeitschrift für die Geschichte des Oberrheins* 125 (1977): 3–20; Hans K. Schulze, "Reichsaristokratie, Stammesadel und fränkische Freiheit. Neuere Forschungen zur frühmittelalterlichen Sozialgeschichte," *Historische Zeitschrift* 227 (1978): 353–73, esp. 370ff. Wilhelm Schneider treats the entire problematic meticulously in his essay "'Adel,' 'Oberschicht,' 'Herrenstand,'

'Aristokratie': Notwendige Begriffsbestimmungen für die Geschichte der germanischen Zeit und des frühen Mittelalters," in W. Schneider, *Wider die These von "Adelsherrschaft,"* Arbeiten zur alemannischen Frühgeschichte, Heft IX (Tübingen, 1980), 429–65.

3. In a passage in his "Reichsaristokratie, Stammesadel und fränkische Freiheit" (p. 373) Schulze aptly puts his finger on the problem. "Ultimately, scholarship on the nobility operates with the axiom that all those persons who are not explicitly referred to as 'unfree' [*Unfreie*] or 'less free' [*Minderfreie*] belonged to the nobility. Since it is indeed impossible to separate the medieval authors, witnesses to documents, the inhabitants of monasteries and the persons whose names appear in the memorial books (*Gedenkbücher*) into noble and nonnoble, even a nonspecific definition of the nobility can get us into a good deal of trouble." "Being noble" and "belonging to the nobility" are thus regarded as one and the same thing, as if the nobility were simply a bag full of nobles—and as if there were a tangible reality behind every word. And yet as early as the late 1950s K. Schmid demonstrated that there was no obvious relationship between nobility and nobles in the early Middle Ages, and that one cannot really even speak of nobles: All we find at that time are "noble communities of persons" or "groups of persons," namely, noble families or clans, noble prayer fraternities (*Verbrüderungsgruppen*), and noble monastic communities. See Karl Schmid, *Gebetsgedenken und adliges Selbstverständnis im Mittelalter. Ausgewählte Beiträge, Festgabe zu seinem sechzigsten Geburtstag* (Sigmaringen, 1983), 183–267, 363–87, 532–97. This important insight implicitly poses the question that interests me here: If there was no self-evident and continuous relationship between the individual *nobilis* and the nobility, when and how was the nobility as the collectivity of all nobles created—and created in such a way that we largely still believe in the self-evidence and continuity of this relationship even today?

4. The distance between nobles and the nobility in the High Middle Ages is emphasized terminologically in a remarkable synthesis by Robert Fossier of scholarship on the nobility, which inspired him to place the term "noblesse" in quotation marks. See his *Naissance de l'Europe Xe–XIIe siècles. Aspects économiques et sociaux*, Nouvelle Clio, 17 bis (Paris, 1982), 965. I myself have had the opportunity to emphasize the sociohistorical significance of the gap between nobles and the nobility, the neglect of which may explain some of the problems in the historical discourse on the crisis of the nobility in the Late Middle Ages. See Joseph Morsel, "Crise? Quelle crise? Remarques à propos de la prétendue crise de la noblesse allemande à la fin du Moyen Age," *SOURCES. Travaux historiques* 14 (1988): 17–42, S. 31ff.

5. On the changing meaning and applications of the term *nobilis*, see Karl-Ferdinand Werner, "Adel," in *Lexikon des Mittelalters*, vol. 1 (1980), 124; Schreiner, "Adel oder Oberschicht?" 282; and Schneider, " 'Adel,' 'Oberschicht,' 'Herrenstand,' 'Aristokratie,' " 336–47.

6. Pierre Bourdieu, Jean-Claude Chamboredon, and Jean-Claude Passeron, *Le métier de sociologue*, Textes de sciences sociales, 1 (Paris, Berlin, and New York, 1973), 28.

7. These include some 1,365 official documents, 620 letters, 355 extracts from various registers (of fiefs and vassals, debts, payments, or appointments) and account books, and the records of 90 court cases from the state archives of Bamberg, Marburg, Munich, Nuremberg, and Würzburg, the archive of the Julius-Spital at Würzburg and private archives in Franconia, as well as a number of narrative texts (some 250 extracts from chronicles, autobiographical writings, etc.)—all of them texts whose lowest common denominator is that they mention members of the Franconian family vonThüngen. I may

be permitted in this context to mention my *thèse, Une société politique en Franconie à la fin du Moyen Age: Les Thüngen, leurs princes, leurs pairs et leurs hommes (1275–1525)*, University of Paris-IV, 1993 (microfiche), and its forthcoming publication as *Une noblesse contre le prince: L'espace sociale des Thüngen à la fin du Moyen Age (Franconie, 1250–1525)*, Beihefte der Francia (Sigmaringen, 2000). Without being unusual, the Thüngen family was one of the more prominent Franconian noble dynasties, and may thus be considered representative of other families. They participated very actively in all the forms of organization of the Franconian knightly class—leagues, assemblies, castles held in coparcenary (*Ganerbenburgen*), tournaments, noble societies, confraternities, etc.—but were never the initiators. The body of texts compiled in the course of this research, of which the Thüngen are the "lowest common denominator" rather than the focus, permits us to cut a cross section of Franconian society and grasp certain phenomena quite precisely, yielding suggestions whose import goes beyond the Thüngen themselves and even beyond Franconia.

8. In late medieval chronicles the position in the *Heerschildordnung* (literally, "army shield ranking") was still central for the way individual noblemen were referred to. See Helga Möhring-Müller et al., "Spätmittelalterliche Adelsterminologie bei Hermann Korner, Andreas von Regensburg und seinen Übersetzern, Veit Arnpeck und Sigismund Meisterlin," in *Zweisprachige Geschichtsschreibung im spätmittelalterlichen Deutschland*, ed. Rolf Sprandel, Wissensliteratur im Mittelalter, 14 (Wiesbaden, 1993), 421.

9. This is substantiated by an observation in Werner, "Adel," in *Lexikon des Mittelalters*, 124. On the polysemy of "nobilis," of which the current sense seems to have become fixed only at the end of the Middle Ages, see Schreiner, "Adel oder Oberschicht," 282.

10. Bayerisches Staatsarchiv Würzburg (henceforth cited as StAW), Würzburger Urkunden, no. 2771. From a later period see also the chronicle from the time of Emperor Sigismund in *Die Chroniken der fränkischen Städte—Nürnberg*, vol. 1, Die Chroniken der deutschen Städte vom 14. bis in's 16. Jahrhundert, 1 (Leipzig, 1862), 382.

11. These are the *Monumenta Boica*, vols. 38–46 (Munich, 1866–1905); *Hennebergisches Urkundenbuch*, vols. 2–7 (Meiningen, 1847–1877); *Hohenlohisches Urkundenbuch*, vols. 2–3 (Stuttgart, 1901–1912); the series *Quellen und Forschungen zur Geschichte des Bistums und Hochstifts Würzburg* (Würzburg, 1950–; 44 vols. to date). The *Hohenlohische Urkundenbuch* gives evidence of a rather vague and singular mention of the word *adel*, dated ca. 1377. Here the term may refer to some small vassals of the lord of Hohenlohe: *Hohenlohische Urkundenbuch*, vol. 3 (1351–1375), no. 90 (Lehnsregister Gerlachs von Hohenlohe, 1356ff.), 117.

12. *Wörterbuch der mittelhochdeutschen Urkundensprache (WMU), auf der Grundlage des Corpus der altdeutschen Originalurkunden bis zum Jahr 1300* (1. Lieferung) ed. Bettina Kirschstein and Ursula Schulze (Berlin, 1986), 35; compare with the *Corpus der altdeutschen Originalurkunden bis 1300*, vol. 1, ed. Friedrich Wilhelm (Lahr im Schwarzwald, 1932), 204 (no. 222); *Urkundenbuch der Vögte von Weida, Gera und Plauen*, vol. 1, ed. Berthold Schmidt, Thüringische Geschichtsquellen, N.F. 2 (Jena, 1884), no. 174; *Urkundenbuch der Deutschordensballei Thüringen*, vol. 1, ed. Karl H. Lampe, Thüringische Geschichtsquellen, N.F. 7 (Jena, 1936), no. 263; *Corpus der altdeutschen Originalurkunden bis zum Jahr 1300. Regesten zu den Bänden I–IV*, ed. Helmut De Boor and Dieter Haacke (Lahr im Schwarzwald, 1963), 27. Jacob and Wilhelm Grimm, *Deutsches Wörterbuch*, vol. 1 (Leipzig, 1854; reprint Munich, 1984), 176–77 (which contains a single medieval example from the end of the fifteenth century). Matthias Lexer, *Mittelhochdeutsches Handwörterbuch*, vol. 1 (Leipzig, 1872), 20; compare with Georg Benecke and Wilhelm Müller, *Mit-*

telhochdeutsches Wörterbuch, vol. 1 (Leipzig, 1854; reprint Hildesheim, Zurich, and New York, 1986), 7–8; cf. also Hermann Paul, *Deutsches Wörterbuch* (Tübingen, 1976), 14, and the new edition revised by Helmut Henne and Georg Objartel (Tübingen, 1992), 17.

13. Christian Gellinek and Heidi Rockwood, *Häufigkeitswörterbuch zur deutschen Prosa des 11. und 12. Jahrhunderts* (Tübingen, 1973); Clifton D. Hall, *A Complete Concordance to Wolfram von Eschenbach's Parzival*, Garland Reference Library of the Humanities, 995 (New York and London, 1990); R.-M. S. Heffner, *Collected Indexes to the Works of Wolfram von Eschenbach* (Madison, Wis., 1961), 2–178.

14. *Die Chroniken der fränkischen Städte (Nürnberg)*, vols. 1–5, Die Chroniken der deutschen Städte vom 14. bis in's 16. Jahrhundert, 1–3 and 10–11 (Leipzig, 1862–1874). Interestingly, Erhard Schürstab's account of the war between the city of Nuremberg and Margrave Albrecht of Brandenburg (*Die Chroniken der deutschen Städte*, vol. 2) uses the word *adel* only in the preface and the introduction to his account of the war, i.e., in the discursive part of the text, while in the description of the events he painstakingly records individual names and title: thus *adel* is less a descriptive than a discursive term which serves to portray and construct the members of the princely opposing party as a united social formation.

15. In the Nuremberg chronicles the shift occurs between 1430/40 and 1450. A fifteenth-century Shrovetide play from Nuremberg entitled *Pope, Cardinal, and Bishops* (*Vom babst, cardinal und von bischoffen*), which was composed before 1483 and should probably attributed to Hans Rosenplüt (which would date it to after 1430), mentions the nobility several times in the sense that interests us here. See *Fastnachtspiele aus dem fünfzehnten Jahrhundert*, vols. 2 and 3, ed. Adalbert von Keller, Bibliothek des litterarischen Vereins, 29 and 30 (Stuttgart, 1853), 642 and 1076 and (wrongly numbered 79) 1457; see also Heinrich Kurz, *Geschichte der deutschen Literatur mit ausgewählten Stücken*, vol. 1 (Leipzig, 1876), 730–37 (text on 732–33), and Ingeborg Glier, "Rosenplütsche Fastnachtspiele," in *Die deutsche Literatur des Mittelalters: Verfasserlexikon*, ed. Kurt Ruh, vol. 8 (Berlin and New York), 211–32.

16. The *Novum glossarium mediae latinitatis ab anno DCCC usque ad annum MCC* (vol. M–N), ed. Franz Blatt (Copenhagen, 1958–1959), 1300–1, records some fifteen mentions of the term *nobilitas*, of which several clearly come directly from Roman usage. According to Du Cange's *Glossarium mediae et infimae latinitatis*, vol. 4 (reprint Graz, 1954), 596–97, *nobilitas* should not be understood as including the totality of aristocrats. This finding is substantiated by Léopold Génicot in the discussion of his contribution "Naissance, fonction et richesse dans l'ordonnance de la société médiévale. Le cas de la Noblesse du Nord-Ouest du Continent," in *Problèmes de stratification sociale. Actes du colloque international de Paris (1966)*, ed. Roland Mousnier (Louvain and Ghent, 1968), 100. See also Fossier, *Naissance de l'Europe*, 964–65.

17. Johannes Fried (ed.), *Die abendländische Freiheit vom 10. zum 14. Jahrhundert. Der Wirkungszusammenhang von Idee und Wirklichkeit im europäischen Vergeich*, Vorträge und Forschungen, 39 (Sigmaringen, 1991); Bernhard Jussen, *Spiritual Kinship as Social Practice: Godparenthood and Adoption in the Early Middle Ages*, trans. Pamela E. Selwyn (Newark, Del., 2000); Thomas Eichenberger, *Patria. Studien zur Bedeutung des Wortes im Mittelalter (6.–12. Jahrhundert)* Nationes, 9 (Sigmaringen, 1991). On the differing flexibility of the Latin and German languages in adapting to social reality see, with reference to the nobility, Möhring-Müller et al., "Spätmittelalterliche Adelsterminologie," 427–28.

18. Fossier, *Naissance de l'Europe*, 965. Shortly before this R. Fossier also points to "the extraordinary rarity of the term [*nobilis*] or of the words derived from it [*nobilitas* among them]."

19. Even in the High Middle Ages, *adel* was used not as a term referring to a social formation, but as an expression of a quality, whether of birth (see esp. Benecke and Müller, *Mittelhochdeutsches Wörterbuch*, 7–8) or of nature (see Konrad von Megenberg, *Das Buch der Natur*, ed. Franz Pfeiffer (Stuttgart, 1861; reprint Hildesheim and New York, 1971), 21, 89, 208, 269, 280, 365, 377, 404. It appears that the word can be traced back to an old Germanic and even Indo-European root, but that it has only been used as a term to refer to the entire nobility since the fifteenth century. See Willy Krogmann, "Adel und Udel," *Zeitschrift für deutsche Philologie* 63 (1938): 189–91; Oswald Szemerényi, "The Etymology of German Adel," *Word* 8 (1952): 42–50; Émile Benveniste, *Le vocabulaire des institutions indo-européennes*, vol. 2 (Paris, 1969), 85–88; Aaron I. Gurevich, "Représentations et attitudes à l'égard de la propriété pendant le haut moyen âge," *Annales É.S.C.* 27 (1972): 525–30.

20. For a fundamental approach to this issue, see Luc Boltanski, *Les cadres. La formation d'un groupe social* (Paris, 1982), esp. 47–59. See also Jacques Le Goff, "Les trois fonctions indo-européennes, l'historien et l'Europe féodale," *Annales É.S.C.* 34 (1979), esp. 1189.

21. The term *adlige Personengemeinschaften* (communities of noble persons) was coined by Karl Schmid in his article "Über das Verhältnis von Person und Gemeinschaft im früheren Mittelalter" (1967), in *Gebetsgedenken und adliges Selbstverständnis im Mittelalter*.

22. The representational, objectivating, and formalizing categories of the social are, to be sure, produced within social relations, but they are also indispensible for the maintenance of these social relations. See Godelier, *L'idéel et le matériel. Pensée, économies, sociétés* (Paris, 1984), esp. 221–28. They also have remarkable social effects because of the "actualizing" dimension of these categories, in that they permit us at once to apprehend objectivated social reality and to produce this social reality through categorization: cf. Peter L. Berger and Thomas Luckmann, *The Social Construction of Reality: A Treatise in the Sociology of Knowledge* (New York, 1966), and on the case of the trifunctional scheme, see Otto Gerhard Oexle, "Perceiving Social Reality in the Early and High Middle Ages: A Contribution to a History of Social Knowledge," in this volume.

23. See Robert Fellner, *Die fränkische Ritterschaft von 1495–1524* (Berlin, 1905), esp. 79–86; Lore Köberlin, *Die Einungsbewegung des fränkischen Adels bis 1494*, Ph.D. diss., University of Erlangen, 1924; Ernst Schubert, *Die Landstände des Hochstifts Würzburg*, Veröffentlichungen der Gesellschaft für fränkische Geschichte, IX, 23 (Würzburg, 1967), esp. 63–77; Angela Kulenkampff, *Einungen mindermächtiger Stände zur Handhabung Friedens und Rechtens 1422–1565*, Ph.D. diss., University of Frankfurt am Main, 1967, and "Einungen und Reichsstandschaft fränkischer Grafen und Herren 1402–1641," *Württembergisch Franken* 55 (1971): 16–41.

24. See, most recently, Holger Kruse et al., *Ritterorden und Adelsgesellschaften im spätmittelalterlichen Deutschlands. Ein systematisches Verzeichnis*, Kieler Werkstücke, D, 1 (Frankfurt am Main, Berne, New York and Paris, 1991; Andreas Ranft, *Adelsgesellschaften. Gruppenbildung und Genossenschaft im spätmittelalterlichen Reich*, Kieler Historische Studien, 38 (Sigmaringen, 1994).

25. See *Das ritterliche Turnier im Mittelalter. Beiträge zu einer vergleichenden Formen- und Verhaltensgeschichte des Rittertums*, ed. Josef Fleckenstein, Veröffentlichungen des

Max-Planck-Instituts für Geschichte, 80 (Göttingen, 1985); William Henry Jackson, "The Tournament and Chivalry in German Tournament Books of the Sixteenth Century and in the Literary Works of Emperor Maximilian I," in *The Ideals and Practice of Medieval Knighthood*, ed. Christopher Harper and Bill and Ruth Harvey, Papers from the First and Second Strawberry Hill Conferences (Woodbridge, 1986), 49–73; Hans Pöschko, *Turniere in Mittel- und Süddeutschland von 1400 bis 1500. Katalog der Kampfspiele und der Teilnehmer* (microfiche Ph.D. diss., University of Stuttgart, 1987); Kruse et al., *Ritterorden und Adelsgesellschaften*; Joseph Morsel, "Le tournoi, mode d'éducation politique en Allemagne à la fin du Moyen Age," in *Éducation, apprentissages, initiation au Moyen Age*, vol. 2, Cahiers du CRISIMA, 1 (Montpellier, 1993), 310–31; Morsel, *Une société politique en Franconie*; Andreas Ranft, "Die Turniere der Vier Lande: genossenschaftlicher Hof und Selbstbehauptung des niederen Adels," *Zeitschrift für die Geschichte des Oberrheins* 142 (1994): 83–102; and Ranft, *Adelsgesellschaften*.

26. See Fellner, *Die fränkische Ritterschaft*; Schubert, *Die Landstände des Hochstifts Würzburg*; and Morsel, *Une société politique en Franconie*.

27. See Georg Landau, *Die hessischen Ritterburgen und ihre Besitzer*, vol. 3 (Kassel, 1836); Martin Schütz, *Die Ganerbschaft vom Rothenberg in ihrer politischen, juristischen und wirtschaftlichen Bedeutung* (Nuremberg, 1924); Karl-Ernst Demandt, "Die Reichsganerbschaft Lindheim in der Wetterau," *Hessisches Jahrbuch für Landesgeschichte* 6 (1956): 77–137; Henning Becker, *Familiensoziologische Untersuchungen hessischer Ganerbenfamilien des 14. bis 17. Jahrhunderts am Beispiel der Schenken zu Schweinsberg und der von Hatzfeld* (Ph.D. diss., Free University of Berlin, 1983); Friedrich Karl Alsdorf, *Untersuchungen zur Rechtsgestalt und Teilung deutscher Ganerbeburgen*, Rechtshistorische Reihe, 9 (Frankfurt am Main, Berne, and Cirencester, 1980); Morsel, *Une société politique en Franconie*; Klaus Rupprecht, *Ritterschaftliche Herrschaftswahrung in Franken. Die Geschichte der von Guttenberg im Spätmittelalter und zu Beginn der Frühen Neuzeit*, Veröff. d. Gesellsch. f. fränk. Gesch., IX, 42 (Neustadt a. d. Aisch, 1994), esp. 377–83.

28. Alfred Friese, "Die Rittergesellschaft 'mit dem Greifen' (1379). Ein Beitrag zur Kulturgeschichte Wertheims im späten Mittelalter," *Frankenland* 5 (1961): 61–75, *Hennebergisches Urkundenbuch*, vol. 4, ed. Georg Brückner (Meiningen, 1861), 31–34; Kruse et al., *Ritterorden und Adelsgesellschaften*, 100–2, 139–42, 156–65; Ranft, *Adelsgesellschaften*, 37–116, 189–90, 194; *Monumenta Zollerana*, vol. 6, ed. Rudolf von Stillfried (Berlin, 1852), nos. 29 and 33, *Regesten des fränkischen Geschlechts von Schaumberg*, vol. 2, ed. E. von Guttenberg et al., nos. 356 and 358 (in which the dating given in the *MZ* is corrected); *Des Teutschen Reichs-Archiv*, vol. 12, Partis Specialis Continuatio, 3, ed. Johann Christian Lünig (Leipzig, 1713), section 2, no. 112.

29. Hans-Peter Baum, *Der Lehenhof des Hochstifts Würzburg im Spätmittelalter (1303–1519). Eine rechts- und sozialgeschichtliche Studie*, vol. 1 (Habil. Thesis, Würzburg, 1990), 20–22 and 277.

30. See Philippe Dollinger, "Patriciat noble et patriciat bourgeois à Strasbourg au XIVᵉ siècle," *Revue d'Alsace* 90 (1951), reprinted in *Pages d'Histoire. France et Allemagne médiévales, Alsace*, Collection de l'Institut des Hautes Études Alsaciennes, 25 (Paris, 1977), 204–13; Schubert, *Die Landstände des Hochstifts Würzburg*, 36; Baum, *Der Lehenhof des Hochstifts Würzburg*, 1:198–99, 277–78; Thomas Zotz, "Adel in der Stadt des deutschen Spätmittelalters. Erscheinungsformen und Verhaltensweisen," *Zeitschrift für die Geschichte des Oberrheins* 141 (1993): 29–42. Werner Paravicini, *Die Preußenreisen des eu-*

ropäischen Adels, vol. 1, Beihefte der Francia, 17/1 (Sigmaringen, 1989), 154. Since the pair of terms *edel/unedel* (noble/commoner), which appeared in the fourteenth century, exists alongside other pairs such as clerical/lay, male/female, etc. (an example from 1366: "with all his people, nobles and commoners, priests and laymen, women and men, spiritual and worldly" [mit allen sinen lueten, edeln vnd vnedeln, pfaffen vnd leyen, frauwen vnd mannen, geystlich vnd werltlich], *Monumenta Boica*, vol. 45, Munich, 1899, 232), one should regard it less as the expression of a split than as a way of thinking in terms of *ordines*, i.e., a manner of classification that welds many and diverse elements into a whole. Cf. Otto Gerhard Oexle, "Ordo (Ordines)," in *Lexikon des Mittelalters* 6 (1993), 1436.

31. See Lünig, *Reichs-Archiv*, vol. 12, nos. 112–34; *Deutsche Reichstagsakten*, ältere Reihe, vol. 6, ed. J. von Weizäcker (1887, reprint Göttingen, 1956), no. 234; *Monumenta Castellana*, vol. 1, ed. P. Wittmann (Munich, 1890), no. 521; *Sammlung alter historischer Schrifften und Documenten*, vol. 1, ed. Johann Friedrich Schannat (Fulda, 1725), 99–102; *Reichsritterschaftliches Magazin* 8, ed. Johann Mader (Frankfurt a.M. and Leipzig, 1786), no. 1; *Geschichte der Grafen von Wertheim von den ältesten Zeiten bis . . . 1556*, vol. 2, *Wertheimisches Urkundenbuch*, ed. Joseph Aschbach (Frankfurt a.M., 1843), no. 194; Thüringisches Staatsarchiv Meiningen, Gem. Henneb. Archiv, K 7, F°25′–30; and section 2, no. 180; Bayerisches Staatsarchiv Nürnberg (henceforth StAN), Reichsstadt Rothenburg, Akten, no. 324/142, Reichsstadt Windsheim, Urkunden, no. 207; StAW, Würzburger Urkunden, no. 15/169, Würzburger Urkundenlibelle, no. 181, Ritterschaft, no. 586; Reichsritterschaft, no. 718, Standbücher, no. 947, F°6–6′. The *Austrag* or arbitration clause was the only constantly recurrent clause, which was often followed by the assistance clause (*Hilfe*).

32. Baum, *Der Lehenhof des Hochstifts Würzburg*, vol. 1, quotations on 270 and 278.

33. Baum, *Der Lehenhof des Hochstifts Würzburg*, 1:94–96: a new, agnatic succession (within the family, name, "shield," and "helmet") for the noble fiefs, and not for censive (nonnoble) fiefs. This new succession led to nobles converting an ever increasing number of allodial estates into fiefs, since the allods were supposed to follow the normal *landrechtlich* (i.e., according to the general law of the country) succession, which called for complete distribution among the male and female heirs. A similar phenomenon may also be observed for the neighboring Franconian and Middle German feudal courts (particularly the other important feudal court of the Burggravate of Nuremberg/Margravate of Brandenburg-Ansbach).

34. Schubert, *Die Landstände des Hochstifts Würzburg*, 133. Rolf Sprandel, "Die Ritterschaft und das Hochstift Würzburg im Spätmittelalter," *Jahrbuch für fränkische Landesforschung* 36 (1976): 117–43, here 130ff. Gerhard Fouquet, *Das Speyerer Domkapitel im späten Mittelalter (ca. 1350–1540). Adlige Freundschaft, fürstliche Patronage und päpstliche Klientel*, Quellen und Abhandlungen zur mittelrheinischen Kirchengeschichte, 57 (Mainz, 1987), esp. 113–17, 289–92.

35. Kurt Andermann, *Studien zur Geschichte des pfälzischen Niederadels im späten Mittelalters. Eine vergleichende Untersuchung an ausgewählten Beispielen*, Schriftenreihe der Bezirksgruppe Neustadt, 10 (Speyer, 1982), 225; see also Georg Schmidt, "Ulrich von Hutten, der Adel und das Reich um 1500, in Ulrich von Hutten in seiner Zeit," in *Schlüchterner Vorträge zu seinem 500. Geburtstag*, ed. Johannes Schilling and Ernst Giese, Monographia Hassiae, 12 (Kassel, 1988), 21.

36. See the present author's "Das Geschlecht als Repräsentation. Beobachtungen zur

Verwandtschaftskonstruktion im fränkischen Adel des späten Mittelalters," in *Die Repräsentation der Gruppen*, ed. Andrea von Hülsen-Esch and Otto-Gerhard Oexle, Veröffentlichungen des Max-Planck-Instituts für Geschichte, 141 (Göttingen, 1998).

37. See Joseph Morsel, "A quoi sert le service princier? Carrières, gains, attentes et discours dans l'aristocratie franconienne à la fin du Moyen Âge," in *S.H.M.E.S. Les serviteurs de l'État au Moyen Âge* (Paris, 1999).

38. Schubert, *Die Landstände des Hochstifts Würzburg*, 63–76. On multiple vassalage, see Rolf Sprandel, "Mittelalterliche Verfassungs- und Sozialgeschichte vom Blickpunkt einer Landschaft: Mainfranken," *Zeitschrift für historische Forschung* 7 (1980), esp. 410–12; Baum, *Der Lehenhof des Hochstifts Würzburg*, 1:183–91.

39. See *Die Geschichten und Taten Wilwolts von Schaumburg*, ed. Adelbert von Keller, Bibliothek des Literarischen Vereins, 50 (Stuttgart, 1859), 156.

40. Philippe Contamine, "De la puissance aux privilèges: doléances de la noblesse française envers la monarchie aux XIVe et XVe siècles," in *La noblesse au Moyen Age, XIe– XVe siècle. Essais à la mémoire de Robert Boutruche*, ed. P. Contamine (Paris, 1976), 235–37.

41. See the mentions of the word in the text of the *Reformatio Sigismundi. Reformation Kaiser Siegmunds*, in Monumenta Germaniae Historica, Staatsschriften des späteren Mittelalters, 6, ed. Heinrich Koller (Stuttgart, 1964); in an account from Nuremberg of a meeting of towns held in Konstanz in 1441, *Deutsche Reichstagsakten unter Kaiser Friedrich III.*, vol. 2, Deutsche Reichstagsakten, ältere Reihe, 16, ed. Ludwig Quidde (1928, reprint Göttingen, 1957), 85; in a 1444 letter from Ulm, Harro Blezinger, *Der schwäbische Städtebund in den Jahren 1438–1445*, Darstellungen aus der württembergischen Geschichte, 39 (Stuttgart, 1954), 112 and 160. Around 1450 the word *adel* was regularly used in Franconia to refer to nobles as a group, as evidenced by Erhard Schürstab's chronicle (see above n. 14) and also the song "Die Städte" (The Cities) which was composed at the time of the war between Nuremberg and the Margrave (1449–1450). *Historische Volkslieder der Deutschen vom 13. bis 16. Jahrhundert*, vol. 1, ed. Rochus von Liliencron (Leipzig, 1865), 417–18. See also the Shrovetide play mentioned in n. 15 above.

42. See the letter of 13 August 1441 from Nuremberg to the Swabian League of Towns (summary in Blezinger, *Der schwäbische Städtebund*, 149).

43. That the Swiss Confederation represented a dreaded example of princely and noble power is plainly apparent in texts from the German southwest in the years after 1440; see Blezinger, *Der schwäbische Städtebund*, 112; Thomas A. Brady, *Turning Swiss: Cities and Empire, 1450–1550* (Cambridge, 1985), esp. 34–42; Guy P. Marchal, "Die Antwort der Bauern," in *Geschichtsschreibung und Geschichtsbewußtsein im späten Mittelalter*, ed. Hans Patze, Vorträge und Forschungen, 31 (Sigmaringen, 1987), 757–90.

44. Compare, for example, Ulman Stromer's chronicle with that penned by Erhard Schürstab (see n. 14).

45. Klaus Graf, "Feindbild und Vorbild. Bemerkungen zur städtischen Wahrnehmung des Adels," *Zeitschrift für die Geschichte des Oberrheins* 141 (1993): 121–54, here 126–27. The earliest conflicts between nobles and nonnobles over participation in tournaments, which have been emphasized by Thomas Zotz, also arose in this period. See his "Adel, Bürgertum und Turnier in deutschen Städten vom 13. bis 15. Jahrhundert," in Fleckenstein, *Das ritterliche Turnier im Mittelalter*, 485–89.

46. See Oexle, "Perceiving Social Reality in the Early and High Middle Ages," Chapter 3 of this present volume.

47. Studying the case of families of the lower nobility in the region known as

Franconian Switzerland, Wolfhard Vahl has shown that family coats of arms and names were largely fixed by the early thirteenth century. See his *Fränkische Rittersiegel. Eine sphragistisch-prosopographische Studie über den fränkischen Niederadel im 13. Und 14. Jahrhundert* (Neustadt a.d. Aisch, 1997), 300, 307.

48. On the "house archives," see Sprandel, "Die Ritterschaft und das Hochstift Würzburg," 124–25. The cartularies are scarcely viewed in this context in the contributions to the colloquium *Les cartulaires*, ed. Olivier Guyotjeannin et al. (Paris, 1993), see 409–10; it does, however, appear significant to me that the first noble cartularies from Franconia that have come down to us date from the years 1420–1440 (Seinsheim, Guttenberg, Thüngen), i.e., precisely that period when the discourse on noble *Geschlechter* and the discourse on the nobility apparently became mutually dependent and supporting.

49. On the connection between the establishment of the inheritability of lordship, which was promoted by the discourse on noble families, and the practice of feuding, see Joseph Morsel, " 'Das sy sich mitt der besten gewarsamig schicken, das sy durch die widerwertigen Francken nit nidergeworfen werden'. Überlegungen zum sozialen Sinn der adligen Fehdepraxis am Beispiel des spätmittelalterlichen Franken," in *Strukturen der Gesellschaft im Mittelalter—Interdisziplinäre Mediävistik in Würzburg*, ed. Joachim Schneider and Dieter Rödel (Würzburg, 1996). It thus appears that there was no reason, from either the political or kinship point of view, for feuds to become less frequent in Franconia as long as princes could not, or would not, assume the "monopoly of legitimate violence." According to contemporary sources a number of princes, unlike the town authorities, showed little interest in combating noble feuds. Cf. Heinrich Schmidt, *Die deutschen Städtechroniken als Spiegel des bürgerlichen Selbstverständnisses im Spätmittelalter*, Schriftenreihe der Historischen Kommission bei der Akademie der Wissenschaften, 3 (Göttingen, 1953), esp. 32ff., 57ff., and 76ff. and, from a French perspective, Philippe de Commynes, *Mémoires*, ed. Philippe Contamine (Paris, 1994), 355.

50. On the significance of social structuring through conflict regulation for the aristocratic groups, see (for earlier periods) the works of the American school of legal anthropology (Stephen D. White, Fredric L. Cheyette, Patrick J. Geary).

51. For a more detailed exposition of the remarks that follow, see Joseph Morsel, "Changements anthroponymiques et sociogenèse de la noblesse en Franconie à la fin du Moyen Age," in *Genèse médiévale de l'anthroponymie moderne*, vol. 3, ed. Monique Bourin and Pascal Chareille, Enquêtes généalogiques et données prosopographiques (Tours, 1995), and his essay "Personal Naming and Representation of Feminine Identity in Franconia in the Thirteenth and Fourteenth Century," in *Personal Naming and the History of the Family*, ed. M. Bovrin and George Beech, forthcoming.

52. StAW, Würzburger Urkunden, no. 45/109c (1489).

53. What was fundamentally new about these anthroponymic and sphragistic changes was, on the one hand, that every intermediate position a woman assumed was the object of a process of naming and representation, and on the other, that the announced framework of membership in a birth or matrimonial kin group was, systematically, the noble *Geschlecht*, while an analysis of the persons who played a role in marriage negotiations and contracts shows that the kin groups involved on both sides were broad and not only patrilinear. These changes must thus be understood as genuinely discursive—as components of a discourse on kinship.

54. On the generally integrative function of the tournament, see below text to notes 56–59. On the prominent place of women in the world of the tournament see An-

dreas Ranft's recent *Adelsgesellschaften*, 95–111, 170, and Morsel, "Das Geschlecht als Repräsentation."

55. See Morsel, "Changements anthroponymiques." Two different logics of first names existed side by side: one within the context of noble families (traditional first names), and the other within the context of the nobility (knightly first names).

56. Baum (*Der Lehenhof des Hochstifts Würzburg*, 200–202) shows that the number of vassals bearing the title of knight fell steadily during the fourteenth and fifteenth centuries. Furthermore, the fact that a single nobleman (Michel von Ehenheim, Wilwolt von Schaumberg) might be knighted more than once may indicate that the value of the accolade had diminished.

57. The text is published in Morsel, "Le tournoi," 326–28.

58. See Morsel, "Le tournoi."

59. The 1478 circular letter on the revival of the tournament (see n. 57) reveals that the tournament was understood as one of the most important sites for the maintenance of the nobility through chivalrous behavior. Similarly, the famous Ludwig von Eyb the Younger wrote in his 1519 book of tournaments, "the tournament is not the least [thing] that may move the nobility to good, knightly and honorable things" (als der turnir nit das minst ist, den adl zu guten, ritterlichen und eerlichen sachen bringen mag). *Das Turnierbuch des Ludwig von Eyb (cgm 961). Edition und Untersuchung mit einem Anhang: die Turnierchronik des Jörg Rugen*, ed. Heide Stamm, Stuttgarter Arbeiten zur Germanistik, 166 (Stuttgart 1986), 93.

60. See Zotz, "Adel, Bürgertum und Turnier," 450–51, and "Adel in der Stadt," 40–41. See also the title of the Feyerabend edition of Rüxner's *Turnierbuch*, in n. 86 below. Noble societies also regularly met in the cities. See Andreas Ranft, "Adel und Stadt im späten Mittelalter. Ihr Verhältnis am Beispiel der Adelsgesellschaften," in *Die Kraichgauer Ritterschaft in der frühen Neuzeit*, ed. Stefan Rhein, Melanchthon-Schriften der Stadt Bretten, 3 (Sigmaringen, 1993), 47–64; and the same author's "Die Turniere der Vier Lande," 94, and "Adelsgesellschaften," 232–49.

61. On the jurisdiction of the royal law court in the *parlement*, see Étienne Dravasa, *Vivre noblement. Recherches sur la dérogeance de noblesse du XIVe au XVIe siècles* (Bordeaux, 1965), and Jacques Mourier, "Nobilitas, quid est? Un procès à Tain-L'Hermitage en 1408," *Bibliothèque de l'École des Chartes*, 142 (1984): 255–69. In all cases what was at stake was deciding who should be taxed by the king (nonnobles) and who should not (nobles).

62. See Luc Boltanski, *Les cadres. La formation d'un groupe social* (Paris, 1982), 480–82.

63. On the literature, state of research and critiques, see Morsel, "Crise? Quelle crise?" 20–23, and Ulrich Andermann, *Ritterliche Gewalt und bürgerliche Selbstbehauptung. Untersuchungen zur Kriminalisierung und Bekämpfung des spätmittelalerlichen Raubrittertums am Beispiel norddeutscher Hansestädte*, Rechtshistorische Reihe, 91 (Frankfurt a.M., Berne, New York, and Paris, 1991), 27–33 and 45–58. See also Morsel, "Das sy sich mitt der besten gewarsamig schicken."

64. See the recent study by Hillary Zmora, *State and Nobility in Early Modern Germany: The Knightly Feud in Franconia, 1440–1567* (Cambridge, 1997).

65. The term "Städtefeindschaft" (opposition to cities) was coined by Graf, "Feindbild und Vorbild." The term "Adligenfeindschaft" (opposition to nobles) appears to me better than "Adelsfeindschaft" (opposition to the nobility) because, as will become clear below, what was at issue was not (yet) the principle of nobility itself, but rather the embodiment of nobility by nobles. Similarly, Graf's "Städtefeindschaft" must be clearly

distinguished from "Stadtfeindschaft" (opposition to the city), which would imply that we are dealing with a mere conflict between two social types, while what is really at stake is a discursive conflict between concrete cities and nobles over the domination of space, the creation of sociopolitical identities, and concrete claims to power.

66. One of the oldest clear pieces of evidence for the use of *adel* to refer to nobles as a group (and as an active subject) refers to just such an accusation: "after . . . one had to see clearly that the nobility had become very much given to robbery" (nachdem . . . man clerlichen siehen mochte, das der adel sich der rawbrei seer angenomen he^{a}tten) (1441): see Reichstagsakten 16 (cf. n. 41), 85.

67. Norbert Elias, *The Court Society*, trans. Edmund Jephcott (New York, 1983), 66–68. Municipal legal restrictions of the noble lifestyle, such as existed in Nuremberg in the 1430s, point in a similar direction. See Zotz, "Adel, Bürgertum und Turnier," 487–89. The above-mentioned Shrovetide play by Rosenplüts (esp. 646–47) portrays the gap between the two logics, the "aristocratic" and the "burgher," by having the Fool advise the urban audience to leave the nobles and their social values out of their monetarized economy, while the knight (like the duke before him, p. 645) presents war as the instrument for maintaining the status scale against such a disintegration of the prevailing order through money. Cf. Gadi Algazi, "The Social Use of Private War: Some Late Medieval Views Reviewed," *Tel Aviver Jahrbuch für deutsche Geschichte* 22 (1993): 259–62.

68. See the above-mentioned Shrovetide play by Rosenplüts, which was performed publicly before the town community. Basically, it addresses the problem of the common good (why are the "poor," that is "the peasants and the town," always under attack?) and ends with the Fool comparing the towns and the nobility.

69. For Nuremberg, see Martial Staub, "Memoria im Dienst von Gemeinwohl und Öffentlichkeit. Stiftungspraxis und kultureller Wandel in Nürnberg um 1500," in *Memoria als Kultur*, ed. Otto Gerhard Oexle, Veröffentlichungen des Max-Planck-Instituts für Geschichte, 121 (Göttingen, 1995), 285–334.

70. Klaus Graf, "Schlachtgedenken in der Stadt," in *Stadt und Krieg, 25. Arbeitstagung in Boblingen 1986*, ed. Bernhard Kirchgässner and Günter Scholz, Stadt in der Geschichte, 15 (Sigmaringen, 1989), 83–104; and Graf, "Feindbild und Vorbild," 128–29.

71. On Ulm, see Zota, "Adel in der Stadt," 26–27, und Graf, "Feindbild und Vorbild," 146–47. On Augsburg, see *Fastnachtspiele aus dem fünfzehnten Jahrhundert*, vol. 3, 1357–68. On Cologne, see Wolfgang Herborn, "Bürgerliches Selbstverständnis im spätmittelalterlichen Köln. Bemerkungen zu zwei Hausbüchern aus der ersten Hälfte des 15. Jahrhunderts," in *Die Stadt in der europäischen Geschichte. Festschrift Edith Ennen*, ed. Werner Besch (Bonn, 1972), 490–520, esp. 503–7.

72. See Klaus Schreiner, *Sozial- und standesgeschichtliche Untersuchungen zu den Benediktinerkonventen im östlichen Schwarzwald*, Veröffentlichungen der Kommission für geschichtliche Landeskunde in Baden-Württenberg, B, 31 (Stuttgart, 1964), 94–112, as well as "Religiöse, historische und rechtliche Legitimation spätmittelalterlicher Adelsherrschaft," in Oexle and Paravicini, *Nobilitas*, 376–430; Otto Gerhard Oexle, "Aspekte der Geschichte des Adels im Mittelalter und in der Frühen Neuzeit," in *Europäischer Adel 1750–1950, Geschichte und Gesellschaft*, Sonderheft 13, ed. Hans-Ulrich Wehler (Göttingen, 1990), 53–56; Graf, "Feindbild und Vorbild," 146–54.

73. See the song, mentioned above in n. 41, composed during the war against the Margrave: "they . . . call themselves the Roman Empire / now they are nothing but peasants after all" (si . . . nennen sich das römisch reich / nun sind si doch nur pauren).

See also Graf, "Feindbild und Vorbild," 131–32, and Schmidt, *Die deutschen Städtechroniken*, 69.

74. Klaus Schreiner, "Consanguinitas—Verwandtschaft als Strukturprinzip religiöser Gemeinschafts- und Verfassungsbildung in Kirche und Mönchtum des Mittelalters," in *Beiträge zu Geschichte und Kultur der mittelalterlichen Germania Sacra*, ed. Irene Crusius, Veröffentlichungen des Max-Planck-Instituts für Geschichte, 93 (Studien zur Germania Sacra, 17 [Göttingen, 1989], 213–14).

75. See, for example, StAW, *Libri diversarum formarum*, no. 15, p. 426.

76. As king of the tournament society "With the Unicorn" (zum Einhorn) Dietrich (V) von Thüngen was charged in 1483 with the task of confirming the noble descent of Melchior Truchseß von Pommersfelden, a candidate for a benefice in the cathedral chapter of Mainz. *Die Protokolle des Mainzer Domkapitels*, vol. 1, ed. Fritz Herrmann and Hans Knies (Darmstadt, 1976), no. 1505. In 1480, Balthasar von Ostheim justified the participation of Wilhelm von der Kere in the next noble tournament by stating that Wilhelm and his siblings "were good knightly nobles from both their four paternal and maternal ancestors and have demonstrated their four ancestors in the cathedral chapter of Würzburg according to the laudable custom of that chapter" (von iren vir annen vatterer und mutterer gute rittermessige edelleut sein und ir vir annen uff deme thumstifft zu Wirzpurg nach lobliger gewonheyt desselben stiffts bewissen haben). Stadtarchiv Frankfurt am Main, Reichssachen 1, no. 6053.

77. See also Graf, "Feindbild und Vorbild," 142–53; Oexle, "Aspekte der Geschichte des Adels," 48–56; for a more general sociological discussion, see Boltanski, *Les cadres*, 298–301.

78. See esp. *Memoria. Der geschichtliche Zeugniswert des liturgischen Gedenkens im Mittelalter*, Münstersche Mittelalter-Schriften, 48, ed. Karl Schmid and Joachim Wollasch (Munich, 1984), and *Gedächtnis, das Gemeinschaft stiftet*, ed. Karl Schmid (Munich and Zurich, 1985). On the community of the living and the dead, see esp. Otto Gerhard Oexle, "Die Gegenwart der Toten," in *Death in the Middle Ages*, ed. Herman Braet and Werner Verbeke, Mediaevalia Lovanensia, 1, 9 (Louvain, 1983), 19–77, and "Die Gegenwart der Lebenden und der Toten. Gedanken über Memoria," in Schmid (ed.) *Gedächtnis, das Gemeinschaft stiftet*, 74–107.

79. Otto Gerhard Oexle, "Memoria, Memorialüberlieferung," in *Lexikon des Mittelalters* 6 (1993), 510.

80. See Franz Machilek, "Frömmigkeitsformen des spätmittelalterlichen Adels am Beispiel Frankens," in *Laienfrömmigkeit im späten Mittelalter. Formen, Funktionen, politisch-soziale Zusammenhänge*, ed. Klaus Schreiner, Schriften des Historischen Kollegs, Kolloquien, 20 (Munich, 1992), 168, as well as Morsel, "Das Geschlecht als Repräsentation" and *Une noblesse contre le prince*.

81. See Kruse et al., *Ritterorden und Adelsgesellschaften*, 26–27, and Ranft, *Adelsgesellschaften*, 85–92, 156–61.

82. Cf. the statutes of the coparcenary of Rothenberg, whose first clause stipulates that masses be said for all deceased members: StAN, Reichsstadt Nürnberg, D-Ladenurkunden, no. 705.

83. The main characteristic of princely *memoria* appears to me to be the historical and genealogical justification offered for the princes' legitimate power (see Gert Melville, "Vorfahren und Vorgänger. Spätmittelalterliche Genealogien als dynastische Legitimation zur Herrschaft," in Peter-Johannes Schuler, ed., *Die Familie als sozialer und historischer*

Verband. Untersuchungen zum Spätmittelalter und zur frühen Neuzeit, Sigmaringen, 1987, 203–309), a legitimation which in my view asserted itself particularly against the other aristocrats.

84. See the claims of a Roman origin for the Franconian and Swabian nobility in *Die Geschichten und Taten Wilwolts von Schaumburg* (6), and in Thomas Lirer's chronicle; see Klaus Graf, *Exemplarische Geschichten. Thomas Lirers "Schwäbische Chronik" und die "Gmünder Kaiserchronik,"* Forschungen zur Geschichte der älteren deutschen Literatur, 7 (Munich, 1987), or also the nobles' justification for their refusal to pay the *Gemeiner Pfennig* tax in 1495. They argued that the nobility of Franconia and the Empire (*Francken und deß Reichs vom Adel*) had always (*jederzeit*) served the Empire with their bodies and their military skills, as if the nobility had always existed. *Codex Diplomaticus Equestris cum continuatione, oder Reichs-Ritter-Archiv*, ed. Johann Stephan Burgermeister (Ulm, 1721), 1335–36). Cf. the remembered Swabian castles in Graf, "Feindbild und Vorbild," 141; see also his *Exemplarische Geschichten*, 120ff; for the example of the commemoration of battles see Graf, "Schlachtgedenken in der Stadt." On the example of the existence of the land of Swabia, which was explained historically and in relation to the nobility in the so-called Thomas Lirer, see Graf, *Exemplarische Geschichten*, 81–157.

85. See Stamm (ed.), *Das Turnierbuch des Ludwig von Eyb*, 145ff.; Dorothea A. Christ, *Das Familienbuch der Herren von Eptingen, Kommentar und Deskription* (Liestal, 1992), 342ff.; Georg Rüxner, *Anfang, Ursprung und Herkomen des Thurniers inn Teutscher nation . . .* (Simmern, 1532).

86. Particularly apparent in the title of Rüxner's book of tournaments, edited by Sigmund Feyerabend: *Thurnierbuch. Von Anfang, Ursprung und herkomen der Thurnier im heyligen Roemischen Reich Teutscher Nation, Wieviel offentlicher Landthurnier von Keyser Heinrich dem ersten dieses Namens an biß auff den jetztregierenden Keyser Maximilian den andern, unsern Allergnädigsten Herrn, und in welchen Stetten die alle gehalten, Auch durch welche Fuersten, Graffen, Herrn, Ritter und vom Adel dieselben jederzeyt besucht worden* (Book of Tournaments. Of the Beginning, Origins and Descent of the Jousters in the Holy Roman Empire of the German Nation. How many public Tournaments from Emperor Henry the First of that name onward to the now-reigning Emperor Maximilian the Second, our most gracious Lord, and in which places all of them were held, also which Princes, Counts, Lords, Knights and their Nobility have visited them each Time, Frankfurt a.M., 1566). Henry I was regarded as the first organizer of a tournament in the German lands by Max Würsung (*Wann und umb welicher Ursachen Willen das loblich Ritterspiel des Turniers erdacht und zum ersten geübet worden ist*, Augsburg 1518) as well as by Ludwig von Eyb and Jörg Rugen. See Stamm (ed.), *Das Turnierbuch des Ludwig von Eyb*, 104–5 and 245–46.

87. See, for example, the two ambiguous fourteenth-century cases mentioned above (nn. 12 and 13, *Wörterbuch der mittelhochdeutschen Urkundensprache*, and the works cited for comparison with it). The existence of other, perhaps clearer, mentions cannot be excluded, but they were doubtless only scattered before the years 1430–1440.

88. See F[riedrich] Lippmann, *Lucas Cranach. Sammlung von Nachbildungen seiner vorzüglichsten Holzschnitte und seiner Stiche* (Berlin, 1851), no. 35; F. W. H. Hollstein, *German Engravings, Etchings and Woodcuts, ca. 1400–1700*, vol. 6 (Amsterdam, 1955), no. 112 (p. 89); Max Geisberg, *The German Single-Leaf Woodcut: 1500–1550*, vol. 2 (New York, 1974), no. G.624 (p. 591). The dimensions of the woodcut itself are 24.7 cm by 16.6 cm.

89. The rhymed commentary reads: "A proverb says, it is well-known / Throughout

the German lands / When Adam dalf and Eve span / Who was then the gentleman? / Tis right enough, yet as it's sure / Nobility is God's order true / We should pay it honor due / As St. Paul taught us to / Let the nobility too think hereupon / Like Emperor Maximilian: / The equal of any man I be / Only 'twas God who honored me. / C.M.O." (Ein Sprichwort heist, ist wol bekant / Durchaus im gantzen Deutschenland / Da Adam reut und Eva span, / Wer war doch da ein Edelman? / Es ist wol war, Doch weil gewis / Der Adel Gottes ordnung ist, / Soln wir im sein gebürlich ehr / Erzeigen, nach S. Pauli lehr, / Auch soll der Adel dencken dran, / Wie Keiser Maximilian: / Ich bin gleich wie ein ander Man, / Nur das mir Gott die Ehre gan. / C.M.O.) Cf. Christian Schuchardt, *Lucas Cranach des Aeltern Leben und Werke, nach urkundlichen Quellen bearbeitet*, vol. 2 (Leipzig, 1851), 279; F. W. H. Hollstein, *German Engravings*, 89 (only the beginning and end of the text), and Eberhard Freiherr Schenk zu Schweinsberg, "Die Wandlungen des Adelsbildes in der Kunst," in *Deutscher Adel 1430–1555*, Büdinger Vorträge 1963, Schriften zur Problematik der deutschen Führungsschichten in der Neuzeit, vol. 1, ed. Hellmuth Rössler (Darmstadt, 1965), esp. 1–2 (modernized version).

90. The accompanying text juxtaposes three social discourses: first, the German version of the English rebel John Ball's famous speech of 1381 ("When Adam dalf and Eve span / Where was then the gentleman?"), second, a reference to the Epistle of St. Paul to the Romans (13:1ff.), which is frequently cited in connection with the legitimation of secular government, and was for many years used to legitimize the *militia*, particularly within the concept of the three orders (e.g., in the Anglo-Saxon monk Ælfric's replacement of "the authorities" by the *bellator* as sword bearer around the year 1000); and third, a statement attributed to the Emperor Maximilian, who is said to have grounded his noble (princely) superiority in the honor bestowed upon him by God. For materials to aid in deciphering this argument, see Arnold Angenendt, "Der eine Adam und die vielen Stammväter. Idee und Wirklichkeit der Origo gentis im Mittelalter," in *Herkunft und Ursprung. Historische und mythische Formen der Legitimation*, ed. Peter Wunderli (Sigmaringen, 1994), 27–52; Gerhard Herm, *Der Aufstieg des Hauses Habsburg* (Vienna and New York, 1992), 169; Rodney H. Hilton, *Bond Men Made Free: Medieval Peasant Movements and the English Rising of 1381* (London and New York, 1973); Jan-Dirk Müller, *Gedechtnus. Literatur und Hofgesellschaft um Maximilian I.*, Forschungen zur Geschichte der älteren deutschen Literatur, 2 (Munich, 1982); Oexle, "Perceiving Social Reality" in this volume; Klaus Schreiner, "Zur biblischen Legitimation des Adels. Auslegungsgeschichtliche Studien zu 1. Kor. 1, 26–29," *Zeitschrift für Kirchengeschichte* 85 (1974): 317–57.

91. Max Weber, *Wirtschaft und Gesellschaft. Grundriß der verstehenden Soziologie* (Tübingen, 1972), 534–38.

PART III

STABILIZING

(Royal) Favor

A Central Concept in Early Medieval Hierarchical Relations

Gerd Althoff

"The king used the numerous festivities, walks and excursions as a reward or punishment for those who were or were not invited. As he realized that he did not have enough favours to dispense to make a permanent impression, he replaced real rewards with imaginary ones, by exciting jealousy, by petty everyday advantage, by his partiality. No-one was more inventive in this respect than he."[1] The king in question was no medieval monarch, but rather Louis XIV, whose name is inextricably linked with the absolutist form of rule. What Louis's reserved critic, Saint-Simon, describes here in his memoirs makes one thing perfectly clear: the ruler's favor or grace functioned as an instrument of reward and punishment; it could both encourage and discipline, but it could also do more. Yet another peculiarity of royal favor has been aptly illustrated for absolutist court society: The bestowing of favor would have been impossible outside of the existing social hierarchy. Indeed, certain people had a claim to favor which resulted directly from their rank. This claim found its visible expression in intricate court etiquette, in ceremonial which had absorbed the multifarious forms of displaying royal favor. Thus only members of certain ranks could claim the right to hold the candlestick at the king's couchee or to hand the queen the first article of clothing at her levee.[2]

According to the literature, it is here—and in the many comparable details of court ceremonial—that we can see the tenacity of a system that persisted despite an increasing loss of political functions and the reduction of its scope of influence to the court itself.[3] This is most likely one of the reasons why the court and courtly life have been subjected to such massive criticism ever since the high Middle Ages, for which we have impressive literary evidence ranging from the works of John of Salisbury and Sebastian Brant to those of Friedrich Schiller.[4]

When a system is so tenacious and effective, though, it makes sense to inquire into the early phases of its history—and this is where medieval historians come in. How did a hierarchical system centered on a single individual (the monarch) function, we might ask, and what role did royal favor play in this system? Under what circumstances did it fulfill its function as an instrument of reward and discipline; and under what circumstances and when did the above-mentioned losses of function, phenomena that ultimately characterized the system as a whole, occur?

Such questions put medieval historians on the spot, for they have, to be sure, frequently encountered the term "favor" in the sources, generally in the form of the Latin word *gratia*, but have not hitherto treated—nor, most probably, recognized—the phenomenon as one of the central concepts of medieval hierarchical systems or ways of life.[5]

Most of those who have addressed the problem come from the neighboring disciplines, mainly legal history and literary studies. The former, the legal historians, encounter the punitive measure of withdrawing favor, a threat found in countless medieval documents.[6] The order to do or avoid doing particular things if one wished to retain the favor of the lord or ruler is a common formula of royal, papal, and also private documents. Legal historians also however encounter favor in questions involving mercy in the law and the right of pardon.[7] It was a prerogative of monarchs or lords to show mercy when they saw fit. This procedure was associated with favor, which also lay in the discretion or caprice of the lord or ruler.[8]

Literary scholars encounter favor not only in lyrics of the troubadours and minnesingers, where the favor of the beloved is usually described as unattainable,[9] but they have also provided us with well-researched semantic-field studies, for example on the Old High German vocabulary for the concepts of grace, favor, and love.[10] They have discovered that the word *huldi* (modern German *Huld*: favor, or grace) was "originally largely [associated with] the sphere of the Germanic system of fealty." It could refer both to the "benevolent attitude" of the liege lord and the "free devotion" of the liegeman. *Huldi* was also, however, used to refer to a "relationship on an equal basis" such as was called for and common among kin groups or friendly tribes.[11]

The results of these studies are corroborated by the historical sources in the narrower sense. Nevertheless, here we find the term mainly in the field of hierarchical relations.[12] Favor (*gratia*) was bestowed not only by the feudal lord on his vassal; the vassal also bestowed favor on his lord, which probably found its most striking expression in the homage paid to the magnates within the framework of the installation of the ruler.[13] Favor was thus probably taken over into vassalage from the system of fealty. What, however, is the content and meaning of this form of conduct, which is expressed above all through gesture or ritual? Someone who bestows favor or is well disposed toward someone else signals his readiness to continue to fulfill the duties that result from an existing bond. He signals his satisfaction with the bond and his continued good conduct. The evidence of favor may, naturally, also appear at the inception of a bond and represent a first promise of good conduct for the future. What all of the acts that were used to show favor have in common, however, is a distinctly demonstrative character. They are directed not only at the person whom favor is being shown in a given case, but also at an audience who then become the witnesses and guarantors of this act, an act that is in many cases of a legally symbolic or ritual nature. We will return presently to a discussion of what this meant in individual cases.

At this point we should turn our attention to a problem that is probably responsible for historians' lack of interest in the phenomenon of favor up until now. Medieval authors address the subject matter that we describe using the term "favor" in widely varying ways. Medievalists encounter this problem in many fields, but we must also take it into account here.[14] The authors frequently use the term *gratia* when they mean the favor of the lord or sovereign, but they refer to the same subject matter when they report that a great *familiaritas* or *pietas* existed between persons,[15] that persons treated each other *honorifice* or *benignissime*, that they conversed frequently and intensively,[16] or presented each other with munificent gifts.[17] Such messages were readily understandable to contemporaries—in each of these cases the persons demonstratively emphasized that their relationship was wholly untroubled. We, in contrast, overlook such hints all too easily because this complex arena of gesture, ritual acts, and their meanings has become foreign to us.[18] It thus appears appropriate to begin by introducing concrete examples of acts of bestowing and withdrawing favor before proceeding to the question of what basic conditions underlay these acts.

Let us begin with the withdrawal of favor, which generally, but by no means always, proceeded from the lord or sovereign. In the documents, a whole series of misdeeds carry with them the threat of a withdrawal of favor. Any violation of commands whatsoever could bring with it the loss of the lord's favor.[19] One could also fall into disfavor without any misconduct of one's own, either by membership in a kin group in some way hostile to the sovereign, or through particular circumstances that incurred his displeasure.[20] Finally—and this appears to be a significant characteristic—no formal judicial proceedings, in which the king or lord asked the accused's equals in rank or clan members for a judgment, which he then joined, were necessary for the suspension of favor.[21] Apparently, it was the lord alone who ordered and took responsibility for the withdrawal of favor. Such a measure was a signal that put firm pressure on the party in question to change his behavior.

The following factors are important for an understanding of this procedure: since favor could only be lost where it had once been present, this procedure applied only to groups of persons bound to each other by hierarchy, friendship, or kinship. In the case of dissent or conflicts, such groups were mainly interested in conciliation through satisfaction, whereby peace and favor were restored.[22] For this reason favor was generally not irrevocably lost. Instead, the sources usually only mention the loss of favor after it has already been regained by spectacular acts of redress. In other words, the affected party was moved by the suspension of favor to make amends for his previous misconduct and thus to remove the source of contention. This process of giving satisfaction (*satisfactio, compositio*) is also very significant for the understanding of how the medieval state functioned.[23] I will return to this point presently.

But what consequences did the withdrawal of lordly favor have for a medieval person in the first place? To be sure there are cases in which the individual involved also found himself stripped of his offices, fiefs, or even all of his property; but it was by no means the case that the withdrawal of favor automatically entailed the confiscation of assets.[24] Yet the loss of favor in itself, even without other measures, still had serious consequences. Gregory of Tours already had Bishop Berthram of Bordeaux argue against an episcopal *confrater*: "Hear now, O brother and fellow bishop; thou hast not the favour of the king; wherefore thou mayst not have our friendship either, unless thou first gain the king's pardon."[25] The loss of favor brought exclusion; it made it impossible to coexist in a group in which mutual favor existed. It was scarcely conceivable, under such circumstances, to remain or appear at a court diet (*Hoftag*)—as one may easily imagine—since the king or lord would not speak to the person in question, would probably not even acknowledge his presence or at most look upon him grimly, and not affably and cheerfully as he did the other members of the party.[26]

The ruler's withdrawal of favor thus isolated those it singled out, and also affected their other ties, since further contacts with one who had fallen out of favor were regarded as affronts to the lord. It should nevertheless be emphasized that relatives and friends often chose to stand by those affected by a loss of favor, indeed even actively supported them, so that the intended effect of isolation remained in vain.[27] As a rule, though, his presence near the lord would have become difficult, and we read not infrequently of people leaving the ruler's vicinity secretly, that is, without observing the prescribed departure ceremonial.[28] The sources can also tell quite a different story, however: the service regulations for the ministers of the archbishop of Cologne in the mid-twelfth century stipulated how a ministerial who had lost the archbishop's favor should be treated.[29] He was not to be expelled from the community, but rather given the opportunity for the period of one year to gain, through the performance of services, an intercessor and mediator from among the most powerful and influential men at the archbishop's court, who would regain his lord's favor on his behalf. If this did not succeed, he had the possibility of entering the service of another lord.[30] Here we have a concrete example of the quasi-institutionalized role of the intermediary, who enjoyed particular significance in all medieval conflicts.[31] His task was to negotiate an appropriate satisfaction; he agreed on the forms in which satisfaction would be given, and he also guaranteed that the lord would keep the promises he made in the course of such negotiations.[32] The intermediary's sphere of activities in the Middle Ages by no means appears to have been restricted to resolving conflicts. Intervenients—another name for mediators—were apparently called on in many areas where something stood to be achieved or prevented.[33] The function of the mediator reveals a peculiarity of medieval communication, which was crucial to the functioning of medieval ways of life. People did not choose a direct or frontal means of voicing their desires, claims, or concerns, but rather a confidential one. Mediators or friends presented the matter to the addressee—the king, for example—in such a way as to ensure, as far as possible, a favorable response. We may also observe this manner of proceeding in the relationship between medieval people and God, for he, too, was approached primarily through intercessors—that is, the saints—and put in a gracious—that is, favorable—mood.[34]

But let us return to the Cologne service regulations. The rules affecting anyone found guilty of slaying a fellow official were more complicated still. He, too, lost the archbishop's favor, but in addition was turned over to his authority (*in potestatem domini sui*) by court order.[35] He had to continue to follow the archbishop wherever he went and to serve him with three horses and two servants; at the same time, however, he had to stay out of his lord's sight; indeed, if he chanced upon him he had to avoid the encounter.[36] Even in this case, however, the miscreant had one year to search for an intermediary among the first men of Cologne, here referred to as *domini terrae*, or anyone else who would help him to recover his lord's favor (*pro recuperandi gratia domini sui*).[37]

These regulations can help us better to understand a famous eleventh-century case of the withdrawal of favor, in which a quite similar aspect emerges, which has gone unnoticed up until now. The case in question is the conflict between King Konrad II and his stepson, Duke Ernst, which proceeded through several dramatic acts, ending in tragedy and death for Duke Ernst. For that reason, among others, the case evoked a broad response both in the contemporary sources and later literature.[38] Up until now scholars have understood neither the consistency with which the king acted nor the bitterness that clearly motivated his stepson. Wipo—our main source of information about these events—reports as follows on the initial phase of the conflict: "Full of disdain for them [that is, his opponents and Duke Ernst] King Konrad resolved to travel to Italy with his troops. Duke Ernst, however, accompanied him in humility (*humiliter*) as far as Augsburg, where the king, after long resisting the intercessions of his mother, the queen, his very young brother Heinrich, and other princes, finally took him back into his favor."[39]

If we consider, against the background of the above-cited Cologne regulations, what it meant in concrete terms for the duke to accompany the campaign as a *humiliter* who had fallen out of favor until he was finally returned to the king's good graces by the efforts of mediators, there can be little doubt that he will have behaved—and had to behave—as was also expected of the Cologne officials: he avoided contact with the sovereign, but had to display his willingness to serve until the mediators had effected his return to Konrad's favor. Any further explanation of what it meant for the duke's prestige to be publicly excluded and, finally, an object of royal mercy, is doubtless unnecessary.[40]

Let us return once again to the brutal minister of Cologne, the treatment of whom is further detailed in the service regulations. If his efforts to find a mediator who could regain the favor of his lord remained unsuccessful after one year, he was to be held in a chamber of the archbishop's palace and only allowed three days' leave three times a year in order to search for an intermediary. Anyone who wished to visit him was free to do so at any time. A child conceived by his wife during such a visit would, however, be considered illegitimate.[41] More important than this detail is the emphasis here, too, on the role of the intermediary, whose task it was to regain for the prisoner the favor of his lord by negotiating the proper satisfaction.

The document does not mention what kind of amends were to be made to the archbishop. The satisfaction offered to a king apparently consisted in a demonstrative act of public, unconditional subordination, for which something akin to a ceremonial existed. Barefooted and dressed in penitential robes—sometimes also with a sword at their necks—those who had lost favor approached the king, and did so as publicly as possible.[42] In the case of one such subordination the Altaich annalist comments, "barefoot, as the *honor regius* demanded."[43] Such acts are attested for major feast days and for the ruler's walk to attend mass, but also for similarly solemn occasions, such as coronations or royal weddings.[44] Several authors concretely state that the person seeking favor expressed his unconditional submission with the words, "Do with me what you will."[45] We may assume that this sentence, too, belonged to the ceremonial.

This subordination was, however, only apparently unconditional. Rather, the mediators had negotiated what would happen after this act of submission, and they guaranteed that the agreements would be honored. The person subordinating himself generally regained the ruler's favor—sometimes his exalted position was restored, and sometimes he was placed under arrest, but imprisonment was only brief and quasi-symbolic, and ended with demonstrative acts similar to those already practiced during the subordination.[46] Frequently, however, he also had to accept material losses. Interestingly enough, it was not only the ruler who was compensated here; the mediators also profited. What is characteristic of this entire scenario or drama, though, is that it afforded satisfaction to the person whose favor was being sought in an incredibly demonstrative and public manner. It showed the public not merely the extent of his power, but also, simultaneously, that he knew how to handle this power with mercy and a readiness to forgive. This demonstration partially, or indeed wholly, concealed the fact that he was, in reality, not as much in control of the situation as was suggested, but had instead already committed himself—and been compelled to commit himself—to restoring his favor.

The possibility of withdrawing favor thus certainly provided the kings and lords of the Middle Ages with an instrument capable of fulfilling disciplinary functions. We would only understand half of the process, though, if we forgot that favor had to be restored once appropriate satisfaction was offered. It was not the lord, or at least not he alone, who decided what was appropriate in an individual case. Rather, the intermediaries also played a role, and they had the affected party's interests in mind and thus placed limits on the lord's caprices.

If historians have paid little attention to the process of withdrawing favor, they have been even less interested in how favor was actually bestowed, what range of demonstrations of favor was available to a given lord or ruler, and what rules had to be followed in the process. A sketch of the two extremes may make the problem clearer. The one extreme is described by Tacitus in connection with his remarks on the Germanic system of vassalage. He observed a fierce struggle for position among vassals, each of whom wanted to be first in rank after his lord. According to Tacitus, only the lord could decide such questions of hierarchy.[47] Put another way, his favor established the hierarchy and could change it at will. To be sure, it would be quite natural to suspect Tacitus of idealizing certain circumstances here in order to hold them up to his fellow Romans as a model.[48] The problem existed throughout the Middle Ages, however—to what extent could the lord bestow his favor freely, that is, independently of the existing hierarchy?

This already brings up the other extreme—did the hierarchy not produce a claim to favor that robbed the lord of any freedom to show favor as he saw fit, and thus necessarily lead to those losses of function which, as indicated at the beginning of the paper, characterized the ceremonial of absolutist court society? In actual practice in the Middle Ages we encounter neither the freedom to bestow favor described by Tacitus nor its absolute tie to the hierarchy. Characteristic instead is the dialectic between the two principles, even if the trend was doubtless one from greater freedom to greater restriction.

What were the preferred fields for demonstrating favor in the Middle Ages?

Without claiming to be exhaustive, we should emphasize three areas: (1) the broad field of gifts, (2) honoring persons by drawing attention to and showing preferences for them in public and, not least, (3) the confidential conversation. Scholars have already addressed the function of gifts as expressions of favor.[49] Because gifts made favor visible to all, they were chosen with great care and usually reflected the exact degree of esteem that they were intended to express. That it was also interpreted in this way by all those who attended the public presentation of the gifts is demonstrated by a letter that the Carolingian king Louis the Younger sent to his kinsman Louis the Stammerer in the year 878 along with a number of exquisite gifts. He wrote that the gifts were intended as a pledge of the continuation of the bond between them.[50] The gifts included an excellent horse and the saddle that the king himself had used, and a costly wall hanging. The recipient—as his kinsman wrote—should hang the latter when he consulted with his nobles as a clear sign of their mutual affection (*dilectio, devotio, affectio*), so that all of the evil gossip about their relationship would cease.[51] The gifts were thus indicators of the state of their relations and were universally interpreted as such.

That gifts had to take account of the recipient's rank is also substantiated by Notker of St. Gallen's report on the gift-giving practices of Louis the Pious at Easter: "On this day he also distributed gifts among all those who served at the palace and attended at the king's court, according to who each individual was, so that all of the more distinguished among them received sword-belts or girdles and valuable articles of clothing; the lesser, however, were given Frisian mantles of all colors, while grooms, bakers, and cooks were rewarded with linen and woolen clothing and short swords."[52]

Such gifts presented to all according to their rank and occupation must certainly be distinguished from those bestowed upon individuals as demonstrative rewards. Thus, for example, when in 1041 Henry III presented Margrave Luitpold of Austria with the horse and its saddle embellished with silver and gold which he had just received from the Duke of Bohemia as part of his subordination, it was a mark of public distinction. The Altaich annalist refers to this affirmation and distinction, which was expressed through gift giving, as *gratia maxima*.[53] This brings us to the area of honorable special treatment, which in this case was a response to extraordinary military successes. In this instance we have no evidence of negative reactions on the part of other magnates. When special treatment became too blatant, however, the response could be quite different, as we can see in the case of Hagano of Lorraine, a minion of King Charles the Simple, who made him powerful through his favor (*ex mediocribus potentem effecerat*).[54] The magnates of the kingdom considered this "indignum";

it aroused their "indignatio,"[55] which they expressed in the following way: when Duke Robert, who claimed the king's "maior gratia," was expected to sit at the king's right and Hagano at his left, he considered it beneath his dignity and also an insult to the other magnates. Robert suppressed his anger but scarcely spoke to the king and rose from table sooner than was customary in order to consult with his allies.[56] His behavior, however, drew the king's attention to his "indignatio," which meant the cancellation of his favor. When Charles the Simple refused, despite the efforts of intermediaries, to drop Hagano, this signaled a break between the duke and the king.[57]

Only when we consider that placement at table or in counsel rendered hierarchies visible do the numerous medieval disputes over seating plans become understandable, disputes that not infrequently escalated into armed conflicts or at least occasioned the indignant departure of those who felt that they had been improperly seated.[58] Lords who wished to avoid serious discord did well to observe the rules of these seating plans, and to bestow their favor within the framework thus established.

The examples mentioned here are but a few among many: favor bestowed in an unusual way aroused *indignatio* or at least *invidia*, envy. In the vita of Bishop Bernward of Hildesheim the connection between favor (shown toward one man) and the envy of all others is the central theme used to treat Bernward's rise.[59] His grandfather had already "taken him into his closest confidence and did not make the slightest decision without first asking his advice. . . . And although envy easily creeps in with so much *familiaritas*, Bernward managed to suppress it altogether by exercising the greatest caution."[60] At the court of the Empress Theophanu, Bernward quickly attained the *summa familiaritas* of the empress, who even entrusted him with the upbringing of her son. The result, however, was that Bernward incurred the *invidia quorundam*, the envy of other courtiers.[61] According to the vita he was also bound to his pupil Otto III by a *praecipua* (particular) *familiaritas*; so it is no wonder that this once again evoked the envy and *indignatio* of many. This *praecipua familiaritas* even aroused the anger and *indignatio* of the archbishop of Mainz, who, like many others, was envious that another man stood higher in the emperor's favor than he did.[62]

That *familiaritas* indeed referred to a relationship marked by particular favor may be demonstrated by a phrase from the roughly contemporaneous copybook of Gerbert of Aurillac, who reassured a fellow bishop on behalf of Adalbero of Reims that "Him whom you believe lacking in the king's favor [*gratia*] is not excluded from any form of *familiaritas*."[63]

Nonetheless, if the relationship between two persons was marked by the greatest favor and *familiaritas*, then the confidential conversation played a signif-

icant role. Bernward's vita and its account of the bishop's meeting with Otto III in
Rome illustrates in detail what a favorable reception looked like as well as the
importance of conversation for such encounters:

Accompanied by the grace of God, Bernward stepped onto Roman soil on 4 January.
When the pious and humble emperor learned of this, he was so filled with longing to see
his beloved teacher that he could hardly wait. Because, however, he did not wish to put
him to the trouble of coming to him, he set forth at once to meet him, going almost two
miles to St. Peter's church, received him with the greatest love, embraced and kissed him
like his best friend and accompanied him to his lodgings. There he conversed with him for
a long while and bade him come to the palace the following day. . . . The next morning the
emperor invited the Pope to receive his beloved guest. As the latter approached, the two
men went to meet him in the entrance hall and welcomed him warmly. He was also not
permitted to return to his lodgings; instead, the emperor offered him excellent apartments next to his own. Then the two sat down together, now in the emperor's apartments,
now in the bishop's, and discussed judicial disputes and affairs of state.[64]

These were the points that were emphasized, then, when one wished to describe a
relationship characterized by particular favor, although there is naturally no
guarantee of the factual correctness of the individual details.

The familiar and confidential conversation appears as a sign of the greatest
favor in other contexts as well. Two further examples may be cited here: Otto the
Great was reportedly so pleased by the arrival of Bishop Ulrich of Augsburg in
Ravenna, that, according to Ulrich's vita, he "rushed off to meet him . . . shod on
one foot and barefoot on the other in order to receive him full of love. Then the
two sat together in his apartments in amicable conversation—the empress, too,
was called to join them."[65] The author of the vita needed to say no more in order
to show that Bishop Ulrich enjoyed the emperor's highest favor.

The confidential and gracious conversation could also be the opening act of
an official decision, such as an appointment to an office. Thus Thietmar of
Merseburg reports as follows on the events that occurred after the death of the
Magdeburg archbishop Tagino: "Then we were called into the palace and entered
the king's private chambers. But only Walthard was admitted, and they conversed
alone together until tierce. When Walthard emerged he wore a ring on his hand,
showed it to us and declared, 'Here you see the pledge of future favor.' "[66]

It is worth dwelling for a moment on why it was that a confidential conversation on an important matter should go together with, and indeed be so important to, particular favor. If we consider that in the Middle Ages kings and lords
were obliged to discuss the matters at hand with their loyal followers, without any
precise stipulations on who should be involved in such discussions, then it makes
sense that being consulted on all matters, and enjoying the ruler's confidence,
placed an individual in an important position.[67] This kind of consultation was a

mark of particular favor; it provided the only opportunity to exert influence. For—and this cannot be emphasized enough in this context—those who did not have the ear of their lord or king had scarcely any chance of asserting their interests or claims.[68] It was not usual for people to present their wishes to the king unsolicited, let alone to assert claims publicly. Rather, the rules of the game prescribed other forms, which the above-cited Thietmar expressed as follows: "Then I asked the king for the favor of granting me a conversation on the affairs of my church."[69] If we take this situation into account, then the envy that particular intimacy aroused had a very real background. As a rule, the other magnates of the kingdom took swift action when a king particularly favored one of their number in this respect. This sort of excessive *familiaritas* was the undoing not only of the above-mentioned Hagano, but also of the bishops Liudwart of Vercelli and Adalbert of Hamburg-Bremen, famous favorites of the ninth and eleventh century, respectively.[70]

Up until now, we have only presented the manifestations of favor from the vantage point of lords. This manner of proceeding is justified by the sources, which report far more frequently on lords' bestowal and withdrawal of favor than they discuss this in relation to their liegemen or vassals. It should nonetheless be emphasized once again that favor was a mutual responsibility, that is, that men also bestowed favor or withdrew it from their lords. From the perspective of vassals, however, showing favor primarily involved a promise of *fides*, or loyalty, and the behavior that went along with it.[71] For this reason *fides* or *fideliter* are terms central to the favor shown by vassals, just as *gratia* was for lords. Their conduct was also probably more strongly determined by strict norms, more ritualized, than we have been able to see in the case of lords. All the same, vassals too not infrequently vented their *indignatio*, either by removing themselves or failing to go to their lords in the first place, wearing an earnest or grim expression, speaking little, or giving whatever other signs were usually used to signal that relations with their lord were seriously troubled.[72] On the other hand, they showed their favor not only within the context of the king's installation or entry into a relationship of vassalage, in which they underwent the ceremony of the joined hands (*Handgang*), together with a promise of loyalty and a kiss. They also, for example, performed ritual services such that of the *strator*, in which the vassal led his lord's horse by the reins and held the stirrup, thus symbolically demonstrating his willingness to serve.[73] The services performed by dukes as marshals, cupbearers, stewards (*Truchseß*), and chamberlains, for example, which are mainly attested to for the coronation banquets of newly installed kings, also belong to this conceptual world.[74]

A tale told by Dudo of St. Quentin about the establishment of ties of vassalage between the Norman duke Rollo and the king of West Francia, Charles the Simple, shows how strongly, despite all ritualization, such displays of favor and the concrete forms they took captured the imagination of contemporaries.[75] Despite Dudo's anecdotal exaggeration, the forms in which the self-assured Norman could be moved to accept vassalage show how loaded with meaning any ritual act in this arena was. Rollo agreed to the joined hands common in the acceptance of vassalage, although "neither his father nor his grandfather nor any of his ancestors had ever done this with anybody."[76] The king alleviated the degrading significance of the joined hands by giving Rollo his daughter Gisela in marriage—and presenting him with land not as a fief but as his property.[77] Then, however, according to Dudo, a crisis arose. Rollo firmly refused to kiss the king's foot as he had been requested to do. "Never," he said, "have I bent my knee before anyone's foot, and I shall kiss the foot of no man."[78] The compromise reached after negotiations stipulated that one of Rollo's warriors should kiss the king's foot in his stead.[79] The performance of this ritual, which was, after all, intended as a display of homage, makes abundantly clear what was at stake here: "He [the warrior] immediately raised the king's foot, brought it to his mouth and completed the kiss standing upright, causing the king to fall backwards. This evoked much laughter and great agitation among the people."[80]

This story is naturally fictive, and it transmits but one important message: a Norman warrior bows his head before no man.[81] It is precisely the fiction, however, that shows what vassals' displays of homage were also, or even primarily, about. They were supposed to demonstrate submission, of which kissing the foot was an extreme—and for the Normans unacceptable—form of expression. Vassals' displays of homage also apparently reflected their rank and their distance from the lord. If, however, this distance became altered, so did the forms of displaying homage. They may thus be used as indicators of the state of hierarchy, even if the only evidence we have of them is anecdotal.

The sketch presented here urgently needs to be summarized and integrated into a broader context of research. First, it has doubtless become clear that both displaying and withholding favor were among the behaviors most central to the hierarchical relations of the Middle Ages. They were very flexible instruments for both discipline and reward, encouragement and warning; but they were also sensitive ones, which could not be applied without precise observation of the prevailing conditions and rules of the game in these fields of power. The conditions were set in large part by the hierarchy prevailing within the ruling stratum, a hierarchy which became ever more firmly entrenched over the course of the Middle Ages. This hierarchy established the duty to show favor, which directly reflected each person's position in it. This connection surely promoted those losses of function spoken of at the beginning of this essay. But even in the centuries of the early Middle Ages, it is apparent that displays of favor were never wholly free of the exigencies of hierarchy. Rather, the frequency with which favor aroused envy and discord in these centuries may be regarded as a strong indication that lords were in the process of being obliged to respect the hierarchy—a process that was by no means always linear.[82] By the tenth century at the latest, with the recognition of dynastic succession, by means of which the kings largely dispensed with the strongest displays of favor—the bestowal of offices and fiefs[83]—favor had been successfully tied to hierarchy. This does not mean that no efforts were made thereafter to show favor by circumventing this hierarchy, however.

Second: when we address the theme of favor and its multifarious guises in the medieval hierarchical system and way of life, we address a topic that cries out for integration into a larger framework. Favor is only one manifestation in the broad field of rituals, gestures, and rules the sum of which represents the peculiarity of political interactions in the Middle Ages, in other words, the nature of the medieval state. Research in this field has long been neglected in favor of other approaches, and I believe that it is high time that we changed this. Only then can we reach an appropriate understanding of how a system that is, after all, worlds apart from our own, functioned. It managed—largely—without literacy, without institutions, established jurisdiction or administrative channels and, not least, without a monopoly on the use of force. Instead, it practiced verbal consultations among constantly changing categories of people, a large number of ceremonies from the liturgical to the courtly, and very specific forms of conducting and settling conflicts, among other things. In order to take all of these elements seriously as characteristics of the medieval state, we must undertake a substantial reorientation.[84] In the light of the medieval sources' norm-oriented and stereotypical mode of representation, we need, not least, to collect all of the scattered information, accounts, and stories that afford us concrete glimpses of political events and the conceptual world emerging behind them.[85]

A concluding reference to modern times may also be in order here. I may have awakened the impression that the phenomenon of favor is some relic of archaic ages without relevance or meaning for people today. This would, however, be a misunderstanding, for favor—even if we do not use the term—still determines many of our interactions nowadays. I am not speaking of the activities of those crowned heads who wave from balconies or carriages, much to the delight of their subjects, aged eight to eighty.[86] What I have in mind are, rather, contemporary communication strategies: how people greet each other; who speaks with whom and for how long, and which special attentions are offered to whom, particularly when they are in the public eye.[87] We may find the phenomenon that was referred to in the Middle Ages as "favor" everywhere. Verbally, but almost more so nonverbally through gestures, signs, and rituals, we show each other our esteem, admiration, or willingness to be of service, and these signs are oriented toward the rank accorded to the recipient of these signals in the particular world in which the act takes place. Favor is thus a widespread anthropological theme and phenomenon, even if the terms used to refer to it may vary greatly from one era to another.

Notes

This essay, which originated as an inaugural lecture given on 29 January 1991 at the University of Gießen, is translated from Gerd Althoff, "Huld: Überlegungen zu einem Zentralbegriff der mittelalterlichen Herrschaftsordnung," *Frühmittelalterliche Studien* 25 (1991): 259–82. Many thanks to my Gießen colleagues Xenia v. Ertzdorff, Diethelm Klippel, and Heinz Schilling for their valuable ideas on aspects of the topic that cross epochal and disciplinary boundaries.

1. Quoted in Norbert Elias, *The Court Society* (New York, 1984), 120; on the phenomenon of royal favor in absolutism, see Heinz Schilling, *Höfe und Allianzen. Deutschland 1648–1763*, Das Reich und die Deutschen 6 (Berlin, 1989), 19–20; Heinz Duchhardt, *Das Zeitalter des Absolutismus*, Oldenburger Grundriss der Geschichte 11 (Munich, 1989), 36ff. and 166ff. with additional bibliography.

2. For a fundamental account see Elias, *The Court Society*, 89ff.; Juergen Freiherr von Kruedener, *Die Rolle des Hofes im Absolutismus*, Forschungen zur Sozial- und Wirtschaftsgeschichte 19 (Stuttgart, 1973), 60ff.

3. Elias uses the apt image of a "ghostly *perpetuum mobile* that continued to operate regardless of any direct use-value, being impelled, as by an inexhaustible motor, by the competition for status and power of the people enmeshed in it." *The Court Society*, 86.

4. On this see Claus Uhlig, *Hofkritik im England des Mittelalters und der Renaissance* (Berlin, 1973); Helmuth Kiesel, *"Bei Hof, bei Höll." Untersuchungen zur literarischen Hofkritik von Sebastian Brant bis Friedrich Schiller*, Studien zur deutschen Literatur 60 (Tübingen, 1979); C. Stephen Jaeger, *The Origins of Courtliness* (Philadelphia, 1985); Joachim Bumke, *Höfische Kultur. Literatur und Gesellschaft im hohen Mittelalter*, 2 vols. (Munich, 1986), 2: 583ff.; Peter von Moos, *Geschichte als Topik* (Hildesheim, Zürich, New York, 1988), 509ff., 570ff., and passim; most recently in the collection of essays *Curialitas. Studien zu Grundfragen der höfischritterlichen Kultur*, ed. Josef Fleckenstein, Veröffentlichungen des Max-Planck-Instituts für Geschichte 100 (Göttingen, 1990), particularly Thomas Szabó's contribution "Der Mittelalterliche Hof zwischen Kritik und Idealisierung," 350–91, with a wealth of evidence of criticisms of the court and court life since the ninth century.

5. This becomes clear, for example, in the brief and not particularly informative article "Huld, -verlust" in the *Lexikon des Mittelalters*, 5, 1. Lief. (Munich and Zurich, 1990), col. 183. In contrast, the phenomenon receives a good deal of attention in the older literature on constitutional history. See, for example, Georg Waitz, *Deutsche Verfassungsgeschichte*, 8 vols., 2d ed., revised by Gerhard Seeliger (Berlin, 1880–1896), 6:576ff.; Eugen Rosenstock-Huessy, *Königshaus und Stämme in Deutschland zwischen 911 und 1250* (Leipzig, 1914; reprint, Aalen, 1965), 313ff.; in his *Lehnrecht und Staatsgewalt* (Weimar, 1933; reprint, Darmstadt 1958), 481ff., in contrast, Heinrich Mitteis treats *Huld* only in connection with the vassal's oath of loyalty as an "institution of feudal law," a fact which apparently had a major impact on the further interest of researchers.

6. See Georg Cohn, "Die Strafe des Huldeverlustes im deutschen Recht" (Jur. Diss., Universität Göttingen, 1907); Rudolf Köstler, *Huldentzug als Strafe. Eine kirchenrechtliche Untersuchung*, Kirchenrechtliche Abhandlungen 62 (Stuttgart, 1910); see also the articles "Hulde" and "Huldeverlust" in the *Handwörterbuch zur deutschen Rechtsgeschichte*, ed. Adalbert Erler and Ekkehard Kaufmann, vol. 2 (Berlin, 1978), cols. 256–62; most recently, with an extensive historical review of the literature, see Jürgen Weitzel, *Dinggenossenschaft und Recht. Untersuchungen zum Rechtsverständnis im fränkisch-deutschen Mittelalter*, Quellen und Forschungen zur Höchsten Gerichtsbarkeit im Alten Reich 15, 1–2 (Cologne and Vienna, 1985), 1169ff. and 1176ff.

7. See Konrad Beyerle, *Von der Gnade im Deutschen Recht* (Göttingen, 1910); see further references in the articles "Gnade" in *Handwörterbuch zur deutschen Rechtsgeschichte*, 1 (Berlin, 1971), 1714–19, and "Gnadenrecht" in *Lexikon des Mittelalters*, 4 (Munich and Zurich, 1988), 1521–22.

8. On this see Beyerle, *Von der Gnade*, 5–6; Weitzel, *Dinggenossenschaft und Recht*, 1186ff.

9. Among the very abundant literature see Rüdiger Schnell, *Causa amoris. Liebeskonzeption und Liebesdarstellung in der mittelalterlichen Literatur*, Bibliotheca Germanica 27 (Berne and Munich, 1985), esp. 77ff. and "Die 'höfische' Liebe als 'höfischer' Diskurs über die Liebe," in *Curialitas*, ed. Joseph Fleckenstein, 231–301; Bumke, *Höfische Kultur* 2:503ff. with bibliography, 835ff.

10. See Paul Wahmann, *Gnade. Der althochdeutsche Wortschatz im Bereich der Gnade, Gunst und Liebe*, Neue deutsche Forschungen 125, Abteilung Deutsche Philologie 4 (Berlin, 1937); Marianne Steimer, *Die Wörter huldi, helpa, anst, mildi und andere Synonyme im Heliand* (Ph.D. diss., Universität Berlin, 1937); Gottfried Rupprecht Leuthold, "Gnade und Huld" (Ph.D. diss., Universität Freiburg, 1953); Marianne Ohly-Steimer, "Huldi im Heliand," *Zeitschrift für deutsches Altertum und deutsche Literatur* 86 (1955–56): 81–119; Dennis Howard Green, *The Carolingian Lord. Semantic Studies on Four Old High German Words balder—frô—truhtin—herro* (Cambridge, 1965), esp. 140ff.

11. See the cited terms in Ohly-Steimer, "Huldi im Heliand," 82–83.

12. Since the terms used to refer to behavior within communal and kinship bonds have been intensively studied, and the word *gratia* is not encountered there, it seems certain that the term was not or was only seldom used in these types of relationships to refer to the behavior called for and practiced here. Of the fundamental studies on the terminology of the conduct demanded in kinship and communal groups, see Reinhard Schneider, *Brüdergemeine und Schwurfreundschaft*, Historische Studien 388 (Lübeck and Hamburg, 1964); Pierre Michaud-Quantin, *Universitas. Expressions du mouvement communautaire dans le moyen age latin* L'église et l'état au Moyen Age 13 (Paris, 1970); Otto Gerhard Oexle, "Gilden als soziale Gruppen in der Karolingerzeit," in *Das Handwerk in vor- und frühgeschichtlicher Zeit*, ed. Herbert Jankuhn et al., 2 vols., Abhandlungen der Akademie der Wissenschaften in Göttingen, Phil.-hist. Klasse 3. Folge, 122–23 (Göttingen, 1981–1983), 1:284–354; Alexander Callander Murray, *Germanic Kinship Structure. Studies in Law and Society in Antiquity and the Early Middle Ages* (Toronto, 1983); most recently, Gerd Althoff, *Verwandte, Freunde und Getreue. Zum politischen Stellenwert der Gruppenbindungen im früheren Mittelalter* (Darmstadt, 1990), 31ff.

13. See the bibliographies in the articles on "Huldigung" in *Handwörterbuch zur deutschen Rechtsgeschichte*, 2:262ff. and in the *Lexikon des Mittelalters*, 5:184.

14. See the corresponding findings of the studies on the medieval terms referring to

community and groups in Michaud-Quantin, *Universitas*; Oexle, "Gilden als soziale Gruppen," 292, or the corresponding observations in *Gilden und Zünfte. Kaufmännische und gewerbliche Genossenschaften im frühen und hohen Mittelalter*, ed. Berent Schwineköper, Vorträge und Forschungen 29 (Sigmaringen, 1985), of which the contributions by Ruth Schmidt-Wiegand, Franz Irsigler, and Otto Gerhard Oexle are the most relevant here; see also Karl Brunner, *Oppositionelle Gruppen im Karolingerreich*, Veröffentlichungen des Instituts für österreichische Geschichtsforschung 25 (Vienna, Cologne, and Graz, 1979), 14ff., with analyses of the terminology in the area of political opposition; most recently see Althoff, *Verwandte, Freunde und Getreue*, esp. 86, 90–91, and passim.

15. The term *familiaritas* is frequently glossed with *huldi/hulde*, on this see Leuthold, "Gnade und Huld," 25; in the Latin sources as well we encounter *gratia* and *familiaritas* as a synonymous pair of concepts; see, for example, Lampert of Hersfeld, "Annalen," in *Lamperti monachi Hersfeldensis opera*, ed. Oswald Holder-Egger, MGH SSrG (Hanover and Leipzig, 1894), a.1072, 134: "receptu non modo in gratiam et familiaritatem, sed pene in regni consortium et omnium quae publice vel privatim agenda erant societatem." Adalbert's position is thus described as *primus in palatio*; see below, n. 70. Thietmar of Merseburg, for example, uses the term *pietas* for favor (*Huld*). *Die Chronik des Bischofs Thietmar von Merseburg und ihre Corveyer Überarbeitung*, ed. Robert Holtzmann, MGH SSrG NS 9 (Berlin, 1955), VI, 54 and 66; see, more generally, Wilhelm Dürig, *Pietas liturgica. Studien zum Frömmigkeitsbegriff und zur Gottesvorstellung der abendländischen Liturgie* (Regensburg, 1958), esp. 166–67. *Gratia* was, incidentally, already familiar in classical Latin as a term for "favor" or "grace" in the arena of political power; on this see Hans Drexler, *Politische Grundbegriffe der Römer* (Darmstadt, 1988), 159–87; the account first appeared in *Romanitas*, 1971, 85–126.

16. On the conversation as an expression of favor see below, at n. 64ff.

17. See below at n. 49.

18. On this field of research, see Hanna Vollrath, "Das Mittelalter in der Typik oraler Gesellschaften," *Historische Zeitschrift* 233 (1981): 571–94; Ruth Schmidt-Wiegand, "Gebärdensprache im mittelalterlichen Recht," *Frühmittelalterliche Studien* 16 (1982): 363–79; August Nitschke, *Bewegungen in Mittelalter und Renaissance. Kämpfe, Spiele, Tänze, Zeremoniell und Umgangsformen*, Historisches Seminar 2 (Cologne, 1987), with numerous textual examples; Jean-Claude Schmitt, *La raison des gestes dans l'Occident médiéval* (Paris, 1990), each of which provides further examples; see also below, n. 26.

19. See the material-rich accounts in Köstler, *Huldentzug als Strafe*, 10ff.; Weitzel, *Dinggenossenschaft und Recht*, 1169ff., with all further references.

20. Thus, for example, Otto the Great refused to make Gero, a member of the Saxon high nobility, archbishop of Cologne because he was angry with his brother, the margrave Thietmar, for various reasons; see *Die Chronik des Bischofs Thietmar von Merseburg*, II, 24. This account, which was visibly embroidered into a miracle tale, is highly interesting for the issues addressed here because, according to Thietmar of Merseburg, the emperor himself asked for forgiveness and reestablished good relations by appointing Gero archbishop of Cologne after all: "Eique protinus venienti curam baculo pastoralem commisit et indulgentiam humiliter efflagitavit" (ibid., 68). Humble apologies are usually more the affair of the ruler's opponents. On this, see below nn. 42–43. On the role that *ira* and *furor* played as kingly modes of behavior particularly for this emperor, see Karl J. Leyser, *Rule and Conflict in an Early Medieval Society: Ottonian Saxony* (London, 1979).

21. The question of whether favor was withdrawn through legal proceedings remains

controversial among legal historians; see, most recently, Weitzel, *Dinggenossenschaft und Recht*, 1170ff., with its justifiably critical remarks on the notions of "arbitrary procedures" according to *Hausrecht* (i.e., the sovereign's own law) that exist in the literature. He too, however, still assumes that favor was withdrawn through legal proceedings (1172–73); a judgment based not least on the assumption that the withdrawal of favor and confiscation of goods necessarily belonged together. On this see below, n. 24. On the course and forms that judicial proceedings took in the Middle Ages, see the article "Gerichtsverfahren" in *Lexikon des Mittelalters*, vol. 4 (Munich and Zurich, 1989), 1330–35; see also Wolfgang Schildt, *Alte Gerichtsbarkeit. Vom Gottesurteil bis zum Beginn der modernen Rechtsprechung* (Munich, 1985), with impressive illustrations and many concrete references.

22. See Rudolf His, *Das Strafrecht des deutschen Mittelalters*, 2 vols. (Leipzig and Weimar, 1920–1935; reprint Aalen, 1964), 1:263ff.; Hermann Krause, *Die geschichtliche Entwicklung des Schiedsgerichtswesens in Deutschland* (Berlin, 1930), 3ff.; see also the article "Buße (weltliches Recht)," *Lexikon des Mittelalters*, vol. 2 (Munich and Zurich, 1983), 1144ff.; and "Schiedsgericht" in *Handwörterbuch zur deutschen Rechtsgeschichte*, vol. 4 (Berlin, 1990), 1386ff.; on the controversial history of research in this field, see also Weitzel, *Dinggenossenschaft und Recht*, 691ff.

23. The process is dealt with in legal history under the headings of "penance" or "system of compositions" (see the corresponding entries in *Handwörterbuch zur deutschen Rechtsgeschichte*); see also the references in n. 22. What is absent is a treatment of the phenomenon beyond the judicial arena, where it is also frequently encountered in attempts to avoid conflicts and restore peace; on the *deditio* as a frequently practiced form of giving satisfaction, see Timothy Reuter, "Unruhestiftung, Fehde, Rebellion, Widerstand: Gewalt und Frieden in der Politik der Salierzeit," in *Die Salier und das Reich*, ed. Stefan Weinfurter, 3 vols. (Sigmaringen, 1990), 3:297–325, here 320–21.

24. This should be recalled as a counterpoint to Weitzel's argumentation (*Dinggenossenschaft und Recht*, 1172ff.), for it is surely correct that the withdrawal of favor went hand in hand with confiscations of goods, but we have no reason to assume any automatism in the opposite direction.

25. Gregory of Tours, *Libri historiarum X*, ed. Bruno Krusch and Wilhelm Levison, MGH SS. rer. Merov. I, 1 (Hanover, 1951), V, 18, 223: "Audi, o frater et coepiscope, quia regis gratiam non habes, ideoque nec nostram caritatem uti poteris, priusquam regis indulgentia merearis." Engl. trans. *History of the Franks*, trans. O. M. Dalton (Oxford, 1927), 2:191–92. On the case in question see Georg Scheibelreiter, *Der Bischof in merowingischer Zeit* (Vienna, 1983), Veröffentlichungen des Instituts für Österreichische Geschichtsforschung, 28, 142–43 with n. 50; Weitzel, *Dinggenossenschaft und Recht*, 1186ff. One finds stipulations similar to those of the Merovingian period in the twelfth-century service regulations for ministerials in the Ahr (Rhineland), who were forbidden to treat a man who had fallen out of favor as a *socius*, and were indeed expected to regard him as an *inimicus*; see the "Ahrer Dienstrecht," in *Urkundenbuch für die Geschichte des Niederrheins*, ed. Theodor Lacomblet, 4 vols. (Düsseldorf, 1840–1858), 4, no. 624, 774–75: "Quicunque uero earum que prescripte sunt legum transgressor fuerit et propterea gratiam meam perdiderit. omnes suos compares non ut socios sed ut inimicos habeat. omnes contra eum sint. donec vel uolentem vel nolentem michi subiciant. Quod si quis eorum aliud aliquid cum eo commune vel sociale habuisse conuictus fuerit. eandem michi compositionem faciat quam ipse reus facere deberet."

26. On gestures of favor and disfavor, see Erhard Lommatzsch, *System der Gebärden*,

dargestellt auf Grund der mittelalterlichen Literatur Frankreichs, Ph.D. diss., Berlin, 1910; Dietmar Peil, *Die Gebärde bei Chretien, Hartmann und Wolfram. Erec-Iwein-Parzival*, Medium Aevum. Philologische Studien 28 (Munich, 1975), 85ff. and 223ff. (he does not, however, incorporate gestures of favor and disfavor into his account). Heinrich Fichtenau, *Lebensordnungen im 10. Jahrhundert, Studien über Denkart und Existenz im einstigen Karolingerreich*, Monographien zur Geschichte des Mittelalters, 30.1–2 (Stuttgart, 1984), 53–54. Louis XIV still referred to those who had incurred his disfavor with the devastating sentence "I do not know him"; quoted in Schilling, *Höfe und Allianzen*, 19. On cheerful composure (*hilaritas*) as an ideal for medieval gentlemen and rulers, see Hatto Kallfelz, *Das Standesethos des Adels im 10. und 11. Jahrhundert*, Ph.D. diss., Würzburg, 1960, 67ff.; Jaeger, *The Origins of Courtliness*, 168ff.; Fichtenau, *Lebensordnungen im 10. Jahrhundert*, 53 with n. 19 and 88 with n. 66.

27. See Althoff, *Verwandte, Freunde und Getreue*, esp. 119ff., and "Königsherrschaft und Konfliktbewältigung im 10. und 11. Jahrhundert," *Frühmittelalterliche Studien* 23 (1989): 265–90, both with numerous examples; see also Timothy Reuter, "Unruhestifung, Fehde, Rebellion, Widerstand: Gewalt und Frieden in der Politik der Salierzeit," in *Die Salier und das Reich*, ed. Stefan Weinfurter, 3 vols. (Sigmaringen, 1990), 3:297–325.

28. It should be emphasized in this context that it was necessary to obtain the king's permission (*licentia*) before traveling home from a court diet (*Hoftag*), for example; cf. Waitz (*Deutsche Verfassungsgeschichte*, vol. 6, 441) with extensive examples. For accounts of secret departures from the royal army, see Widukind of Corvey (*Die Sachsengeschichte des Widukind von Korvei*, ed. Paul Hirsch and Hans-Eberhard Lohmann, MGH SSrG, 5th ed., Hanover, 1935, III, 9) and the *Continuator Reginonis* (*Reginonis abbatis Prumiensis chronicon cum continuatione Treverensi*, ed. Friedrich Kurze, MGH SSrG, Hanover, 1890, a. 951) of Duke Liudolf, son of Otto the Great.

29. See the edition of the Cologne *Dienstrecht* in *Ausgewählte Urkunden zur Erläuterung der Verfassungsgeschichte Deutschlands im Mittelalter*, ed. Wilhelm Altmann and Ernst Bernheim, 2nd rev. ed. (Berlin, 1895), 148–53; see also Jakob Ahrens, *Die Ministerialität in Köln und am Niederrhein*, Ph.D. diss., Leipzig, 1908, 43ff.

30. Cf. the Cologne *Dienstrecht*, Art. 3, 149: "Item si archiepiscopus alicui ministerialium suorum quacumque occasione offensus fuerit, ita quod gratiam suam ei denegat et bonis suis eum exheredat, ille ministerialis nobiles terre et eos precipue, qui summi officiales curie vocantur, precibus et obsequio invitare debet, quatinus ipsi apud dominum suum pro recuperanda gratia eius intercedant. Quod si ipse infra annum eam recuperare non valuerit, expleto anno ad alium dominum se transferre poterit, ut illi serviat, ita tamen ut nec rapinas nec incendia contra dominum suum archiepiscopum exerceat. Si autem archiepiscopus eum non exheredat, sed tantummodo gratiam suam ei denegat, ipse post predictum annum expletum servitium suum domino suo archiepiscopo subtrahere potest, donec gratiam suam recuperet."

31. For the early Middle Ages see Reinhard Schneider, "Zum frühmittelalterlichen Schiedswesen," in *Aus Theorie und Praxis der Geschichtswissenschaft. Festschrift für Hans Herzfeld*, ed. Wilhelm Kurze (Berlin and New York, 1972), 389–403; from the perspective of legal history see especially Krause, *Die geschichtliche Entwicklung des Schiedsgerichtswesens*, and Karl Siegfried Bader, "*Arbiter arbitrator seu amicabilis compositor*," *Zeitschrift der Savigny-Stiftung für Rechtsgeschichte: Kanonistische Abteilung* 77 (1960): 239–76; for the French region see Patrick J. Geary, "Vivre en conflit dans une France sans état: Typologie de mécanisme de règlement de conflit (1050–1200)," *Annales É.S.C.* 41 (1986):

1107–26; more recently Gerd Althoff, "*Colloquium familiare—colloquium secretum—colloquium publicum.* Beratung im politischen Leben des früheren Mittelalters," *Frühmittelalterliche Studien* 24 (1990): 145–67, esp. 160ff.; Reuter, "Unruhestiftung, Fehde, Rebellion, Widerstand," 303 with n. 32, and 306–7 with further cases and references.

32. See Althoff, "*Colloquium familiare*," 161ff., with numerous examples, which reveal among other things that mediators took an oath guaranteeing that the agreements would be honored; cf. ibid., n. 51.

33. I am grateful to Helmut Beumann of Marburg for his suggestion that the role of intervenients in the documents might be discussed anew from this point of view; on this problem, see Hermann Krause, "Königtum und Rechtsordnung in der Zeit der sächsischen und salischen Herrscher," *Zeitschrift der Savigny-Stiftung für Rechtsgeschichte: Germanistische Abteilung* 82 (1965): 1–98, 72; Alfred Gawlik, "Zur Bedeutung von Intervention und Petition," in *Grundwissenschaften und Geschichte. Festschrift Peter Acht*, ed. Waldemar Schlögl and Peter Herde, Münchener Historische Studien. Abteilung Geschichtliche Hilfswissenschaften 15 (Kallmünz, 1976), 73–77, and, more recently, the article on "Intervenienten" in *Lexikon des Mittelalters*, vol. 5, 3.Lief. (Munich and Zurich, 1990), 470.

34. On this see Patrick J. Geary, *Furta sacra: Thefts of Relics in the Central Middle Ages, 800–1100* (Princeton, 1978), 25; Aron I. Gurevich, *Mediaeval Popular Culture: Problems of Belief and Perception*, trans. János M. Bak and Paul A. Hollingsworth (Cambridge and Paris, 1988), chap. 2, "Peasants and Saints." On the consequences of this mediating function within medieval relic practices, see Heinrich Fichtenau, "Zum Reliquienwesen des früheren Mittelalters," *Mitteilungen des Instituts für österreichische Geschichtsforschung* 60 (1952): 60–89, reprinted in Fichtenau, *Beiträge zur Mediävistik. Ausgewählte Aufsätze*, 3 vols. (Stuttgart, 1975–86), 1:108–44; cf. more recently, Arnold Angenendt, *Das Frühmittelalter. Die abendländische Christenheit von 400 bis 900* (Stuttgart, Berlin, and Cologne, 1990), 190.

35. Cf. the Cologne *Dienstrecht*, Art.8, 150: "Item nullus ministerialium beati Petri cum altero ministeriali sancti Petri monomachiam inire potest, quicquid unus adversus alium fecerit. Quod si unus alterum pro libitu suo et sine iusticia occiderit, proximi illius occisi querimoniam coram domino suo archiepiscopo de occisore deponent, et si occisor factum confessus fuerit, ipse in potestatem domini sui iudicabitur"; on this, see Ahrens, *Die Ministerialität in Köln und am Niederrhein*, 65ff.

36. Cologne *Dienstrecht*, Art.8, 150: "Postquam in potestatem domini sui iudicatus est, sequetur dominum suum omni tempore, quocumque dominus ierit, cum tribus equituris et duobus servis, ita quod nullo tempore se conspectui domini sui sponte ostendat, nisi forte inscienter vel in via, ubi dominus exinopinato per viam quam venit subito revertitur."

37. Ibid.: "Sic autem dominum suum continue sequetur, ut semper apud priores Colonienses et dominos terre et apud omnes quos potest studiose laboret pro recuperanda gratia domini sui et ut inimicis suis de morte occisi reconcilietur."

38. See Heinrich Mitteis, *Politische Prozesse des früheren Mittelalters in Deutschland und Frankreich*, Sitzungsberichte der Heidelberger Akademie der Wissenschaften, Phil.-Hist. Klasse 17 (Heidelberg, 1927), 29ff.; Helmut Maurer, *Der Herzog von Schwaben. Grundlagen, Wirkungen und Wesen seiner Herrschaft in ottonischer, salischer und staufischer Zeit* (Sigmaringen, 1978), 138ff., 147ff., and passim; Adelheid Krah, *Absetzungsverfahren als Spiegelbild von Königsmacht*, Untersuchungen zur deutschen Staats- und

Rechtsgeschichte N.F. 26 (Aalen, 1987), 347ff.; Odilo Engels, "Das Reich der Salier—Entwicklungslinien," in *Die Salier und das Reich*, ed. Stefan Weinfurter, 3:479–541, 496–97; on comparable conflicts, see Althoff, "Königsherrschaft und Konfliktbewältigung," esp. 278ff.; Reuter, "Unruhestiftung, Fehde, Rebellion, Widerstand"; Hanna Vollrath, "Konfliktwahrnehmung und Konfliktdarstellung in erzählenden Quellen des 11. Jahrhunderts," in *Die Salier und das Reich*, 3:279–96.

39. See *Wiponis Gesta Chuonradi II. imperatoris*, MGH SSrG, ed. Harry Bresslau, 3rd ed. (Hanover and Leipzig, 1915), cap. 10, 32: "Quos omnes rex Chuonradus parvi pendens iter suum in Italiam cum copiis destinavit. Sed dux Ernestus humiliter iter eius prosecutus usque Augustam Vindelicam interventu matris suae reginae et fratris sui Heinrici adhuc parvuli aliorumque principum multum renuente rege vix in gratiam eius receptus est."

40. On this see Althoff, "Königsherrschaft und Konfliktbewältigung," 276 with n. 38, citing well-known cases in which persons who had performed a ritual of subordination rose up against the ruler again soon afterwards; see also the similar assessments of the effects of rituals of subordination on the participants in Reuter, "Unruhestiftung, Fehde, Rebellion, Widerstand," 322–23.

41. See the Cologne *Dienstrecht*, Art. 7, 151: "Quod si hoc infra annum et diem obtinere non valuerit, tunc advocatus Coloniensis et camerarius pariter recludent eum in camera que proxima est capelle beati Thome sub palatio archiepiscopi, ideo proxima capelle ut per fenestram in capellam intrantem singulis diebus divinum officium audire possit. . . . Nunquam siquidem, prout dictum est inde egredietur nisi certis temporibus anni, scilicet in nativitate Domini, in pascha et in festo sancti Petri; habet etenim licentiam egrediendi in natali Domini per tres dies, in pascha per tres dies, in sollempnitate beati Petri, quando synodus episcopalis celebratur, per tres dies, ut tunc universos priores ecclesie et dominos terre ac omnes amicos et condomesticos suos moneat et roget, quantinus pro eo intercedant, et post hoc triduum statim in cameram suam non inpetrata gratia revertetur et sicut prius illic inclusus permanebit. . . . Quamdiu autem in camera perseveraverit, per totum diem amici et cognati et noti sui ad eum licite ingredi et egredi poterunt et loqui et esse cum eo, ita tamen ut ingredientes et egredientes filum et sigilla neque rumpant neque ledant; uxor quoque sua poterit ad eum ingredi et manere cum eo, si tamen prolem de ea intus genuerit, proles illa legitima non erit et secularis iuris expers manebit."

42. For cases, see Althoff, "Königsherrschaft und Konfliktbewältigung," 273 and 286–87, including the (in this respect) particularly impressive subjugation of the Saxons by King Henry IV in 1075; see *Carmen de bello Saxonico*, ed. Oswald Holder-Egger, MGH SSrG (Hanover, 1889), III/2, vv. 28ff.: "Castra petunt humiles Saxonum quique valentes, / Iam diffidentes armisque dolisque fugaeque, / Armis exuti, demissi colla superba / Nudatique pedes, cuncti cum supplice voto / Regi se dedunt omni sine conditione." Rahewin tells of the executioner's sword which was held to the necks of the Milanese during their subjugation to Barbarossa's army in 1058; see Bishop Otto of Freising and Rahewin, *Die Taten Friedrichs oder richtiger Chronica*, trans. Adolf Schmidt, ed. Franz-Josef Schmale, Ausgewählte Quellen zur deutschen Geschichte des Mittelalters. Freiherr vom Stein-Gedächtnisausgabe 17 (Darmstadt, 1965), III, 51, 500: "Talibus pacis conditionibus utrimque receptis, Mediolanum in gratiam reditura hoc ordine talique specie, fide publica accepta, cum suis ad curiam venit. Inprimis clerus omnis et quique fuerant ecclesiastici ordinis ministri cum archiepiscopo suo, prelatis crucibus, nudis pedibus, humili habitu; deinde consules et maiores civitatis, item abiecta veste, pedibus nudis,

exertos super cervices gladios ferentes." On comparable cases, see Althoff, "*Colloquium familiare*," 161–62.

43. *Annales Altahenses maiores*, ed. Edmund L. B. Oefele, MGH SSrG (Hanover, 1891), a. 1041, 27: "venit dux die condicto cum plerisque suis principibus et regiis, ut dignum erat, muneribus, et caesare sedente in palatio cum caetu seniorum, procidit ille ante consessum illorum discalciatus, ut poscebat honor regius, iam plus humiliatus, quam antea supra se fuerit exaltatus."

44. Henry, brother of Otto the Great, prostrated himself before his royal brother when the latter went to church on Christmas night. See Althoff, "Königsherrschaft und Konfliktbewältigung," 274 with n. 29; the acts were, so to speak, built into the ceremonial of elevation to kingship at the coronation of Konrad II; cf. ibid., 276 with n. 37; Duke Lothar of Supplinburg, in contrast, obtained the pardon of Henry V in 1114 when he publicly expressed his unconditional submission on the occasion of the ruler's wedding festivities; see Otto von Freising, *Chronicon sive historia de duabus civitatibus*, ed. Adolf Hofmeister, MGH SSrG (Hanover and Leipzig, 1912), VII, 15, 329: "In ipsa nuptiarum sollempnitate Lotharius dux Saxonum, nudis pedibus sago indutus coram omnibus ad pedes eius venit seque sibi tradidit." Otto von Freising added the comment: "Tantus enim usque ad id temporis timor omnes regni principes invaserat, ut nullus rebellare auderet vel rebellans cum maximo dampno sui vel etiam vitae detrimento in gratiam eius non rediret."

45. This is evidenced, for example, by the annals of Altaich (*Annales Altahenses maiores*, a. 974, 12) for the case of the subordination of Henry the Quarreler to Otto II: "sine ulla dilatione se praesentavit domino imperatori cum eis omnibus, qui erant in eo consilio, ut ille ex eis fecisset, quicquid sibi placuisset." This is also doubtless what Widukind of Corvey (*Die Sachsengeschichte*, II, 13, 78) meant when he wrote, on the occasion of the subjugation of Duke Eberhard of Franconia to Otto I: *Evurhardus adiit regem, supplex veniam deposcit, se suaque omnia ipsius arbitrio tradens*. Thietmar of Merseburg's (*Die Chronik des Bischofs Thietmar von Merseburg*, VI, 2, 276) assessment of the conditions stipulated by Henry II in his negotiations with mediators in the case of the subjugation of Margrave Henry of Schweinfurt is similar: "prefato comiti suimet gratiam ea ratione indulsit, ut predium sibi suisque fautoribus et incolatum redderet, ipsum autem, quamdiu voluisset, in custodia detineret. Heinricus vero se nimis in omnibus culpabilem lacrimabiliter professus more et penitentis regi se tradidit . . ." According to the Vita Bernwardi, the same applied to the subjugation of the inhabitants of Tivoli to the rule of Otto III, which came about through the mediation of the pope and Bernward. Thangmar, *Vita Bernwardi episcopi Hildesheimensis*, ed. Georg Heinrich Pertz, MGH SS 4 (Hanover, 1841), 754–82, cap. 23, 769): "Nam cuncti primarii cives praescriptae civitatis assunt nudi, femoralibus tantum tecti, dextra gladios, laeva scopas ad palatium praetendentes, imperiali iuri se suaque subactos; nil pacisci, nec ipsam quidem vitam; quos dignos iudicaverit, ense feriat, vel pro misericordia ad palam scopis examinari iubeat. Si muros urbis solo complanari votis eius suppetat, promptos libenti animo cuncta exequi, nec iussis eius maiestatis dum vivant contradicturos."

46. On mediators' guarantees that agreements would be kept, see above, n. 32. On the practice, expressly attested to in two cases, of admonishing the king from the pulpit to release someone who was under arrest, see Gerd Althoff, "Die Billunger in der Salierzeit," in *Die Salier und das Reich*, 1:309–29, esp. 323 with n. 70. Here, too, it seems likely that the admonition was arranged beforehand with the king and was thus a ritual procedure intended to demonstrate his gentleness and mercy.

47. P. Cornelius Tacitus, *Germania*, ed. Allan A. Lund, Wissenschaftliche Kommentare zu griechischen und lateinischen Schriftstellern (Heidelberg, 1988), cap. 13, 80: "gradus quin etiam ipse comitatus habet iudicio eius quem sectantur; magnaque et comitum aemulatio quibus primus apud principem suum locus, et principi cui plurimi et acerrimi comites." From a medievalist's point of view see also Walter Schlesinger, "Herrschaft und Gefolgschaft in der germanisch-deutschen Verfassungsgeschichte," *Historische Zeitschrift* 176 (1953): 225–75; reprinted in Schlesinger, *Beiträge zur deutschen Verfassungsgeschichte des Mittelalters*, 2 vols. (Göttingen, 1963), 1:9–52, esp. 21ff.

48. See Hans Drexler, *Tacitus. Grundzüge einer politischen Pathologie* (Darmstadt, 1970); Lund, Introduction to *Germania*, 44–69, esp. 65f. with further references.

49. On the significance of gifts in archaic societies more generally, see Marcel Mauss, *The Gift: The Form and Reason for Exchange in Archaic Societies* (New York, 1990); Wilhelm Grönbeck, *Kultur und Religion der Germanen*, 2 vols., 5th ed. (Darmstadt, 1954), 2:7ff. and 55ff.; Georges Duby, *Guerriers et paysans* (Paris, 1973), 50ff.; on the Middle Ages in particular see the rich collection of evidence in Percy E. Schramm and Florentine Mütherich, *Denkmale der deutschen Könige und Kaiser*, vol. 1, 2nd ed., Veröffentlichungen des Zentralinstituts für Kunstgeschichte II (Munich, 1981), 15ff., esp. 74ff.; there is also a wealth of material in Percy E. Schramm, *Herrschaftszeichen: gestiftet, verschenkt, verkauft, verpfändet*, Nachrichten der Akademie der Wissenschaften in Göttingen, Phil.-Hist. Klasse 5 (Göttingen, 1957); see, more recently, Jürgen Hannig, "Ars donandi. Zur Ökonomie des Schenkens im früheren Mittelalter," in Richard Van Dülmen (ed.), *Armut, Liebe, Ehre. Studien zur historischen Kulturforschung* (Frankfurt, 1988), 11–37.

50. *Collectio Sangallensis*, ed. Karl Zeumer, MGH Formulae (Hanover, 1886), no. 27, 412: "Ut autem foedus inter nos condictum firmiter permaneat, mittimus vobis pro arrabone . . ."

51. The sentence cited above n. 50 continues, ". . . mittimus vobis pro arrabone cavallum, viribus et velocitate, non statura et carnibus probabilem, et sellam, qualem nos insidere solemus, ut nos fortitudine et utilitate, non luxu et inanitate delectari noveritis. Mittimus etiam cortinam praestantissimam, qua in palatio vestro tempore consilii pro signo dilectionis nostrae suspensa, omnia maledicorum seminaria contabescant, dum et meam apud vos devotionem hoc munere et vestram erga nos affectionem ipsa viderint et extimuerint ostentatione."

52. *Notkeri Balbuli Gesta Karoli magni imperatoris*, ed. Hans F. Haefele, MGH SSrG NS 12 (Berlin, 1962), II, 21, 92: "In qua etiam cunctis in palatio ministrantibus et in curte regia servientibus iuxta singulorum personas donativa largitus est, ita ut nobilioribus quibuscumque aut balteos aut fasciones preciosissimaque vestimenta a latissimo imperio perlata distribui iuberet; inferioribus vero saga Fresonica omnimodi coloris darentur. Porro custodibus equorum pistoribusque et cocis indumenta linea cum laneis semispatiisque, prout opus habebant, proicerentur."

53. *Annales Altahenses maiores*, a. 1041, 28: "Idem Liutpoldis Radasponae regi redeunti obviam venit et gratias maximas cum meritis muneribus accepit, inter alia equum optimum, ducis Boemi donum, quem ipse regi detulerat, cum sella miri ponderis et operis, quae tota ex argento et auro fabrefacta fuerat." On the details, see Ernst Steindorff, *Jahrbücher des deutschen Reiches unter Heinrich III.*, 2 vols., Jahrbücher der deutschen Geschichte (Berlin, 1874–1881), 1:102ff., esp. 111.

54. Richer von Reims, *Historiarium liber IV*, 2 vols., ed. Robert Latouche, Les classiques de l'histoire de France au moyen âge, 12 and 17 (Paris, 1930–1937), 1, XV, 38:

"Nam cum multa benignitate principes coleret, praecipua tamen beatitudine Haganonem habebat, quem ex mediocribus potentem effecerat . . ." The assessment is taken from the annals of Flodoard; *Les Annales de Flodoard*, ed. Philippe Lauer, Collection des textes 39 (Paris, 1905), a. 916.

55. Richer, *Historiarium liber IV*, 38: "Etenim primates id ferentes indignum, regem adeunt ac apud eum satis conqueruntur hominem obscuris parentibus natum, regiae dignitati multum derogare, cum acsi indigentia nobilium ipse tamquam consulturus regi assistat, et, nisi a tanta consuetudine cesset, sese a regis consilio penitus discessuros."

56. Ibid., 38–39: "Inter quos [sc. principes Galliae], cum Rotbertus, in majore gratia apud regem sese haberi putaret, utpote quem ducem in Celtica omnibus praefecerat, cum rex in palatio sedisset, ejus jussu dux dexter, Hagano quoque ei levus pariter resedit. Rotbertus vero dux tacite indignum ferebat, personam mediocrem sibi aequari, magnatibusque praeponi. At, iram mitigans, animum dissimulabat, vix regi pauca locutus. Celerius ergo surgit ac cum suis consilium confert."

57. Ibid., 39: "Quo collato, regi per legatos suggerit sese perferre non posse sibi Haganonem aequari primatibusque anteferri; indignum etiam videri hujusmodi hominem regi haerere et Gallorum nobilissimos longe absistere; quem nisi in mediocritatem redigat, sese eum crudeli suspendio suffocaturum. Rex dilecti ignominiam non passus, facilius se omnium colloquio quam hujus familiaritate posse carere respondit. Quod nimium Rotbertus indignatus, cum optimatibus plerisque injussus Neustriam petit ac Turonis sese recipit, multam ibi de regis levitate indignationem habens, plurima etiam ut in se transfundatur rerum summa apud suos caute pertractans."

58. Cf., for example, the famous "Goslar seating dispute" of 1063, which was sparked by the placement at table of the bishop of Hildesheim and the abbot of Fulda; see Lampert (cf. n. 15) a. 1063, 81ff.; in 1184 a similar dispute arose at a court gala in Mainz over the placement of the abbot of Fulda and the archbishop of Cologne; cf. *Arnoldi chronica Slavorum*, ed. Georg Heinrich Pertz, MGH SSrG (Hanover, 1868), III, 9, 88ff.; cf., more recently, Peter Moraw, "Die Hoffeste Kaiser Friedrich Barbarossas von 1184 und 1188," in *Das Fest. Eine Kulturgeschichte von der Antike bis zur Gegenwart*, ed. Uwe Schultz (Munich, 1988), 70–83, 74–75.

59. Thangmar, *Vita Bernwardi episcopi Hildesheimensis*; on the Life of Bernward see Knut Görich and Hans-Henning Kortüm, "Otto III., Thangmar und die Vita Bernwardi," *Mitteilungen des Instituts für österreichische Geschichtsforschung* 98 (1990), 1–57, which provides clues suggesting that the vita was not written until the twelfth century. It will require further investigation, however, to determine exactly which parts of the vita are contemporary or based on contemporary sources, since many details provided in the text reflect very specific Saxon positions of the late tenth century and thus can scarcely have been written down for the first time in the twelfth century.

60. *Vita Bernwardi*, cap. 1, 759: "In quo quia salutaris consilii stationem saluberrimam repperit, familiarius sibi adiunxit, ut ne minimum quidem sine eius consultu ageret. Ebd. cap. 2, S. 759: Et quamvis in huiusmodi familiaritate invidia facile subrepat, hanc maxima cautela in plerisque declinabat." For a detailed account of this aspect of the vita, see Francis J. Tschan, *Saint Bernward of Hildesheim*, 3 vols. (South Bend, Ind., 1942–1952), 1:35ff.

61. *Vita Bernwardi*, cap. 2, 759: "Quo defuncto, ad palatium se contulit, in servitium videlicet tercii Ottonis imperatoris, qui septennis adhuc puer, cum venerabili et sapientissima matre domna Theuphanu augusta rebus praeerat. A qua hic venerabilis iuvenis

Bernwardus benignissime suscipitur, atque in brevi summae familiaritatis locum apud illam obtinuit, adeo ut domnum regem fidei illius literis imbuendum moribusque instituendum consensu cunctorum procerum commendaret. In quo ita excelluit, licet quorundam invidia morderetur, ut puer imperialis in discendo mirifice proficeret, et tamen ad cuncta foris obeunda liberalissimo negocio eius ingenium feriaret"; on this, see Tschan, *Saint Bernward of Hildesheim*, 1:42ff.

62. *Vita Bernwardi*, cap. 3, 759: "Unde domnus rex utroque parente desertus, totum se regendum in stationem fidissimi magistri contulit. Huius consilio examinabat, quodcumque alii adulando persuadebant; quia, quamvis in puerilibus auspiciis ociaretur, altiori tamen industria quorundam simulationes praevidebat. Praecipua itaque familiaritate magistrum suum amplectebatur, nec ab ullo inferius tractabatur, quem universali virtutum decore respersum venerabatur." Ibid., cap. 6, 760: "Nam tercio Ottoni imperatori affectuosissimo animo pro scire ac posse obsequebatur. Unde et multorum invidiam in se commovebat, qui indignabantur, illum vigilantiori studio rei publicae negocia obire." Ibid., cap. 18, 766–67: "Hanc autem iram et indignationem archiepiscopi adversus venerandum praesulem creavit maxime praecipua familiaritas domni imperatoris, qua illum speciali devotione pietatis caeteris familiarius percoluit. Affectuosissimo namque obsequio devinxit sibi imperatorem, quia cuncta, quae ad gratiam illius competere sciebat, vigilantissimo studio obibat; et ob hoc animositatem invidiamque plurimorum in se commovebat, adprime quoque Mogontini episcopi, qui indignabatur, aliquem praeter se familiaritatis locum apud imperatorem habere"; on this, see Tschan, *Saint Bernward of Hildesheim*, 1:157ff. with a detailed treatment of the Gandersheim dispute between Bernward and Willigis; see, more recently, Gerd Althoff, "Gandersheim und Quedlinburg. Ottonische Frauenklöster als Herrschafts- und Überlieferungszentren," *Frühmittelalterliche Studien* 25 (1991): 123–44, with additional references. Otto III expressed the same idea, that preferential treatment excites envy, in his famous oration to the Romans: "Causa vestra, dum vos omnibus proposui, universorum in me invidiam et odium commovi." *Vita Bernwardi*, cap. 25, 770.

63. *Die Briefsammlung Gerberts von Reims*, ed. Fritz Weigele, MGH Die Briefe der deutschen Kaiserzeit 2 (Berlin, Zurich and Dublin, 1966), no. 73, 104: "Is, quem caruisse regali gratia putastis, a nulla familiaritate seclusus est."

64. *Vita Bernwardi*, cap. 19, 766–67: "Dei gratia comitatus, ad votum rebus cedentibus, secundo Nonas Ianuarii Romam ingressus est. Quod humillimus ac piissimus imperator audiens, miro affectu dilectum magistrum videndi flagrans, ad suam praesentiam tamen eum fatigare nolebat, sed festinus a palatio fere duo miliaria ad Sanctum Petrum illi occurrit, benignissimeque susceptum, inter amplexus familiarissime deosculatum, ad hospitium deduxit, diuque cum illo confabulans, sequenti die ad palatium illum venire rogavit . . . Mane vero domnum apostolicum convocavit in occursum carissimi hospitis, venientem quoque foris in atrium obviam procedentes libentissime susceperunt, nec permissus est ad suum domicilium reverti, sed iuxta ubi ipse domnus imperator habitabat, splendidissimum illi habitaculum exhibebat. Vicissim quoque nunc imperatoris cubiculo, interdum episcopi considentes, et forenses causas et rei publicae necessaria conferebant."

65. Gerhard, *Vita sancti Oudalrici episcopi Augustani*, ed. Georg Waitz, MGH SS 4 (Hanover, 1841), cap. 21, 407: "Imperator vero cum eum in tanta vicinitate manere agnovisset, uno pede calciato et alio adhuc incalciato, causa humilitatis et flagrantia divini

amoris, eum ad suscipiendum amabiliter festinavit. Cumque in cubiculo, accersita imperatrice, suavi colloquio fruerentur"; on the vita, see Ernst Karpf, *Herrscherlegitimation und Reichsbegriff in der ottonischen Geschichtsschreibung des 10. Jahrhunderts*, Historische Forschungen 10 (Stuttgart, 1985), 105ff.

66. Cf. Thietmar of Merseburg, *Chronik*, VI, 66, S. 356: "et post hanc in urbem vocati ivimus usque ad caminatam regis. Et ibi solus intromittitur Walterdus et ibi usque ad terciam soli colloquebantur; et egressus tunc Walterdus anulum portat in manu sua et ostendens nobis: 'Ecce habetis', inquid, 'pignus subsecuturae pietatis!'" On the function of gifts as an honor see also, for example, Norbert, *Vita Bennonis II. episcopi Osnabrugensis*, ed. Harry Bresslau, MGH SS 30, II (Leipzig, 1934), cap. 6, 874: "Reversus igitur ad suam sedem incolumis episcopus cum sociis tantis eum honoribus, ubicunque sibi oportunum et possibile reperisset, ampliavit et donis, ut merito praecipuus apud omnes haberetur et clarus." See also the literature cited in n. 49.

67. On the place of advice in the Middle Ages see Fritz Kern, *Gottesgnadentum und Widerstandsrecht im früheren Mittelalter* (Leipzig, 1914; reprint Darmstadt, 1954), particularly n. 280, and pp. 269ff., 283, and 278ff.; Francois L. Ganshof, *Was waren die Kapitularien?* (Darmstadt, 1961), 53ff.; Jürgen Hannig, *Consensus fidelium. Frühfeudale Interpretationen des Verhältnisses von Königtum und Adel am Beispiel des Frankenreiches*, Monographien zur Geschichte des Mittelalters 27 (Stuttgart, 1982), 3ff.; and more recently Althoff, "*Colloquium familiare*," 145ff. with additional references.

68. On the technique of approaching rulers indirectly and in confidence see Althoff, "*Colloquium familiare*," 153 ff. with corresponding examples; this peculiarity probably also explains the eminent significance of intermediaries in all areas of life; see above nn. 33 and 34. Conversely, if a ruler took a vassal into his confidence this was regarded as a direct proof of favor. See, for example, the assessment in *Brunos Buch vom Sachsenkrieg*, ed. Hans-Eberhard Lohmann, MGH Deutsches Mittelalter 2 (Leipzig, 1937), cap. 13, which relates in detail the pricks of conscience suffered by a *familiaris* of Henry IV's because he believed he would lose the *gratia* of his heavenly king if he maintained that of his earthly sovereign. In this account favor meant above all participation in the *secreta regis*, the secret council. On the function of *Brunos Buch vom Sachsenkrieg* see Gerd Althoff and Stephanie Coué, "Pragmatische Geschichtsschreibung und Krisen, Teil I: Zur Funktion von Bennos Buch vom Sachsenkrieg," in *Pragmatische Schriftlichkeit im Mittelalter. Erscheinungsformen und Entwicklungsstufen*, ed. Hagen Keller et al. (Munich, 1992), 95–107.

69. Thietmar of Merseburg, *Chronik*, VI, 67, 365: "Deinde regiam interpellabam pietatem, ut de aecclesiae necessitatibus meae aliquid loqui cum eo dignaretur."

70. See Althoff, *Verwandte, Freunde und Getreue*, 15–16, with additional references.

71. On the vassals' concept and promise of loyalty see Mitteis, *Lehnrecht und Staatsgewalt*, 43ff.; François L. Ganshof, *Was ist das Lehnswesen?* (Darmstadt, 1967), 25ff., esp. 35–36; more recently, with a wealth of material, Walther Kienast, *Die fränkische Vasallität von den Hausmeiern bis zu Ludwig dem Kind und Karl dem Einfältigen*, ed. Peter Herde, Frankfurter wissenschaftliche Beiträge: Kulturwissenschaftliche Reihe 18 (Frankfurt, 1990), esp. 73ff. with additional references.

72. On this see Fichtenau, *Lebensordnungen im 10. Jahrhundert*, 48ff.; Althoff, "Königsherrschaft und Konfliktbewältigung," 271–72 with examples in n. 22; see also Lampert of Hersfeld's account (n. 15 above, a. 1066, 101–2) of the toppling of Archbishop Adalbert of Hamburg-Bremen (see also n. 70), in which the princes revealed their inten-

tions to Henry IV in advance by their grim expressions: "Statuta die tristis in regem omnium vultus, tristis erat sententia, ut aut regno se abdicaret [sc. Henry IV] aut archiepiscopum Premensem a consiliis suis atque a regni consortio amoveret."

73. Robert Holtzmann, *Der Kaiser als Marschall des Papstes. Eine Untersuchung zur Geschichte der Beziehungen zwischen Kaiser und Papst im Mittelalter*, Schriften der Strassburger wissenschaftlichen Gesellschaft in Heidelberg, N.F. 8 (Berlin and Leipzig, 1928); on other ritual services performed by vassals see Mitteis, *Lehnrecht und Staatsgewalt*, 479ff.; and more recently Kienast, *Die fränkische Vasallität*, 73ff.

74. On this see Karl Hauck, "Rituelle Speisegemeinschaft im 10. und 11. Jahrhundert," *Studium Generale* 3 (1950): 611–21, esp. 620–21; Percy Ernst Schramm, "Ottos I. Königskrönung in Aachen (936). Die Vorakte und Einzelvorgänge im Rahmen der deutschen Geschichte," in Schramm, *Kaiser, Könige und Päpste. Gesammelte Aufsätze zur Geschichte des Mittelalters*, 4 vols. (Stuttgart, 1968–71), 3:33–58, esp. 48–49; Irmgard Latzke, *Hofamt, Erzamt und Erbamt im mittelalterlichen deutschen Reich*, Ph.D. diss., Frankfurt, 1970, 24ff. with additional references.

75. *Dudonis Sancti Quintini De moribus et actis primorum Normanniae ducum libri tres*, in Migne PL 141 (Paris, 1880), 650f.; the later edition by Jules Lair (Mémoires de la Société des Antiquaires de Normandie 3, Caen 1885) was not available to me. For a more recent account of the anecdote treated here, see Hans Hattenhauer, *Die Aufnahme der Normannen in das westfränkische Reich—Saint Clair-sur-Epte AD 911*, Berichte aus den Sitzungen der Joachim-Jungius-Gesellschaft der Wissenschaften e.V. Hamburg 8, Heft 2 (Göttingen, 1990). He spends a good deal of time (22ff.) trying to demonstrate that the tale recounted here is fictive. This is indeed undisputed, so that we can dispense with Hattenhauer's question marks (36).

76. *Dudonis Sancti Quintini*, 650: "Statim Francorum coactus verbis, manus suas misit inter manus regis, quod nunquam pater eius, et avus, atque proavus cuiquam fecit."

77. Ibid., 650: "Dedit itaque rex filiam suam, Gislam nomine, uxorem illi duci, terramque determinatam in alodo et in fundo, a flumine Eptae usque ad mare, totamque Britanniam de qua posset vivere."

78. Ibid., 650: "Nunquam curvabo genua mea alicuius pedibus, nec osculabor cuiuspiam pedem!"

79. Ibid., 650: "Francorum igitur precibus compulsus, iussit cuidam militi pedem regis osculari."

80. Ibid., 650–51: "Qui statim pedem regis arripiens, deportavit ad os suum, standoque defixit osculum, regemque fecit resupinum. Itaque magnus excitatur risus magnusque in plebe tumultus."

81. The many anecdotes in Dudo's work, which was not written until the early eleventh century, may be based on accounts by Count Rudolf, a member of the Norman ducal house, whom Dudo cites as his source; see Max Manitius, *Geschichte der lateinischen Literatur des Mittelalters 2. Von der Mitte des 10. Jahrhunderts bis zum Ausbruch des Kampfes zwischen Kirche und Staat* (Munich, 1923), 257ff.; as well as the article "Dudo von St.-Quentin," in *Lexikon des Mittelalters*, vol. 3 (Munich and Zurich, 1985), 1438–39. We would be well advised to take such narratives more seriously as building blocks for a concrete history of mentalities; see Gerd Althoff, "Genealogische und andere Fiktionen in mittelalterlicher Historiographie," in *Fälschungen im Mittelalter*, 5 vols., MGH Schriften 33, 1–5 (Hanover, 1988), 1:417–41, and "Gloria et nomen perpetuum. Wodurch wurde man im Mittelalter berühmt?," in *Person und Gemeinschaft im Mittelalter. Karl Schmid zum 65.*

Geburtstag, ed. Gerd Althoff, Dieter Geuenich, Otto Gerhard Oexle, and Joachim Wollasch (Sigmaringen, 1988), 297–313.

82. Let us recall that the process occurred under different circumstances in the different European countries; on this see esp. Heinrich Mitteis, *Der Staat des hohen Mittelalters*, 5th ed. (Weimar, 1955), 154ff.; particularly in the eras of Louis the Pious and Henry IV we may observe instances in which the king's conscious efforts to change or ignore the hierarchy ruffled a good many feathers; on this see Althoff, *Verwandte, Freunde und Getreue*, 158ff. and 178ff.

83. See Hagen Keller, "Grundlagen ottonischer Königsherrschaft," in *Reich und Kirche vor dem Investiturstreit. Gerd Tellenbach zum 80. Geburtstag*, ed. Karl Schmid (Sigmaringen, 1985), 17–34, esp. 25ff., and "Zum Charakter der 'Staatlichkeit' zwischen karolingischer Reichsreform und hochmittelalterlichem Herrschaftsaubau," *Frühmittelalterliche Studien* 23 (1989), 248–64 with numerous additional references.

84. We historians need to take the groundwork already done by anthropologists in this area much more seriously, not by adopting it uncritically, but rather as a broadening of our conceptual horizons; see the excellent overview in Simon Roberts, *Order and Dispute: An Introduction to Legal Anthropology* (Oxford, 1979); see also, more recently, Thomas Schweitzer (ed.), *Netzwerkanalyse. Ethnologische Perspektiven* (Berlin, 1989), which contains contributions on the analysis of social networks that are of methodological interest to medievalists; Werner Schiffauer, *Die Bauern von Subay. Das Leben in einem türkischen Dorf* (Stuttgart, 1987), with a case study which reveals parallels to medieval conditions in a number of its observations; see also Stefan Breuer, *Der archaische Staat. Zur Soziologie charismatischer Herrschaft* (Berlin 1990).

85. This is the aim of the project I directed in Münster, "Träger, Felder, Formen pragmatischer Schriftlichkeit im Mittelalter" (The Protagonists, Fields and Forms of Pragmatic Writing in the Middle Ages). The focus was on the function of historiography in times of crisis, particularly the eleventh century, which saw not least a crisis in the conduct of oral advice and negotiation. See Althoff and Coué, "Pragmatische Geschichtsschreibung und Krisen."

86. After my inaugural lecture, my colleague Klaus Vetter of the Humboldt University in Berlin pointed out the extent to which, until the very recent past, gestures and rituals belonging to the phenomena of homage and favor continued to determine political ceremonial, particularly in the socialist camp.

87. On the caricaturing of this phenomenon, see C. Northcote Parkinson's famous book, *Parkinson's Law* (Boston, 1957). On the multiplicity of modern status symbols and status-oriented behaviors, see Erving Goffman, *Interaction Ritual: Essays in Face to Face Behavior* (Chicago, 1967); George C. Homans, *Social Behavior: Its Elementary Forms* (New York, 1961); and Pierre Bourdieu, *Distinction: A Social Critique of the Judgement of Taste*, trans. Richard Nice (Cambridge, Mass., 1987).

SEVEN

Satisfaction

Peculiarities of the Amicable Settlement of Conflicts in the Middle Ages

Gerd Althoff

The image that modern people had, and still have, of the Middle Ages is highly ambivalent. On the one hand, notions of the Middle Ages as "dark" or "brutish" dominate, evoking the supposedly limited intellectual horizons of medieval people and their predilection for violence. On the other hand, particularly in the past few decades, the Middle Ages have elicited broad interest as the "completely other" era, a "distant mirror" of modern times, and a place in which well-ordered and harmonious circumstances prevailed, out of which one could pick eclectic phenomena such as sacred art or chivalry, the flowering of the Minnesong or architecture, and present a cozy romantic rebirth of the Middle Ages as an alternative to modern alienation.[1]

This essay seeks to approach the basic conditions of medieval life by looking at the use of force, a subject that has been used more often up until now to justify our feelings of distaste for and superiority to the Middle Ages. The intention here is not to establish an opposite position, but rather to correct some widespread (mis)conceptions about the conditions and rules that regulated, and prevailed in, the medieval use of force. One basic fact remains undisputed, however: the Middle Ages were indeed an epoch in which the right to employ armed force was an integral part of aristocratic life, leading to a seemingly endless number of feuds and bloody deeds. The state's monopoly of force is a modern achievement, whose establishment was a long, drawn-out process. Aspects of the conflicts surrounding this process persisted into the twentieth century, as both older and more recent research on the duel demonstrates.[2]

The view of the Middle Ages as a sword-clanking and feud-happy era is by no means restricted to popular publications. Scholarly research also remains dominated by studies of armed conflict, for example in the vast literature on medieval feuds. When historians describe the medieval state, they often do so from the perspective of its deficits, including the absence of a monopoly of force.

Otto Brunner's study *Land and Lordship*, which portrays the peculiarities of medieval political organization not least by means of a description of feuding, has had a fateful and long-lasting effect here. In fact, we cannot understand the basic conditions of medieval life and the ways in which political rule functioned without a description of the consequences and manifestations of the right to use force. Legal and other historians, with the intensive participation of literary historians, already undertook such descriptions before Brunner, and continued to do so after his work was published.[3]

The picture that they sketch is, nevertheless, not a balanced one. Historians have concentrated on the causes of armed conflicts, on legitimate and illegitimate reasons for feuding, and on the means of and rules for carrying out feuds. Much attention has also been paid to attempts to check feuds before they occurred, such as can be seen in particular in the *pax dei* and *pax communis* movements. In contrast, scholars have paid less attention to, and indeed virtually ignored, the forms of amicable conflict resolution that were practiced throughout the Middle Ages, which may be observed before—and, more important, after—armed conflicts, and which also had fixed rules and a fixed group of persons who felt responsible for them. In this way historians have overlooked the fact that the medieval conduct of conflicts consisted in large part of demonstrative, ritualized acts. Only in rare instances did medieval feuds aim to destroy the opponent. Rather, those involved were familiar with and practiced a diverse range of threatening and yielding behavior that ended the feud in an amicable manner before it could escalate into something worse—in other words, before an armed conflict began in the first place. A highly developed tactic of amicable conflict resolution, with established forms and responsibilities, marks the other side of the sword-clanking Middle Ages, one that we need to take account if we do not wish to miss the reality of the Middle Ages.[4]

Only very recently have increasing numbers of scholars begun to point to this field of research and its relevance for assessments of the Middle Ages. One version of this amicable settlement of disputes can already be found in the wergild catalogues of the early medieval *leges*.[5] Wergild, which the relatives of the wrongdoer paid to the injured party, was a penance or conciliatory payment whose acceptance settled the conflict for good. In modern terms one would call it a kind of compensatory damages. Like other payments intended to make up for the violation of rules, the payment of wergild for the amicable resolution of conflicts within the upper class was supplemented, or rather replaced, in the course of the early Middle Ages by another form of compensation, namely, satisfaction. It consisted of one or more demonstrative acts which informed the other party to the conflict and the public that one was prepared to yield and bring the conflict to an end. Naturally, the lines between atonement, penance, and satisfaction cannot be sharply drawn and we need to keep in mind the omnipresence of the theological side of penance and satisfaction in the Middle Ages. In satisfaction, however, the idea of intangible compensatory damages was doubtless in the foreground. This demonstrative act was frequently accompanied by further compensation, such as the payment of a penalty or the loss of fiefs. The party prepared to offer satisfaction could also be sentenced to banishment or imprisonment. The demonstrative act of satisfaction, however, formed the centerpiece of atonement, and regularly occurred before a large audience. A wide range of acts was available, depending upon circumstances; these ranged from gestures of peace to sophisticated acts of submission.[6] Which form was used depended on the social position of the parties to the dispute, their relationship to each other, the extent of hostilities and the losses they had inflicted on each other and, not least, on who was responsible for causing the dispute in the first place. The parties to the conflict did not, however, themselves decide which form of satisfaction would be applied. Instead they used the services of mediators. Interestingly, until very recently no modern scholarly encyclopedia of the Middle Ages devoted an article to these people.[7] The significance and indeed the activities of mediators have been largely ignored by scholarship in several disciplines. This has led to substantial misunderstandings regarding the course of medieval conflicts and thus to erroneous assessments of important processes in medieval orders of life.

We should keep in mind that any medieval conflict immediately involved such mediators, whose function was to bring about an amicable resolution to the dispute. The appropriate candidates for these positions were persons of high rank, above all the king himself, along with bishops, dukes, and influential counts who had well-established relationships to both parties to the conflict.[8] It is still unclear to what extent the king's own activities consisted in such mediation between parties—in other words, whether the king's authority was based largely on his function as supreme mediator. The Ottonian coronation *ordines*, at any rate, already refer to the king as a mediator between the clergy and the people (*mediator cleri ac populi*), which gives some indication of the high status accorded to this task.[9]

Mediators met with the parties separately, negotiated an appropriate satisfaction with them, and guaranteed that the method suggested for ending the conflict would actually be adopted. It was chiefly their responsibility to see that the conflicts did not escalate unduly, for their suggestions for mediation were backed up by substantial authority, even if they were not themselves officeholders or representatives of a state institution. Their activities provide evidence of the binding quality of the rules of archaic societies: a transgression against custom could, in some cases, be far more dangerous than a violation of imposed norms.

And the commonly practiced customs included the use of mediators and obedience to their suggestions. Since these mediators were active from the beginning of the dispute, they also helped to prevent conflicts from escalating.

This function is clearly referred to in a letter written in the late eleventh century by an Augsburg bishop to his brother bishop in Halberstadt. The letter was occasioned by the bishop's presence in the army of King Henry IV, who had taken up arms against the rebellious Saxons, among them the bishop of Halberstadt. He was not in the king's army in order to persecute the Saxons *hostiliter*, he told his episcopal confrater, but rather to win back their favor for the king *amicabiliter*, in emulation of the deeds of the mediator Jesus Christ. Christ, too, had after all seen himself as a mediator between God and man *(mediator Dei et hominem)*. The bishop of Augsburg then asked his Halberstadt colleague to turn over his *causa* to himself, three further bishops and a duke, and greeted him in brotherly love (*in fraterna dilectio*) and in the hope of reconciliation (*spes reconciliationes*).[10]

This case may claim model character, since we also have evidence from other sources of a party to a conflict choosing mediators from among his opponent's entourage.[11] The armed contingents who faced each other in feuds thus also represented potential mediators. The foremost duty of these mediators was to negotiate an appropriate satisfaction. A firm agreement was made and the mediators swore an oath to enforce what the parties had agreed upon. Satisfaction was then given before an audience, who thereby became witnesses to the resolution of the conflict, significantly enhancing the binding quality of the acts.

It appears that in the course of the early Middle Ages a public act of subjugation developed as the most common form of satisfaction, one that was used particularly, but not only, when one of the parties to the conflict was a king. Such an act of subjugation followed fixed rules, which however left some scope for a more or less humiliating procedure. The *honor regius* required that the person subordinating himself be barefoot.[12] He also arrived in penitential garb, a hair shirt or even practically naked, threw himself down at the king's feet and, speaking in humble tones, left everything up to the king's will—satisfaction indeed. In principle, the party who thus distinguished himself as master of the situation and over the fate of the person subordinating himself had various possible reactions at his disposal. He could grant his forgiveness, dispense with any punishment, and return the person in question to office; impose a punishment such as imprisonment or exile; or remain unrelenting, refusing to accept the satisfaction offered, in which case the procedure would be repeated a second and third time. What is decisive for an understanding of such processes, however, is that the behavior in any given case was agreed upon beforehand, all actions were predetermined and guaranteed by the mediators. In other words the acts of subjugation were choreographies in which the actors played set roles. Numerous cases provide evidence of this.[13] One such case, which will be presented in detail here, reports extensively on the forms in which the conflict was carried out and the activities of the mediator. In this case, however, several unforeseen incidents occurred, repeatedly calling into question the intended procedure.

In 1202 a feud broke out in Lower Lorraine between the duke of Louvain and the count of Geldern.[14] The actual cause is not mentioned in the sources. The duke led a large army into the count's territory, to "humiliate him by force of arms." The count, realizing that the situation was hopeless, "came to the duke's camp and sent him a message via friends asking him to make peace." This was nothing other than the deputation of mediators who were supposed to negotiate the conditions of the peace treaty and with it an appropriate satisfaction. The mediators were thus negotiating an end to hostilities before the armed conflict had even begun. The threat of a large army had had the desired effect. Then, however, the conflict escalated anyway, because one of the aides of the count of Geldern, the count of Holland, attacked one of the duke's cities, burning it to the ground, and took the inhabitants away as prisoners. Full of wrath, the duke attacked the count of Holland, defeated his troops and took him prisoner before turning anew to the count of Geldern. Once again the count avoided the apparently hopeless military conflict and asked King Otto IV, Archbishop Adolf of Cologne, and other princes to mediate for him. They agreed to act as mediators, negotiated with the duke, and he "finally relented on the condition that they bring the count personally to Louvain on a certain day to give satisfaction and offer themselves as hostages in guarantee ['seseque pro eo obsides ac fideiussores exponerent']. After receiving their oaths of agreement he ordered a cease-fire, dismissed his army and returned to his country." He thus relied wholly on the agreement and in fact "a few days later Count Otto set off for Louvain, accompanied by King Otto, Archbishop Adolf, and Count Adolf, surrendered himself to the duke and relieved the hostages and guarantors." Thereafter counsel was taken for several days, but the sources do not mention what was discussed. It seems highly likely, however, that the topic was the form satisfaction should take. Two of the mediators, the archbishop of Cologne and Count Adolf, became wary because the negotiations were taking so long and, suspecting that the duke had set a trap, fled secretly. This angered the duke, to be sure, but that did not prevent him shortly thereafter from entering an alliance with the count of Geldern, which was sealed with a payment of six thousand marks and the marriage of the count's son to the duke's daughter.

Thus this feud between the count of Geldern and the duke of Louvain never erupted into armed conflict because the count always declared his willingness to offer satisfaction just in time, and transferred negotiations regarding the procedure to mediators—a sign of surrender that satisfied the duke each time and indeed appeared so trustworthy that he dismissed his army. The behavior that we can observe here in an individual case may be considered typical; feuds were conducted not in a blind rage, but often in a virtually ritualized manner. The corresponding threatening gestures were followed by signs of yielding; the calling in of mediators effected a cessation of military actions, and an amicable resolution to the conflict was set in motion. This, in turn, was accomplished by means of the agreed act of satisfaction.

One part of the rules for setting the parameters of satisfaction was that it not be too exacting. Instead, the victor was to exercise generosity, to make satisfaction a quasisymbolic act which did not offend his opponent's honor too greatly. It was doubtless easier to end disputes that had already led to armed conflict or even injury and death by this means than if the vanquished party had been made to feel the full severity of the victor.

A fine example of such mildness (*mansuetudo*) in exacting satisfaction was displayed by Archbishop Norbert of Magdeburg, according to his vita. For various reasons he had become involved in fierce conflicts with the inhabitants of Magdeburg, where he was besieged and attacked in one of the city's towers, only barely escaping with his life. These incidents had moved unnamed secular princes (*principes terrae*) to ask the archbishop to leave the city. After his departure some of his loyal followers acted as intermediaries and succeeded in bringing matters to a peaceful conclusion: "His adversaries agreed to a kind of satisfaction [*omnimoda satisfactione*] and humbled themselves before him. Norbert greeted them with gentleness and asked of them but one thing, that they bring themselves to make peace with his vassals. They joyfully agreed, repaired the vassal's destroyed house and paid him forty marks in silver for his wounds."[15] In light of numerous parallel cases, it seems certain that this solution was negotiated and guaranteed by the intermediaries. The Magdeburgers could thus offer any satisfaction they wished, in the secure knowledge that the archbishop would demand no more than that cited above. In this way everyone involved could save face.

Those not infrequent cases in which men sought to force a marriage by abducting the bride were also ultimately about preserving honor. Thietmar of Merseburg describes such a case in detail, because it occurred among his own kin.[16] When the father of the bride, Margrave Ekkehard of Meissen, decided for unknown reasons not to respect the formal betrothal of his daughter to Margrave Werner, the bridegroom abducted the girl from Quedlinburg, where she was being educated under the supervision of Abbess Mathilde. Mathilde then made an urgent plea to the Saxon princes to bring the girl back, if necessary by force. Since the abductor had barricaded himself in his castle intermediaries went into action. They learned from the bride that she preferred to remain where she was rather than return to Quedlinburg, and then negotiated an amicable settlement with the abbess. Margrave Werner then came to Magdeburg with his aides and, barefoot, returned the abducted girl. On the recommendation of the princes he was then forgiven. The kidnapped bride at first remained in the care of the abbess of Quedlinburg, and was later married to her abductor. Thus instead of a feud the mediators arranged for an amicable agreement, which, on the basis of public satisfaction, allowed all of the participants to save face. By appearing barefoot, the abductor staged his return of the girl as an act of subjugation, which apparently fulfilled the requirements of the demanded satisfaction.

"Giving satisfaction" and "saving face" also represent the central vantage points from which we should understand Frederick Barbarossa's reconciliation with the inhabitants of Alessandria, that bastion of the Lombard League in the struggle against the Staufers. The pact made in Nuremberg in 1183 stipulated that the inhabitants should submit themselves to the authority of the emperor in the following manner: all inhabitants were to leave the city and remain outside its walls until an emissary from the emperor led them back and returned the city to them, newly founded and renamed Caesarea.[17] In formal terms, this wholly satisfied the requirements of the imperial claim to right and rule. The emperor was the founder of the city, as the new name demonstratively expressed. But this satisfaction also allowed the inhabitants of Alessandria to avoid public shame; one might even ask whether they did not emerge as the political victors.

The disputes between Archbishop Anno and the citizens of Cologne proceeded less peacefully. This was the case, however, because Archbishop Anno did not play by the rules, which expected him to respect the laws of dedication and satisfaction (*ius dedicationis* and *satisfactionis*). The people of Cologne had begun by driving Anno from the city, but then, when he marched on the city with an army, he sent out messengers offering peace. Anno then invited his opponents by episcopal proclamation to give satisfaction: "They all approached forthwith wearing woolen garments over their naked flesh, after attaining with great difficulty the assurance of the men surrounding the archbishop that they could do so without fear."[18] This was, however, not the end of the matter for Anno, who then demanded that the citizens appear again the following day to do penance. Six hundred of the wealthiest merchants thereupon fled to the king to ask him to mediate on their behalf against the archbishop's "raging," as they referred to his behavior. The others kept the archbishop waiting for three days and did not follow the order to "make suggestions for an appropriate satisfaction." We would doubtless not be wrong in assuming that the people of Cologne believed that their submissive procession had already provided adequate satisfaction, since they had, after all, thereby fulfilled the normal requirements of *satisfactio*. For the archbishop's vassals this disregard of their lord was the signal to fall upon the citizens' houses, pillaging and murdering and—as Lampert remarks in Anno's defense—"without the bishop's knowledge, [performing] the work of righteous vengeance with much more abandon . . . than is compatible with the reputation of such an exalted prince of the Church." Plainly, opinions on the appropriate satisfaction diverged widely in this conflict. Vengeance appears here as an active form of taking satisfaction. If one compares Anno's conduct with that of others who claimed satisfaction, his demand for multiple satisfaction appears unusual, not to mention excessive.[19]

King Lothar of Supplinburg, in contrast, behaved according to generally accepted maxims in his dispute with Archbishop Albero of Trier in the year 1131. Albero had received consecration as bishop without requesting investiture from the king. For that reason the king initially withheld investiture and the regalia of office. Since Lothar knew, however, as the archbishop's vita tells us, "that Albero was a man easily capable of inciting his entire kingdom against him," he had declared himself satisfied with a light satisfaction (*leva satisfactio*). On the advice of other princes, the archbishop offered the king an oath as satisfaction, in which he argued that he had done what he had not in order to injure the king's honor, but rather at the pope's insistence. This offer was already sufficient satisfaction for Lothar; he released the bishop from the oath and gave him investiture. Both sides had saved face, which was a significant aspect in the resolution of such conflicts! Interestingly enough, this agreement prevented Albero neither from excommunicating the king's stepbrother, Duke Simon of Upper Lorraine, as an oppressor of the Trier church, at the same court diet, nor from publicly forcing him to leave the festival service—at least according to the rather proud account in the *Vita Alberonis*.[20]

As the cases discussed here doubtless illustrate, there was a very definite connection between an individual's rank and weight and the satisfaction that could be demanded of him. Conversely, it is obvious that in the Middle Ages, as in the modern period, a certain rank was required in order to be capable of giving satisfaction at all.[21] Satisfaction was not only given by persons of lower to persons of higher rank, or between persons of equal status, however. It is a particular characteristic of *satisfactio* that noblemen, including the king, could find themselves compelled, in conflict situations, to give satisfaction to their vassals or other inferiors. Naturally, such satisfaction took other forms than that of subjugation. Nevertheless, these forms are no less characteristic, and persons of higher rank appear to have used them in quite comparable situations to persons of lower rank, namely, when they were in danger of defeat. I will examine a few examples below.

In 1063, Abbot Widerat of Fulda found himself in difficulties when he became involved in the so-called Goslar seating dispute with the bishop of Hildesheim, a conflict that ended in injury and death. It is said that he had to pay enormous sums in order to regain the favor of the king, the court, and his opponent. To this end he sold the lands attached to the Fulda monastery, which greatly angered the monks, already dissatisfied with their abbot's conduct of office. The following occurrence, however, represented the last straw: the monastery had been presented with a valuable horse for the salvation of the soul of the Fulda standard-bearer Reginbodo, who had been killed during the conflict in Goslar. The abbot, however, had immediately passed the horse on to a layman. Boiling over with rage, the monks had demanded that the gift be returned, saying that they had withstood the abbot's tyranny long enough and would seek help against his violent deeds. Matters escalated to such an extent that it became clear to the abbot that only an act of satisfaction could alleviate the conflict. He changed his tactic, pleading and weeping and asking his monks to give him just a little time, promising that "if he could ever breathe freely again after such suffering he would not merely replace, but double that which had been taken from them."[22] The older and more mature monks (*aetate et sensu matutiores*) immediately understood these gestures and words as satisfaction and were prepared to end the conflict. The younger men, however, as is their custom (*more suo*, that is, unreasonably), refused to be satisfied, took the conflict to the royal court and failed utterly, arousing not the slightest sympathy for their undertaking. The older monks of Fulda were doubtless correct in their assessment. They considered the abbot's tearful speech to be satisfaction enough and were prepared to set aside the conflict. It was apparently one of the rules of the game not to cast doubt on what was said in the course of satisfaction.

Lampert of Hersfeld reports on a comparable case in the context of a conflict between King Henry IV and Duke Berthold of Carinthia, the Zähringer. Henry had taken the latter's duchy and given it to a certain Markward. When the king, however, "cleared himself with the most sacred declarations" and claimed that Markward had done all this without his knowledge, Berthold accepted it as *satisfactio*, although he knew Henry's account to be factually incorrect.[23] Only in this way could both have saved face and settled the conflict. Despite all of Henry IV's efforts, however, he failed at the end of his reign and lifetime, when his son Henry V, the papal legate, and also the participating nobles refused to adopt Henry IV's repeated offers of appropriate *satisfactio*. It is nevertheless remarkable how stubbornly Henry tried in the last letters he wrote to rescue his rule by means of *satisfactio*. As his last offer, in a manner of speaking, he even declared himself prepared to go to Rome and "either clear himself of the charges or humbly give satisfaction" before the pope and the Roman clergy.[24] This vividly illustrates the proposition that any conflict could be resolved by a suitable satisfaction.

If we look at the forms of conflict resolution in the Middle Ages, we notice a phenomenon that is of more general significance for assessing forms of interaction and communication in this period. Conflicts were ended by means of demonstrative acts, whose function was to give satisfaction to one's adversary and thus eliminate the conflict. Such acts were staged in front of an audience in order to increase the binding nature of what had been done or promised. The ritual of giving satisfaction certainly also owed its higher degree of binding force to the peculiar circumstance that it could not be repeated between the same persons.

The public staging of the ritual required more actors than just the direct participants, however. Such resolutions of conflicts would have been inconceivable without preparatory negotiations, and for this reason the highest importance was accorded to the persons who organized these negotiations. These confidential transactions were the province of one or more mediators who always went into action when a conflict broke out. All men of high rank were potential mediators, and it improved their chances of efficacy if they had a relationship to each of the parties in the conflict. In any case they needed to be neutral and independent, and they drew their great authority from their temporary function. Their actions, which consisted of often long and drawn-out negotiations with both sides, aimed to arrive at a mutually agreed effort that would eliminate the cause of the conflict. Whether one calls this effort penance, atonement, compensatory damages, or satisfaction, what appears to be characteristic—at least in conflicts between members of the elites—is that the corresponding exercise consisted particularly of an act performed in public, which gave the opposing side satisfaction in the specific meaning of the word. There were fixed rules governing this act, and these were generally known. These rules governed the clothing, conduct, and even the smallest details of such a scene. The rules might be varied according to the situation and the rank of the participants, but certainly not at will. One ground rule was apparently maintained with particular strictness: satisfaction could be given only once. A participant who continued or resumed hostilities after satisfaction had been given could no longer rely on the hope of reconciliation, and was severely punished.[25] Another obstacle to understanding the phenomenon should at least be mentioned here: how could giving satisfaction be reconciled with saving face? Doubtless, nobody underwent a ritual of subjugation or any other act of satisfaction gladly. Nevertheless, it must be emphasized that the affected person suffered no recognizable disadvantages after performing the act.

The system of conflict resolution, which was based on mediators and the performance of satisfaction, was characterized not least by its ability to dispense almost totally with the law courts. Beginning in the eleventh century, however, one may observe an increasing trend for kings to have those disputes in which they were themselves involved, in particular, regulated by the decision of royal courts. This procedure clearly aimed to replace mediators with the assessors (*Urteiler*) of the royal court. The change does not appear to have gained wide acceptance in either the eleventh or the twelfth century, as a long series of sentences for contumacy against members of the high nobility demonstrates.[26] They had all refused to appear before such a court at all and in fact there is a glaring difference between this method and that of conflict resolution by mediation: mediators were chosen by the parties themselves, while the assessors of the royal court were appointed by the king, even when he himself was one of the opposing parties. It would doubtless be anachronistic, and a serious misunderstanding, to conceive of such assessors as very independent of the expectations of the court's overlord.

The displacement of conflict resolution away from the parties to the conflict themselves to the royal and other courts in the choice of mediators thus marks an important step on the way to the formation of state structures. This change occurred extremely slowly, as is demonstrated not least by the development of a system of arbitral jurisdiction in the late Middle Ages.[27] It was from here that the idea of amicable conflict resolution, or arbitration, entered the modern judicial system. In addition, arbitrators continue to play an important role even today in the resolution of disputes between states. Especially in the more embattled fields such as modern environmental law, the calls for a well-directed use of mediators to solve conflicts outside the courts are becoming ever louder these days, since court decisions in these sensitive areas no longer meet with enough acceptance among broad segments of the population.[28] Interestingly enough, this has engendered a problem that existed in a quite similar way in the Middle Ages: the problem of finding mediators whom the conflict parties trust and also respect enough to accept their decisions.

While the mediator as an extrajudicial instance for the amicable resolution of conflicts has retained his functions in various fields with an astounding degree of continuity, the same cannot be said of the act of satisfaction. To be sure, it would be difficult to find evidence of public rituals of subjugation in penitential garb and bare feet in the modern period. Yet remnants survive even today in the form of public and private apologies, which are, after all, nothing but acts of satisfaction intended to end or avoid conflicts. A closer examination of modern forms of conflict resolution would surely diagnose other behaviors, both verbal and nonverbal, as satisfaction, thus demonstrating the *longue durée* of such behaviors in cases of conflict.

Notes

This chapter is expanded from Gerd Althoff, "Genugtuung (satisfactio): Zur Eigenart gütlicher Konflikbeilegung im Mittelalter," in *Modernes Mittelalter. Neue Bilder einer populären Epoche*, ed. Joachim Heinzle (Frankfurt am Main and Leipzig, 1994), 247–65.

1. See, in particular, the works of Otto Gerhard Oexle, "Das Bild der Moderne vom Mittelalter und die moderne Mittelalterforschung," *Frühmittelalterliche Studien* 24 (1990), 1–22; "Das entzweite Mittelalter," in Gerd Althoff (ed.), *Die Deutschen und ihr Mittelalter* (Darmstadt, 1992), 7–28; "Das Mittelalter und das Unbehagen an der Moderne. Mittelalterbeschwörungen in der Weimarer Republik und danach," in *Spannungen und Widersprüche. Gedenkschrift für Frantisek Graus*, ed. Susanna Burghartz, Hans-Jörg Gilomen, Guy P. Marchal, Rainer C. Schwinges, and Katharina Simon-Muscheid (Sigmaringen, 1992), 125–53.

2. Ute Frevert, *Ehrenmänner. Das Duell in der bürgerlichen Gesellschaft* (Munich, 1991).

3. Otto Brunner, *Land und Herrschaft. Grundfragen der territorialen Verfassungsgeschichte Österreichs im Mittelalter*, 5th ed. (Vienna, 1965), Engl.: Land *and Lordship: Structures of Governance in Medieval Austria*, trans. Howard Kaminsky and James V. Melton (Philadelphia, 1992); Gerhard Dilcher, "Mittelalterliche Rechtsgewohnheiten als methodisch-theoretisches Problem," in G. Dilcher (ed.), *Gewohnheitsrecht und Rechtsgewohnheiten im Mittelalter*, Schriften zur Europäischen Rechts- und Verfassungsgeschichte 6 (Berlin, 1992).

4. Of the rich literature on this subject see Simon Roberts, *Order and Dispute: An Introduction to Legal Anthropology* (Oxford, 1979); Patrick Geary, "Vivre en conflit dans une France sans état: Typologie de mécanisme de règlement de conflit (1050–1200)," *Annales É.S.C.* 41 (1986), 1107–126; Geoffrey Koziol, *Begging Pardon and Favor: Ritual and Political Order in Early Medieval France* (Ithaca, N.Y., 1992); Stephan White, "Pactum . . . legem vincit et amor iudicium: The Settlement of Disputes by Compromise in Eleventh-Century Western France," *American Journal of Legal History* 22 (1978), 281–301. See, most recently, Gerd Althoff, *Spielregeln der Politik im Mittelalter. Kommunikation in Frieden und Fehde* (Darmstadt, 1997), "Einleitung," 1–17, with a review of the literature.

5. For a general account see Ruth Schmidt-Wiegand, *Stammesrecht und Volkssprache. Ausgewählte Aufsätze zu den Leges barbarorum*, ed. Dagmar Hüpper and Clausdieter Schott, Acta humaniora (Weinheim, 1991); Clausdieter Schott, "Leges," in *Lexikon des Mittelalters* 5 (Munich, 1990), 1802–3.

6. On this see Gerd Althoff, "Das Privileg der deditio. Formen gütlicher Konfliktbeendigung," in *Spielregeln der Politik im Mittelalter*, 99–125, and in *Nobilitas. Funktion und Repräsentation des Adels in Alteuropa. Festschrift für Karl Ferdinand Werner zum 70. Geburtstag*, ed. Otto Gerhard Oexle and Werner Paravicini, Veröffentlichungen des Max-Planck-Instituts für Geschichte, 133 (Göttingen, 1997), 27–52.

7. This lacuna has been filled by the present author's article "Vermittler," in *Lexikon des Mittelalters* 8 (Munich, 1997), 1555–57.

8. See Hermann Kamp, "Vermittler in Konflikten des hohen Mittelalters," in *La Giustizia nell' Alto Medioevo II (secoli IX–XI)*, Settimane di studio del Centro Italiano di studi nell' Alto Medioevo, 44 (Spoleto, 1997), 675–710.

9. Rudolf Schieffer, "Mediator cleri et plebis. Zum geistlichen Einfluß auf Ver-

ständnis und Darstellung des ottonischen Königtums," in *Herrschaftsrepräsentation im ottonischen Sachsen*, ed. Gerd Althoff and Ernst Schubert, Vorträge und Forschungen 46 (Sigmaringen, 1998), 345–61.

10. Bishop Embricho of Augsburg to Bishop Burchard of Halberstadt, in *Briefsammlungen zur Zeit Heinrichs IV.*, ed. Carl Erdmann and Norbert Fickermann, MGH Briefe der deutschen Kaiserzeit V (Weimar, 1950), no. 54, 100–1.

11. See the examples in Gerd Althoff's "Konfliktverhalten und Rechtsbewußtsein. Die Welfen im 12. Jahrhundert," in *Spielregeln der Politik im Mittelalter*, 57–84; "Staatsdiener oder Häupter des Staates," in ibid., 126–53; and "Heinrich der Löwe in Konflikten. Zur Technik der Friedensvermittlung im 12. Jahrhundert," in *Heinrich der Löwe und seine Zeit. Herrschaft und Repräsentation der Welfen 1125–1235*, vol. 2, *Essays*, ed. Jochen Luckhardt and Franz Niehoff (Munich, 1995), 123–28.

12. *Annales Altahenses maiores*, ed. Edmund L. B. Oeffle, MGH SSrG (Hanover, 1891), a. 1041, 27.

13. On this see Gerd Althoff's essays "Königsherrschaft und Konfliktbewältigung im 10. und 11. Jahrhundert," "Konfliktverhalten und Rechtsbewußtsein. Die Welfen im 12. Jahrhundert," "Demonstration und Inszenierung. Spielregeln der Kommunikation in der mittelalterlichen Öffentlichkeit," all in his *Spielregeln der Politik im Mittelalter*; and "(Royal) Favor: A Central Concept in Early Medieval Hierarchical Relations" in the present volume. See also Timothy Reuter, "Unruhestiftung, Fehde, Rebellion, Widerstand: Gewalt und Frieden in der Politik der Salierzeit," in Stefan Weinfurter (ed.), *Die Salier und das Reich*, vol. 3 (Sigmaringen, 1990), 297–325.

14. See *Chronica regia Coloniensis*, ed. Georg Waitz, MGH SSrG (Hanover, 1880), a. 1202, 171–72. "Eodem anno circa festum sancti Egidii Heinricus dux Lovanie multifaria comitis de Gelre permotus impudentia, iam diutius eius insolentias pati ratus sibi fore pudori, copiosum educens exercitum, terram eius invadere ipsumque utpote totius beneficii ac benignitatis ingratum sub armis humiliare disposuit. Cuius manum potentem et brachium extentum iam dictus comes ferre non prevalens, adhuc illo longe agente, per se ipsum adventum eius prevenire satagens, ad castra ducis devenit, per amicos legationem misit, rogans ea que pacis sunt. Interea comes Hollandie, in auxilium predicti comitis evocatus, civitatem novam nomine Bushc, quam ipse dux summo labore ac studio maximisque sumptibus exstruxerat, penitus igne consumpsit, viros ac mulieres vinctos abduxit, armenta boum et equorum greges, ovium aliarumque diversarum rerum innumeram multitudinem asportavit. Itaque de pace inter agendum, cum iam ab omnibus pacis et concordie speraretur effectus, ecce subito rumor et clamor, miserabilis dolor et gemitus intolerabilis cuncta ducis castra replevit, ipseque dux ultra quam credi potest animo consternatus ac nimia exacerbatione excitus, predictum comitem de Gelre huius mali conscium eiusque consilio factum suspicatur; unde pax, que iam obsidibus et fidei sacramento confirmanda sperabatur, interrumpitur. Adunato igitur exercitu, dux e vestigio comitem cum preda secure procedentum insequitur, marteque constanti magnanimitate commisso, exercitus comitis partim occiditur, partim in fugam vertitur, preda tam hominum quam iumentorum excutitur, ipse cum aliis quam pluribus captivis abducitur. Hac felici victoria dux animatus, Novimaium devenit, Oie castrum satis munitum expugnavit, comitem de Clieve, licet puerum, amicitie sue copulavit, omnibusque pro libitu et utilitate ibidem dispositis, in festo sancte crucis Xantum preteriens, in ira magna et multitudine gravi terram comitis intravit; postera die ex iudicio et sententia super ea examinaturus. Comes vero cernens se totius honoris ac dignitatis inevitabili circumvalla-

tum dispendio, hominesque suos tam vite quam rerum supremo periclitari discrimine, licet invitus, sera tamen penitudine ductus, Ottonem regem, Adolfum archiepiscopum aliosque principes pro pace sollicitare opere pretium duxit. Dux itaque tantorum legatorum continua interpellatione pulsatus tandemque devictus, annuit, hac tamen conventione, ut ipsum comitem die designato sibi satisfacturum Lovanie exhiberent seseque pro eo obsides ac fideiussores exponerent."

15. *Vita Norberti archiepiscopi Magdeburgensis*, ed. Roger Wilmans, in MGH SS 12 (Hanover, 1856), 670–706, cap. 20, p. 700. "Adversarii namque convenientes omnimoda satisfactione coram ipso humiliati sunt, quos ipse in mansuetudine suscipiens, hoc solum ab eis exigit, ut vulneratum militem suum placare non erubescerent. Quod illi libentissime accepantes, dirutam domum militis restauraverunt, eique pro inflicto vulnere quadraginta marcas argenti contulerunt."

16. *Die Chronik des Bischofs Thietmar von Merseburg und ihre Korveier Überarbeitung*, ed. Robert Holtzmann, MGH SSrG, 2nd ed. (Berlin, 1955), IV, 40–42, 176–80.

17. *Reconciliatio Alexandriae*, ed. Ludwig Weiland, in *Constitutiones et acta publica imperatorum et regum* 1, MGH Legum Sectio 4, 1 (Hanover, 1893), 407. Cf. Knut Görich, "Der Herrscher als parteiischer Richter. Barbarossa in der Lombardei," *Frühmittelalterliche Studien* 29 (1995), 273–88.

18. Lampert of Hersfeld, *Annalen*, ed. Oswald Holder-Egger, MGH SSrG (Hanover and Leipzig, 1894), a. 1074, 191. "Protinus omnes nudis pedibus, laneis ad carnem induti processerunt, vix et aegre impetrata pace multitudinis, quae circa episcopum erat, ut hoc tuto facere sinerentur."

19. Barbarossa, however, behaved similarly in the case of Milan (see Gerd Althoff, "Das Privileg der deditio," 104ff.), as did the Welfs at the end of the Tübingen feud (see Gerd Althoff, "Konfliktverhalten und Rechtsbewußtsein," 71).

20. *Gesta Alberonis archiepiscopi auctore Balderico*, ed. Georg Waitz, in MGH SS 8 (Hanover, 1848), 243–60, cap. 13, 250–51. "Preterendum non est, quod cum dominus Albero archiepiscopus venisset Aquisgrani ad curiam imperatoris, Lotharius rex noluit eum investire regalibus, eo quod ante recepisset consecrationem episcopalem, quam suam requisivisset investituram; et omnio, ut credebatrur rex se ie opposuisset, nisi quod ipsum talem virum esse sciebat, qui facile totum orbem sui imperii contra ipsum commoveret; unde et levem satisfactionem ab ipso recepit. Cum enim ex comuni consilio principum iuramentum regi obtulisset, quod non ad diminutionem sui honoris hoc factum esset, sed a domino papa coactus ad consecrationem accessisset, dominus rex iuramentum ei remisit, et regalia sceptro regni ei concessit. In eadem quoque curia Lotharinigae ducem Symonem, fratrem regis, excommunicatum pronunciavit, et in die sancto paschae, dum legeretur euangelium, eum exire aecclesiam compulit."

21. For the modern period see Norbert Elias, "Die satisfaktionsfähige Gesellschaft," in N. Elias, *Studien über die Deutschen. Machtkämpfe und Habitusentwicklung im 19. und 20. Jahrhundert*, ed. Michael Schröter (Frankfurt am Main, 1989), 61–158.

22. See Lampert of Hersfeld, *Annalen*, a. 1063, 85. "si ab tantis malis vita comite unquam respirasset, non modo adempta redditurum, sed duplicatis quoque muneribus cumulaturum."

23. Lampert of Hersfeld, *Annalen*, a. 1073, 153. "Casu quoque nuper advenerat, nescio quid privatae causae acturus in palacio, Bertoldus dux quondam Carentinorum. Huic rex quam sanctis obtestacionibus se purgabat, quod ducatum eius nulli alii tradidisset, sed Marcwardum privata presumptione fines alienos invasisse, nec ei quicquam de iure suo

propterea imminutum esse, si suo iniussu, sine consulto principum honores publicos homo ineptissimus temerasset. Ille licet haec ficta esse sciret et regis maliciam non tam voluntate quam fortunae violentia correctam esse, tamen suscepit satisfactionem, promisitque operam suam rei publicae utilitatibus nusquam defuturam."

24. *Die Briefe Heinrichs IV*, MGH Deutsches Mittelalter 1, ed. Carl Erdmann (Leipzig, 1937), no. 37, 50. "ubi presente Romano clero et populo, remoto odio et invidia et ceteris, que iusticie sunt contraria, liceret de obiectis vel digne purgare vel humiliter satisfacere." On this, see Stefan Weinfurter, *Die Salier. Grundlinien einer Umbruchzeit* (Sigmaringen, 1991).

25. See the references in the introduction to Gerd Althoff, *Spielregeln der Politik im Mittelalter*.

26. See Heinrich Mitteis, *Politische Prozesse des früheren Mittelalters in Deutschland und Frankreich*, Sitzungsberichte der Heidelberger Akademie der Wissenschaften, Phil.-Hist. Klasse, 17 (Heidelberg, 1927).

27. See Uta Rödel, *Königliche Gerichtsbarkeit und Streitfälle der Fürsten und Grafen im Südwesten des Reiches, 1250–1313* (Cologne and Vienna, 1979).

28. See Wolfgang Hoffmann-Riem, *Konfliktmittler in Verwaltungshandlungen*, Forum Rechtswissenschaft, 22 (Heidelberg, 1989).

EIGHT

Peace Through Conspiracy

Otto Gerhard Oexle

Peace by Monarchical Authority—Peace by Association—Peace by Conspiracy

Legal historians of the Middle Ages generally distinguish between two basic forms of peace: *pax ordinata*, or "commanded" peace ordered from above, and "sworn peace" or *pax iurata*, which is based on a consensus, association, or oath. As a result it was always clear that "during the whole Middle Ages one always had to reckon with both factors"—"the idea of peace conceived in monarchical (sovereign) terms and the notion that preserving peace is a matter for the interested parties, who were left to achieve peace by means of association."[1] Nevertheless, for many years historians and legal historians continued to concentrate their interest and perceptions largely on the manifestations of commanded peace.[2] In doing so, they were influenced by the historical pattern of interpretation according to which familial, dynastic, and clan peace had to be overcome by the monarchy, the "state," which "with an increasing intensification of political rule" arrogated "the maintenance of peace to itself as its foremost task." This process was a historically necessary one, it was claimed, because family, dynastic, and clan peace was always of a purely particular and private nature and thus also synonymous with the "feud." The measures taken by the monarchy thus signaled the transition from a "group society to the earliest beginnings of a state society" within the context of preserving peace. And in the state's very act of arrogating the preservation of peace to itself, peace became stripped of its "chance—more social or political than legal—character and was raised from the private to the public arena."[3] The transition of the preservation of peace from the private to the public sphere through the monarchy thus also meant the transition from chance to necessity.

Proponents of this shift of emphasis in favor of quasi-state peace ordinances imposed from above could certainly feel justified in citing medieval reflections on peace. We know of numerous medieval examples,[4] rooted in antique traditions, in which peace in the political, legal, and social sense was tied to the cosmos and its *ordo*, and with it to the validity of command and obedience.

When in his famous definition Augustine understands peace (*pax*) as "the tranquillity and order of all things" (omnium rerum tranquillitas ordinis) (*De civitate Dei* XIX, 13), he defines this "order" that signifies peace as the interplay of "house" (*domus*), *civitas*, and cosmos. In the immanence of this world, domestic peace and peace in the community of citizens—*pax domestica and pax civilis*—are rooted in the harmony between command and obedience, the *concordia imperandi et oboediendi*. The chance of having an order obeyed is, of course, the basis for all authority. The creation of peace through political rule was—following Augustine—thus that form of peace which initially received the most attention in medieval reflections upon peace, for example in statements about the monarchy and the duties of rulers.[5] We find the same element in the canonist Rufinus, whose *De bono pacis* of about 1180 provides the first systematic medieval text on this subject.[6] Rufinus, following Augustine, regards true peace in this world as based on tacit agreement (*pactio tacita*), and on the covenant (*foedus*) between ruler and ruled, *rex* and *populus*.[7] Thus medievalists could consider themselves justified in directing most of their attention to the forms of peace established by monarchical authority.

Only recently has there been a clear shift, indeed a reversal in perceptions, within medieval studies. "Breaking with previous views, we should accord the elements of agreement and association the decisive role in peacemaking," noted the legal historian Hans-Jürgen Becker in 1989.[8] To be sure, historians might have noticed sooner that reflection on the contrast between peace by monarchical authority (the only genuine peace, in Rufinus's opinion) and peace (ostensible, but in truth reprehensible) by association or sworn association was already present in the High Middle Ages—particularly in the work of the above-mentioned Rufinus[9]—and that subsequently, from the early fourteenth century on, the moment of agreement, and the elucidation of agreement and monarchical rule appear in famous and oft-cited peace treatises and plans as contradictory constitutive elements of peace. In his *Monarchia* Dante explains that *pax universalis* is best ensured by the universal monarch: "the monarchy is necessary in order best to guide the world, for that which one man may accomplish is better done by one than by many."[10] At the very same time, Pierre Dubois was promoting the opposite principle that peace could best be ensured by agreement and association.[11] According to Dubois, *pax universalis* should be rooted not in the command of the one but in the consensus of the many: "Pacem firmari taliter expedit quod una sit respublica."[12] His suggestion that a court of arbitration be established to maintain peace between states is also based on this principle. A few years later (1324) Marsilius of Padua made a similar argument in his book on the "Defender of the Peace" (*Defensor pacis*). According to him, peace was "a good state for the city or the kingdom" (*bona disposicio civitatis seu regni*), in which "each part is capable of fulfilling the tasks allocated to it by reason and destiny." In particular, peace meant "mutual relations between the citizens and the exchange of their products, mutual aid and support, and in general the possibility of fulfilling their individual and common tasks without outside interference, and also of participation in the common advantages and burdens to a degree appropriate to each."[13] This state of peace is guaranteed by the polity (*civitas seu regnum*), which is in turn constituted by the estates (peasants, artisans, warriors, merchants, priests, and judges or counsellors) working in concert.

One could thus organize the history of European ideas on peace and peace programs from the Middle Ages to the modern era according to whether they regarded peace as better ensured by the political authority of the one[14] or the agreement of the many.[15] The latter group would also include Immanuel Kant, who in his 1795 treatise *On Perpetual Peace* named as one of the most important conditions of lasting peace that "the law of nations should be based on a federalism of free states" and that all states be republics constituted through a division of powers ("The civil constitution of each state should be republican"). After all, if "(as must necessarily be the case under this constitution) the consent of the state's citizens is required in order to determine whether or not there is to be a war, nothing could be more natural than that they should give very careful thought indeed to beginning such a terrible game . . . since they must resolve to bring upon themselves all the hardships of war."[16] But what was the origin of the underlying idea of agreement as a constitutive moment of peace, which was applied by Pierre Dubois (that is, as early as the Middle Ages) even to the forms of rule and the cooperation of those orders which were themselves based on command and obedience? Is it possible that Dubois borrowed the principle of conflict resolution through arbitration, which is implied in his plan for peace, from the sphere of associations, and transferred it to that of international law?

This question demands a broadening of our field of vision. It is no longer a matter of learning more about the idea or notions of peace or peace programs in the Middle Ages.[17] What also interests us here are real and in a sense lived peace ordinances,[18] which were grounded in the social actions of individuals,[19] and their connections with the intellectual justifications for peace. That peace tied to, agreed upon, and made by groups, in particular, deserves thorough and comparative discussion.

The highly varied types of group formation and ties, which also always served—albeit in different ways—the creation and maintenance of peace[20] included the house (*domus*)[21] and kin,[22] godparenthood,[23] *amicitia*,[24] vassalage,[25] the monastic and clerical community,[26] as well as all those forms of "fraternal alliances," that is, groups based on consensus and pact, that were so numerous precisely in the early Middle Ages, from the eighth to the tenth century.[27]

The most influential of these was surely the *coniuratio*[28]—the oath association (*Schwur-Einung*) or sworn association (*geschworene Einung*)[29]—which always appeared to outsiders as an ominous and dangerous conspiracy. It was so very effective because it emerged from a particular form of social action in which individuals banded together with others on the basis of consensus in order to achieve objectives they had set themselves.[30] In the early and high Middle Ages, *coniuratio* appeared in two guises: the guild and the commune. The chief difference between the two forms is that as a guild, the *coniuratio* was a purely personal association, while as a commune the *coniuratio* also had a spatial substrate, that is, it represented an association of persons that was essentially "locally rooted."[31] We should keep in mind, however, that there is evidence as early as the ninth century of *coniurationes* that had formed within the context of a regional or local substrate, and thus were also spatially rooted.[32]

All types of group formation in early medieval society were characterized by specific modes of creating and maintaining peace. In what follows the main focus will be on peace in the associations, and more particularly the *sworn associations*, that is, on peace by association.

Several medievalists have recognized the outstanding significance of the *coniuratio* for the maintenance of peace, above all within the context of the communal movement of the eleventh century in Italy and France. In a 1966 monograph, Albert Vermeesch points out the connection between the Peace of God movement of the eleventh century in France and the communal movement of the second half of that century. He clarifies the connection between *pax* and *pactum*,[33] characterizes the commune primarily as an institution of peace ("la commune est avant tout une institution de paix"), and notes, in regard to the content of communal statutes (communal law created by consensus and *Willkür*)[34] that the chief aim of these statutes was to bring about peace: "La loi communale est avant tout une paix."[35] This does not mean that the communal movement can be traced back to the Peace of God movement.[36] Rather, these two movements shared common aims but pursued them in quite different ways,[37] as is also evidenced by the demonstrable existence, as early as the ninth century, of spatially rooted *coniurationes* as instruments for the maintenance of peace.[38] At the same time as Vermeesch, but independently of him, Gerhard Dilcher came to similar conclusions in his 1967 monograph on the genesis of the Lombard communes: "The commune was set up as a . . . peace association," it was a *foedus pacis*. It was "each citizen's act of binding himself to the communal oath," that brought about peace. Thus a *carmen* from Bergamo, in the early days of the communal movement, reads, "For golden peace firmly unites the citizens, / poor and rich alike coexist in the peace association."[39] Put another way, *pax* was a "synonym for *coniuratio*."[40] Among historians, Hagen Keller substantiated this

view when he elaborated the underlying mental structures of the Italian communes, which were *caritas, dilectio, fraternitas, unanimitas,* and *humilitas:* "It
was the idea of Christian brotherhood," the "idea of the Christian community of
love and peace, that gave both the Peace of God and communal movements their
strength."[41] And the explanation for the only rare mentions of the Peace of God
in Italian texts after 1040 may be "precisely that the communes themselves had
taken the place of the Peace of God movement."[42] This finding also speaks for the
shared goals but differing quality of these two phenomena and processes.

It appears typical of the continuing split in medieval studies between intellectual and constitutional history and between intellectual and social history that
the many publications that have appeared in recent years on "ideas on peace,"
"concepts of peace," and "programs for peace" in the Middle Ages[43] have paid no
attention whatsoever to the communal principle as a bundle of maxims for social
action for many people, and thus as a basis for the formation of groups and even
institutions in the name of maintaining peace. This is all the more surprising
given that recent research on the early modern period, which frequently incorpo-
rates the late Middle Ages, has quite impressively pointed out the connections
between the need for peace and "communalization" or, conversely, the significance of self-imposed (*gewillkürt*) communities of consent for the maintenance
of peace.[44] According to this view, the fact that peace is a "central category of
communal regimes"[45] does not only apply to the early and high Middle Ages.
With this in mind, we should pay even closer attention to the significance of the
communal principle for the creation and maintenance of peace in the earlier
centuries of the Middle Ages as well.[46]

The Culture of Coniuratio *and the Culture of Peace*

Each social group produces a specific culture of its own, in which its contribution
to the creation and maintenance of peace is also rooted. The term "culture"
implies a fabric of norms and values, which provide the foundation for social
action. Social action refers to the conduct of other persons[47] whereby this action
creates material and immaterial objectifications—for example institutions[48]—a
process that is constantly renewing itself because all objectifications are reinter-
nalized by thought, so that the three moments of externalization, objectification,
and internalization are continually being related to each other in the consciousness, and are mutually interpenetrating. All kinds of social groups entail a specific culture in this sense, because each culture rests on the specific norms and
central ideas about human coexistence that prevail in a given group, and thus
also produces its own forms of behavior and action. What, then, are the basic

elements of the culture of a *coniuratio* that constitute its peacemaking effect, and how does this effect manifest itself?

The peacemaking effect rests in the idea of mutual aid, *mutuum adiutorium* or *mutuum consilium et auxilium*, which is entered into by those persons who recognize their weakness within an existing political and social order because, and so long as, they are isolated; the recognition of this situation leads people to seek a remedy in newly created bonds.[49] This occurs primarily with the help of the mutual promissory oath,[50] whose constitutive and not simply declaratory significance we should keep in mind.[51] It was only the power of this oath and the "conspiracy" it created that enabled the individual to leave or relativize his previous social ties and at the same time to band together with others to settle and discuss conflicting interests, to reach a consensus and form pacts, and to agree upon the objectives they should set themselves. The power of the oath and the bond it created thus constituted joint social action, which was intended to be permanent or at least of long duration. It was just this that the statutes of a twelfth-century London clerics' guild expressed when they noted of the bond of voluntary consensus established by oath ("unusquisque fratrum sacramento corporaliter prestito huic fraternitati se sponte obligavit") and its mutual character ("mutuata sit caritatis vicissitudo") that it was the strongest possible bond between men ("nulla obligatio maior est quam voluntaria").[52]

Outsiders always recognized this effect clearsightedly and found it daunting, fearing, for example, that the members of a (communal) *coniuratio* would "stick together like the scales of a fish, so that not the slightest breath of air could penetrate"—quite an apt metaphor.[53] This explains why the history of associations and sworn associations in late antiquity, the Middle Ages, and the early modern period is also a history of attacks on them from outside and of the resulting prohibitions imposed upon them.[54] The peacemaking influence of *coniurationes*, in particular, was denied. Around 1180, in his *De bono pacis*, the above-mentioned Rufinus, canonist in Bologna, and later bishop first of Assisi, and then of Sorrento, defined three forms of peace among humankind: "The peace of man and man, which is created and maintained between men, takes three forms: Una est pax Aegypti, alia Babyloniae, tertia Jerusalem."[55] *Pax Jerusalem* was peace among Christians within the context of the *christianae societatis fraternitas*; *pax Babyloniae* was secular peace as the absence of war and violence, which presupposed a community of goods and rested on *iustitia*, *humanitas*, and *prudentia*; *pax Aegypti*, however, was "the conspiration of the evil for evil" (*malorum in unam pravitatem conspiratio*) or the "community of crime" (*communio criminum*)—the Devil's work—which was based on *superbia*, *impunitas*, and *pertinacia*. Rufinus, too, invokes here in concise form some of the age-old reservations about sworn associations and accusations against them.[56] It was thus only consistent for Rufinus to contrast what he viewed as only apparent peace by sworn association with true peace by monarchical authority. In his view it was, after all, the contract, the tacit agreement (*pactio tacita*) or the covenant (*foedus*) between ruler and ruled (*rex* and *populus*) that ensured peace, because the ruler provided protection and exercised justice and could thus claim obedience in return.[57] It was only under these conditions that *humanitas* could emerge, which, (in the sense of the trifunctional interpretative scheme; see Chapter 3) contributed—through "mutual support in the necessities of human life" (*humanarum necessitatum collativa subventio*), "reciprocal acts of assistance" (*mutua suffragia*), and exchange of goods—to maintaining a stable order, in such a way "that the warriors protect the peasants with their arms and the peasants endeavor with their work in the fields to provide the warriors with food."[58] Those who terminated the pact between ruler and ruled by refusing to give legitimate rule (*legitima dominatio*) its due (obligations and taxes), rejecting its representatives, disdaining its laws, and thus arrogating to themselves an illegitimate liberty (*libertas illicita*), however, were rebels against such a worldly peace.[59]

We see that in Rufinus's reflections on the conditions for true and lasting peace, the idea of pact and consensus or of agreement and mutuality appears, but that ultimately he ties peace not to association, but to monarchical authority. It is the pact or the understanding between ruler and ruled that brings about true peace—in sharp contrast to the only apparent peace of conspiration, whose agreement rests on equality (parity)[60] and which is intended to recreate it constantly. For Rufinus, the reciprocity of mutual support and reciprocal assistance is not the basis of peace but its effect, a consequence of the power relationship of protection and obedience. Rufinus correctly recognized the contradiction between "peace by monarchical authority" and "peace by sworn association," and was quite just in his negative assessment of the self-interpretations of a *coniuratio*. The reciprocal promissory oath was supposed to create not only close ties among the oath takers, but also a bond that was directed against all others. It was not simply a matter of mutual aid, *mutuum auxilium*, but rather—and this is the content of the oath formulas that have come down to us—of *mutuum auxilium contra omnes*.[61] Thus, for example, the famous and much discussed "Pacta quietis et pacis" (here, once again, a case of peace by sworn association) made by three Swiss valley communities (*Talschaften*) in August 1291 states, "they promised to stand by each other with aid, counsel and every type of favor, in regard to persons and things, in the valleys and outside, with all of their strength and efforts, against all and each individual."[62] This objective of *mutuum auxilium contra omnes* is typical precisely within the context of the peacemaking effects of *coniurationes*, as will be discussed in the final section of this essay.

It was doubtless Max Weber, in his interpretation of the *coniuratio* as a fraternal alliance (*Verbrüderung*), who most clearly addressed the nature of the specific culture of the *coniuratio*, which also provided the basis for its peacemaking and peace-maintaining effects. According to Weber, the oath is "one of the most universal forms of all alliance pacts." The fraternal alliance, which was created by a reciprocal promissory oath, signified "a transformation in the overall legal status, universal position, and social habitus of persons." To ally oneself by means of a pact thus by no means simply meant guaranteeing each other certain "usable services" for "concrete purposes," or promising "that from now on one would have a new and in a certain sense meaningfully qualified total relationship to one another." Rather, it meant "that one 'became' something qualitatively other than before. . . . The participants must allow another 'soul' to enter them."[63] In his great but unfinished essay "Die Stadt' " (published posthumously in 1920–21)[64] Weber sought to show how the occidental city of the Middle Ages, and consequently of the period that followed, as a communal sworn association differed fundamentally from the cities of other cultures—of antiquity, India, China, and Islam.[65] He paid particular attention to the genesis of a special urban law, the self-imposed (*gewillkürt*) communal law, because for him it represented the most important reason for the emergence of an urban burgher class as a new estate. This does not, however, mean that he reduced the phenomenon of the *coniuratio* to aspects of the law, legal history, or constitutional history—on the contrary. It is precisely Weber's characterization of the commune as a fraternal alliance (*Verbrüderung*) that draws our attention to the fact that it was a way of life in which all dimensions of existence, thought, conduct, and political and social action are integrated and thus worthy of equal attention.

Thus the *coniuratio* as a type of group formation possessed an "ethos" of its own.[66] This ethos constituted a bundle of norms of behavior and action, which it imposed on individuals as binding, and which exerted a broad influence on the genesis and history of ideas and mentalities, ritual and religion; on the law, constitutions, and the creation of institutions; on the economy and even the arts. The association and the sworn association emerge on the basis of a *pactum*, which at the same time creates legal and social bonds. For that reason associations and sworn associations are contractual relationships governed by such central behavioral norms as *fraternitas*, *caritas*, *pax*, and *concordia*.[67] It was precisely the interconnections between and indeed the identity of the sworn association and the alliance that produced social, constitutional, and political influences of far-reaching consequence and long duration, particularly in the creation and maintenance of peace. Associations and above all sworn associations are self-created spheres of law and peace, in other words, legal special communities with a self-imposed *Willkür* law and their own jurisdiction and a typical form of constitution, which is characterized by the development of autonomous procedural rules, by co-optation, by the legal concepts of delegation and representation,[68] as well as by the election of officeholders for a limited tenure. Here, too, we are speaking of institutions established with permanence in mind, albeit in a different way from those in the sphere of monarchical rule. We need to ask how enduring the two forms of institutional creation were in ensuring lasting peace in a given case; certainly the question will not always be answered in favor of peace by monarchical authority.

It is also worth noting that this culture of sworn associations undermines the ever-popular juxtaposition of individual and community and community and society in modernist interpretations of the Middle Ages as well as in modern scholarship.[69] On the one hand, associations are contractual relationships, and in this sense are constituted not by community (*Gemeinschaft*) but by society (*Gesellschaft*). On the other, associations and sworn associations are the product of the actions of individuals; they are expressions of individual social action. For that reason, they are indicators of and factors in a medieval culture of the individual, and not some medieval "culture of community" (*Gemeinschaft*) that modern writers are constantly invoking. The extent to which this is the case may be seen in the fact that the central phenomena and concepts of the culture of sworn associations, namely the terms referring to agreements and contracts (*conventio, foedus, pactum*), to the solemn assumption of ties (*promittere, promissio*), and to agreed rules (*statuere, statutum*) were also imbued with theological meanings in the twelfth and thirteenth centuries. They were key concepts in scholastic theology, to the extent that they reflected upon the relationship between God and humanity in the sense of God's voluntary bond with humankind, which also implied the notion of a personal independence of the human being before God.[70] Presumably, though, what the value system of *fraternitas, caritas, pax*, and *concordia* meant to medieval guilds and communes was expressed nowhere more clearly than in the visual arts. For that reason let us recall Ambrogio Lorenzetti's painting in the Palazzo Pubblico in Siena (1337/39), which provides an allegorical representation of the city as a commune, with members of the citizenry united by the bond of *concordia*, and an incomparable depiction of the beauty and grace of *Pax* herself.[71]

Internal and External Peace

The section that follows will discuss the effects of the *coniuratio* on the creation and maintenance of peace from two perspectives—those of internal and external effects. Let us begin with two examples. They come from one of the most interesting and momentous incarnations of *coniuratio* in the history of the Occident, that is, the emergence around the year 1200 of the institution of the university.[72]

An early thirteenth-century chronicler recounts a serious conflict (*gravis dissensio*) that arose between students and the townspeople of Paris in the year 1200.[73] At that time a *nobilis scholaris Teuthonicus*, who was at the same time an elect of Liège, was studying in Paris, and his manservant became involved in an incident in a tavern where he was buying wine. After the matter had become common knowledge, a number of German clerics (*clerici Teuthonici*) banded together, forced their way into the tavern, and beat the tavern keeper so severely that they left him half-dead. This provoked great unrest among the townsfolk: "For that reason, there arose a great clamor among the people, and the city fell into agitation," so that the *prévôt*, the royal governor of the city, mustered the city's militia and ordered an attack on the house (*hospitium*) of the German students, in the course of which several students lost their lives. The university teachers (*magistri*) thereupon lodged a complaint with the king of France, Philip August, which proved successful. The *prévôt* and some of his henchmen were arrested; others, who had managed to flee, had their houses, vineyards, and gardens destroyed by royal order. The *prévôt* was supposed to submit to trial by ordeal and—should the outcome be unfavorable—be hanged. The students then suggested to the king (out of pity, the chronicler writes) that he should have the miscreants flogged instead, saying "that the *prévôt* and his accomplices should, following the custom of the scholars in their groups, be flogged, but then released and their property returned to them." Peace was thus to be restored by turning the malefactors over to the punitive authority of the scholars. This was going too far from the king's perspective, however, since he regarded it as detrimental to the royal honor "if someone other than himself were to punish the malefactors under his authority." Since, on the other hand, Philip August feared that the *magistri* and scholars would leave Paris if not provided with appropriate compensation and a restoration of the peace, he gave them satisfaction by exempting the *clerici* from secular jurisdiction: "When a *clericus* commits an offence, he should turn himself over to the bishop and be punished according to the law of the clerics." He also ordered that the *prévôt* of Paris should henceforth swear an oath of loyalty to the *magistri* and students, "regardless of his loyalty to the king," to be sure. The king, in turn, promised protection, security, and peace ("rex dedit scholaribus firmam pacem suam, et eam eis carta sua confirmavit") and "drew up a document to this effect."

These events were, of course, connected with the beginnings of the University of Paris[74] and the inception of a *coniuratio* of the *magistri* with their students, which however only became visible in the years that followed. Even if the text cited does not explicitly mention a *coniuratio*, *societas*, or *universitas*, it reveals the peacemaking power of this group which constituted itself through consensus and oath, and which succeeded in convincing its opposite number—the king—to behave and act peacefully, although, and probably precisely because, it was not in a position to deploy armed force. What it did bring to bear was the power of group consensus and the resulting power of joint action.

The second example, which draws our attention to the internal effects of the *coniuratio*, also refers to the turbulent circumstances of student life in late twelfth-century Paris. Jacques de Vitry also looks back on this era in his *Historia occidentalis* of circa 1220, in which he describes the lamentable "state of the city of Paris" in those days,[75] which had, he emphasizes, greatly improved since then. He vividly recalled the social and moral troubles and abuses then prevailing among the *magistri* and students, particularly the harsh competition among the *magistri* and their groups of students (*sectae*); the hectic activity of the *magistri*, which was motivated by ambition and a craving for admiration (*scientia inflat*); their fight for every single student and also conflicts of other kinds among the *magistri* and students, for example during disputations or in daily life, because of prejudices arising from "national," meaning ethnic and regional, differences.[76] "They also argued amongst themselves because of their diverse origins [*pro diuersitate regionum*], insulting and reviling each other, hurling affronts and abuse back and forth. . . . And because of insults of this kind words often turned into blows" (*de uerbis frequenter ad uerbera procedebant*). Jacques de Vitry offers a long list of such prejudices: the English were lascivious drunkards; the French arrogant weaklings; the Germans brutal and given to obscenity; the Lombards miserly, cowardly, spiteful, and so on. In this respect as well the *coniuratio* of *magistri* and students in Paris apparently became a vehicle of peace—of internal peace. It had to develop rules and institutions to prevent such internal disputes if possible, and to punish inappropriate behavior with the help of a group-based and mutually agreed-upon special law and its penal norms and group-specific jurisdiction.[77] One may describe this process as a significant contribution to the civilizing process in Europe, a process that was facilitated not only by the monarchy as the medieval apparatus of political power, as Norbert Elias puts it in his theory of civilization,[78] but also, to a large extent (which remains to be defined more precisely), by social groups, above all those that rested on voluntary commitment, consensus, and agreement. A contemporary document chosen almost at random, such as the highly complex agreement on the modalities of electing the rector of the *universitas ultramontanorum* in Bologna in 1265, which was negotiated by sworn *arbitratores* and *compositores*, shows vividly how difficult it could be in an individual case to mediate among the divergent interests of the various *nationes* (thirteen in this case) and come to some compromise, turning *discordia* back into *bonum pacis et concordiae*.[79]

The two sections that follow will outline the internal and external peace-making effects of guilds and communes.

The Peace of the Guild

The medieval sworn association was based on consensus. This found expression in the principles of free entry and co-optation, which were "two quite essential constitutional elements" of the guilds, which had "a close reciprocal relationship to each other." The principle of free entry underlines that "the association—and with it the social relations among the individuals encompassed by it—rested on a voluntary consensus between aspirants and those who were already members, and thus had its legal basis in a private contract." Co-optation, for its part, represented the "instrument" by means of which "the principle of free entry was realized"; in it the will of the community and "the contrast to a decision determined by outside authority became visible."[80] The guild, which was based on the consensus of its members, had its visible foundation in a self-imposed (*gewill-kürt*) legal regime laid down in regulations. Its highest organ was the meeting of members, which was also responsible for maintaining internal peace. It elected an executive and other committees or individual members for the various offices and tasks, for leadership functions and administration, for the external representation of the guild, and also for the exercise of disciplinary authority. The guild delegated particular competences to these members for limited periods on the rotation principle, while they remained responsible to the body of members in the exercise of their duties.[81]

The internal peace of the group thus rested on the peaceful behavior and attitude of the members among themselves; on the maintenance of the self-imposed legal regime, which was also a peace ordinance; and on the interaction between members and the institutions which they themselves had created and put in place. This also included the duty to refer all internal conflicts to the communal court and not to take them before outside authorities, and to submit to any sanctions imposed for violating the statutes.[82]

In the earlier Middle Ages such regulations may be found mainly in the merchant guilds, since the early medieval traveling merchants, like the twelfth-century *magistri* and students, were at first strangers to each other and their environments. They were thus in particular need of peace. The earliest surviving statutes of merchant guilds demonstrate very clearly what peace meant in this situation—first and foremost, the absence of violence and a basically friendly attitude. The statutes of the early merchant guilds thus show on the one hand the measures taken to prevent violence and on the other the conditions for creating a peaceful attitude. Both were rooted in brotherly love (*fraterna dilectio*) and led to harmony or *concordia*. It was a central value for the *coniuratio*, in commune and guild alike.[83] Within the context of the guild (and of the commune) *pax* was defined above all by *concordia*. The peace of the association was *concordia* in the maintenance of the sworn *pactum*, of consensus. Thus one of these early statutes stipulates that "no man who hates one of our brothers may be accepted into our guild,"[84] while another, referring to outer nonviolence and inner disposition as prerequisites for membership and participation in guild meetings, states that "they should come peacefully, and each should maintain peace towards the other regarding past or present events."[85]

The avoidance of any use of violence and all disturbances of the peace in the everyday life of the group was regulated in particular detail.[86] For that reason no weapons were allowed at guild meetings or anywhere in the guild hall, and the same prohibition applied to objects, such as wooden shoes or hobnailed boots, which could be used as weapons.[87] The entire range of hurtful, offensive, or disruptive behavior, including verbal abuse, emotional outbursts of all kinds, noise, restlessness, jumping up from one's seat, and the like, is exhaustively catalogued. The regulation of disciplinary punishments on the part of the executive or guild court is similarly noted in detail. The behavior of members outside the guild hall, to the extent that it had any bearing on the maintenance of peace, was accordingly also subjected to norms. Thus injuries of all kinds, such as insults to or physical assaults on a member by others, had to be testified to by witnesses.[88] The typical responsibility to carry a weapon in public, both within and outside the city, in order to be prepared at any time to defend guild brothers against the injurious behavior of others,[89] also served the maintenance of peace, which demonstrates the external effects of the guild in ensuring peace.

We may add a late medieval example from the south to the example of the early medieval merchant guild north of the Alps: the Collegia Iudicum, the sworn associations of professional jurists in the cities of Upper Italy in the thirteenth to fifteenth centuries, which appear, by their structure, to have been guilds.[90] Their statutes also address the theme of *pax et concordia*, and, as we might expect from lawyers, they do so in exhaustive detail. They thus provide us with a wealth of reflections on, and indications of, social action around the making and maintenance of peace.

These jurists were chiefly concerned with the sole and absolute responsibility of the internal judicial authority.[91] The arbitration and resolution of disputes played a large role in their considerations, and they sometimes also developed subsidiary procedures for those cases in which the decisions of the court did not directly produce a resolution of the conflict.[92] It is instructive to note that these jurists' guilds had specially elected *consiliarii* (a "very important and in some respects decisive constitutional organ") alongside the *prior* and *consules* (*anziani* or the like) as a measure for the maintenance of peace. The task of these *consiliarii* was to represent those members not entrusted with some guild office before the executive "and to make sure that their interests were taken into account and that the statute was enforced."[93] A number of regulations applying to professional practice, which touched on the principles of fraternity and group solidarity, also served the cause of *pax et concordia*: for example, the duty to advise colleagues *sine fraude et dolo* in difficult cases; the honest sharing of fees in cases of joint representation of a client; the equal distribution of contracts for advisory services, and the like.[94] A high value was also placed on expressions of mutual respect and esteem during trials. If one of the lawyers were "insulted by the other side during the trial, the latter's counsel, according to his oath, was required to voice his disapproval, reprimand his party sharply, and lay down his mandate, thereby expressing that he took what had been done or said to his brother as if it had been directed at him."[95]

It is also instructive to learn that these jurists referred to the social and constitutional structure of their *coniuratio* on the whole as a guarantee of *pax* and *concordia* and described it as such, for example in the 1308 statutes of the Collegium Iudicum of Treviso.[96] The elected executive, or *caput collegi*, was not an organ of authority but rather a "limb," which—as these statutes state—was responsible for the *communia negotia* and for carrying out "what has been decided by the *collegium*." This cooperation between the head and limbs was essential for the existence of the *collegium* as a "proper body" (*corpus certum*), and for that reason the adherence of the executive's conduct to the statutes was to be submitted to additional scrutiny by the *anciani* and *consiliarii*; this was an important condition of "vera pax, concordia et laudabilis unio animorum," as the section "De pace et concordia facienda" explains.

Other institutions of the guild type could also be elucidated from the vantage point of maintaining peace. They include the late medieval journeyman's guilds or the noble societies constituted as sworn associations, with their apparatus for internal and external peacemaking,[97] or the so-called confraternities. We now know much better than before that the latter were defined not merely by their religious and charitable aims, to which the members devoted most of their attention, but also by the fact that they belonged, if not to the sworn associations, then to the associations (*Einungen*), since they, too, were founded on consensus and *pactum*.[98] I cannot discuss them further here. Rather, I shall focus on another aspect of the maintenance of peace by sworn associations and other associations of the guild type, in which the external effects of the preservation of peace manifested themselves. Let us turn our attention to the significance of guilds and associations for the peace of the city as a whole.

It is above all Gerhard Dilcher who has pointed to the importance of the "intensive associational (*einungsrechtlich*) . . . life" of the city for the "cohesion, and the community of peace and law of the larger citizenry, whose numbers were often growing at a dizzying rate." The "rapid enforcement" of peace in the medieval city, which "never ceases to surprise us," may be explained by the "solid foundation" and the "social substructure in the subdivision of large segments of the urban population into brotherhoods and guilds."[99] This statement could be applied equally, for example, to the Italian cities of the late Middle Ages, as relatively recent studies, particularly on Florence, have shown.[100] In late medieval Florence the confraternities were also voluntary associations. As Ronald Weissman has shown, they may be regarded, on the basis of their structures, as "communes in miniature," which offered their members an "education in republican civic procedure and culture."[101] They allowed the individual to transcend familial, household, parish, and neighborhood ties as well as those of occupation and estate in a way that encompassed the entire city. This also signified the creation of much farther-reaching ritually and religiously based bonds that rested on obligatory reciprocity. Each of these individual bonds contributed to the maintenance of peace in the city as a whole. For that reason it is not surprising that the humanists, from Coluccio Salutati to Pico della Mirandola and Marsilio Ficino, emphasized the significance of the confraternities for the body politic and, at the same time, for the emergence of a Christian humanism: "This movement toward an extended sense of civic responsibility was encouraged both by political exigencies and the desire of a large segment of the laity to participate directly in that round of acts of charity which would make them worthy in the sight of God. *Quattrocento* ritual and ceremony firmly placed the laity in sacral space as they literally acted out the *imitatio Christi*; the confraternities were centers in which this burgher drama was to unfold. A close connection obtained between laic spirituality and Florentine humanism; confraternities were the locale for the delivery of sermons and orations by leading humanists." Furthermore, the "culture resonating from the confraternities was part of a network of ideals serving as a bridge to a larger society, with religion and civic veneration interlaced."[102] And once again it was the visual arts that most vividly documented this culture.[103] The humanists saw in the *caritas* practiced by these confraternities and their forms of socialization and community-building their most important contribution to the body politic—education for *pax* and *concordia*.[104]

The Peace of the Commune

As was mentioned above,[105] recent research has largely recognized and described the connections between peace and the commune. Not insignificant in this context is the fact that—as already indicated[106]—the history of the commune as a sworn association that not only represented cooperation among individuals but also had local or regional roots did not begin with the cities of the eleventh century. We have evidence of the existence of local or regional sworn associations dedicated to maintaining peace, particularly against external enemies, as early as the ninth century. Probably the most interesting of these groups are those referred to in the sources as guilds (*geldae*), which arose in the villages of the western Frankish kingdom in the late ninth century to protect the population against attackers and therefore to maintain the peace in a specific area.[107] One may thus refer to these groups as village or peasant communes. In a period when the order previously guaranteed by the monarchy was breaking down, they took the maintenance of peace and law in their village communities into their own hands, and were indeed founded for this express purpose.[108]

We also encounter regionally oriented sworn associations for the maintenance of peace in the early tenth century, in England as well as the empire, where they were promoted to this end by the monarchy. In his so-called Castle Order of 926 King Henry I deployed *agrarii milites*, or armed peasants, to defend the country against the Hungarians, and the sources permit the interpretation (one thinks of Widukind of Corvey's "assemblies and all meetings in the cities" ("concilia et omnes conventus atque convivia in urbibus") as well as the *conventicula* of the *Miracula Sancti Wigberhti*) that these groups of armed peasants were sworn associations or guilds.[109] At the same time, in the England of King Athelstan (924–39) we know of a so-called peace guild in London (its self-designations were *ferscipe*, *societas*, and *gildscipa*), which was charged with the task of maintaining the public peace and protecting the population against robbery and plunder. Its surviving written legal foundation, the *Iudicia ciuitatis Lundoniae*, displays a peculiar blend of royal law, law agreed upon by bishops and other Anglo-Saxon magnates, and self-imposed guild law.[110] The regional associations formed by the inhabitants of various towns have yet another, communal, character. One example is the peace agreement (*pactum pacis*), motivated by years of famine and other catastrophes, between the inhabitants of Amiens and Corbie in the first half of the eleventh century (1033–36), which was established by reciprocal oath, and intended to serve the creation of *pax et iusticia* ("peace and justice come together, and it seems as if the reign of Saturn is about to return" ["una conveniunt pax et iusticia; iamiam placet redire Saturnia regna"]) in the sense of a complete peace, that means for each day of the week: they bind themselves to the vow of this promise and seal the vow with an oath."[111] This agreement was regarded as a *nova religio*, out of which arose a customary law statute (*consuetudo*), whereby the *pactum* was renewed annually: "Conflicts were settled, and the parties returned to peaceful relations. . . . The statutes of both towns were renewed and explained to the people, and thus they came to their senses."[112]

From here we have a view of the public peace and leagues of cities created by sworn associations in a later era,[113] or of such a stirring phenomenon for contemporaries as the sworn association of the *Caputiati* in the Auvergne in the 1280s, in which town and country, urban and rural folk made common cause against gangs of mercenaries.[114]

The internal and external peacemaking effects of the urban communes may be demonstrated using a few examples from the late eleventh and early twelfth centuries. One of the earliest texts of its kind, the 1114 statute of Valenciennes, tellingly refers to itself as a "Pax," to its members, the *coniurari*, as men of the pact (*homines* or *viri pacis*), and to its officeholders as *iurati pacis* and *domini pacis*.[115] Statutes of this type may serve as examples here of the peacemaking regulations concerned with security and public safety, communal jurisdiction, and penal legislation, which also addressed and punished disturbances of the peace in the surrounding region ("ambitus pacis; reus erit violate pacis ac si in villa commisisset").[116] No less instructive are the occasional glimpses we gain into the manner of creating communal law and the internal forms for reaching consensus. An example of this is offered by the record, in the form of an episcopal document certifying the resolution of a dispute (*discordia*) in the commune of Pisa by Bishop Daibertus around 1090, in the course of which the communal sworn association was renewed at the same time.[117] This is the earliest surviving documentation of the existence of a commune in Pisa.[118] The occasion for the dispute was a violation of the stipulated maximum height for eaves, stories, and towers, but underneath it all were deeper disruptions of the peace ("in view of the ancient plague of pride in the city of Pisa, which daily caused countless murders and perjuries and illicit marriages, and above all on the occasion of the destruction of houses, and in regard to other innumerable evils"). The bishop, together with several knowledgeable men (*viri sapientes*) he consulted in the case, devised a settlement which he—referring to the earlier communal oath sworn by all ("ex nomine sacramenti quod fecistis")—now suggested could be applied to the resolution of the prevailing *discordia* as a new *pax et concordia*. Anyone who did not agree to this settlement placed himself outside the reaffirmed community of peace and law and its *securitas*. It was a matter here not merely of detailed measures for equalizing the towers ("their height should be aligned, and no one should build anything in wood or stone that is higher than this line") and preventing all sorts of tricks that might be used to circumvent this regulation. (The extent to which a uniform height of eaves was regarded as an expression and "representation" of a more general communal equality also becomes clear here, by the way.) What was also at stake, as was emphasized frequently, was a renewed stabilization of communal institutions such as the communal general meeting or *commune colloquium civitatis*, the highest authority in all disputes. It was also important to recall the fundamental guideline for the conduct of each individual—the *communis utilitas civitatis*. The threats of punishment were also characteristic; anyone who preferred not to maintain *pax et concordia*, who had not previously taken the oath and did not intend to do so now, was to be excommunicated, and all members of the community should avoid him "like a condemned heretic separated from God's Church" and have "no association with him, either in church or on a ship"[119]—a sentence that effectively combines the foundations and aims of a commune and expresses its simultaneous character as an ecclesiastical, economic, legal, and peace community.

Accounts of the inception of urban communes also speak quite plainly of the maintenance of peace as a central motive. In the cases of the Upper Italian communes the main focus appears to have been on maintaining the internal *pax urbana*.[120] Unfortunately, the surviving accounts are few and far between and also generally quite laconic. Giovanni Codagnelli's early thirteenth-century account of the establishment of the communal association in Piacenza around 1090, which he placed at the beginning of his annals,[121] recounts the great conflict between the *populus* and the *milites*, which was only turned around by divine intervention and both sides' dawning recognition of their own sinfulness, maliciousness, and stupidity, a *conversio* expressed in rivers of tears and cries of "Pax, pax." He writes of reciprocal kisses instead of an oath here: "The *milites* left the city, and approached the *populus*, weeping and lamenting, and they kissed each other by turns." Together, the *populus* and *milites* returned to the city, thus establishing *pax* and *concordia*: "And so they walked back into the city, and the *concordia* and *pax* proclaimed by a speaker reigned among them in the entire city of Piacenza and its environs."

Much more realistic, precise, and detailed was the account (also only written down later, in the twelfth century) of the founding, around 1070, of the commune of Le Mans,[122] the oldest French commune.[123] At the same time it draws our attention to some peculiarities of sworn peace regimes in guilds and communes, which will be treated systematically in the following section.

The account vividly illustrates how the commune arose out of the prevailing political chaos and absence of any public order ("the city . . . was crushed by all manner of sedition") and the war in the county of Maine,[124] which—after the death of Count Heribert—had been annexed by William the Conqueror (now in England) to his Norman duchy. The most distinguished men of Le Mans (*proceres Cenomanensium*), together with the *populus*, thus abandoned their loyalty to William and sent to Italy for the Margrave Azzo of Este, son-in-law to the last count of Maine, with his wife Gersendis and son Hugo (as the new pretender). William's knights were driven from the cities and their hinterland, which Bishop Arnald, who was loyal to the duke and new king of England, was powerless to prevent. When he returned from a visit to England the citizens refused to allow him entry into the city. Only after mediation by the clergy could concord be established between them. In the meantime Azzo had lost his faith in the loyalty of the Cenomanensians and in the efficacy of his money and gifts and had returned to Italy; he left his wife and child in the care of Gaufried of Mayenne, "an extremely sly man of the nobility," who, in the role of "tutor and quasi-husband," now worked his way up to the position of actual ruler and proceeded to burden the citizens with additional duties (*novis quibusdam exactionibus*). For that reason, "they began to discuss how they might resist his evil undertakings, and avoid suffering unjust oppression from him or any other man." The commune thus arose out of the hardships of war and oppression. The demand for peace was, therefore, coupled with that for freedom,[125] a circumstance expressed in a reciprocal oath: "And they made a conspiracy (*conspiratio*), which they called a commune (*communio*), all binding themselves to each other by oaths as equals (*sese omnes pariter sacramentis astringunt*),[126] and they began to force the said Gaufried and the other *proceres* of the region, against their will, to join their conspiracy (*conspiratio*) by an oath. And in the unprecedented presumptuous-ness of such a *coniuratio* they committed countless crimes, sentenced a great many people to death without any proper conviction, had a number of people blinded *pro causis minimis* and others—it is shameful to report (*quod nefas est referre*)—hanged for the most paltry misdemeanors. The fortresses in the coun-tryside surrounding the city were also senselessly torched during Lent and even during Easter week." When one of the noblemen of the county resisted the sacred institutions of the *coniurati* ("plotters" or "conspirators") they raised an army with the bishop at its head and the clerics of the individual parishes carrying crosses and banners, and with them a large number of peasants from the sur-rounding countryside; it suffered a terrible defeat, however, at the hands of the contingent raised by Gaufried of Mayenne and his noble allies. This is not the place to relate the highly varied events that subsequently occurred inside and outside the city. Finally, Duke William returned from England, and it came to peace talks (*colloquium de pace*) between him and the most distinguished men of the city (*proceres civitatis*). William took an oath promising them that they would not be punished and that the communal statutes would be respected, "and they accepted his oath, as regards both exemption from punishment for their dis-loyalty and the maintenance of the ancient legal customs and rights of the city, and then turned themselves and their property over to his rule and authority." The customary law (*consuetudo*) laid down by the commune could thus be saved.

The account of the establishment of the commune of Le Mans is of extraor-dinary importance. It shows that the lack of peace, security, and public safety was the reason for the creation of the communal conspiracy, which sought to oppose chaos with its own newly established regime of peace and law (*consuetudo*), and whose members included not only the citizens of the town (*cives*), but also the bishop and clergy, as well as peasants from the surrounding countryside. To be sure, the account tells us little of its internal organization, but we learn all the more about how it was supposed to influence outside events: first by enforcing compulsory membership upon nonmembers (particularly the nobility of Maine); then by exercising criminal jurisdiction over all those who were unwilling to join; and finally by raising an army which was supposed to assert the communal peace ordinance by force.[127] Two further aspects are remarkable here. It is surprising how the perspectives of observation from outside and inside are interwoven in this account, for example in the phrase "they made a conspiracy, which they called commune." The author leaves no room for doubt that he rigorously condemns the undertaking, and yet he does not deny the legitimacy of the attempt to resist oppression and the absence of rights and to restore peace by one's own means.[128] We even hear the voices of the *coniurati* themselves,[129] for example in the precise description of the procedure of reciprocal oaths. This interweaving of two opposing perspectives also draws our attention to something else, however, which remains to be discussed—the paradoxes of conspiracy.

The Paradoxes of Conspiracy

What interests us here is the contradiction between inside and outside—between group-based exclusivity, indeed group egotism, and attempts to act in the outside world—that is, the problem of group norms and the group social behavior based upon them, which, after all, also influenced the society surrounding such a group. This is what the spoken oath formulas hint at, which were used to found the sworn associations and express their aims: *mutuum auxilium contra omnes*.[130] To put it another way, what is at stake here is the tension between an intended, explicit particularity and an implicit universality. This contradiction, paradox, or polar tension expressed itself in multiple guises and was thus also repeatedly perceived and acknowledged by outsiders and contemporaries in the era of the medieval *coniurationes*.

First, the matter is expressed in the juxtaposition of self-imposed special law (*voluntas*) and the universal law imposed by the king (*lex*), a contrast Alpert of Metz held up to the merchant guild of Tiel in the eleventh century: "the judgments [of their court] are spoken not according to universal law (*lex*), but rather according to their special law (*voluntas*)."[131] Here, too, we can hear the voices of guild brothers in the critique and condemnation "from outside." For *voluntas* is *Willkür* in both senses of the word (willed and arbitrary). It is—viewed from the inside—enacted special law created by the group according to regulations. Viewed from the outside, however, this *Willkür* is arbitrary law in the sense of injustice. What was the competition between particular *voluntas* and the universal *lex* whose validity was restricted by *voluntas*? The author of the history of the bishopric of Le Mans also discusses this question in his account of the commune of Le Mans. The commune created its own law and applied it, against outsiders as well as inhabitants, sometimes even resorting to violence. In doing so it made use of its own jurisdiction as well as its armed contingent. This justice—viewed from outside and from the perspective of the future chronicler—was thus arbitrary justice, or injustice and violence. It was every bit as unjust as the deployment of military force with which the *coniuratio* not merely protected itself but also sought to impose its will on its political and social surroundings. Similarly, in a letter to Hugo, deacon of the cathedral of Beauvais, Bishop Ivo of Chartres explained that the self-imposed legal order (*pacta et constitutiones*) that had been asserted by the local commune (*communio*) in a tumultuous manner, enforced by oath (*turbulenta coniuratio*), was null and void, despite its establishment through an oath, because it was created in violation of the *leges ecclesiasticae* and Canon law and the authority of the holy father (*contra leges canonicas et auctoritates sanctorum Patrum*)[132] which Ivo considered to be a universal and absolute norm.

Second, we are dealing with the religious, spiritual, and normative justifications for *coniuratio*—with *caritas*, *fraternitas*, and equality in the sense of parity. What was the relationship here between particularity and universality?

Caritas, *fraternitas*, and brotherly love (*fraterna dilectio*) were at all periods the basic norms of voluntary associations. *Caritas*, understood and practiced in the sense of an exclusive, group-based reciprocity, was already the basic norm of the clerics' guilds of the sixth and seventh centuries.[133] And *caritas* was invoked in a virtually programmatic manner in the statutes of the early merchants' guilds, for example those of the merchant guild of Valenciennes, in whose first section Jesus' commandment to his disciples to love one another (here according to John 13:34) was uninhibitedly extended to the practice of this one group.[134] The influence and assertive power of the group over outsiders and foreigners (*estrangiers*) was directly attributed to the power of mutual love (*dilection fraternelle*), which created harmony and banished discord.[135] Indeed, this guild went so far as to refer to itself as *caritas* or *caritet*,[136] and if an emergency befell a member when he was outside the city he could summon his brothers *en nom de caritet*, that is, in the name of *caritas* and of the group itself.[137] But how could *fraternitas*, *caritas*, *fraterna dilectio*, and *dilection fraternelle* be group-specific norms and a basis for group-specific social action if, as everybody knew, they were by their very nature universal norms that commanded all people to treat their fellows in a fraternal and loving manner? This objection was raised against sworn associations throughout the Middle Ages.[138]

This also applies to equality, or parity, which was created through reciprocal oaths among the *coniurati*. We find the same contradiction here, which could in turn be used against the *coniurationes*. In regard to the sworn association of the *Caputiati* in the 1180s (founded to protect against and fight bands of mercenaries),[139] the author of the history of the bishopric of Auxerre describes soberly and aptly how these "hooded men" banded together in *mutua caritas* to maintain peace.[140] Furthermore, "they bound themselves to each other by oath, promising that they would help all with mutual advice and assistance in times of trouble."[141] This, the account informs us, they called their *libertas*, and in so doing they referred to the possession of this freedom by the progenitors of the human race at the beginning of Creation. But, it was objected, could this liberty and equality exist in the world and in society after the Fall?[142] And should they exist? The answer, naturally, was negative, for the negation, as manifested in this *coniuratio*, of transcendentally justified differences of estate, and with it of monarchical authority, was considered essentially evil. The *mutua caritas* referred to here could thus only be a ruse, and the will to make peace thus proved to be a mere feigned semblance of good, a *simulata boni species*. In truth it was nothing but "an all too terrible and dangerous arrogance," an insurrection, an uprising of those "below" against those "above" (*rebellio superiorum et [in] exterminium potestatum*), a "pernicious and devilish venture" (*diabolicum et perniciosum inventum*).[143] The particular, group-based claim to equality and freedom thus competes and comes into conflict with a universal, transcendently justified inequality and lack of freedom, with the principle of a society of classes, harmony in inequality (see Chapter 3)—and is condemned for this reason.

This contradiction between particularity and universality in the law and in the grounds for and practice of *caritas* and *fraternitas*, parity and *libertas* (one might also say liberty, equality, and fraternity)[144] also plays a role in the third contrast that interests us here, that between peace and violence. "They pretend that they wish to make peace, but in reality they use violence" was the criticism levied by the historian of the bishopric of Auxerre against the *Caputiati* around 1180, and by the historian of the bishopric of Le Mans against the local *coniurati* around 1070; the aim was to make peace, but this very intention led to violence, arbitrary justice, and militant aggressivity and thus to a deserved downfall. This accusation, too, reflects the problem of particularity and universality. How can a particular group expect to justify, establish, and enforce peace for itself when peace is, after all, a universal good, which should benefit all and can only be constituted by universal—in this case transcendental—preconditions? It was in this sense that Jacques de Vitry spoke of the communes "or rather conspirations," which were bound together "like thorny bundles of twigs,"[145] using such brutal violence against their neighbors, the nobility and the church, and above all destroying ecclesiastical law and *libertas*. It was the duty of the laity to obey; they had no right to give orders. The lack of peace in the communes resulted from this grave violation of the proper order of the world and society: the commune meant war with the outside world and terror within.[146] Ivo of Chartres argued with the same intentions, not in moral and metaphysical, but in legal terms. In 1114, in a letter to King Louis VI of France, he intervened on behalf of Bishop Godfrey of Amiens, who was greatly distressed by the commune that had been set up in his see, and by the resulting unrest. "He told us in tears of the unbearable misery and oppression that the disturbers of the peace had caused him." Ivo contrasts the alleged peace ordinance of the commune, which was in reality nothing but a violation of the peace, with the *pactum pacis* created by the king, and reminds the ruler of his duties: "You must not permit the peace agreement that you have consolidated in your kingdom with God's help to be violated out of consideration for friendship or out of sloth."[147] As we know, in his treatise *De bono pacis* the canonist and bishop Rufinus also presents a (more fundamental) contrast between peace by monarchical authority (*dominatio*) and peace by conspiracy (*conspiratio*) as a contrast between good and evil.[148]

It is important that we recognize this tension between particular and universal norms, between particular, group-based conduct and actions that transcended it. It is this tension which explains the outside world's recurring resistance to the *coniurationes*, as well as their failure in many individual cases. It also explains something else, though—the historic success of the *coniurationes* as a whole in the history of the West.

As forms of coexistence of people and groups, the medieval association and the *coniuratio* in their various incarnations conflicted with other varieties of group formation. They conflicted with those groups that human beings formed on the basis of natural ties (family, dynasty, kinship), as well as those groups, like the "house," that were founded from the beginning on the "harmony of command and obedience."[149] Similarly, they conflicted with a society of classes and its basic norm of harmony in inequality. The *coniuratio* always permitted the individual to come together with others, to formulate aims agreed upon by balancing interests and negotiating, and to work toward their realization. It was a form of expression for individual action, which certainly had its foundations in Christianity, but which just as certainly only developed a broader influence in the Middle Ages. This is what Max Weber sketches in outline in his essay on "The City."[150] While in other cultures individual ties of estate or caste appear irrevocable, or people's integration into cult and familial or kinship groups dominates, the western Middle Ages produced, in the *coniuratio*, sworn association and fraternal alliance, consensual ties, which at once presupposed individual action and permitted joint consensual action for the achievement of common goals.[151] Herein lies the significance of the *coniurationes*, the reason for their apparent attractiveness for the people of that era, and also the explanation for their unusual influence in history.

A result of this attractiveness, and one of these influences, was the making and maintenance of peace—peace by conspiracy. The history of peace and its realization cannot thus be properly understood if we portray it as a history of the necessary transcending of "private" and "particular" peace regimes by the monarchy, or of family, dynastic, and clan peace by a kingship that, with the growing intensification of its authority, arrogated to itself the maintenance of peace as its foremost task, in order to transcend "group society" and establish true peace in "state society."[152] Such a viewpoint takes sides in a dispute which, as we now know, was already fought out in the Middle Ages, a dispute over the question of how to make and maintain peace—by monarchical authority or sworn association, by the *pactio tacita*, the contract between ruler and ruled, or the *pactum*, *fraternitas*, the *coniuratio* of equals. In contrast to the views prevalent in the scholarly literature, what made the societies of the medieval Occident "group societies" was the fact that they contained not only family, dynastic, and kinship units, but also associations and sworn associations, and in such large numbers that they significantly influenced political and social events. The history of peace in the West as a history of real and imagined peace regimes was thus shaped by both ideas and by both forms of organizing peace, by monarchical authority and *coniuratio*, whereby the highly conflicted tension between them itself represents a significant element in the history of the European Occident.

For that reason, what we discover in the culture of the *coniuratio* is not the much discussed medieval community, with its supposed opposition to individuals, who did not exist in the Middle Ages, because they had allegedly been absorbed by the community,[153] in which all conflicts then came to rest. Such views of the Middle Ages are projections, ideals of the modern age, in which modern people express their own deficits and discontent with the present.[154] What we see in the culture of *coniuratio* is, rather, a culture of conflict inhabited and used by individuals, which offered the tools for creating and maintaining consensus, for integration, for the control and resolution of conflict, for peacemaking within and outside the group. To acknowledge this is to acknowledge something of the modernity of the Middle Ages,[155] and indeed to recognize a significant element of occidental culture, whose relevance transcends the history of the Middle Ages and which, precisely because of its unusual historical depth, remains to be rediscovered in the present in new contexts.[156]

In the process of modernization the medieval *coniuratio* initially underwent multiple transformations, only to disappear in the decorporatization of the late eighteenth century. It has nevertheless left a number of marks on the modern world.[157] The idea and reality of peace by conspiracy have also disappeared, unable to survive the emerging modern state's monopoly of the use of force, which began to assert itself gradually in the late Middle Ages and gained momentum particularly in the early modern period. To be sure, the idea of peace by agreement which underlies peace by *coniuratio* is alive and well. Whether peace can most lastingly be made and maintained from above, that is, by command and obedience, or by agreement, that is, by consensus, remains an absorbing question at the end of the twentieth century, and particularly in these times—perhaps more than ever before.

Notes

This chapter is slightly abridged from Otto Gerhard Oexle, "Friede durch Verschwörung," in *Träger und Instrumentarien des Friedens im Hohen und späten Mittelalter*, ed. Johannes Fried, Vorträge und Forschungen 43 (Sigmaringen, 1996), 115–50.

1. Ekkehard Kaufmann, "Friede," in *Handwörterbuch zur deutschen Rechtsgeschichte*, 1 (1971), cols. 1275–92, 1275–76. In regard to definitions of *Einung* (agreement, association) and *coniuratio*, let us recall the definition of guild as a term used in the sources and scholarship. It is, first, an *Einung* because it is based on consensus and agreement. This consensus is, second, based on a mutual promissory oath; the guild is thus a sworn *Einung, Schwureinung,* and *coniuratio*. The third characteristic is the comprehensiveness of objectives. See Otto Gerhard Oexle, "Conjuratio und Gilde im frühen Mittelalter. Ein Beitrag zum Problem der sozialgeschichtlichen Kontinuität zwischen Antike und Mittelalter," in *Gilden und Zünfte. Kaufmännische und gewerbliche Genossenschaften im frühen und hohen Mittelalter*, ed. Berent Schwineköper, Vorträge und Forschungen 29 (Sigmaringen, 1985), 151–214, esp. 156ff.; and Oexle, "Gilde," in *Lexikon des Mittelalters* 4 (1989), cols. 1452–53.

2. In his "Rechtsordnung und Friedensidee im Mittelalter und der beginnenden Neuzeit," in *Christlicher Friede und Weltfriede. Geschichtliche Entwicklung und Gegenwartsprobleme*, ed. Alexander Hollerbach and Hans Maier (Paderborn, 1971), 9–34, Hermann Conrad discusses the "church as a vehicle for the idea of peace," the "state as a vehicle for the idea of peace," and the "idea of peace on a supra-national basis." This corresponds to the assumption that peace is always tied to the "development of the state." See, for example, Herfried Münkler, *Gewalt und Ordnung. Das Bild des Krieges im politischen Denken* (Frankfurt am Main, 1992), 22. Here he attempts a typology of war and peace, referring for historical background to the study by Helmut Berve, *Friedensordnungen in der griechischen Geschichte* (Munich, 1967).

3. Kaufmann, "Friede," 1275 and 1283. One finds a similar view in Reinhold Kaiser, "Selbsthilfe und Gewaltmonopol. Königliche Friedenswahrung in Deutschland und

Frankreich im Mittelalter," *Frühmittelalterliche Studien* 17 (1983), 55–72. Kaiser contrasts the king's maintenance of peace to "self-help"—which is reduced to "blood vengeance" and above all the "feud"—as "the distinguishing characteristic of the medieval state" (56). See below, n. 46.

4. See the various contributions in the article "Friede" in *Lexikon des Mittelalters* 4 (1989), cols. 919–21.

5. See Eugen Ewig, "Zum christlichen Königsgedanken im Frühmittelalter," in *Das Königtum. Seine geistigen und rechtlichen Grundlagen*, Vorträge und Forschungen, 3 (1956, reprint Darmstadt, 1963), 7–73, especially 63–64 (on the influence of the biblical and Augustinian ideas of peace in the Carolingian period); Hans Hubert Anton, *Fürstenspiegel und Herrscherethos in der Karolingerzeit*, Bonner historische Forschungen, 32 (Bonn, 1968), 69ff.; Otto Eberhardt, *Via regia. Der Fürstenspiegel Smaragds von St. Mihiel und seine literarische Gattung.* Münstersche Mittelalter-Schriften, 28 (Munich, 1977), 653–54; Kaiser, "Selbsthilfe und Gewaltmonopol," 57ff. On the role of the bishops see Karl Ferdinand Werner, "Observations sur le rôle des évêques aux Xᵉ et XIᵉ siècles," in *Medievalia Christiana: Hommage à Raymonde Foreville* (Paris, 1989), 155–95.

6. Reproduced in Jacques-Paul Migne, *Patrologia latina* 150, cols. 1591–1638. New edition: *Magistri Rufini Episcopi de Bono Pacis*, ed. A. Brunacci and G. Catanzaro (Assisi, 1986). On this, see Klaus Arnold, "De bono pacis—Friedensvorstellungen im Mittelalter und Renaissance," in Jürgen Petersohn (ed.), *Überlieferung, Frömmigkeit, Bildung als Leitthemen der Geschichtsforschung* (Wiesbaden, 1987), 133–54, 137ff.

7. Rufinus, *De bono pacis* II, 9, *Patrologia latina* 150, col. 1617. "Unde cum rex instituitur, pactio quaedam tacita inter eum et populum initur, ut et rex humane regat populum, et populus regem statutis tributis et inlationibus meminerit venerari. See Brunacci and Catanzaro, *Magistri Rufini Episcopi de Bono Pacis*, 155. See below, text to nn. 55–59.

8. Hans-Jürgen Becker, "Friede I," in *Lexikon des Mittelalters* 4 (1989), col. 919. For earlier work on the connections between peace and (sworn) associations see in particular Wilhelm Ebel, *Der Bürgereid als Geltungsgrund und Gestaltungsprinzip des deutschen mittelalterlichen Stadtrechts* (Weimar, 1958), 1ff. and 202ff.; Gerhard Pfeiffer, "Die Bedeutung der Einung im Stadt- und Landfrieden," *Zeitschrift für bayerische Landesgeschichte* 32 (1969), 815–31. The significance of (sworn) associations has gone unrecognized in the political theory of war and peace in history, however. See above n. 2 and below, n. 156. In *Gewalt und Ordnung* (44ff.) Münkler thus places the idea of the confederation of states (see below, n. 11) in proximity to Dante's universal monarchy, and in a curious historical construction sees its counterpart in the idea of the balance of powers, which was borrowed from "mercantile accounts in the economic field," and which in turn gave rise to the "egalitarian model of a political pluriversum" (47–48).

9. See below, text to nn. 55–59.

10. Dante Alighieri, *Monarchia*, ed. Pier Giorgio Ricci (n.p., 1965), 163. See Waldemar Voisé, "Dante et sa vision de la paix mondiale," *Revue de synthèse* 59–60 (1970): 221–31.

11. See Otto Gerhard Oexle, "Utopisches Denken im Mittelalter: Pierre Dubois," *Historische Zeitschrift* 224 (1977): 293–339; Günther Hödl, "Ein Weltfriedensprogramm um 1300," in *Festschrift Friedrich Hausmann* (Graz, 1977), 217–33.

12. C.-V. Langlois (ed.), *De recuperatione terre sancte. Traité de politique générale par Pierre Dubois* (Paris, 1891), 3. Most instructive here are the national stereotypes that appear in the comparative assessments of Dante's and Pierre Dubois's plans for peace, for

example in Carlo Schmid's 1937 essay "Dante und Pierre Dubois. Idee und Ideologie des Abendlandes an der Wende von Mittelalter und Neuzeit," which is reprinted in C. Schmid, *Europa und die Macht des Geistes*, Gesammelte Werke in Einzelausgaben, vol. 2 (Berne, Munich, and Vienna, 1973), 9–31. Schmid saw in the works of Dante and Dubois "the two most different images of the united Occident . . . that one could imagine, both of them representing, in their attitude and meaning, everything that the centuries to follow have brought," in the sense of the "contrast between idea and ideology, between the idea of empire and that of a league of nations." While the one text represented a "song of praise for empire," the other was a "cunning model for a league of nations" (11–12), an expression of "vulgar Aristoteleanism" and the "spirit of civilization" (23), of "western humanism, filled with hedonism and faith in progress" (27), and directed toward the "intellectual and political hegemony of France over the world" (25). "Ultimately, then, a political conception of the world whose objective was the general increase of civilized comforts, a conception of the world that regards peace as no more than the absence of unpleasant disturbances and justice as no more than the organization of the exchange of goods and of the desired political reality" (29–30). Such statements also express the persistent German unease with the idea of association (as opposed to that of rule) and with the principle of consensus and contract (as opposed to the idea of community); on this see Otto Gerhard Oexle, "Das Mittelalter und das Unbehagen an der Moderne. Mittelalterbeschwörungen in der Weimarer Republik und danach," in *Spannungen und Widersprüche. Gedenkschrift für Frantisek Graus*, ed. Susanna Burghartz et al. (Sigmaringen, 1992), 125–53.

13. "Civium conversacio mutua et communicacio ipsorum invicem suorum operum, mutuumque auxilium atque iuvamentum, generaliterque suorum propriorum operum et communium exercendi ab extraneo non impedita potestas, participacio quoque communium commodorum et onerum secundum convenientem unicuique mensuram." Marsilius of Padua, *Defensor pacis* I, 19 §2, ed. Richard Scholz (Hanover, 1932), 125–26.

14. Examples here are Rufinus, Dante, Engelbert of Admont, and Christine de Pizan (*Le livre de la paix*, 1412/14).

15. Apart from Pierre Dubois and Marsilius of Padua, examples include Philippe de Mezières (*Le songe du vieil pélerin*, 1389) and the peace plan of the Bohemian king George of Podiebrad (*Tractatus pacis toti Christianitati fiendae*, 1462/64).

16. Immanuel Kant, "Zum ewigen Frieden. Ein philosophischer Entwurf," in I. Kant, *Kleinere Schriften zur Geschichtsphilosophie, Ethik und Politik*, ed. Karl Vorländer, Philosophische Bibliothek 47/I (reprint Hamburg, 1973), 126ff.

17. On the history of the idea of peace in the Middle Ages see Conrad, "Rechtsordnung und Friedensidee"; Wilhelm Janssen, "Friede," in *Geschichtliche Grundbegriffe*, ed. Otto Brunner, Werner Conze, and Reinhard Koselleck, vol. 2 (1975), 543–91; *La pace nel pensiero, nella politica, negli ideali del Trecento*, Convegni del Centro di Studi sulla Spiritualità Medievale, 15 (Todi, 1975); Thomas Renna, "The Idea of Peace in the West, 500–1150," *Journal of Medieval History* 6 (1980): 143–67; Hans Hattenhauer, *Pax et iustitia*, Berichte aus den Sitzungen der Joachim Jungius Gesellschaft der Wissenschaften e.V., Hamburg, vol. 1, no. 3 (1982–83); James Hutton, *Themes of Peace in Renaissance Poetry* (Ithaca, N.Y., 1984); Werner Conze, "Sicherheit, Schutz," in *Geschichtliche Grundbegriffe*, vol. 5, ed. Brunner, Conze, and Koselleck (Stuttgart, 1984), 831–62, here 833ff.; *Frieden in Geschichte und Gegenwart*, ed. Historisches Seminar der Universität Düsseldorf, Kultur und Erkenntnis, 1 (Düsseldorf, 1985); Wolfgang Sellert, "Friedensprogramme und Friedenswahrung im Mittelalter," in *Wege europäischer Rechtsgeschichte. Festschrift Karl*

Kroeschell (Frankfurt am Main, 1987), 453–67; Arnold, "De bono pacis"; Evamaria Engel, "Friedensvorstellungen im europäischen Mittelalter," *Zeitschrift für Geschichtswissenschaft,* 37 (1989): 600–607; Hans-Joachim Diesner, *Stimmen zu Krieg und Frieden im Renaissance-Humanismus,* Abhandlungen der Akademie der Wissenschaften in Göttingen, Phil.-hist. Kl., 3rd series, 188 (Göttingen, 1990); Dietrich Kurze, "Krieg und Frieden im mittelalterlichen Denken," in *Zwischenstaatliche Friedenswahrung in Mittelalter und Früher Neuzeit,* ed. Heinz Duchhardt, Münstersche Historische Forschungen, 1 (Cologne and Vienna, 1991), 1–44.

18. On the topology and history of the forms of real, lived peace in the High Middle Ages, see Otto Gerhard Oexle, *Formen des Friedens in den religiösen Bewegungen des Hochmittelalters, 1000–1300,* in *Mittelalter. Annäherungen an eine fremde Zeit,* ed. Wilfried Hartmann, Schriftenreihe der Universität Regensburg, Neue Folge, 19 (Regensburg, 1993), 87–109.

19. See below, n. 47.

20. The recent findings of biological behavioral research and sociobiology on the inhibition of aggression and the maintenance of peace among groups of animals through the development of hierarchies and particular forms of conduct that bind the group together—referred to as rites, rituals, or ceremonies—should be taken into account here. See Otto Gerhard Oexle, "Gruppenbindung und Gruppenverhalten bei Menschen und Tieren. Beobachtungen zur Geschichte der mittelalterlichen Gilden," *Saeculum. Jahrbuch für Universalgeschichte* 36 (1985): 28–45, 31ff. and 33ff.

21. See Otto Gerhard Oexle, "Haus und Ökonomie im früheren Mittelalter," in *Person und Gemeinschaft im Mittelalter. Festschrift Karl Schmid* (Sigmaringen, 1988), 101–22.

22. See Klaus Schreiner, "Consanguinitas—Verwandschaft als Strukturprinzip religiöser Gemeinschafts- und Verfassungsbildung in Kirche und Mönchtum des Mittelalters," in *Beiträge zur Geschichte und Struktur der mittelalterlichen Germania Sacra,* ed. Irene Crusius, Veröffentlichungen des Max-Planck-Instituts für Geschichte, 93 (Göttingen, 1989), 176–305, esp. 260ff.

23. Bernhard Jussen, *Spiritual Kinship as Social Practice: Godparenthood and Adoption in the Early Middle Ages,* trans. Pamela E. Selwyn (Newark, Del., 2000).

24. Gerd Althoff, *Verwandte, Freunde und Getreue. Zum politischen Stellenwert der Gruppenbindungen im früheren Mittelalter* (Darmstadt, 1990), 88ff.

25. See Walter Ullmann, *Individuum und Gesellschaft im Mittelalter* (Göttingen, 1974), 40ff.

26. Augustine describes how the peace of the "house," *pax domestica,* was secured by the harmony between orders and obedience. The Benedictine rule, which in many respects structured the monastic community according to the domestic model, also explicitly ties the "preservation of peace and love" (*pacis caritatisque custodia*) to the abbot's authority to give orders (c. 65), to which the monks' willingness to obey was supposed to correspond (ibid., Prologue 3: "oboedientiae fortissima atque praeclara arma").

27. The standard account is Karl Schmid, "Mönchtum und Verbrüderung," in *Monastische Reformen im 9. und 10. Jahrhundert,* ed. Raymund Kottje and Helmut Maurer, Forschungen und Vorträge, 38 (Sigmaringen, 1989), 117–46.

28. We should also recall the Frankish institution of sworn friendship (*Schwurfreundschaft*), which is allied to *coniuratio,* and which has been aptly described as "a self-help relationship that serves the preservation of peace." Wolfgang H. Fritze, *Papst und Frankenkönig,* Vorträge und Forschungen, Sonderband 10 (Sigmaringen, 1973), 21ff., quotation on 27.

29. On the definition of the terms *Einung* and *coniuratio* see above, n. 1.

30. See Otto Gerhard Oexle's "Gilden als soziale Gruppen in der Karolingerzeit," in *Das Handwerk in vor- und frühgeschichtlicher Zeit*, ed. Herbert Jankuhn et al., part I, Abhandlungen der Akademie der Wissenschaften in Göttingen, Phil.-hist. Kl., 3rd series, 122 (Göttingen, 1981), 284–354; "Conjuratio und Gilde"; "Die Kaufmannsgilde von Tiel," in *Untersuchungen zu Handel und Verkehr der vor- und frühgeschichtlichen Zeit in Mittel- und Nordeuropa*, part VI: *Organisationsformen der Kaufmannsvereinigungen in der Spät- antike und im frühen Mittelalter*, ed. Herbert Jankuhn and Else Ebel, Abhandlungen der Akademie der Wissenschaften in Göttingen, Phil.-hist. Kl., 3rd series, 183 (Göttingen, 1989); Ernst Cordt's relatively recent account *Die Gilden. Ursprung und Wesen*, Göppinger Arbeiten zur Germanistik, 407 (Göppingen, 1984) is a dissertation inspired and super- vised by Otto Höfler (4), which is based on the state of research ca. 1940, as shown by the review of the literature on guilds, which ends with the works of H. Planitz (34ff.). Cordt seeks to support O. Höfler's thesis, which was flawed from the beginning, on the origins of the guilds in Germanic male organizations (*Männerbünde*) (151ff.).

31. Gerhard Dilcher, *Die Entstehung der lombardischen Stadtkommune*, Untersuch- ungen zur deutschen Staats- und Rechtsgeschichte, N.F. 7 (Aalen, 1967), 158.

32. See Oexle, "Gilden als soziale Gruppen," 307–8.

33. Albert Vermeesch, *Essai sur les origines et la signification de la commune dans le Nord de la France (XIe et XIIe siècles)*, Études présentées à la Commission Internationale pour l'Histoire des Assemblées d'États, 30 (Heule, 1966), 20. On what follows, see also Knut Scholz, *"Denn sie lieben die Freiheit so sehr. . . ." Kommunale Aufstände und Entsteh- ung des europäischen Bürgertums im Hochmittelalter* (Darmstadt, 1992).

34. On the term *Willkür*, which referred to laws established by agreement, see Max Weber, *Wirtschaft und Gesellschaft*, Studienausgabe, 5th ed. (Tübingen, 1972), 416–17. Cf. Wilhelm Ebel, *Die Willkür. Eine Studie zu den Denkformen des älteren deutschen Rechts*, Göttinger rechtswissenschaftliche Studien, 6 (Göttingen, 1953).

35. Vermeesch, *Essai sur les origines*, 179–80. See also the earlier account by Charles Petit-Dutaillis, *Les communes françaises. Caractères et évolution des origines au XVIIIe siècle* (reprint Paris, 1970), 72ff. "At its inception the commune was, above all, an instrument of concord and peace" (376).

36. On the controversies over this see Joachim Deeters, "Die Kölner Coniuratio von 1112," in *Köln, das Reich und Europa*, Mitteilungen aus dem Stadtarchiv von Köln, 60 (Cologne, 1971), 125–48, 136ff., and Hans-Werner Goetz, "Gottesfriede und Gemeinde- bildung," *Zeitschrift für Rechtsgeschichte, Germ. Abt.*, 105 (1988): 122–44.

37. Vermeesch, *Essai sur les origines*, 175–76; and Goetz, "Gottesfriede und Gemein- debildung." The differences are also made clear in a study by Theodor Körner, which takes ritual into account: *Iuramentum und frühe Friedensbewegung (10.–12. Jahrhundert)*, Münchener Universitätsschriften, Juristische Fakultät, Abhandlungen zur rechtswissen- schaftlichen Grundlagenforschung, 26 (Berlin, 1977).

38. See Oexle, "Gilden als soziale Gruppen," 307–8.

39. Dilcher, *Die Entstehung der lombardischen Stadtkommune*, 153. The quotation from the *carmen* of Bergamo comes from the same source.

40. Ibid., 144.

41. Hagen Keller, "Die Entstehung der italienischen Stadtkommunen als Problem der Sozialgeschichte," *Frühmittelalterliche Studien* 10 (1976): 169–211, 204. See also the same author's "Die soziale und politische Verfassung Mailands in den Anfängen des kommunalen Lebens," *Historische Zeitschrift* 211 (1970): 34–64, 51ff.; and "Einwohnerge-

meinde und Kommune: Probleme der italienischen Stadtverfassung im 11. Jahrhundert,"
ibid.: 561–97, 570ff. "The foundation of the commune is, ultimately, a religious idea"
(570).

42. Keller, "Die Entstehung der italienischen Stadtkommunen," 195.

43. See above, n. 17.

44. Peter Blickle, "Friede und Verfassung. Voraussetzungen und Folgen der Eidgenossenschaft von 1291," in *Innerschweiz und frühe Eidgenossenschaft. Jubiläumsschrift 700
Jahre Eidgenossenschaft* (Olten, 1991), 13–202.

45. Peter Blickle, "Kommunalismus. Begriffsbildung in heuristischer Absicht," in
Landgemeinde und Stadtgemeinde in Mitteleuropa. Ein struktureller Vergleich, ed. P. Blickle
(Munich, 1991), 5–38, 15.

46. See Gerhard Dilcher, "Reich, Kommunen, Bünde und die Wahrung von Recht
und Friede. Eine Zusammenfassung," in *Kommunale Bündnisse Oberitaliens und Oberdeutschlands im Vergleich*, ed. Helmut Maurer, Vorträge und Forschungen, 33 (Sigmaringen, 1987), 231–47. Reinhold Kaiser's narrowing of nonmonarchical (nonroyal)
preservation of the peace to "self-help" and of this self-help to "blood vengeance" and
particularly the "feud" proves questionable; see above, n. 3.

47. The term "action" is used here in the Weberian sense as a "human behavior . . . if
and to the extent that the actor or actors associate(s) a subjective meaning with it," and
"social action" as an action "which, according to the meaning intended by the actor or
actors, is applied to the behavior of others and oriented therein in its process" (Max
Weber, *Wirtschaft und Gesellschaft*, 1).

48. On this approach, following E. Husserl and A. Schütz, see Peter L. Berger and
Thomas Luckmann, *The Social Construction of Reality* (New York, 1966); cf. Hans-Georg
Soeffner, "Appräsentation und Repräsentation. Von der Wahrnehmung zur gesellschaftlichen Darstellung des Wahrzunehmenden," in *Höfische Repräsentation. Das Zeremoniell
und die Zeichen,* ed. Hedda Ragotzky and Horst Wenzel (Tübingen, 1990), 43–63. On the
applicability of this approach to medieval studies see Otto Gerhard Oexle, "Deutungsschemata der sozialen Wirklichkeit im frühen und hohen Mittelalter. Ein Beitrag zur
Geschichte des Wissens," in *Mentalitäten im Mittelalter. Methodische und inhaltliche Probleme*, ed. Frantisek Graus, Vorträge und Vorschungen, 35 (Sigmaringen, 1987), 65–117,
esp. 68ff. See the English translation in the present volume, "Perceiving Social Reality in
the Early and High Middle Ages: A Contribution to a History of Social Knowledge."

49. Pierre Michaud-Quantin, *Universitas. Expressions du mouvement communautaire dans le Moyen-Age latin*, L'Église et l'État au Moyen Age, 13 (Paris, 1970), 160 on the
commune.

50. The standard work here is Michaud-Quantin, *Universitas*, 233ff. See, more recently, Lothar Kolmer, *Promissorische Eide im Mittelalter*, Regensburger Historische Forschungen, 12 (Kallmünz, 1989), esp. 168ff.; André Holenstein, *Die Huldigung der Unter-
tanen. Rechtskultur und Herrschaftsordnung (800–1800)*, Quellen und Forschungen zur
Agrargeschichte, 36 (Stuttgart and New York, 1991), esp. 17ff.; Paolo Prodi, *Il sacramento
del potere. Il giuramento politico nella storia costituzionale dell'Occidente*, Annali dell'Isti-
tuto storico italo-germanico, Monografia 15 (Bologna, 1992).

51. On this, see Oexle, "Conjuratio und Gilde," 156ff.

52. Gilles Gérard Meersseman, *Ordo fraternitatis. Confraternite e pietà dei laici nel
Medioevo*, vol. 1 (Rome, 1977), 176.

53. The metaphor comes from the canonist Stephan of Tournai. See *Lettres d'Étienne*

de Tournai, new edition, ed. Jules Desilve (Valenciennes and Paris, 1893), 299, no. 242. Further judgments of this kind, which repeatedly emphasized the impenetrability of communal ties from outside, are discussed in Achille Luchaire, *Les communes françaises* (1911, reprint Geneva 1977), 235ff., esp. 242ff.

54. See Oexle, "Gilden als soziale Gruppen," esp. 309ff. and 314ff., and the same author's "Die Kaufmannsgilde von Tiel," 180ff.

55. Rufinus, *De bono pacis* II, 1, Migne, *Patrologia latina* 150, col. 1611: "Pax igitur, quae hominis ad hominem est, et quae inter homines habetur et colitur, et ipsa quoque in tres species propagatur. Una est pax Aegypti, alia Babyloniae, tertia Jerusalem. Pax Aegypti est malorum in unam pravitatem conspiratio. Pax Babyloniae est tam malorum quam bonorum ab externo vel civili bello privatave rixa tuta conversatio. Pax Jerusalem Christianae societatis fraternitas aestimatur. Pax Aegypti communionem criminum, pax Babyloniae communionem rerum, pax Jerusalem communem virtutem omnium exigit facultatem. Pacem Aegypti diabolus, pacem Babyloniae mundus, pacem Jerusalem conciliat Christus. Pacem Aegypti facit superbia, fovet impunitas, firmat pertinacia. Pacem Babyloniae facit justitia, alit humanitas, firmat prudentia. Pacem Jerusalem facit charitas, nutrit pietas, firmat humilitas." Cf. Brunacci and Catanzaro, *Magistri Rufini Episcopi de Bono Pacis*, 131.

56. Oexle, "Conjuratio und Gilde," 170ff. and 203ff.

57. Rufinus, *De bono pacis* II, 9, Migne, *Patrologia latina* 150, col. 1617.

58. Rufinus, *De bono pacis* II, 9, col. 1616.

59. Rufinus, *De bono pacis* II, 12, cols. 1619–20: "Rebelles nos computamus, qui jugum legitimae dominationis quaerentes excutere, et libertatem illicitam sibi usurpare, legatos publicos etiam rejiciunt, regalia decreta contemnunt, non pensitantes fiscalia, nec tributa praebentes. Contra quos Dominus: Reddite quae sunt Caesaris, Caesari." Cf. Brunacci and Catanzaro, *Magistri Rufini Episcopi de Bono Pacis*, 163. On communal freedom, see Johannes Fried, "Die Kölner Stadtgemeinde und der europäische Freiheitsgedanke im Hochmittelalter," in *Der Name der Freiheit. Ergänzungsband zur Ausstellung des Kölnischen Stadtmuseums*, ed. Werner Schäfke (Cologne, 1988), 23–34; Hagen Keller, "Die Aufhebung der Hörigkeit und die Idee menschlicher Freiheit in italienischen Kommunen des 13. Jahrhunderts," in *Die abendländische Freiheit vom 10. zum 14. Jahrhundert. Der Wirkungszusammenhang von Idee und Wirklichkeit im europäischen Vergleich*, ed. Johannes Fried, Vorträge und Forschungen, 39 (Sigmaringen, 1991), 389–407. On the "libertas scolastica" (i.e., autonomy of association) of the university *coniurationes*, see Otto Gerhard Oexle, "Alteuropäische Voraussetzungen des Bildungsbürgertums—Universitäten, Gelehrte und Studierte," in *Bildungsbürgertum im 19. Jahrhundert*, Part I: *Bildungssystem und Professionalisierung in internationalen Vergleichen*, ed. Werner Conze and Jürgen Kocka, Industrielle Welt, 38 (Stuttgart, 1985), 33 and 42–43.

60. See Gerhard Dilcher, "Zur Geschichte und Aufgabe des Begriffs Genossenschaft," in *Recht, Gericht, Genossenschaft und Policey. Symposion für Adalbert Erler*, ed. G. Dilcher and Bernhard Diestelkamp (Berlin, 1986), 114–23.

61. There is as yet no thorough study of the wording of oaths. See also below, n. 141.

62. Traugott Schiess (ed.), *Quellenwerk zur Entstehung der Schweizerischen Eidgenossenschaft* 11 (Aarau, 1933), 776ff., no. 1681, p. 778. See, more recently, Blickle, "Friede und Verfassung," 24ff., also on the topic of the longstanding dispute over whether this was a peace ordinance or a revolutionary act.

63. Weber, *Wirtschaft und Gesellschaft*, 401–2.

64. Max Weber, "Die Stadt. Eine soziologische Untersuchung," *Archiv für Sozial-wissenschaft und Sozialpolitik* 47 (1920–21): 621–772. The text is reprinted under another (wrong and misleading) title in Weber, *Wirtschaft und Gesellschaft*, 727–814. On this text see Christian Meier (ed.), *Die okzidentale Stadt nach Max Weber. Zum Problem der Zugehörigkeit in Antike und Mittelalter* (Munich, 1994).

65. See Otto Gerhard Oexle, "Kulturwissenschaftliche Reflexionen über soziale Gruppen in der mittelalterlichen Gesellschaft: Tönnies, Simmel, Durkheim und Max Weber," in Meier, *Die okzidentale Stadt*, 115–59; and "Les groupes sociaux du Moyen Âge et les débuts de la sociologie contemporaine," *Annales É.S.C.* 47 (1992): 751–65.

66. On this concept of "ethos," see Max Weber, *Gesammelte Aufsätze zur Religionssoziologie*, vol. 1 (Tübingen, 1978), 234–35 and 238, as well as 40 (note).

67. On older monarchical uses of the formula *pax et concordia*, see Josef Semmler, "Eine Herrschaftsmaxime im Wandel: Pax und concordia im karolingischen Frankenreich," in *Frieden in Geschichte und Gegenwart*, 24–34. On the (Roman) origins of this pair of terms, see Hattenhauer, *Pax et iustitia*, 19–20.

68. The existence of these legal concepts can be demonstrated quite early in the area of early medieval peasant sworn associations. On this, see Otto Gerhard Oexle, "Gilde und Kommune. Über die Entstehung von 'Einung' und 'Gemeinde' als Grundformen des Zusammenlebens in Europa," in *Theorien kommunaler Ordnung in Europa*, ed. Peter Blickle (Munich, 1996), 75–97, 78ff.

69. On this problem, see Otto Gerhard Oexle's "Das Bild der Moderne vom Mittelalter und die moderne Mittelalterforschung," *Frühmittelalterliche Studien* 24 (1990): 1–22, 18ff.; "Kulturwissenschaftliche Reflexionen," and "Les groupes sociaux du Moyen Âge." See also the same author's "Das entzweite Mittelalter," in *Die Deutschen und ihr Mittelalter*, ed. Gerd Althoff (Darmstadt, 1992), 7–28.

70. Berndt Hamm, *Promissio, Pactum, Ordinatio. Freiheit und Selbstbindung Gottes in der scholastischen Gnadenlehre*, Beiträge zur historischen Theologie, 54 (Tübingen, 1977).

71. See Aldo Cairola, *Simone Martini e Ambrogio Lorenzetti nel Palazzo Pubblico di Siena* (Florence, n.d.); Wolfgang Pleister and Wolfgang Schild (eds.), *Recht und Gerechtigkeit im Spiegel der europäischen Kunst* (Cologne, 1988), 137ff.; and the contributions in Hans Belting and Dieter Blume (eds.), *Malerei und Stadtkultur in der Dantezeit. Die Argumentation der Bilder* (Munich, 1989). See also the contribution by Klaus Arnold, "Bilder des Krieges, Bilder des Friedens," in *Träger und Instrumentarien des Friedens im hohen und späten Mittelalter*, ed. Johannes Fried, Vorträge und Forschungen 43 (Sigmaringen, 1996), 561–86, 574ff. On pictorial and other representations (symbols) of peace, see Gernot Kocher, "Friede und Recht," in *Sprache und Recht. Festschrift für Ruth Schmidt-Wiegand*, vol. 1 (Berlin and New York, 1986), 405–15.

72. On the early university as a *coniuratio*, see Oexle, "Alteuropäische Voraussetzungen des Bildungsbürgertums," 30ff.

73. *Chronica Magistri Rogeri de Houedene*, ed. William Stubbs, vol. 4 (London, 1871), 120–21 (*De dissensione quae fuit inter scholares et cives Parisius*). Here, too (see below, n. 125) the connection between *pax* and *securitas* is hinted at. Cf. Conze, "Sicherheit, Schutz," in *Geschichtliche Grundbegriffe*. This account may be compared to that of Matthew of Paris on a similar incident in 1229 (*De discordia orta Parisius inter universitatem cleri et cives, et de discessione cleri*), which led to the famous secession of the *magistri* and students: *Matthaei Parisiensis chronica majora*, ed. Henry Richard Luard, vol. 3 (London, 1876), 166ff. Here, too, it was the power of action negotiated by consensus that finally

forced the recalling of the departed *universitas* and the restoration of peace: "pax est clero et civibus reformata, et scolarium universitas revocata" (ibid., 169). See also Louis IX's diploma of August 1229 (H. Denifle and E. Chatelain [eds.], *Chartularium universitatis Parisiensis*, vol. 1 [Paris, 1899], no. 66, pp. 120ff.), which takes up once again the previous privilege of his predecessor Philip August.

74. See also Denifle and Chatelain, *Chartularium universitatis*, vol. 1, 59ff., no. 1. On this, see A. B. Cobban, *The Medieval Universities: Their Development and Organization* (London, 1975), 75ff.

75. John Frederick Hinnebusch, *The Historia Occidentalis of Jacques de Vitry: A Critical Edition*, Spicilegium Friburgense, 17 (Fribourg, 1972), 90ff., cap. 7 (De statu Parisiensis ciuitatis).

76. See Ludwig Schmugge, "Über 'nationale' Vorurteile im Mittelalter," *Deutsches Archiv für Erforschung des Mittelalters* 38 (1982): 439–59.

77. On the jurisdiction of the (student) rectors in Bologna, see Walter Steffen, *Die studentische Autonomie im mittelalterlichen Bologna. Eine Untersuchung über die Stellung der Studenten und ihrer Universitas gegenüber Professoren und Stadtregierung im 13./14. Jahrhundert*, Geist und Werk der Zeiten, 58 (Bern, 1981), 106ff.

78. Norbert Elias, *The Civilizing Process* (Oxford, 1994), see esp. 263–86.

79. M. Sarti and M. Fattorini (eds.), *De claris archigymnasii Bononiensis professoribus a saeculo XI usque ad saeculum XIV*, vol. 2 (Bologna, 1888–96), 18f., no. 8.

80. Ulrich Meyer-Holz, *Collegia Iudicum. Über die Form sozialer Gruppenbildung durch die gelehrten Berufsjuristen im Oberitalien des späten Mittelalters, mit einem Vergleich zu Collegia Doctorum Iuris*, Fundamenta Juridica. Hannoversche Beiträge zur rechtswissenschaftlichen Grundlagenforschung, 6 (Baden-Baden, 1989), 198.

81. Meyer-Holz, *Collegia Iudicum*, 204.

82. Ibid., 210–11.

83. On *concordia* as a central concept, see Dilcher, *Die Entstehung der lombardischen Stadtkommune*, 153ff. See above, n. 67. On strangers, see Marie Theres Fögen (ed.) *Fremde der Gesellschaft. Historische und sozialwissenschaftliche Untersuchungen zur Differenzierung von Normalität und Fremdheit* (Frankfurt am Main, 1991); Rudolf Stichweh, "Der Fremde—Zur Evolution der Weltgesellschaft," *Rechtshistorisches Journal* 11 (1992), 295–316.

84. Charter of the merchant guild of Valenciennes at the end of the eleventh century. H. Caffiaux, "Mémoire sur la charte de la frairie de la halle basse de Valenciennes (XIe et XIIe siècles)," *Mémoires de la Société Nationale des Antiquaires de France* 38 (1877): 1–41, 30, §17.

85. Statutes (*consuetudines*) of the merchant guild (*gilda mercatoria*) of Saint-Omer at the end of the eleventh century. G. Espinas and H. Pirenne, "Les coutumes de la gilde marchande de Saint-Omer," *Le Moyen Age* 14 (1901): 189–96, 193, §4.

86. For a wealth of information on this subject, see Manfred Weider, *Das Recht der deutschen Kaufmannsgilden des Mittelalters*, Untersuchungen zur Deutschen Staats- und Rechtsgeschichte, 141 (Breslau, 1931), 248ff.

87. S. Omer, Espinas and Pirenne, "Les coutumes," 193 and 196, §§7 and 26.

88. Valenciennes, Caffiaux, "Mémoire sur la charte," 28, §§5–6.

89. Valenciennes, Caffiaux, "Mémoire sur la charte," 28–29, §§8–9.

90. Meyer-Holz, *Collegia Iudicum*. On the guild character of these organizations, see 193ff. and 198ff.

91. Ibid., 213.

92. Ibid., 210.

93. Ibid., 74; cf. 210.

94. Ibid., 218ff.

95. Ibid., 219.

96. Ibid., 204ff.

97. Wilfried Reininghaus, *Die Entstehung der Gesellengilden im Spätmittelalter*, Vierteljahrschrift für Sozial- und Wirtschaftsgeschichte, Beiheft 71 (Wiesbaden, 1981); Herbert Obenaus, *Recht und Verfassung der Gesellschaften mit St. Jörgenschild in Schwaben. Untersuchungen über Adel, Einung, Schiedsgericht und Fehde im fünfzehnten Jahrhundert*, Veröffentlichungen des Max-Planck-Instituts für Geschichte, 7 (Göttingen, 1961). Obenaus has described this society as a "peace community": "arbitration and the avoidance of legal disputes, the elimination of feuds: this describes the interest and thus also the scope of activity of the inner circle of the association with the shield of St. George" (38). The connection between the influences on internal and external peace thus becomes very clear here. See, most recently, Andreas Ranft, *Adelsgesellschaften. Gruppenbildung und Genossenschaft im spätmittelalterlichen Reich*, Kieler Historische Studien, 38 (Sigmaringen, 1994), 171ff. and 194ff.

98. Ludwig Remling, *Bruderschaften in Franken. Kirchen- und sozialgeschichtliche Untersuchungen zum spätmittelalterlichen und frühneuzeitlichen Bruderschaftswesen*, Quellen und Forschungen zur Geschichte des Bistums und Hochstifts Würzburg, 35 (Würzburg, 1986).

99. Gerhard Dilcher, "Die genossenschaftliche Struktur von Gilden und Zünften," in Schwineköper, *Gilden und Zünfte*, 71–111, here 109 and 106.

100. Marvin B. Becker, "Aspects of Lay Piety in Early Renaissance Florence," in *The Pursuit of Holiness in Late Medieval and Renaissance Religion*, ed. Charles Trinkaus and Heiko A. Oberman, Studies in Medieval and Reformation Thought, 10 (Leiden, 1974), 177–99; Richard C. Trexler, "Ritual in Florence: Adolescence and Salvation in the Renaissance, in ibid., 200–264, and *Public Life in Renaissance Florence* (New York and London, 1980); Charles M. de la Roncière, "Les confréries à Florence et dans son contado aux XIVe–XVe siècles," in *Le mouvement confraternel au Moyen Age. France, Italie, Suisse*, Collection de l'École Française de Rome, 30 (Geneva, 1987), 297–342. See also the contributions by Ulrich Meier in *Stadtregiment und Bürgerfreiheit. Handlungsspielräume in deutschen und italienischen Städten des Späten Mittelalters und der Frühen Neuzeit*, ed. Klaus Schreiner and Ulrich Meier (Göttingen, 1994), 37–83 and 147–87.

101. Ronald F. E. Weissman, *Ritual Brotherhood in Renaissance Florence* (New York, 1982), quotation 58. Weissman also cites Lauro Martines's *Lawyers and Statecraft in Renaissance Florence* (Princeton, 1968) with a comparison between guild organization and the republic, and notes that "the milieu of the guild was in its way an education in statecraft, a preparation for politics" (53).

102. Becker, "Aspects of Lay Piety," 190ff. The quotations are on 190 and 195.

103. See the polyptych of the Madonna della Misericordia painted by Piero della Francesca after 1444 for the Confraternità della Misericordia in Sansepolcro (now in the Pinacoteca Comunale of Sansepolcro). On this work, see Carlo Bertelli, *Piero della Francesca*, trans. Edward Farrelly (New Haven and London, 1992), 26ff. and 172ff.

104. See de la Roncière, "Les confréries à Florence," 318–19. See also Paul O.

Kristeller, "Lay Religious Traditions and Florentine Platonism," in Kristeller, *Studies in Renaissance Thought and Letters* (Rome, 1956), 99–122.

105. See above, text to nn. 33–46.

106. See above, text to nn. 33–46.

107. Oexle, "Gilden als soziale Gruppen," 304ff.

108. Ibid., 305.

109. Ibid., 349–50.

110. Oexle, "Conjuratio und Gilde," 186.

111. *Miracula S. Adalhardi Corbeiensis* c. 4, MGH SS 15.2, 861. On this see Ludwig Huberti, *Studien zur Rechtsgeschichte der Gottesfrieden und Landfrieden*, vol. 1 (Ansbach, 1892), 190ff.; Körner, *Iuramentum und frühe Friedensbewegung*, 97ff. See also Hartmut Hoffmann, *Gottesfriede und Treuga Dei*, Schriften der Monumenta Germaniae historica, 20 (Stuttgart, 1964), 64–65, who assumes that this "pax" was "set in motion by the count and the bishop," for which the text, however, offers no evidence.

112. *Miracula S. Adalhardi Corbeiensis* c. 8 (862): "Adoleverat etiam inter Ambianenses et Corbeienses nova quaedam religio, et ex religione pullulaverat consuetudo, quae etiam reciprocabatur omni anno."

113. See Gottfried Partsch, "Ein unbekannter Walliser Landfrieden aus dem 12. Jahrhundert," *Zeitschrift für Rechtsgeschichte: Germ. Abt.* 75 (1958): 93–107; Pfeiffer, "Die Bedeutung der Einung." On the communal pacts of the high and late Middle Ages see the collection of essays *Kommunale Bündnisse Oberitaliens und Oberdeutschlands im Vergleich*, ed. Helmut Maurer. Here the "tried and tested constitutional structure of the commune . . . in its essential characteristics was raised to a higher super-municipal level: the legal basis was a peace pact designed and sworn to by the representatives of the cities, which however, through the swearing in of the citizenries, was expanded into a personal tie among all participating citizens of the town" (Dilcher, "Reich, Kommunen, Bünde," 245).

114. On the *Caputiati* see, most recently, Rolf Köhn, "Freiheit als Forderung und Ziel bäuerlichen Widerstandes (Mittel- und Westeuropa, 11.–13. Jahrhundert), in *Die abendländische Freiheit von 10. zum 14 Jahrhundert. Der Wirkungszusammenhang von Idee und Wirklichkeit im europäischen Vergleich*, ed. Johannes Fried, Vorträge und Forschungen, 39 (Sigmaringen, 1991), 325–87, 360ff.; Otto Gerhard Oexle, "Die Kultur der Rebellion. Schwureinung und Verschwörung im früh- und hochmittelalterlichen Okzident," in *Ordnung und Aufruhr im Mittelalter. Historische und juristische Studien zur Rebellion*, ed. Marie Theres Fögen, Ius Commune, Sonderhefte, 70 (Frankfurt am Main, 1995), 119–37, esp. 126ff.

115. The text is reproduced in MGH SS 21, 605ff. A new edition with an extensive commentary, mainly from the perspective of legal history, is P. Godding and J. Pycke (eds.), "La paix de Valenciennes de 1114. Commentaire et édition critique," *Bulletin de la Commission royale pour la publication des anciennes lois et ordonnances de Belgique* 29 (1979): 1–142. On the occasions and conditions for the emergence of the commune see the remarks in Vermeesch, *Essai sur les origines*, 116ff.

116. C. 29, Godding and Pycke, "La paix de Valenciennes," 122.

117. For the text see Francesco Bonaini (ed.), *Statuti inediti della città di Pisa dal XII al XIV secolo*, vol. 1 (Florence, 1854) 16ff., no. 1. On Bishop Daibertus, see B. Hamilton, "Daimbert (Daibert), Patriarch von Jerusalem," in *Lexikon des Mittelalters* 3 (1986), cols.

433–34. For interpretations, see Uwe Prutscher, *Der Eid in Verfassung und Politik italien-ischer Städte. Untersuchungen im Hinblick auf die Herrschaftsformen Kaiser Friedrich Barbarossas in Reichsitalien*, Ph.D. diss., University of Gießen, 1980, 63ff.

118. Dilcher, *Die Entstehung der lombardischen Stadtkommune*, 129; Prutscher, *Der Eid in Verfassung und Politik*, 66.

119. Bonaini, *Statuti inediti della città di Pisa*, 17: "Volumus deinde vos scire, quod quisquis, superbia qualibet inflatus, hanc pacem et concordiam servare noluerit, sacramentum quod factum est non fecerit vel facere noluerit, propterea sit excommunicatus; et omnes custodite vos ab eo sicuti ab heretico damnato et ab ecclesia Dei separato, neque in ecclesia neque in navi cum eo aliquam communionem habeatis."

120. Dilcher, *Die Entstehung der lombardischen Stadtkommune*, 135ff. On the ritual of *conversio*, out of which the commune arose, see Keller, "Die soziale und politische Verfassung Mailands," 51–52. On the ritual of the kiss in peacemaking see Klaus Schreiner, " 'Gerechtigkeit und Frieden haben sich geküßt' (Ps. 84, 11). Friedensstiftung durch symbolisches Handeln," in *Träger und Instrumentarien des Friedens im hohen und späten Mittelalter* (Sigmaringen, 1996), 37–86.

121. *Iohannis Codagnelli Annales Placentini*, ed. Oswald Holder-Egger, MGH SSrer-Germ (Hanover and Leipzig, 1901), 1ff. See Dilcher, *Die Entstehung der lombardischen Stadtkommune*, 136–37.

122. In the history of the bishopric of Le Mans, G. Busson and A. Ledru (eds.), *Actus pontificum Cenomannis in urbe degentium*, Archives historiques du Maine, 2 (Le Mans, 1901), 374ff.

123. Vermeesch, *Essai sur les origines*, 81ff.

124. For details, see Robert Latouche, *Histoire du Comté du Maine pendant le Xe et le XIe siècle* (Paris, 1910).

125. Similar events led to the creation of the famous commune of Laon (1109/12), which was described by Guibert of Nogent. See Guibert de Nogent, *Autobiographie*, III, 7ff., ed. Edmond-René Labande, Les classiques de l'histoire de France au Moyen Age, 34 (Paris, 1981), 316ff. The underlying motives were, on the one hand, the legal insecurity that arose in the bishop's absence, and the disturbance of "public order" by acts of violence (*rapinae et caedes*, 316): "Furta, immo latrocinia per primores et primorum apparitores publice agebantur. Nulli noctibus procedenti securitas praebebatur, solum restabat aut distrahi aut capi aut caedi" (320). According to Guibert's account this very circumstance was used by the clergy, the archdeacons and *proceres* (cf. 316), in order to demand additional taxes—and to permit the creation of a commune in exchange: "Quod considerantes clerus cum archidiaconis ac proceres, et causas exigendi a populo pecunias aucupantes, dant eis per internuncios optionem, ut, si pretia digna impenderent, communionis faciendae licentiam haberent" (320). On the connection between *pax* and *securitas*, which has already been mentioned here (see above, nn. 73 and 125), see Werner Conze's article, "Sicherheit, Schutz," in *Geschichtliche Grundbegriffe*.

126. See also Guibert of Nogent's description of the creation of the commune of Laon as the expression of a *mutuum adjutorium*: "Facta itaque inter clerum, proceres et populum mutui adjutorii conjuratione," *Autobiographie*.

127. On the significance of the show of military strength and of the communal army for the "nature," i.e., the definition, of the commune, see Joachim Deeters's apt account in "Die Kölner Coniuratio von 1112," in *Köln, das Reich und Europa*, Mitteilungen aus dem Stadtarchiv von Köln, 60 (Cologne, 1971): 125–48, 130ff. and 136ff.

128. The same is true of the account by Guibert of Nogent on the commune of Laon (see above, n. 125) and of other descriptions of both peasant and urban communes. On this "polyvocality" of the accounts see the author's study of early medieval peasant communes, "Gilde und Kommune," 78ff.

129. One gains the impression that an older text was incorporated into the account of the history of the bishopric, above all because of the occasional shifts of narrative perspective, which are indicated by terms such as "our people" (*nostri*). See G. Busson and A. Ledru (eds.), *Actus pontificum Cenomannis*, 378 and 380.

130. See above, text to n. 61.

131. Alpertus Mettensis, *De diversitate temporum* II, 20, ed. Hans Van Rij (Amsterdam, 1980), 80. On this text, see Oexle, "Die Kaufmannsgilde von Tiel," esp. 187ff. On the character of medieval legal customs (*consuetudines*), see, most recently, Gerhard Dilcher, "Mittelalterliche Rechtsgewohnheit als methodisch-theoretisches Problem," in *Gewohnheitsrecht und Rechtsgewohnheiten im Mittelalter*, ed. G. Dilcher et al., Schriften zur Europäischen Rechts- und Verfassungsgeschichte, 6 (Berlin, 1992), 21–65.

132. Ivo of Chartres, ep. 77, Migne, *Patrologia latina* 162, col. 99. On the context of Ivo's comment, see Vermeesch, *Essai sur les origines*, 103ff. The 1212 synod of Paris under the leadership of the papal legate Robert of Courçon took a similar view of matters. Mansi, *Sacrorum conciliorum nova et amplissima collectio* 22, col. 851, c. V, 8: "Cum . . . sint . . . fere in singulis urbibus et oppidis et villis totius regni Franciae pertinacissime synagogae constitutae, quas vulgariter communias vocant: quae diabolicae instituta, ecclesiasticis institutis contraria penitus in conversionem totius ecclesiasticae jurisdictionis adinvenerint," etc.

133. Oexle, "Conjuratio und Gilde," 170ff.

134. Caffiaux, "Mémoire sur la charte," §1 (see n. 84), 25–26.

135. Ibid., 25: "Nous, très-amet Frère, avons voet à nostre Signeur emsamble awarder le loyen de dilecion, pour coi besoing seroit que quelconques cose que nous faisons encontre les estrangiers, entre nous au mains ire ne estinchielle de discorde nullement aièche vigueur . . ."

136. Caffiaux, "Mémoire sur la charte," §6 (see n. 84), 28.

137. Ibid. §10, 29: "Après che li Frère seront issut ensamble de cheste ville, li uns demeurèche avoecq l'autre tout partout u besoins sera et adiès li uns admonestèche l'autre, en non de caritet, et par avant promettèche se foi qu'il a besoing de li."

138. For the example of the Merovingian clerical guilds, see Oexle, "Conjuratio und Gilde," 171ff.

139. See above, n. 114.

140. "Gesta pontificum Autissiodorensium," in L.-M. Duru (ed.), *Bibliothèque historique de l'Yonne*, vol. 1 (Auxerre, 1850), 445ff.

141. On the formula of the oath, see above n. 62. The tension between a firm condemnation and simultaneous close scrutiny of matters as they were and attention to the 'voices' of those involved, who were, after all, being condemned at the same time (see above text to nn. 127–29) can also be found in the anonymous chronicle of Laon (Bouquet, *Recueil des historiens des Gaules et de la France* 18, 705): the chronicler calls the group of Caputiati a *societas* and a *fraternitas pacis* and a *conjuratio contra hostes pacis* (namely against the *ruptarii* or "gangs" as well as against the "princes who do not keep peace"), describes the statutes and initiation ritual in precise detail, emphasizes the superregional character and social composition across estate lines ("omnes diversae conditionis et or-

dinis, episcopi etiam et omnes inferiorum ordinum, quasi una inspiratione animati")—
and nonetheless considers the whole thing the expression of a mad fury (*insana rabies*),
which also, ultimately, had come about because of an outrageous treachery. See Oexle,
"Die Kultur der Rebellion," 129.

142. See the history of the bishopric of Auxerre ("Gesta pontificum Autissiodorensium," 446): "sed in eam libertatem sese omnes asserere conabantur, quam ab initio
condite creature a primis parentibus se contraxisse dicebant, ignorantes peccati fuisse
meritum servitutem. Hinc etiam sequebatur, quod minoris majorisve nulla esset dis-
tinctio, sed potius confusio que rerum summam, que nunc superiorum moderamine ac
ministerio auctore Domino regitur, brevi tempore traheret in ruinam." On the history of
such modes of argumentation, see Wolfgang Stürner, *Peccatum und Potestas. Der Sünden-
fall und die Entstehung der herrscherlichen Gewalt im mittelalterlichen Staatsdenken*,
Beiträge zur Geschichte und Quellenkunde des Mittelalters, 11 (Sigmaringen, 1987).

143. See also the remarks of Guibert of Nogent on the effect of the commune, that the
serfs (*servi*), "semel ab jugi exactione emancipati," should return "ad modum pristinum"
(322, 324).

144. On the problem of the ultimate universalization of group-related life norms at
the beginning of the modern period and within the context of the decorporatization of
the premodern society of groups at the end of the eighteenth century, see Oexle, "Das Bild
der Moderne vom Mittelalter," 18ff.

145. See the metaphor used by Stephan of Tournai to refer to the same phenomenon,
above at n. 53.

146. The text is reproduced in detail in Luchaire, *Les communes françaises à l'époque
des Capetiens directs*, 242ff.

147. Ivo of Chartres, ep. 253, Migne, *Patrologia latina* 162, col. 259. Cf. Vermeesch,
Essai sur les origines, 113ff., 115–16.

148. See above, 290–91.

149. See above, 286.

150. See above, n. 64.

151. On this, see Otto Gerhard Oexle, "Kulturwissenschaftliche Reflexionen," and
"Les groupes sociaux du Moyen Age," 751–65.

152. See above text to n. 3.

153. This thesis is raised again in Aron Iakovlevich Gurevich, *Categories of Medieval
Culture*, trans. George L. Campbell (London, 1985), 185ff., 295ff., and passim.

154. On this see Oexle, "Das Mittelalter und das Unbehagen an der Moderne," and
"Das entzweite Mittelalter."

155. See Oexle, "Das Bild der Moderne vom Mittelalter."

156. We have as yet no study of this phenomenon. For reflections on this subject
from a systematic perspective, but without the necessary historical depth, see Helmut
Dubiel, "Der Fundamentalismus der Moderne," *Merkur. Deutsche Zeitschrift für eu-
ropäisches Denken*, 46 (1992): 747–62.

157. This, too, is a central concept in Max Weber's sociology of law, political authority, and religion. See Otto Gerhard Oexle, "Kulturwissenschaftliche Reflexionen," and
"Les groupes sociaux du Moyen Age."

Contributors

Gerd Althoff is professor of medieval history at the Westfälische Wilhelms-University in Münster, Westphalia.

Arnold Angenendt is professor of medieval and modern church history at the Westfälische Wilhelms-University, Münster.

Thomas Braucks is a research fellow in the interdisciplinary program on "Symbolic Communication and Transmission of Values" at the Westfälische Wilhelms-University, Münster.

Rolf Busch is a Ph.D. candidate in medieval and modern church history at the Westfälische Wilhelms-University, Münster.

Bernhard Jussen is a research fellow at the Max Planck Institute for History in Göttingen and teaches at the University of Göttingen.

Thomas Lentes is research director of the interdisciplinary project on "Cultural History and Theology of the Image in Christianity" at the Westfälische Wilhelms-University, Münster.

Hubertus Lutterbach teaches medieval and modern church history at the Westfälische Wilhelms-University, Münster.

Joseph Morsel is maître de conférence at the University of Paris I, Sorbonne.

Otto Gerhard Oexle is director of the Max Planck Institute for History in Göttingen and professor at the University of Göttingen.

Index